Mississippi River Open School for Kinship and Social Exchange

EXPERIMENTAL MODES OF TEACHING AND LEARNING FOR THE PLANETARY EMERGENCY

Contents

Introduction

Dio Cramer, John Kim, and Jeremy Meckler

The Mississippi River Open School for Kinship and Social Exchange (Open School) (2022–ongoing) has collaboratively imagined and practiced experimental modes of teaching and learning for the planetary emergency. A concept that has situated much of this work is the Anthropocene, the proposal that we have entered a new epoch characterized by widespread human-caused changes to Earth systems. A core aspect of our activities has been to engage pressing issues at the intersections of race, environment, and extraction in partnership with communities, many on the frontline of struggles in response to the Anthropocene. As articles in this collection suggest, the Anthropocene allows us to connect disparate crises ("polycrises") experienced along the Mississippi River, including biodiversity loss, racial disparities in health, the rapid expansion of mining, destruction of wetland habitats, the erosion of river infrastructure, and flooding, as ways of seeing and understanding interrelated changes to Earth systems. In ways that we introduce below, the concept has also been subject to critical evaluation, because of its limitations when conceived in a way that does not account for the river's complex social and colonial history.

This introduction is written from the perspective of an editorial team that was tasked with curating a selection from the Open School's growing archive. It is impossible to represent the work of the dozens of collaborators who have contributed to this project. We sought to foreground recent activities because of their relevance. In addition, this book could only be a partial representation of the Open School as we never prioritized writing as a preferred mode of engagement or form of documentation. Contributors have explored an expansive array of creative practices and activist art interventions, which we have illustrated throughout the book in inserts with brown background pages. Selections of earlier collaborations have also been included, because they have been crucial reference points, precedents, and influences on the Open School's activities on the river. Just because earlier texts have been included does not suggest that these authors continue to actively work on the Open School.

The notion of an Open School is shorthand for our spatially dispersed and multimodal activities along the river spanning roughly 2,300 miles. We aspire to grow and sustain a distributed community of care, consisting of educators, activists, artists, researchers, and others who connect this distance. "School" is not meant in the conventional sense of formal accreditation (though our study away partner, River Semester, has offered university credits), but as a spatial reorganization in the way in which we think of the institution. The Open School consists of six regional locations, which we refer to as river hubs, spanning the entirety of the Mississippi from its headwaters to the Gulf of Mexico. The northernmost river hub is coordinated by water protectors, land stewards, and artist-activists as a space for land-based education and action against impending threats to the environment. The Upper Mississippi hub foregrounds Indigenous and Black perspectives and histories around southeast Minnesota and southwest Wisconsin. Along the vast midsection of the Mississippi's meander, a constellation of people are working on issues of race, ecology, and place at three additional hubs, located in St. Louis, Missouri, southern Illinois, and Memphis, Tennessee. The Gulf South Open School, located in and around New Orleans, Louisiana, is the southernmost river hub and is comprised of artist organizers, activists, and educators. The Open School is a multiscalar ecosystem of people and partner organizations that operates at the macro and hub level. We encourage readers to research these hubs by looking at the credits section of this book in order to learn more about our partners' life-sustaining work along the river.

Referenced throughout this collection are earlier iterations of our work together. It is important to review some of this history here in order to acknowledge the considerable efforts that contributed to the formation of the Open School. Initiated by the Haus der Kulturen der Welt and the Max Planck Institute for the History of Science, "Mississippi. An Anthropocene River" (2018–2021) was a research project that explored the river as a critical zone of habitation and long-term human-environment interaction. The Anthropocene River was part of a decade-long series of programs about the Anthropocene, known as the Anthropocene Curriculum (AC). The signature event of the AC was the Anthropocene Campus, and many Open School contributors continue to organize them. (We recognize that there are lots of terms and names here that can be confusing. For this reason, we define them throughout the book in editors' notes and include a glossary in the back matter of this book.) Because this collection dips from an eclectic history, the writing style and form of contributions vary. This also accounts for regional and cultural differences in the spellings of some words.

The use of the term "Anthropocene" has not been without controversy. Over the years we have worked closely with members of the Anthropocene Working Group, a research team established in 2009 to provide scientific evidence for the formal recognition of the Anthropocene within the geological time scale. (Members of this group have contributed an essay to this collection.) Without denying the public impact of this characterization of the Earth, some of the authors in this collection push back against its codification as a strictly scientific concept, because of the partial way in which it renders sociohistorical processes that led to Anthropocenic conditions. Within this collection, you'll find a number of critiques. For example, given the Open School's geographical context in the Mississippi River watershed, some argue that the Anthropocene has not been theorized sufficiently with regard to colonialism and slavery. To address these shortfalls, a number of the contributors, especially during the Anthropocene River period, draw on the Colonial and Black Anthropocene as critical counterformulations.

A second reason for the resistance to the Anthropocene is the term's accessibility. To some, the concept floats in the stratosphere only visible from ivory towers; it has little use in the lived experience of those mobilizing action against the polycrises associated with the concept. Many of our contributors have sought to situate their work in collaboration with communities on these frontlines; they share a healthy skepticism of the utility of rarefied concepts and employ them strategically in recognition of audience.

The rejection of the Anthropocene as a new epoch by the International Commission on Stratigraphy (ICS) in March 2024 has made these conversations even more vital and centered the role of the arts, culture, and the humanities in producing insights into the subject. A number of contributors to this collection continue to explore the Anthropocene's implications for scientific and cultural research. We eagerly look forward to the reconsideration of the epoch's validity. The incontrovertible evidence that the Earth has entered a new geological time is everywhere around us, and the Anthropocene's relevance is in the inspiration it has kindled in a multitude of scientific-creative expressions. We will continue to contribute to this paradigm shift in the way in which we comprehend our relationship to the Earth.

Building on the momentum that was created in earlier collaborations, we continued to work together. From 2022–2026, we've met annually in person ("Confluences"); planned classes and public educational programming that connected hubs across regions; sent students and guests down the river on sailboats, canoes, and riverboats multiple times; welcomed each other to our river hubs; shared our approach with others during Anthropocene Campuses in distant locations, even outside the watershed; gifted recipes, seeds, stories, camaraderie, and songs; curated joint art exhibitions; and lots, lots more. In sum, we've aspired to create a sense of the river as a coherent interconnected ecological corridor, or biocultural region, that teaches along its entire length. Water circulates between the river, the Gulf, and the ocean, where it evaporates into rain. At times, the lower Mississippi feels like a future towards which we are heading; at other times, the headwaters feel more that way. But really, it's the river's run in endless recirculation that simultaneously creates our collective past, present, and future.

To find out more about our ongoing work visit our website: www.mississippiriver.school

ABOUT THE BOOK'S DESIGN

A collection of projects, experiences, writings, and creative makings like these don't lend themselves easily to the limitations of a traditional book. Many of these teaching and learning experiments are ongoing, whereas the nature of a printed and edited collection implies a finality that does not apply here. Much of our early work on this book project involved trying to make sense of the overlapping relationships, programs, and containers that made up the previous iterations of these projects and formatting them into a new container. Pieces chosen for the book were selected by a small team to help craft a narrative across time and geography, but they by no means tell the whole story. Many of these pieces were originally created for varying editorial spaces and are thus formally and stylistically distinct; only a handful were made specifically for this publication. This speaks to the nature of the Open School: the combination of learning through academic writing, narrative storytelling, visual media, and collected fragments. The book's illustrations and handwritten quotations seek to remind us of the many hands that worked on this collective project and to situate these pieces within a larger narrative.

For the format of this printed collection, we decided to follow the river. This book is arranged spatially, following the flow of water from the headwaters of the Mississippi down to the Gulf, and contributions are grouped into these geographies. Each section of the book begins with a map to loosely orient the pieces in geographic relation to each other on the river. As with any mapping project, the limitations make the map. *What makes a river? How can marks on a paper reflect the expansive and ever-changing movements of water?* They can't, but in attempting to transcribe the river the best way we know how, we hope to honor it, and to help our readers honor it, too. Drawn here are lines of the Mississippi River and some of her tributaries. We opted to leave off place names from these maps because they were not needed to orient the pieces to each other, and because many place names carry such deep histories of harm and erasure within them.

The pieces that are printed on brown pages are excerpts of larger projects, and thus should be interpreted as fragments. Some are supplemented with diagrams and sketches, editorial additions that attempt to offer readers a slightly fuller contextualization for these stories. These pieces are arguably truest to the nature of this anthology, as this whole book seeks to piece together fragments of expansive experiences and creative works. We honor the fragments as we honor the waters. We honor the people who influenced and experienced this work, regardless of whether their names are printed in these pages. We honor the people who will be influenced by this collection as it continues to make ripples along the river.

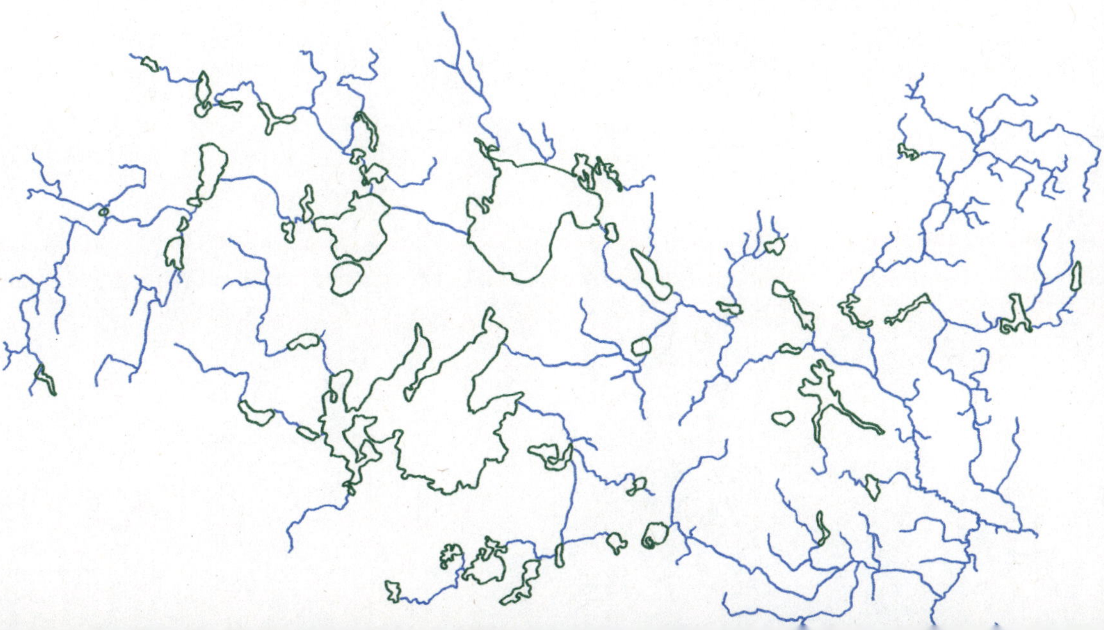

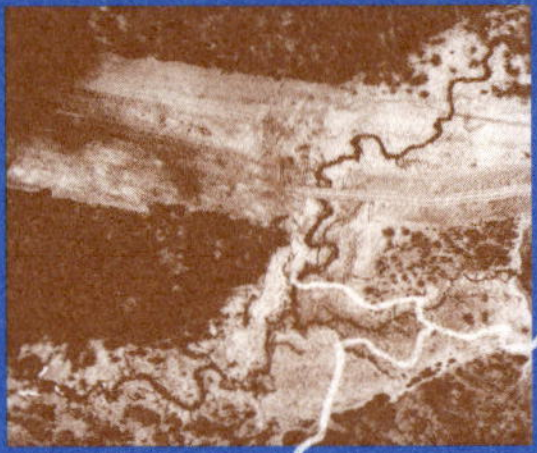

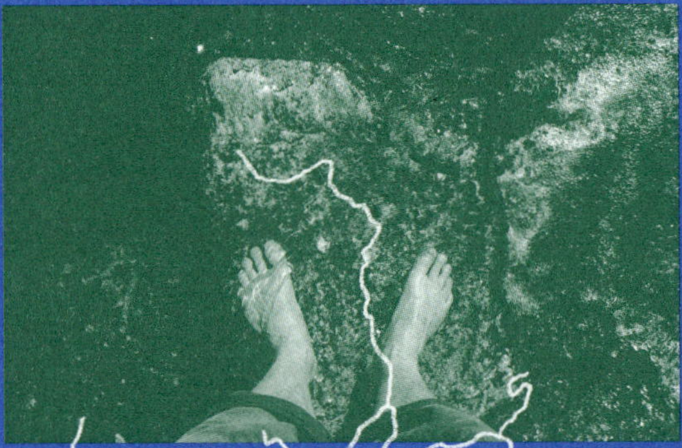

Mississippi Headwaters

The northernmost river hub considers portions of the river north of the Twin Cities, Minnesota, up to its primary source, Lake Itasca, known to the Ojibwe as Omashkoozo-zaaga'igan (Elk Lake). From here the river flows 2,340 miles to the Gulf of Mexico. The river hub is coordinated by water protectors, land stewards, and artist-activists as a space for land-based education and action against threats to the environment.

Head Waters at the Headwaters

Jamie Allen

Knowledge of the precise geographical location of a river's source can bestow considerable power. Yet, as the example of the Mississippi attests, a river's headwaters designation is far from clear-cut. Jamie Allen reflects on Lake Itasca as the source of a mythic fabulation that contributes to the collective consciousness of the U.S.

Photograph by Jamie Allen

The United States of America is just under ten million square kilometers in surface area. Its most conterminous landmass is a topology of creases and folds, mountains and ridges, chasms and embankments. These create, among other divides, hydrological continental separations, sloped divisions for watersheds that flow into either the Great Lakes and Saint Lawrence River or the Missouri-Mississippi complex. These great, tectonic gutters cascade erosive, mineralized waters into the Atlantic Ocean or the Gulf of Mexico, respectively.

The Upper Mississippi River runs from its "headwaters" at Lake Itasca to its "confluence" with the Missouri River at St. Louis, Missouri—and from there, everything heads south. The areas called the "headwaters" are ambiguously and somewhat arbitrarily defined, signifying a something that is resonant, oscillatory, fabricated and factual, real and illusory. We could say that the source waters of the mighty Mississippi are almost anywhere along its varying route, as its watersheds include two Canadian provinces and almost half the landmass of the continental United States. These—all feeding lake, river, rain, and spring waters—remind us that where a river "starts," exactly, is not so simply or easily defined.

Yet, a shallow, tiny stream, dotted with a line of boulders that contemporary pilgrims walk or stumble across, is arranged and maintained as a tourist attraction by the Minnesota Conservation Corps. A carved tree stump indicates that this is where the Mississippi "begins to flow on its winding way 2,552 miles to the Gulf of Mexico."

Photograph by Jamie Allen

Standing at the headwaters, we stand at the "beginning" of America's greatest river, and so, somehow, at the beginning of an American myth. These are lands charged with elevation, energetic potential, territorial and human beauty and violence. This is a launching point for inner and external geographies, insistent flows of meaning that sensitize and affect us all, including those of us embarking on the Anthropocene River Journey.* Emotions well up within us, sentiment dissolving linear planning and logistical thought—"mental rivers wear away abstract banks," as Robert Smithson would have it. There are waters flowing inside us, and those that flow without. We are leaky creatures, never contained or containable, too much for our watery selves. That which makes us sweat or cry, appearing at the limit of exertion and sensation, is the same stuff that washes and wears on the world. At these headwaters, we find ourselves pent-up, pulled in, made raw, and released by an ambiguous start, the anxious demand—"go!"—of a yet-to-be-realized deluge.

* Anthropocene River Journey was a collaboration in 2019 between Mississippi. An Anthropocene River and the River Semester to bring students, researchers, activists, artists, and others to journey by canoe from the headwaters of the Mississippi River to the Gulf of Mexico to research, document, and critically examine the Anthropocene as a site-specific concept on and along the river.

Mark Twain wrote of the Mississippi that we "cannot curb it or confine it, cannot say to it, Go here, or Go there, and make it obey; cannot save a shore that it has sentenced; cannot bar its path with an obstruction which it cannot tear down, dance over, and laugh at." Steady land is left for the sinuous flows of an untamable and lawless, southbound waterway.

A version of this article was originally published on the website Anthropocene Curriculum (Summer 2019).

Bookends from the River Semester by Meira Smit, page 24.
Photograph by Joachim Mueller Jung

Talon Mine Tours

An extractive industry tour company by SHANAI MATTESON

When Rio Tinto - Kennecott proposed a new nickel mining district in my home community on the Mississippi—purportedly for Tesla electric vehicle batteries—I became more aware of how vulnerable we are to greenwashing by extractive industries.

With other local artist activists, I decided to start an educational mine tour company that offers viewpoints and critical information about this proposed nickel-sulfide mine, through images and stories gathered by local residents.

We call it "Talon Mine Tours" and our tagline is simple: The Talon Mine does not exist.

Although no nickel mine has been permitted or built yet, special guest "tour guides" from nearby Native and rural communities share their personal experiences and knowledge of the mining industry, as well as the importance of local places to their identity and lifeways. This includes former miners and mining opponents, environmental scientists, and community activists.

Unlike the mining company that also offers tours, we encourage visitors to ask open-ended questions about who bears the most risk and who benefits from extraction, reflecting together on the answers.

THE OVERBURDEN / OVERLOOK PROJECT

Visitors are invited to climb atop a mobile "mine view" or "overlook" sculpture built on a travel trailer. A placard prompts them to consider the altered landscape, their viewpoints, and their relationships with extractive industries, as well as local places.

Because no mine currently exists here, viewmasters with images of other mining disasters and local wetlands, lakes, rivers, and wild rice beds offer contrast and a sense of what is at stake.

In conversation with guides, we talk about how these relationships shape our sense of place and possibility, and what each of us can do to resist corporate greenwashing and destruction.

COPPER-NICKEL MINING IN MINNESOTA

Although iron ore has been mined in our region of northeast Minnesota for nearly 150 years, copper-nickel mining has never been done here. It's a more destructive and risky type of mining, because targeted minerals are bound in high-sulfide rock, creating waste that turns to acid when it comes into contact with air and water.

Minnesota is water rich and one of the only places in the world where manoomin or wild rice is still abundant. Manoomin is an aquatic plant that has cultural, spiritual, and economic significance for Anishinaabe people, who retain their inherent rights to hunt, fish, and gather in treaty territory.

Wild rice is sensitive to changes in water level and chemistry, and all types of mining impact both. Iron ore mining has already polluted nearby waterways and manoomin beds, but newly proposed mines pose an even greater risk of harm to this ecosystem, and to the people and other beings who depend on this place for their home, sustenance, and survival.

The Talon Mine Tour project surfaces information and stories about the historic, contemporary, and future impacts of mining on our communities—both Native and non-native—using an accessible public art platform and an invitation to share our stories.

START YOUR OWN TOUR COMPANY:

Global mining companies and other extractive industries use many tactics to manufacture consent for polluting projects. In order to gain what is called by some a "social license to operate," companies need to control the narrative about the benefits and risks, especially among local communities. Artists and educators may not have million dollar marketing budgets, but we have the skills to research and share information, and to encourage connections and relationships. We can create accessible platforms for education and grassroots power-building—and to help others imagine new ways of relating to their places, and take responsibility for collective well-being.

Photographs by Laurie Shaull

WHAT CONNECTS YOU TO THIS PLACE?

WHAT HAS MINING MEANT TO YOU & YOUR FAMILY?

TALON
OFFICE
OVER
LOOK

Bookends: Reflections from the River Semester

Meira Smit

Travelling down the entire length of the Mississippi River as a student in the River Semester, Meira Smit reads a history of U.S. colonialism in agricultural transitions found along the river's banks, from Manomin harvesting in Northern Minnesota to sugarcane and plantation landscapes in Louisiana.

MANOMIN IN NORTHERN MINNESOTA, EARLY SEPTEMBER 2023

Our time with Manomin reminded me a lot of harvesting hay on my family's sheep farm. Harvest time for hay is the hottest part of the summer, and you need to wear long sleeves and pants to keep the sticky, sharp grasses off your skin. Despite obvious discomforts, the work is deeply rewarding. It brings me satisfaction when I see a barn full of hay that will feed the sheep all winter, or when we spread several canoes' worth of rice on a tarp. During our week at the Welcome Water Protector Center* in Palisade Minnesota, we harvested, parched, jigged[1] and winnowed Manomin (wild rice) with Dakota and Ojibwe teachers and elders and members of Honor the Earth. Our group worked together for the first time, and we bonded over meals prepared with the grain that we had labored for, not purchased.

* Welcome Water Protector Center Welcome Water Protector Center was an action camp and community hub in Anishinaabe territory (Palisade, Minnesota) that emerged during the Stop Line 3 movement to oppose the construction of the Enbridge Line 3 oil pipeline across the region. Related activities continue to be organized in a distributed way throughout the region.

In the early morning on wild ricing day, we loaded seven canoes with paddles, PFDs (personal floatation devices), two cedar knockers (ricing sticks used to knock rice into the canoe), and push poles and drove to the lake.

Resembling a grassy meadow, the wild rice grew tall and opened up in pathways for canoes to move through.

I sat in the bed of the canoe using the knockers, while Timea stood in the back, pushing the 12-foot pole against the lake bed. We glided through the meadow of Manomin, stabilized and cradled by the vegetal mass. We had little risk of tipping.

A few hours went by gliding through the rice and the "pit" "pat" "whoosh" of rice grains falling in the canoe. Everyone returned with the bottom of their canoes full of rice and bugs. We bagged the rice and returned to the Welcome Water Protector Center.
I sewed the rest of the day: canvas moccasins to wear while jigging the rice later, and bags for the jigging holes. My new crew mates and generous hosts embodied love, patience, and hard work.

MANOMIN IN SOUTHERN MINNESOTA, MID-SEPTEMBER

It is mid-September, before the equinox. The days are long. Near my origin, at the confluence of the Chippewa River and the Mississippi River. Feels like home. In a back channel of the river where the dam created shallow wetlands, the boat drifts through four feet of nearly still water. Unlike the main channel with sandy banks lined with cotton wood and silver maple, with their feet tangled in a thick understory of vegetation, in this channel the water meets green thickets of tall grass. Manomin is actually a cereal grass, like wheat. I recognize the right conditions for Manomin: shallow, slow moving water, like we encountered in the lakes of northern Minnesota. The tall grain reaches for the sky with equal mightiness, as it anchors in the soft organic muck of the river bed. Manomin is steadfast—despite rising and falling water levels, motor boat currents, and nibbling waterfowl and water mammals, such as Mallard ducks and muskrats. Stifling competition, partnering lily pads shade other aquatic plants like cattails. Manomin invites you to be cradled, in its sturdy stalks and abundant nutrients. In Palisade, Minnesota, Manomin gave us gifts of memory, friendship, hospitality, and food. In an attempt to reciprocate and at the request of Betsy, an Anishinaabe elder, we toss balls of clay laden with Manomin seeds to germinate in the coming spring.

SUGARCANE IN LOUISIANA, NOVEMBER

North of Baton Rouge, on a stretch of the river rightfully called Cancer Alley, smoke clouds produced from the remnants of harvested sugarcane plume behind the levee and dissipate along its banks. This stretch is also called the "Chemical Corridor," by those who profit from it. Despite widely used harvesting methods that are more environmentally and lung friendly, such as using the leaves of the cane for compost or mulch, fire is still used here to burn off the dried leaves and other non-sugar parts of the sugarcane stalk. Burning keeps overhead lower for the sugar industry. We can smell the small particulate matter and other toxic compounds, such as ozone, carbon monoxide, and nitric oxide. This somewhat

"Wild Rice in Northern Minnesota" and "Cumulus Cloud near Whitney Plantation." Paintings by Meira Smit

pleasant, sweet aroma has entered our lungs with a discomforting familiarity on our trip down the Mississippi. Further down the horizon is a cumulus cloud, lonely in the sky among a smattering of high elevation cirrocumulus ripples as depicted in my painting, *Cumulus Cloud near Whitney Plantation*. The cloud stands out from the landscape like a feature in an obnoxious popup card against a 2D-landscape. This phenomenon is evidence of a strange but commonplace human meteorological impact, a byproduct of oil refining in which volatile hydrocarbons coalesce with moisture.

Evidence of human impacts are particularly apparent in Southern Louisiana. In a conversation with a geomorphologist who studies coastal land loss there, I was introduced to the term "palimpsest" in the context of geological formations and sites of extraction along the Mississippi River. Palimpsest refers to something that is changed or changing but resembles and retains traces of its earlier form, and often older layers influence the following layers. This is easy to see in river deltas like the Nile River delta in Egypt, where the soil is rich from layers of silt deposition. Economic wealth is built from the land's ability to produce, and conflict arises over who gets to control those resources. The river delta is like the earth itself. It is made up of layers of sediment going back millions of years. The geomorphologist described how land is formed in certain regions in a way that mimics that of the previous era, influenced by environmental conditions but also by historical events. I am building my own psychogeography, an emotional, mental, and geospatial understanding of this section of the river. Using the concept of a palimpsest helps visualize the patterns of history as they are enacted through extraction, oppression, and production on this land.

I AM BUILDING MY OWN PSYCHOGEOGRAPHY, AN EMOTIONAL, MENTAL, AND GEOSPATIAL UNDERSTANDING OF THIS SECTION OF THE RIVER.

Cancer Alley, once attractive to colonizers for its rich river delta soil and proximity to freshwater and ocean ports, today endures significant burdens on its land, water, and inhabitants. We arrived on our boats for a site visit to the Whitney Plantation in Edgard, Louisiana, and walked over the levee, which was built by enslaved people, in a deposition of historical trauma. At this plantation museum, which memorializes experiences of enslaved people, historian

The first star represents where we harvested Manomin, the second, where we planted those seeds. The third star is the place in Louisiana where we watched plumes of smoke go up from sugarcane fields. Painting by Meira Smit

Ibrahima Seck brought us through the preserved shacks of the enslaved who lived at the edge of this old sugarcane plantation. In catalogs, we read the names of hundreds of children who died from the horrid working and living conditions. In silence, our group soaked in the memorial to the revolutionaries lost in the "German Coast" uprising of enslaved people of 1811.

Leaving the plantation grounds, these ruptures in North American history shined upon all following encounters. Our group walks through a sugarcane field, today being harvested by an air-conditioned tractor. As we climb through the batture (the land between river and levee), we encounter inmates working on a tow boat through a work-release scheme—functionally imprisoned on the tow boat. The density of oppression is put succinctly in the article, "The Barbaric History of Sugar in America." Historian Khalil Gibran Muhammad quotes Whitney's executive director, Ashley Rogers, "You passed a dump and a prison on your way to a plantation...these are not coincidences."[2] The shadow of the plantation economy's continued violence looms over the land while a hydrocarbon cumulus dominates the radiant evening sky.

I am reminded of the stories of family members who toiled in the South and migrated north three generations ago, where their hard work continued. Imagining their labor in this extreme heat and dense humidity evokes a sense of grief, as the scene resembles a distant memory. As a visitor now, immersed in this history and yet still breathing in the so-called successes of globalization and colonial capitalism, I desire to resist numbness and demobilization. I question daily how my upbringing in the North allows ignorance and even complacency of this history and present, simply because we don't have to see it every day. Living in the progressive state of Minnesota protects me from many environmental hazards, and, in many ways I benefit from the suffering of people breathing and drinking pollution elsewhere. I benefit from the ways fellow Black people shaped and suffered for this country. And I benefit from those who still rema in Cancer Alley, doing the labor we choose not to acknowledge, or simply being exposed to the externalities of chemical production. As part of a population of beneficiaries, I wonder if the suffering will catch up to us.

Sailing to the Gulf. Photograph by Meira Smit

IN MANY WAYS, I BENEFIT FROM THE SUFFERING OF PEOPLE BREATHING AND DRINKING POLLUTION ELSEWHERE.

The commodification and subjugation of sugarcane and the land that we see today echoes the same atrocities inflicted on other humans in the past and present. Throughout the model of "conventional" agriculture, which evolved from the plantation system reliant on enslaved labor, the methods involved (not the farmers necessarily) have attempted to sterilize, standardize, and control the soil and supporting ecosystem. This approach has led to increasing use of excessive tillage to make planting easier, artificial agents for bigger and better yields, and militarized defenses against invaders, such as nitrogen fertilizers and herbicides and pesticides. In a vicious cycle that is both expensive and damaging to the health of humans and ecosystems alike, "conventional" agriculture facilitates further abuse and creates degraded soil by violently pummeling the existing life in the soil. Nitrogen and phosphorus fertilizers replace the nutrients created by organic matter, and herbicides and pesticides ensure that nothing but the crop can survive.

In the end, very little organic material—the most essential thing for plants to grow in a healthy ecosystem—remains. Organic material is a complex ecosystem made up of decomposing bacteria, bugs, and fungi that can effectively and efficiently make minerals and nutrients biologically available and enable plants to have natural defenses. How long can these "conventional" practices persist, one might ask, until the soil, no matter how many chemical injections it receives, cannot produce the crops our society depends on?

Considering the impact of these practices, I often think about plants and intra-species interactions and how our relationships with them shape our culture and vice versa. Can our communion with these non-human creatures repair the distraught relationships we have to our human relatives along the river, reflecting how environmental justice is social justice? By paying attention and participating with the natural world, humans can recognize that we are not the only species sharing this planet. What kinds of relationships existed in the past and could exist in the present and future?

Take, for instance, sugarcane. This plant, which becomes a word that hangs heavy and saccharine on the tongue, has a history steeped in exploitation—sown in stolen land with stolen labor to please the taste buds of Europe and the young United States. The cultivation of sugarcane has led to significant environmental degradation, polluting the air with its smoke and making it difficult to breathe. By acknowledging this history and understanding the broader impact of sugarcane cultivation, we can begin to see the interconnectedness of environmental and social justice. Paying attention to the way sugarcane has been produced and the suffering it has caused can lead to a greater awareness of our role in the ecosystem and help foster human humility.

AMENDMENT FROM BACK IN MINNESOTA, JULY

It is easy to forget these scenes. Sensitivity diminishes with time and distance. Looking, smelling, feeling back; those sensations are canned and sealed for me as I read this account. I don't want to forget, but I also don't want to actually feel it again, because it hurts and I'd rather not rot in grief. Remembering the smoke and heat. Drinking water during a drought, while the cracked sand begs for a sip of whatever you're drinking, and while rain refills perpetual puddles on the sidewalk and brings riverwaters to levels unsafe for small vessels. The North is really just beginning to experience the so-called effects of climate change, and climate change is harder and harder to deny when a snowy state doesn't receive snow in a winter. We have much to learn from our neighbors in the South about how to adapt (or not) for what is to come.

An earlier version of the section "Sugarcane in Louisiana, November" was originally published in Imani *(Spring 2024), Macalester College's Black student publication.*

ENDNOTES

1 Threshing or "jigging" separates wild rice from its husk. This is traditionally done in a hole lined with either a hide or canvas. Moccasin-clad feet grind off the husk of the rice in a movement that looks like a dance or a jig.

2 Khalil Gibran Muhammad, "The Barbaric History of Sugar in America," *The New York Times*, August 14, 2019, https://www.nytimes.com/interactive/2019/08/14/magazine/sugar-slave-trade-slavery.html.

Action Camps Everywhere

John Kim

The Mississippi River Open School has explored diverse activities and approaches. John Kim reflects on ones he characterizes as solidarity programs in the Anthropocene: programs that resist conditions that contribute to the Anthropocene and prefigure life after it. An emphasis on solidarity suggests that they flourish with the formation of extraordinary communities that model collective action.

Paul Chiyokten Wagner (Wsaanich / Saanich) teaches people at the Welcome Water Protector Center how to build tarpees, an emergency shelter that Paul developed. Photograph courtesy of John Kim

Since its inception in 2022, the Mississippi River Open School for Kinship and Social Exchange* has explored diverse activities and approaches. The ones I selectively focus on in this introduction I characterize as solidarity programs in the Anthropocene*: programs that resist conditions that contribute to the Anthropocene and can prefigure life after it. I describe how these programs are variously educational, community-centered, research-based, activist, or some combination of these. An emphasis on solidarity suggests that such programs flourish with the formation of extraordinary communities that model collective action by drawing direct learning or inspiration from alternative educational practices, such as forest schools, Indigenous and traditional forms of ecological knowledge, cultural organizing, and diverse histories of mutual aid. The first part of this article reviews examples of this work; the second section steps back to discuss conceptual themes and frameworks that eddy around and through these activities. Together, these sections generate specific recommendations for educational reforms that are responsive to looming social and environmental crises associated with the Anthropocene.

* Proposed as a new geological epoch to follow the Holocene, the Anthropocene refers to widescale earth systems changes caused by human activities, including climate change and mass species extinction. Within the span of a couple decades, the term has become pivotal in mobilizing new research and educational initiatives globally, public activism and engagement, art and documentaries, and more.

The example I would like to discuss first is the Open School's work with the Welcome Water Protector Center, which is often referred to as the Welcome Center. The Welcome Center's original location was on the Great River Road in Palisade, Minnesota, a rural location about two and a half hours north of the Twin Cities. The Welcome Center's physical location on the Great River Road closed in early 2024, but Welcome Center activities continue at alternate locations throughout the region. A diverse group of people were involved in organizing there, and, in order to protect their privacy, I do not name them here. I spent a significant amount of time there contributing to activities, and this makes it easier for me to speak in an informed manner.

From 2022 to 2024, the Open School worked with the Welcome Center to co-create cultural and educational programming in collaboration with Native and non-native elders, artists, organizers, activists, and educators who moved through the space. Because it was a bustling nexus for frontline community organizing, the activities that were convened there were often open to the public and not exclusively for college and university students, but students' needs were considered throughout. We learned about diverse traditional, Native, and non-native cultural and ecological approaches to the teaching of practices of care and living.

As an example, teachers led seasonal camps for visitors to celebrate and learn about nature's seasonal gifts. This involved experiential learning activities about spring sugar bushing, summer foraging, fall harvesting, winter storytelling and art sharing, among others. For those of us who were not raised with these traditions, we were incredibly fortunate to learn from teachers who shared with us elements of this knowledge in ways that were appropriate for their communities.

The Welcome Center's recent history provides backstory for the generosity many showed for that place. The center was located on the banks of the Mississippi River where the Enbridge Line 3 oil pipeline crosses its span. Because of this location, the forest around the Welcome Center itself became an action camp for the Stop Line 3 movement* (2020–2021).[1] Given the significance of the Mississippi River for the region and the entire country, this pipeline crossing was the site of some of the nation's fiercest resistance to pipeline construction.

* Stop Line 3 was a movement to halt the construction of the Enbridge Line 3 tar sands oil pipeline. Enbridge completed the construction of the pipeline in 2021.

After the completion of the pipeline, another environmental threat loomed on the horizon: Tamarack Mine, a proposed copper and nickel sulfide mine just 30 minutes from the Enbridge oil pipeline crossing in Palisade.[2] Northern Minnesota's economic history has been tied to resource extraction for centuries, and the proposed mine is representative of an explosive growth in mining activity around the world in the global hunt for minerals to power the green energy gold rush.[3] The Welcome Center shifted to raising awareness of the threats the mine posed to the region's wetland ecosystems and co-creating learning activities about it, focusing on the differential impacts of so-called "green mining" on rural and Native communities on the mine's front line.

This article focuses on a particular aspect of these learning activities: namely, the *form* of the camp at the Welcome Center. By form, I refer to the camp's social organization and its daily routines, which are powerfully emergent educational experiences. The layered social richness and camaraderie of living and learning as part of this community is difficult to convey, but it gets to the heart of what I want to communicate here.

THE ANTHROPOCENE IS A GEOSOCIAL DISASTER

I compare action camps to what Rebecca Solnit[4] has called extraordinary communities—the self-organized groups that can form in the aftermath of natural disasters. In the days and weeks following a disaster, and in the wreckage left in its wake, it is possible to witness the formation of communities of care that provide essential services to support life, including food, shelter, healthcare, community, and security. Dormant forms of sociality and solidarity emerge as widespread volunteerism and mutual aid. This has been powerfully observed in the aftermath of many disasters, including Hurricane Katrina, the 1985 Mexico City earthquake, and the COVID-19 pandemic.[5]

Kathleen Tierney[6] argues that all disasters are social in origin. Obviously, one cannot stop a hurricane or a massive flood, so what Tierney means is that a disaster's human toll is a consequence of the social infrastructure in affected communities. Communities on the front line of disasters may not have access to sufficient material and financial resources, the expertise, or preparedness to mount an effective emergency response. The ongoing neoliberal rollback of social services, including the underfunding of federal emergency response programs, has direct consequences for the survivability of crises.

Another way in which the survivability of disasters can be understood as social in origin is through a recognition of ongoing social engineering that has been leading to growing isolation, separation, and disconnection from others which can constrain a community's emergency response. Inspired by this work with the Open School, in Spring 2024 I taught a class entitled, "Alone Together: The Contradictions of Social Media." The class's premise was that, notwithstanding the "social" in social media, the media's historical role has often been the distinct opposite. With the endless expansion of commodification into everyday social relations, the media has led to a separation of people into individualized consumers. (We considered the widespread introduction of television into living rooms as an illustration of the media as a technology of mass social isolation.) This digital isolation and separation have had the effect of fomenting perceived political helplessness and real political powerlessness. As Dean Spade[7] argues, "Today, many of us live in the most atomized societies in human history, which makes our lives less secure and undermines our ability to organize together to change unjust conditions on a large scale." It is important to add that this atomization is not only produced by the media but enforced by corporate and capital interests in the form of state-sanctioned police and military violence, governmental neglect, and white supremacy.

The Anthropocene is a geosocial disaster. It is a crisis on a geologic scale, and there's fundamentally this social one as well.

As many critical commentators noted during the COVID-19 pandemic, crises are a portal through which it is possible to discover cracks in the edifice of the neoliberal state.[8] The extraordinary communities that form in action camps are a portal for the reconstruction of sociality as a necessary alternative to atomization. Extraordinary communities exhibit what Victor Turner[9] termed *communitas*, the social connectedness that binds people in solidarity during particular times of cultural change or transition. Within the field of anthropology, communitas has been applied to the study of rituals, specifically the powerful collective feeling and utopian desires that emerge among participants. Rituals loosen the prevailing norms that govern inflexible social hierarchies, allowing people to connect across lines of difference. *Communitas* can be dangerous for a society that is invested in the rigid maintenance of the status quo, as communitas can disrupt, invert, or otherwise upset dominant hierarchies and formations of power.

THE ANTHROPOCENE IS A GEOSOCIAL DISASTER. IT IS A CRISIS ON A GEOLOGIC SCALE, AND FUNDAMENTALLY THIS SOCIAL ONE AS WELL.

Communitas can also exist in the liminal time around a disaster, as is evidenced in the extraordinary communities that come together in the wake of catastrophes.[10] When faced with the consequences of our social separation and atomization, the forces that govern and regulate everyday behaviors, out of necessity, fall away. We require moments of effervescent communitas to disrupt unequal social structures.[11]

ACTION CAMPS AS EXTRAORDINARY LEARNING COMMUNITIES

We live in a time of action camps as extraordinary communities that challenge the unfolding geosocial disaster. In camps, we relearn forms of collective action and solidarity that have nurtured human togetherness for millennia prior to the isolation and separation that characterize our current moment. Action camps are a portal to an emergent space for the repair of damaged sociality. We might know little about how to collectively prepare, cook, and distribute meals for a group of one hundred, but we will quickly learn on the job. A design for an emergency winter shelter might not exist, but with others we will brainstorm, design, and build it.

In "falling together"[12] to create social systems to provide basic services, experiential teaching and learning happens. A decolonized education exists in the creation of learning spaces in which people come to recognize the knowledge and skills they already possess and are moved to share with others. This is how the emergent educational space of action camps differs from traditional schooling. While traditional schools can reinforce obedience from an early age through subjection into hierarchical roles, in camps, everyone has skills and knowledge to contribute and, as such, everyone can teach and learn from each other.

As spaces of learning, action camps did not arise spontaneously but draw from multiple traditions. I want to acknowledge a few sources of influence.

INDIGENOUS-LED RESISTANCE MOVEMENTS

Isabel Huot-Link[13] shares how her understanding of decolonization and social justice was shaped through a relational education at Line 3 pipeline resistance camps: "Residents built relationships with and around particular places through art-making, cultivating gardens, skill-sharing, sharing stories, educating youth, and organizing resistance strategy in response to the geographies of treaty territories, reservations, and pipeline corridors." A long history of Indigenous-led resistance movements has shaped the social organization of action camps. Writing about the Oceti Sakowin camp during protests against the Dakota Access pipeline (DAPL) at Standing Rock, Nick Estes[14] connects the DAPL protests to a history of struggles against settler colonization and the environmental consequences of its logic of extraction. He characterizes the social organization of the Standing Rock camps as an "abolition geography." Put in terms we have been considering in this article, his description of abolition geography resonates with our framework for an extraordinary community where economic equity and social equality can be realized:

> Free food, free education, free health care, free legal aid, a strong sense of community, safety, and security were guaranteed to all...In the absence of empire, people came together to help each other, to care for one another. The #NoDAPL camps were designed according to need, not profit. (There were no prisons or armed bodies of the state.) That's what separated them from the world of cops, settlers, and oil companies that surrounded them. Capitalism is not merely an economic system, but also a social system. And it was here abundantly evident that Indigenous social systems offered a radically different way of relating to other people and the world.[15]

ACTION CAMPS ARE A PORTAL TO AN EMERGENT SPACE FOR THE REPAIR OF DAMAGED SOCIALITY.

COMMUNITY SURVIVAL PROGRAMS

Estes's vision of camps as "a radically different way of relating to other people and the world" is inspired by Black-led abolitionist movements and mutual aid societies. In referring to action camps as solidarity programs I am connecting with analyses of the Black Panthers and their community survival programs in particular. As described by David Hilliard: "We call the program a 'survival' program—survival pending revolution—not something to replace the revolution...but an activity that strengthens us for the coming fight, a lifeboat or raft leading us safely to shore."[16]

The name—solidarity programs—is intended as an acknowledgement of the significant differences between Panther community survival programs and what I am referring to as solidarity programs. The Panthers' efforts were rooted in a long tradition of Black mutual aid that organized the social services needed to support the basic conditions for life.[17] Because of the legacies of slavery and white supremacy, Black communities in the U.S. have often been unable to access equitable social services. Out of necessity, the Panthers created autonomous social systems for security, health care, food distribution, and education. Many of these systems were subject to repression that was notoriously violent, but remarkably, some of them were adopted by the federal government, such as a free lunch program in schools.[18]

Multiple throughlines connect survival programs and contemporary efforts to

The main house at the Welcome Water Protector Center. The banners were lent to the Stop Line 3 movement by Dylan Miner (Métis Nation of Ontario). Photograph by John Kim

cultivate extraordinary communities. One of our project partners along the Gulf South, Monique Verdin (Houma Nation), for example, references this history in her project, "Marooned: Between Water and Land."[19] Having lived through multiple flooding events and facing conditions that grow more precarious with climate change, Monique and her collaborators are developing a camp to "support the co-creation and stewardship of safe refuge for people, plants and other living beings to foster biodiversity, food, medicine, and a sense of autonomy."[20]

A DECOLONIZED EDUCATION EXISTS IN THE CREATION OF LEARNING SPACES IN WHICH PEOPLE COME TO RECOGNIZE THE KNOWLEDGE AND SKILLS THEY ALREADY POSSESS AND ARE MOVED TO SHARE WITH OTHERS.

EARTH SCHOOLS

I have referred to camps in various ways so far, including action, resistance, and seasonal camps. As I have highlighted throughout this article, they provide an educational setting in which learning is experiential and based in nature. An apt comparison here is the Forest School, an educational setting in which outdoor spaces become the classroom for experiential learning. Recent trends in Forest Schools have moved away from a romantic celebration of nature and toward the design of land-based education in the Anthropocene.[21] In living and learning on an extensively controlled and engineered river like the Mississippi for one hundred days, the River Semester is a model for this type of education.

In order to distinguish these types of programs from Forest Schools, I prefer to refer to them as Earth Schools, programs which prioritize a reckoning with the challenges of the Anthropocene. Earth Schools ask: how do we live and learn experientially in disturbed Anthropocenic landscapes? They go beyond instruction about ecological relations between humans, plants, and animals, and extend learning to coinhabitation with other-than-human worlds.[22] Earth Schools incubate forms of action for the care of the planet and its inhabitants against further despoiling by capitalist extraction. Earth Schools are settings in which to repair and relearn social capacities that have been degraded, by design, by pervasive digital isolation and alienation.

ACTION CAMPS EVERYWHERE

Indigenous-led resistance movements, community survival programs, and Earth Schools all contribute knowledge and practical wisdom that inspire the organization of action camps as I've experienced them. The phrase "Action camps everywhere" is a recognition of the opportunities for education modeled on the unique experiential settings found in camps. "Action camps everywhere" opens this education to students, activists, scientists, artists, the public—anyone who needs this knowledge to be prepared for, and even thrive, in the midst of the crises that surround us. "Action camps everywhere" is a call to establish action camps in forests, on riverbanks, in deserts, on college campuses, on oceans, everywhere, because the front line *is* everywhere. We need action camps everywhere as they are emergent spaces for the solidarity programs sharing the knowledge and practices that can get us out of the Anthropocene.

SOLIDARITY PROGRAMS IN THE ANTHROPOCENE

"Action camps everywhere" may be a provocative slogan, but how might we apply it to reimagining education, namely college and university education in the Anthropocene? Can we draw inspiration from action camps as extraordinary communities in this reimagining? What should higher education look like if it were mobilized to get us out of the Anthropocene? In contrast to the previous section of this article, the content below is more theoretical. I reflect on themes in the programmatic approaches that we have tried to implement in our work with the Open School. I also frame this discussion through reflection on the Anthropocene, which puts these ideas into conversation with others who have advocated for educational changes to better respond to contemporary urgencies.

TRANSFORMATION OF MODES OF KNOWLEDGE PRODUCTION

Paul Crutzen, a climatologist who has advocated for the adoption of a new geological epoch characterized by widespread human transformations of Earth systems, said, "What I hope is that the term 'Anthropocene' will be a warning to the world."[23] Crutzen's proposal is motivated by a sense of extreme urgency for research and education to attend to the world's thorny problems. The popularization of the concept of the Anthropocene speaks to how academic research can be made more accessible and productive for debates inside and outside the academy.

Our current planetary emergency and the threats to the inhabitability of the Earth for all living species speak to the stakes of transforming knowledge. The forms of knowledge production that have led us to the Anthropocene are ill-equipped to lead us out of it.[24] Higher education in particular has had a central role in reproducing dominant knowledge practices that contribute to the Anthropocene.[25] A changing planet requires a transformation in the knowledge practices that characterize, understand, mitigate, and educate about these changes.[26]

PROBLEM-FOCUSED RESEARCH AND TEACHING

With the intensity and frequency of polycrises that surround us, communities on the front line of these struggles have responded with reparative, creative, visionary, and emergent strategies. (One tactic has been the formation of extraordinary communities discussed earlier in this article.) Frontline communities have developed sophisticated analyses of their condition and imagined wide-ranging responses. As crises continue to spread to communities and places unaccustomed to them, frontline communities have much knowledge to impart.

Colleges and universities can do more to work in solidarity with frontline communities. Community engagement centers are invaluable for mediating these relationships because of ethical concerns in partnering with groups that may have experienced generations of extractive social relations. Different ways to structure these relationships can be defined depending on needs; a frontline community can provide guidance on the identification of problems, with faculty and students developing projects in consultation with that community. More transformatively, we can also imagine more reciprocal, bidirectional relationships, where students learn directly from frontline communities that are in a better position to understand many of the problems society faces.

We sought to build a reciprocal relationship in our work with the Welcome Water Protector Center. This has taken multiple forms, including supporting the Center's efforts to offer cultural programming and public education about environmental threats facing the region. This relationship, in turn, enabled the Welcome Center to provide additional opportunities for public learning. For campus constituencies, this partnership has opened up possible pathways for research and teaching across divisions and departments, including Environmental Studies (alternatives to extraction through mineral recycling), International Studies (critical digital infrastructure), geography (remote sensing and GIS study of new mines), physics (the electrochemistry of batteries), and geology (the geology of fracking and its threats to water aquifers), among others.

A CHANGING PLANET REQUIRES A TRANSFORMATION IN THE KNOWLEDGE PRACTICES THAT CHARACTERIZE, UNDERSTAND, MITIGATE, AND EDUCATE ABOUT THESE CHANGES.

The reciprocal relationship between the Welcome Center and college and university faculty highlights how a problem-focused curriculum can reorient teaching and research priorities on campuses. In consultation with frontline communities, faculty can identify problems that contribute to defining campus research and educational initiatives and committing resources to promote collaborative work. This should be done in a reciprocal way in which colleges and universities support communities' needs.

TRANSDISCIPLINARITY AS "METADISCIPLINARY SPACES OF TEACHING AND DIALOGUE"

The title of this section is a mouthful, but it means that when dealing with an urgent issue, you make use of all the tools you have at your disposal. I understand interdisciplinarity as a transfer of methods and approaches from one discipline to another. In this sense interdisciplinarity can preserve existing frameworks of disciplinary research and constrain the capacity for interdisciplines to develop distinctive, innovative, or novel methods and approaches to the study of problems. When considering the Anthropocene and its intertwined polycrises that cut across classical divisions of knowledge, a reproduction of disciplinarity can be a hindrance to a critical engagement with problem-focused research and teaching goals.

Transdisciplinarity recognizes methods and approaches that go beyond interdisciplinarity. In accepting the inaugural Professorship of Earth Politics at the University of Cape Town, Professor Lesley Green[27] argued that "transdisciplinarity needs to graduate to a metadisciplinary framework." This is to say that metadisciplinarity unlocks common approaches and processes to mobilize new modes of research, teaching, and action. One way to understand the debate surrounding the definition of the Anthropocene is as a site of tension concerning its status as a metadisciplinary concept. On the one hand, the International Union of Geological Sciences's evaluation of the evidentiary basis for the periodization has sought to apply a disciplinary framework (geology) to the Anthropocene.[28] As a counter-formulation to a narrowly defined geological conceptualization of the Anthropocene, the "colonial Anthropocene" has drawn on ideas of coloniality and resource extraction from humanistic and social scientific fields in examining forces that have contributed to the Anthropocene.[29] As an example of how a metadisciplinary concept can inspire new modes of knowledge production at the intersection of transdisciplinary collaboration, the colonial Anthropocene has been incredibly productive for opening up varying ways to understand Earth systems changes as part of human history.

CONCLUSION

The second part of this article applied the idea of solidarity programs to the reimagining of educational practices that respond to crises in the Anthropocene. Some deconstructive critics would argue that this does not go far enough, and they would call for an abolition of the university in its current form by inverting it so as to offer educational resources to the many on its outside that are excluded from its benefits.[30] Though I am sympathetic to the critique, this sees the problem in only two dimensions: inside or outside, refuge or front line, public or private, professional or unprofessional, university or what Stefano Harney and Fred Moten[31] call undercommons.

Short of abolition, can we think of ways to transform the university into a pedagogical environment that is open to the camps and communities from which it is imperative to learn? How can universities support communities so they can continue their necessary work? How might we create opportunities for students to responsibly learn from and with communities without overburdening them?

Our use of the term "open" in the Open School offers an alternative spatial model for reorienting the way in which we think about the relationship between universities and communities.[32] If we evert the university, that is, turn it inside out, it can become a home for public pedagogy. What was exclusive to the inside can be offered to the outside. Resources that are accessible to students on campuses (including funding, meeting spaces, expertise, training, libraries, etc.) can be made available to communities as well. This suggests novel ways to respond with varied strategies for engagement.

The university can become a welcoming center for social, material, and intellectual reciprocity and exchange. This learning can happen on university campuses, the front porches of communities, and around a campfire. This is one way in which we mean "open" here: an Open School is a reimagining of the location of education. Rather than cloistered in closed universities, an Open School consists of globally distributed hubs as sites of eversion and experimentation for crossing the formal organization of the university.[33] With kinship and social reciprocity, an Open School is an extraordinary community for collective learning and action that resists the geosocial disaster that unfolds around us.

This article is adapted from a talk for the 2024 International Roundtable at Macalester College. The theme of the year's roundtable was "Slowing Down, Seeking Roots, Making Sanctuary": Belonging Beyond the Anthropocene (Summer 2024).

ENDNOTES

1 Thank you to Dr. Malte Vogl for suggesting the term "action" as a broader way to refer to camps.

2 Joseph Mogul, "Indigenous and Rural Organizers in Minnesota Prioritize Clean Water Over 'Green' Nickel Mine," *Prism*, March 3, 2025, https://prismreports.org/2025/03/03/minnesota-mine-ojibwe-manoomin/.

3 Mogul, "Indigenous and Rural Organizers."

4 Rebecca Solnit, *A Paradise Built in Hell: The Extraordinary Communities that Arise in Disaster* (Penguin Books, 2010).

5 Solnit, *A Paradise Built in Hell*; Dean Spade, *Mutual Aid: Building Solidarity During This Crisis (and the Next)* (Verso, 2020).

6 Kathleen Tierney, *The Social Roots of Risk: Producing Disasters, Promoting Resilience* (Stanford University Press, 2020).

7 Spade, *Mutual Aid*, 13.

8 Arundhati Roy, "The Pandemic Is a Portal," *Financial Times*, April 3, 2020, https://www.ft.com/content/10d8f5e8-74eb-11ea-95fe-fcd274e920ca.

9 Victor W. Turner, *The Ritual Process: Structure and Anti-Structure* (Aldine Publishing Company, 1969).

10 Steve Matthewman and Shinya Uekusa, "Theorizing Disaster Communitas," *Theory and Society: Renewal and Critique in Social Theory* 50, no. 6 (2021): 965–984, https://doi.org/10.1007/s11186-021-09442-4.

11 Alain Badiou and Gregory Elliott, *The Rebirth of History* (Verso, 2012).

12 Solnit, *A Paradise Built in Hell.*

13 Isabel Huot-Link, "Resistance as Grounds for Futurity: Placemaking and Unsettling through #StopLine3," *Open Rivers: Rethinking Water, Place & Community* 24 (2023), https://doi.org/10.24926/2471190X.10534.

14 Nick Estes, *Our History is the Future: Standing Rock Versus the Dakota Access Pipeline, and the Long Tradition of Indigenous Resistance* (Verso, 2019).

15 Estes, *Our History is the Future*, 252.

16 David Hilliard and Lewis Cole, *This Side of Glory: The Autobiography of David Hilliard and the Story of the Black Panther Party* (Little, Brown, 1993), 211–12.

17 Jessica Gordon Nembhard, *Collective Courage: A History of African American Cooperative Economic Thought and Practice* (Pennsylvania State University Press, 2014).

18 Nik Heynen, "Bending the Bars of Empire from Every Ghetto for Survival: The Black Panther Party's Radical Antihunger Politics of Social Reproduction and Scale," *Annals of the Association of American Geographers* 99, no. 2 (2009): 406–422, https://doi.org/10.1080/00045600802683767.

19 Monique Verdin, "Marooned: Between Water and Land" (unpublished grant proposal, 2024).

20 Verdin, "Marooned."

21 Katherine Mycock, "Forest Schools: Moving Towards an Alternative Pedagogical Response to the Anthropocene?" *Discourse: Studies in the Cultural Politics of Education* 41, no. 3 (2019): 427–440, https://doi.org/10.1080/01596306.2019.1670446.

22 Donna Jeanne Haraway, *Staying with the Trouble: Making Kin in the Chthulucene*, Experimental Futures (Duke University Press, 2016).

23 Paul Crutzen, quoted in Elizabeth Kolbert, "The 'Epic Row' Over a New Epoch," *The New Yorker*, April 20, 2024, https://www.newyorker.com/news/the-weekend-essay/the-epic-row-over-a-new-epoch.

24 Isabelle Stengers, *Another Science is Possible: A Manifesto for Slow Science*, trans. Stephen Muecke (Polity Press, 2018).

25 Max Liboiron, *Pollution Is Colonialism* (Duke University Press, 2021).

26 Bruno Latour, *Down to Earth: Politics in the New Climatic Regime* (Polity Press, 2018)

27 Lesley Green, "Material Flows as Earth Politics: Concepts, Methods, and Approaches for Transdisciplinary Diagnostics and Repair at Muizenberg East, Cape Town," *Environment and Planning E: Nature and Space* 7, no. 13 (2023): 1279–1298, https://doi.org/10.1177/25148486231219156.

28 Anthony Barnosky and Mary Ellen Hannibal, "Despite Official Vote, the Evidence of the Anthropocene is Clear," *Yale Environment 360*, April 2, 2024, https://e360.yale.edu/features/anthropocene-denied. The governing body's rejection of the epoch in March 2024 is an indication of the limits of disciplinarity in providing intellectual tools needed to address today's problems.

29 Nicholas A. Brown and Sarah E. Kanouse, "An Anti-Racist and Anti-Colonial Anthropocene for Compromised Times," *The Anthropocene Review* 8, no. 2 (2021): 159–168, https://doi.org/10.1177/20530196211000080.

30 See Eli Meyerhoff, *Beyond Education: Radical Studying for Another World* (University of Minnesota Press, 2019). A study of alternative education movements and their critiques of mainstream education in the U.S., which include calls for the abolition of its current form.

31 Stefano Harney and Fred Moten, *The Undercommons: Fugitive Planning & Black Study* (Minor Compositions, 2013).

32 See "Home," Mississippi River Open School for Kinship and Social Exchange, accessed October 13, 2025, https://mississippiriver.school. Our website has more information on the Open School as method in addition to examples of this work.

33 John Kim, "The Fourth Coast, Revisited," *The Anthropocene Review* 8, no. 3 (2021): 241–249, https://doi.org/10.1177/20530196211044620.

Bear Creek
by SARA PAJUNEN

In May 2021, I visited 17 water crossings along Enbridge's Line 3 pipeline construction route through Minnesota—now carrying Canadian tar sands oil to a refinery in Superior, Wisconsin.

I used hydrophones to record the acoustic underwater environment of each water crossing (no two alike) and a drone to capture the construction of the pipeline at

each crossing (mostly in the decking phase leading to drilling). Each environment welcomed me and became my close friend, inviting me into its complexity and essence.

The results draw attention to the interruptionand desecration of these intimate places.

This photo was taken above Bear Creek, between the Mississippi headwaters and Lake Itasca. Bear Creek drains to the Mississippi River. I walked along the creek at sunset and stopped to listen to its underwater song. The creek was gentle and soft and felt so vulnerable in the face of the violent construction.

Photograph by Sara Pajunen

Fluvial Networks of Creative Resistance

Joe Underhill

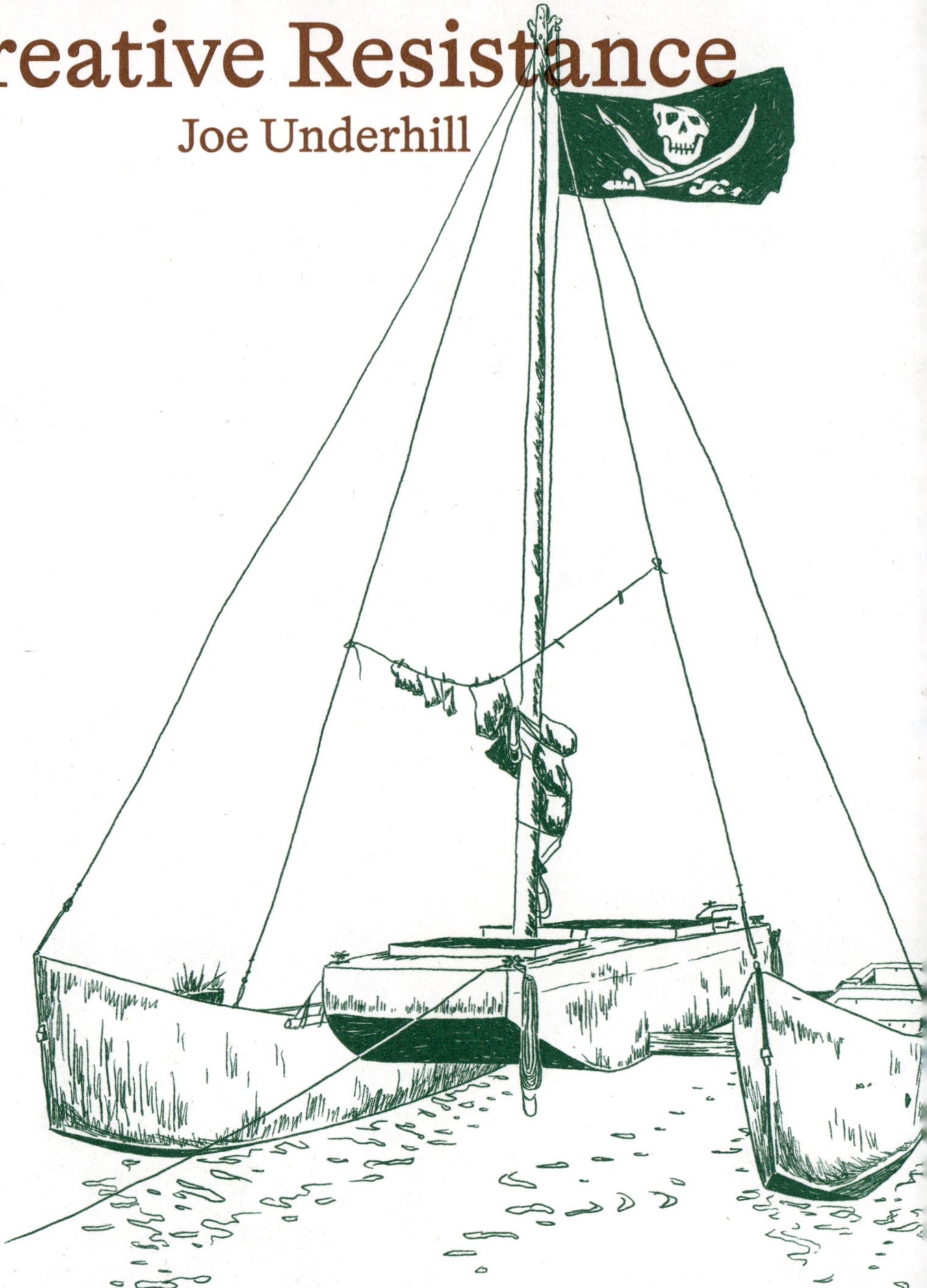

With twenty years of experience in experiential learning, Joe Underhill characterizes rivers as classrooms for "living otherwise." Drawing inspiration from diverse sources, including canoe-based education and Indigenous-led resistance camps, the river as classroom is a pirate pedagogy for the building of joyful and resilient alternatives in the Anthropocene.

> The ship is the heterotopia par excellence. In civilizations without boats, dreams dry up, espionage takes the place of adventure, and the police take the place of pirates.
>
> —Michel Foucault, "Of Other Spaces"

In this article I explore the use of rivers as educational spaces within which to imagine and experiment with alternative ways of living. I draw primarily from my experience over the past twenty years of bringing students out onto the Mississippi River as part of a program that is now called the River Semester offered through Augsburg University's Center for Global Education and Experience. That program is one of a growing number of experimental outdoor and/or experiential education programs that form the basis of an emergent global network—one that I believe should be expanded and strengthened. In the face of multiple and overlapping planetary crises, rivers and watersheds around the world can provide productive alternatives to the range of current social injustices, environmental problems, political dysfunction, and social anomie. Through these alternatives, we can begin to build alternative social forms—what Foucault describes as "heterotopias"—that hold some promise for living well.

What does it mean to live "otherwise" at this moment in time?[1] What lifeways are suggested by a lengthy trip by canoe or sailboat down the Mississippi River? In some ways, one answer is a lived version of "going down to the river to pray." Akin to Michael Pollan's food rules[2]—eat food, mostly plants, not too much—the rules we live by on these river trips amount to little more than consuming less, connecting with the world and with each other, and getting off our digital devices and screens. On these trips we spend almost all our time outside (with the attendant joys and discomforts), cook good food, sing and dance, make campfires virtually every night, swim in the river's muddy waters, learn about its pulse and flow, get plenty of physical exercise, and do what we can to work toward social and environmental justice.

We attend to the mental and physical well-being of the group, using simple medicines, open communication, and honesty about who we are and what we need. These activities and ways of being are a source of joy in the Anthropocene, the contested term for a new geological era in which human activity has become the most significant force shaping the earth.[3] Fluvial networks of creative resistance decrease the harm being done to ourselves and the environment. I give examples of what these forms of living otherwise have been like for us on some of the trips we have taken down the river, and suggests that these activities form the basis—the methodology—for building broader networks as part of the work we need to do to imagine a way home in the Anthropocene.[4]

In the United States today, we face a range of fairly significant social, political, and environmental challenges. In many areas, such as child mortality, education levels, and average lifespan, we have seen substantial improvements over time, but in many areas of our lives there are troubling trends. Wildfires are springing up with increasing frequency and intensity;[5] the political system is characterized by a high level of polarization and animosity, reflected in events such as the January 6, 2021, riots at the U.S. Capitol; the earth's temperature is steadily rising, with 2024 the warmest year in recorded history; the United States has the highest prison population rate in the world,[6] with a disproportionately high number of those prisoners being people of color; there is a growing wealth gap, and rising rates of mental illness and deaths from drug overdose.[7]

Part of finding ways to thrive and live fully in the midst of these trends is to be true to who we are, to bring our whole selves into our work and to create spaces where our students can do that as well.[8] A pedagogy aspiring to authenticity requires that the programs we create reflect who we are as individuals. The practice of outdoor education, and the fairly radical departures from mainstream educational practices described here, are not for everyone. There will need to be all sorts of different ways to navigate our way through the climate crisis, the ongoing effects of racism and settler colonialism, the wars, the gun violence, the carceral state, the various forms of neo-authoritarianism popping up around the globe. The River Semester is itself

Eventually the river opens up to the sea. Here is one of the Water Striders heading out into Lake Pontchartrain near the end of the journey in 2023. Photograph by Tom Turnbull

a reflection of my own predilection for a particular response to the polycrises, which for me has involved exploration, wandering, swimming, sailing, and trying to live close to the land and connected to place. This is my own way of dealing with the various adverse trends listed above, one that amounts to both a diving in and an escape from many of the realities of the contemporary world.

As a teenager growing up in the shadow of Vietnam and in the thick of the nuclear arms race, I attended an outdoor survival school and volunteered on the Hudson River Sloop Clearwater. My first year in college, disenchanted with the scene on campus, I moved out of the dorm and slept in a tent in the pine barrens behind the campus. After a semester of courses taken on board a schooner sailing down the East Coast, I decided to switch schools and move to the West Coast. Rather than driving, a friend and I embarked on a four-month, 7,000-mile bike trip across the country. It was a pilgrimage in search of some alternatives to the polluted, violent, automobile-based, fossil-fueled system we found ourselves in.

Years later, when I began work at Augsburg University in Minneapolis, I began thinking about ways to get students down to the Mississippi, which flowed by just a few blocks from the campus. This exploration of rivers as spaces for educational experimentation began in 2001, with the creation of a course called Environmental and River Politics. The first trip on the river, from St. Cloud to Minneapolis, was part of an expedition organized by Dan McGuinness of the Audubon Society.[9] For that five-day trip we used two wooden dories, or "pulling boats," with oars and sails built by Urban Boatbuilders. Subsequently I began working with the outfitter Wilderness Inquiry, taking progressively longer trips on the river. Other study away trips to New Zealand, Costa Rica, Nicaragua, Tanzania, and Egypt provided additional experience and lessons on the educational value of studying in situ. By the time we had completed a 10-day river trip in August 2014, it seemed feasible to expand to a semester-long expedition, and in 2015 the River Semester program traveled the length of the Mississippi. This was repeated in 2018, and then again in 2019 as part of the international network of scholars, artists, and community practitioners organized by the Berlin-based Haus der Kulturen der Welt (HKW) and the Max Planck Institute for the History of Science, under the title of Mississippi. An Anthropocene River.* Based on that experience, the River Semester then designed and built two river catamarans—dubbed Water Striders—and took them on their maiden voyage during the Covid-19 pandemic in 2021. These new craft worked well and, with some modifications, were used again for the fifth river trip in 2023, as part of the Mississippi River Open School for Kinship and Social Exchange, funded by a grant from the Mellon Foundation. The hope is that this expedition can be a key element of a larger global network of alternative, outdoor educational programming.

This is not what university coursework has traditionally looked like. Higher education has evolved over the centuries, with shifting epistemological paradigms, the rise of new disciplines, adaptation of new technologies, and an increasingly diverse student body.[10] But the basic pedagogical form has remained relatively constant. Students sit in classrooms taking notes, study for exams, and write papers. Today the academy must think through how to educate students to live in a world in which human activity has become the dominant force shaping the planet. This growing set of planetary responsibilities comes at a time of increasing strains in higher education and a widespread sense of embattlement and retrenchment on many college campuses. But even in the face of these political and economic challenges (and in part because of them), there is a need to help students imagine, and live out, alternatives to the contemporary social, economic, and political systems. We need our students to be able to imagine something beyond the current realities and, based on that vision, find ways to take meaningful and productive action. Although utopian imaginaries of authors such as Octavia Butler[11] and José Esteban Muñoz[12] play a role in suggesting alternatives to current realities, it is crucially important to create something here and now that reflects these values and visions.[13] We need programs that invite students, teachers, and community members into the process of building alternatives and enacting new forms of living and education within the context of the problematic present. On our trips down the Mississippi, we have come to think of this as a form of pirate pedagogy.

* Mississippi. An Anthropocene River (2018-2019) explored the vast region encompassed by the world's fourth largest river. The project's aim was to make this landscape legible as a critical zone of habitation and long term human-environment interaction. The project is manifest in a variety of field-research activities, public forums, workshops, and journeys on and along the Mississippi River.

ON OUR TRIPS DOWN THE MISSISSIPPI, WE HAVE COME TO THINK OF THIS AS A FORM OF PIRATE PEDAGOGY.

On our trips traveling in small boats down the Mississippi, we developed the habit of flying the pirate's skull and crossbones flag, or Jolly Roger—a countercultural emblem that reflects aspects of the ethos of the program itself. Though we by no means embraced all aspects of what the flag symbolized, as a radical experiment in university curriculum, these trips do amount to something akin to piracy.[14] Piracy sprung in part from the abuses of power on board sailing vessels in the seventeenth century and sought to redistribute wealth outside the bounds of the existing system of extractive capitalism and colonialism. We take some inspiration from the move toward setting up alternative ways of living, the joyous and mischievous rebelliousness embodied in the figure of the pirate, and the sense of expansive freedom referenced in Foucault's "other spaces." Although not quite the high seas, rivers, particularly ones as large as the Mississippi, provide fertile ground for this kind of educational experimentation qua mutiny.

EDUCATION ON THE MARGINS: RIVERS AS CREATIVE AND LIBERATING SPACES

The changes in the nature of our educational system called for by the current ecological crises encourage us to pay attention to the physical setting for that education. Despite laudable efforts at campus greening, college grounds, buildings, and classrooms still largely reflect the energy-intensive, high-tech, and car-centric culture of contemporary America. For instance, where I teach at Augsburg University, despite decades of working to reduce car commuting, the parking lots, which occupy a significant portion of campus, are overflowing. The newest building, although it achieved a high ranking with the U. S. Green Building Council, consumes more energy than any other building on campus. The life of the mind is premised on the ability to outsource almost all physical labor and avoid most discomfort or inconvenience.[15] The standards for college housing have risen to the point that many on-campus residences resemble luxury condos.[16] These modern conveniences, amenities, and comforts attract students and can increase capacity in many ways, but they come at a cost and are part of the modern, consumerist, energy-intensive train on which we are riding. And all the energy consumption and resource extraction have an impact. College campuses are thoroughly enmeshed in these extractive practices, including their foundation as part of settler colonial and extractivist practices.[17] The cost of higher education is increasing much faster than inflation, while students are reporting higher and higher levels of stress, anxiety, and depression. Campuses are working on responding to this panoply of challenges by offering more mental health counseling, reducing their carbon footprint, and developing some new programs in response to the environmental and social justice challenges of the day. But progress is slow, and—despite serious campus greening efforts—even the switch from fossil fuels to solar energy and electric vehicles still requires a huge amount of mining and raw materials. Think, for example, of the rush to mine the copper, nickel, lithium, and rare earth metals needed to produce the batteries, solar cells, and electrical grid required in turn for the transition to an all-electric renewable energy economy. The extraction of these minerals often comes at the expense of the marginalized communities living in the vicinity of those mining operations.

Sorting and cleaning freshly harvested manoomin at a ricing camp in northern Minnesota with Betsy, an Ojibwe elder, and Giiwedin, an Ojibwe artist. Photograph by Noa Shapiro-Tamir

This is to say that the context and setting for teaching and learning matter. The mindset and physical surroundings—set and setting—are crucially important in the educational experience. Students are learning how to live their lives through the kinds of norms and structures they encounter as they leave home and begin their lives as semiautonomous adults. On campuses, they do so within standard climate-controlled, carpeted rooms, sitting in rows of seats, more often than not facing a screen while a professor gives a lecture with accompanying slide deck, largely isolated from the world around them. Faculty teach their particular specialized disciplines in which they have the required credentials, but the physical structures and daily routines of the college campus are, for the most part, taken for granted. This is not to say that we should stop teaching in classrooms. They are in many ways excellent places to learn. But I would argue that, even while teaching in those spaces, it is worth thinking about the ways in which these settings reinforce the idea that this is the way the world should be, even as, in the world outside, we are experiencing a dramatic increase in the rate of extinctions, and wildfires and violent storms are destroying landscapes and homes.[18]

If the system is so problematic, and existing campus practices are part of that system, it follows that there is great pedagogical benefit to being outside, questioning and critiquing the form and context of education in radical ways. Universities need students to know that there are other ways to live that offer healthier, more joyous, and less destructive ways of living.[19] This means trading the splendid isolation of the air-conditioned ivory tower for muddy, messy, beautifully anarchic spaces, where the pursuit of the liberal arts can be carried out in the thick of the Anthropocene. What are those spaces? There are already many ways in which education takes place off campus. There is a long (though often problematic) history of academic field research, from biological field study to archeological excavations and sociological community-engaged research. Study abroad has become increasingly common at both the undergraduate and graduate level. However, those programs typically use traditional pedagogies and research agendas, even if they take place off campus. Wilderness education, such as the National Outdoor Leadership School (NOLS) and Outward Bound, and ocean-based programs like those run by the Sea Education Association (SEA) constitute alternatives to traditional curricula but have the drawback of being largely disconnected from "normal life" and human communities. They take place in remote wilderness or the open ocean, far from so many of the dynamics that are driving the Anthropocene. As we step outside the confines of modern cities and campuses with their glistening buildings, there is great educational value in what Donna Haraway[20] refers to as "staying with the trouble" and resisting the urge to completely escape into the wild. The challenge remains of how we can live in the Anthropocene, not separate ourselves from it so thoroughly that we are just running away from the problem.

ALTHOUGH NOT QUITE THE HIGH SEAS, RIVERS, PARTICULARLY ONES AS LARGE AS THE MISSISSIPPI, PROVIDE FERTILE GROUND FOR THIS KIND OF EDUCATIONAL EXPERIMENTATION QUA MUTINY.

There are many possibilities for how to live differently within the realities of contemporary society, but I think some of the most promising can be found where the normal rules don't necessarily apply—on the margins and in the liminal spaces. Akin to the fecund ecological spaces constituted by ecotones (regions of transition between ecological communities), it is in vacant lots or graffiti-covered abandoned buildings, on the fringes of urban areas, or on small farms where nature and culture become thoroughly intertwined that we find some of the most creative forms of social experimentation and alterity. We need to work with people and our plant and animal kin in spaces where experimentation is possible, in what are called edgelands, transition zones that are particularly rich sites for dreaming up new ways of living.[21] If home and work are "first" and "second" spaces, and bars, churches, and bowling alleys are "third spaces," these marginal and semianarchic riparian spaces constitute "fourth spaces" or what Evans and Boyte[22] describe as "free spaces" within which social experimentation is possible.[23]

I have come to see rivers and riparian spaces as spaces for alternative ways of learning for a number of reasons. Rivers, generally speaking, have been the sites of some of the most intensive and extensive human activities—the creation of most early civilizations, the building of tens of thousands of large dams, industry, waste disposal, and massive engineering and flood-control projects.[24] At the same time, these spaces are often muddy, overgrown, challenging to navigate, and difficult to access by automobile. On the lower Mississippi River (and other large rivers), the batture—the land between the river's edge and the levee—is especially wild, and long stretches of the lower Mississippi are referred to as "Wild Miles" due to the lack of development along the river. Since the battureland regularly floods, it is not amenable to human control. Overgrown urban riparian spaces, with abandoned postindustrial buildings, provide refuge from the oversight and norms of mainstream society. These are sites of various informal shelters, campfires, encampments for the unhoused, and guerrilla art such as graffiti and primitive sculptures.
Outside the gaze of the authorities and mainstream social norms, rebels and outcasts—those who take issue with mainstream culture—find space at the margins to live otherwise and resist the oppressive workings of the surveillance state.[25]

On our trips on the Mississippi, we found that river islands are particularly unregulated spaces. Islands (and, even more so, boats, which are in a sense moveable islands) often come to be places for alterity, outlawry, or experimentation.[26] Though technically owned by the U.S. Army Corps of Engineers, channel islands on most of the Mississippi River are generally understood to be public domain within certain broad limits. People can spend some time on the islands, as long as no permanent structures are erected, and there is little to no official oversight on the river. The islands in the Upper Mississippi Fish and Wildlife Preserve have posted signs, but the regulations are almost comically permissive. For instance, they limit campers to no more than 14 days per month in any given spot,[27] meaning that you could theoretically camp on islands indefinitely as long as you moved every two weeks. The U.S. Army Corps is focused almost exclusively on keeping the navigational channel open for the large barges, and they pay little attention to who has pitched tents on the islands as long as the tents do not interfere with their dredge operations. Some privately owned islands on the Lower River (mostly used for hunting) are monitored a bit more closely, mainly to make sure other hunters are not poaching game, but on the whole the river islands are relatively free of social controls. They have been used historically as bases for river pirates and wanderers of various sorts and remain spaces largely free from the norms of mainstream culture and economics.[28] For instance, in fall 2023 we camped on Stack Island (between Greenville and Vicksburg, Mississippi). The island itself is now privately owned, but due to the river's meandering course it has over the years been part of both Mississippi and Louisiana, and there has been a long-standing dispute over jurisdiction. It was virtually wiped out by the flooding that occurred in 1811 when a major earthquake, centered in New Madrid, Missouri, caused a kind of "river tsunami".[29] It was a base for river pirates in the eighteenth century, and as recently as the 1970s, it has been used as a hideaway for fugitive criminals. In this constantly shifting space, where legal jurisdiction is fuzzy at best, our group foraged for oyster mushrooms, discussed the war in Palestine, and held a ceremonial water blessing. The space fostered this kind of learning.

Rivers are productive spaces for education in the Anthropocene for a few other reasons. For one, they are particularly well-suited for travel by boat, this being one of the main reasons human civilizations have developed on their banks in the first place.

Beyond facilitating meeting people and seeing new places, this slow-paced and energy-efficient form of mobility can be seen as a response to the multifaceted planetary crises we face. As climate and ecosystems shift, coasts and riverbanks flood, and arid regions dry out, mobility is a form of resilience that allows us to respond to these changes, while at the same time requiring us to simplify, pare down, and travel light. Rivers are also emotionally and spiritually evocative spaces—sites of ritual, baptism, contemplation, sorrow, and loss. Over the course of our journeys down the river, the water blessing ceremony mentioned above became part of a weekly practice on the river's edge. The river was the site of frequent secular "baptisms" and ritual cleansings experienced when we swam or bathed in its waters.

THE CHALLENGE REMAINS OF HOW WE CAN LIVE IN THE ANTHROPOCENE, NOT SEPARATE OURSELVES FROM IT SO THOROUGHLY THAT WE ARE JUST RUNNING AWAY FROM THE PROBLEM.

We had many moments of experiencing community and alterity in these spaces. In what follows, I share a few of the experiences of freedom we had along the river. At their hearts, these experiences amount to a return to a simple, basic, communal form of living that is itself a fairly radical departure from what life is like when we are on campus. These long trips down the river are intense and physically demanding, entail various discomforts, and involve living in close quarters with a group for months on end, but there is nothing particularly profound or intellectually complicated about these experiences. Their core elements involve simply people getting together, usually outside or in some odd or unusual space, with food and drink, music and dance. They offer glimpses of or suggestions for how to keep forging ahead and building a healthy, joyous, resilient, and sustainable future.

The first example comes from eastern Iowa, a part of the country where I did not expect to find one of the wildest dining establishments I have ever visited. Bombfire Pizza, located in Sabula, Iowa, was the creation of Tom Holman, a retired military veteran and Dionysian muse for the pursuit of living otherwise, who had a habit of uttering a loud pirate's "Aarrggh!" whenever he entered the

The Water Striders anchored near the confluence of the Mississippi and Illinois Rivers, September 2025. Photograph by Joe Underhill

establishment. In October 2015, we visited the establishment, and our group of students and staff from Augsburg University and Augustana College joined local residents and an inebriated staff in an evening of joyous abandon. The space overflowed with the oddest assortment of found items, musical instruments, and other flotsam and jetsam gathered from the river. A local musician (with more enthusiasm than talent) banged away at the piano, joined by some of the students. There was a palpable sense of revelry and a degree of abandon about the place that reflected something of the spirit of these liminal spaces along the river. Created by someone on the margins of society, this space was located on the edge of Iowa (in a city actually on the river), with the aim of building community, welcoming everybody, and celebrating life in the ruins of what had once been a thriving river city. That evening, the elements spontaneously came together for a thoroughly memorable experience, a time of feeling alive, and of asserting joy and humanity in the face of all the troubles and crises swirling around us.

Another example of the varied and idiosyncratic aspects of this way of learning occurred during the 2018 River Semester, in the midst of the wettest 12-month period in U.S. history.[30] On the fifth day of the trip, high straight-line winds and the blaring of tornado sirens forced the group into a nearby storm shelter. Six of our eight tents, pitched in a field near some ancient burial mounds on Prairie Island Indian Community, were blown away. Two of the tents (with all their gear inside) ended up in the river. We spent that night in the dystopian environs of the local casino hotel, and the next day salvaged our gear, replaced the damaged tents, and continued downstream. Two weeks later the group was joined by a group of international scholars and environmental advocates for the paddle from Winona, Minnesota, down to La Crosse, Wisconsin. This stretch of river is in the beautiful Driftless (unglaciated)

Region of the Upper Mississippi, marked by high bluffs and complex braided channels. Their first day on the river was hot and humid, and the group paddled along with the students broadcasting Bob Dylan's *The Times They Are a-Changin'* for the amusement of our Norwegian visitors, who were keen to get an authentically American experience. As is typical of people who are new to the river, our guests had arrived with some apprehension about water quality in the Mississippi. Thanks to thousands of pollution control projects prompted by the Clean Water Act, though, the river in many places is now clean enough to swim in safely; during our lunch stop, it didn't take the sweaty group long to happily jump in and float along in the refreshingly cool water. That afternoon's paddle got the group as far as the village of Trempealeau, Wisconsin. When the weather radar showed the approach of yet another set of intense thunderstorms, the group was forced ashore and took shelter in the local "yacht club" (in this case a very modest boat house and restaurant). As the rain poured down outside, two of the Norwegian professors shared insights from their work related to the water culture and politics of the Nile and Ganges Rivers. With severe weather forecast for the next several days the group then had to seek some place to stay. We were directed to contact a local pastor and ended up being hosted by the Mount Calvary Lutheran Church. Over the course of three days, the church parishioners and good people of Trempealeau showed the group amazing hospitality, brought food, offered showers and rides, and invited the students to meet with the Bible study group. It so happened that we were also there for Yom Kippur, and there was a lay rabbi in the group (along with Palestinian and Jordanian water rights advocates). The rabbi led us in an observance of the Day of Atonement in the sanctuary of the Lutheran church. In the quiet of the unlit space, seated in a circle on the floor in front of the altar, the group reflected on their regrets from the year before, on family, loss, missteps, and on hopes for the year to come. By the end of our time of sharing, many of the group were in tears. That evening the international group prepared a meal of Palestinian and Israeli dishes, along with some hotdish and other local fare, and shared the meal with our church hosts. Coming together across lines of difference (global, ideological, age, gender), we sat together as human beings in a town where Donald Trump had received two-thirds of the vote in 2016. To say the least, these moments are hard to replicate within a standard classroom setting. They pointed, in multiple ways, toward strengthening community across lines of difference and recognizing the many forms of knowledge and ways of being found along the river, and around the world.

AS CLIMATE & ECOSYSTEMS SHIFT, COASTS & RIVERBANKS FLOOD, & ARID REGIONS DRY OUT, MOBILITY IS A FORM OF RESILIENCE THAT ALLOWS US TO RESPOND TO THESE CHANGES, WHILE AT THE SAME TIME REQUIRING US TO SIMPLIFY, PARE DOWN, TRAVEL LIGHT.

In March 2019, during a gathering organized as part of the Anthropocene River program, a group of academics, artists, and community members met at the Kanu Haus, a ramshackle abode located in a rough neighborhood in North St. Louis. The group was hosted by "Big Muddy" Mike Clark, a retired elementary school teacher, local river rat, and guide with deep connections to the Mississippi. Before dinner, the group wandered around Cementland, the abandoned ruins of what was to be a fantastical outdoor amusement park. The half-finished project, built in the wreck of an old cement plant, had the air of a postapocalyptic dreamscape, full of wild ambition, decay, and a resurgent urban ecosystem. Later, Mike cooked pork tenderloin over a fire as we discussed our surreal visit to Cementland, planned events for the coming fall, and shared ideas about education in the Anthropocene. There was joy, revelry, companionship, and a sense that other futures were possible. We experienced many such gatherings later that year as part of the

* Anthropocene Commons is a global, decentralized network of researchers, artists, educators, activists, and scientists who work collaboratively to foster a shared understanding of our planetary crises through transformative pedagogies, collective action, and the sharing of knowledge, skills, and resources.

Camped under the roof of one of the abandoned structures at Lincoln Beach. A site for musical performances in the 1950s and '60s, this was where we feasted on oysters brought to us by Moose Jackson. Photograph by Joseph Underhill

2019 River Semester and the Mississippi. An Anthropocene River project, a watershed moment in the creation of the fluvial networks imagined here.

The forms of alternative pedagogy proposed here, and reflected in the work of the Mississippi River Open School for Kinship and Social Exchange, manifested in powerful ways during our participation in a wild rice harvest at the Welcome Water Protectors Center in Palisade, Minnesota, in September 2023. The event grew out of a long-standing collaboration with frontline communities resisting the oil pipelines and new mining projects in northern Minnesota, and was organized by John Kim in partnership with Shanai Matteson, Ojibwe artist Rory Wakemup, Rory's aunt Betsy, and his brother Justin. Our group assisted in setting up the camp, which would be used to educate people about the importance of wild rice to the life and well-being of the Anishinaabeg. We made cedar knockers used to harvest the rice, scoped out ricing locations, and learned how to push canoes through the thick fields of emergent aquatic vegetation. Back at camp we helped with roasting, threshing, and winnowing the rice, and ended up with a full bag of finished rice for our efforts. Bushels of rice were harvested while we were there, and the ricing workshop, which took place the week after we left, was a success. It was a profoundly satisfying and authentically reciprocal experience, grounded in local knowledge and connecting to a vital form of praxis for the Anishinaabeg. Students left with a deep understanding of the importance of menoomin and the importance of preserving those ricing lakes. We carried the rice with us and made soup with it for several meals in the following month. We also made balls of rice seed and mud—dubbed "rice bombs"—which we later hurled into the river as we traveled south.

During our stay in New Orleans in November 2023, we had the good fortune of connecting with Ray "Moose" Jackson,[31] a local poet, artist, and educator. A fellow traveler in the creation of fluvial networks of creative resistance, he is launching a new boat-based coastal restoration enterprise on the Gulf Coast. As we departed New Orleans, the wind dictated that we head toward the Gulf of Mexico through Lake Pontchartrain, and we were looking for spots to camp. Moose suggested that we stop at Lincoln Beach in New Orleans East. Lincoln Beach was an African American space, an amusement park that saw its heyday in the 1940s and '50s. It was shut down after legal (if not de facto) desegregation in the 1960s but is now being revived and stewarded by a local coalition of advocates. Lincoln Beach is another thoroughly liminal space, located on the other side of the tracks and other side of the levee, where itinerants and local BIPOC community gather, celebrate, and relax (despite the occasional alligator sighting). Like many of the islands we stayed on, it is a space where local residents have been able to take some refuge, at least partially insulated from the ongoing racist dynamics in their community.

We arrived at the beach after dark, finding it strewn with evidence of active use by local residents. We did some cleanup, had the place to ourselves, and pitched our tents. Some of us slept on the beach, while others slept under a large concrete structure that had once been a music hall in the amusement park. The next day, one of the local caretakers, Sage Michael, came down to check on the new arrivals and gave his blessing to our temporary stay there. The following day, after yet another night of heavy thunderstorms and tornado warnings, Moose rejoined us with a gift of two bushel bags of oysters, which we proceeded to shuck, roast, and consume under the canopy of the abandoned amusement park structure. After our feast, Moose shared from his epic poem, "The Loup Garou" (the werewolf),[32] before we crawled into our tents to sleep outside for the one hundredth night of our journey. On our departure the following day, Sage Michael came down to see us off, excited about our adventure and talking about his plans for getting more boats for people to use down at the park.[33]

These experiences, and others like them, provide some glimpses into what we might call simple acts of refusal, rebellion, celebration, rejuvenation, and empowerment. In these spaces, we turned away from the normal practices of the classroom to find different ways of learning and of living. From these experiences, students and fellow travelers gained an appreciation for slowing down. We found it a great relief to stop consuming, stop rushing around, stop staring at screens—and return to some of the basic elements of life in community on this planet. This does not require elaborate theorization, or expensive new gadgets, or much of anything beside the desire to do it and an openness to spending time outside under the wide expanse of the stars, in the company of people, using our bodies to move, cook, build, and dance. We need to build up a network of these kinds of programs, spaces, and experiences.

BUILDING FLUVIAL NETWORKS

The experiences and networks described above are part of the process necessary for building and maintaining a movement for thriving in the Anthropocene. The emergent fluvial network imagined here draws on the work of a number of pioneering enterprises in higher education. These include programs like the Higher Education Consortium for Urban Affairs (HECUA), which used urban field-based research with a focus on economic and social justice and close partnership with local activists and artists. HECUA, which grew out of the unrest and civil rights movements of the late 1960s, offered numerous semester-long programs in Minnesota, Italy, Ecuador, Northern Ireland, and New Zealand, all with a focus on social justice. The organization ended in 2022, although efforts to revive portions of it continue. Similarly the network formed through Imagining America brings together academics, organizers, and artists for community-based, experiential education in the humanities. Its annual conferences offer opportunities for community engagement, often in marginal spaces, and provide inspiration for the kinds of networks imagined here. Other projects that inspire us include the Fourth Coast expedition down the Mississippi organized by Brown and Morrish,[34] Wes Modes's Shantyboat project and his "A Secret History of American River People,"[35] and Monique Verdin's many projects, including the Float Lab and Prairie des Femmes.

As mentioned earlier, the network imagined here grows directly out of the convenings organized by the Anthropocene project of HKW and the Max Planck Institute for the History of Science in 2018–2022. That work now continues in the Anthropocene Commons,* which organizes gatherings that take seriously the need to radically rethink pedagogies, curricula, and epistemologies, and that embody this joyful expression of alterity. The newly formed Max Planck Institute of Geoanthropology is further pushing the boundaries between the natural and social sciences, the humanities, and the arts as we live into the complex entanglements of the Anthropocene. The Floating ~~University~~ in Berlin provides another inspiring example of an experimental school, this one based at an old wastewater treatment plant site. As the name implies, it sees itself as not a university, but instead as a place for exploring radical alternatives to the status quo. Numerous artists and community activities and organizations are engaging these spaces in wonderfully creative and inspiring ways.

A range of kindred field-based programs constitute potential elements of this nascent community of river-based or alternative educational programs. The Grand Canyon Semester, offered at times by Prescott College and Northern Arizona University, uses the Grand Canyon as the setting for a multidisciplinary exploration of environmental and social justice issues. Brevard College's Voice of the River, started in 1997, has organized a range of river trips around the U.S. and overseas; it currently takes students on a regional 18-day river trip. The Rio Tinto Field School was a weeklong field seminar in fall 2022 that hiked along Spain's Rio Tinto, one of the most heavily polluted watersheds in the world, birthplace of the Rio Tinto mining company, and site of Columbus's departure from Spain on his first voyage west. Semester in the West looks at environmental politics and climate change as students travel by bus around the western United States. The Adirondacks Semester is a nature-based program at Hamilton College, and Semester-A-Trail allows students to create their own curriculum while hiking the Appalachian Trail. The Oregon Extension, started in 1975, creates an intentional community in the Cascades. In various ways, each of these programs, offered in a range of marginal and riparian contexts, provides inspiration for new ways of learning and living in the twenty-first century. They can function as part of this emerging network of educational programs providing students with alternatives to simply being trained to be part of the modernist enterprise.

A PEDAGOGY THAT RESPONDS TO THE ANTHROPOCENE HAS TO SIT WITH THE TENSION BETWEEN OUR INHERENT GLOBAL INTERCONNECTIONS AND THE NEED TO STAY GROUNDED IN THE LOCAL.

In addition, a number of academic institutes or networks focused on rivers constitute contributing streams in this dendritic structure. These include the River Field Studies Network, an extensive and growing network of practitioners in river studies funded by the National Science Foundation and led by a team of stream ecologists and freshwater biologists. The National Great Rivers Research and Education Center (NGRREC) in Alton, Illinois, carries out a range of research, education, and outreach programs on the Middle Mississippi. Nongovernmental river-advocacy groups such as American Rivers, International Rivers, Riverkeepers, and Friends of the Mississippi River constitute another set of partners and collaborators in this work. There are likewise various river outfitters, such as Wilderness Inquiry in Minnesota; Quapaw Canoe Company in Clarksdale, Mississippi; Big Muddy Outfitters in St. Louis; and Urban Boatbuilders, which teaches boatbuilding and other woodworking skills to urban youth in the Twin Cities.

We can overlay this rich tapestry of organizations with a fluvial network of creative resistance. What might such a network look like? The global connections facilitated by the various forms of digital networks—email chains, shared Google docs, Discord servers, grant-funded meetings, and conferences—are all important in this work. In addition to these kinds of formal or digital networks, I would argue that what we need most are the kinds of river gatherings we have experienced in the course of our trips down the Mississippi. They will need to be multimodal, flexible, and reflective of whatever local realities, needs, and resources are available to make them happen. A pedagogy that responds to the Anthropocene has to sit with the tension between our inherent global interconnections and the need to stay grounded in the local. It must also be able to partake in the duality of groundedness and the virtual and disembodied interconnectedness of the internet. My particular work is on the Mississippi, and others are doing work on their own rivers.

Facilitating these changes on a larger scale will require connecting with kindred programs, and some of that work has already begun. What are the common elements or shared values? They consist of folks drawn together by the sense that things really need to change, by the pull of the rivers themselves, by the joys of community, food, and music, and by a passion for social justice. They are not wilderness retreats, taking place in distant or secluded locales, but they do draw on elements of those wilderness experiences. As in the stories of "pirate pedagogy" discussed above, this fluvial network needs to be based on meetings that are in person, involving a diverse set of participants: academic and nonacademic folks, artists, researchers, practitioners, activists, and nonhuman kin. This is the approach of the Mississippi River Open School for Kinship and Social Exchange, a wonderful regional example of the kind of network and activities proposed here. This network helps students become integrated into a larger community of river stewards, creators, and change agents that can support them and foster shared learning across watersheds. The gatherings work best when they can be outdoors and in marginal, liminal spaces (like Kanu Haus or Lincoln Beach). Other key ingredients for these gatherings include the primal elements of human communal activity: fire, music, dance, ceremony and ritual, and food and drink prepared and consumed together. To the extent that the world has become too complicated, these conditions call for simplifying, going back to our roots, and resisting the pull of modernity. For those so disposed, these practices constitute one important alternative to the curricular status quo. Already we have seen participants in these events and river trips going out into the world to organize, advocate, and create similar kinds of alternative curricula. Alumni are, among other things, advocating for women's rights and environmental protection in Columbia, leading outdoor education programs, participating in movements to protect Indigenous land, and working on organic farms. Through these experiences we are learning how to live otherwise—in ways that reduce our environmental impact, improve our mental health, create strong communities, and connect us to the world. By increasing the interconnections between these efforts across watersheds, we can strengthen and facilitate efforts toward social change.

With a strengthened network of researchers, teachers, artists, and activists engaging in various forms of immersive and extended investigations on rivers such as the Nile, Amazon, Danube, Ganga, Mekong, and Yangtze, among others, what can we create in the riparian ruins, and what signs of hope do we see in these muddied waters? Can we imagine fleets of river boats, vessels trading in alternative realities up and down the rivers of the world?[36] As with any countercultural practice, the alternative will not be an easy sell. It will require work, discomfort, and actively disentangling ourselves from the normal consumerist and extractivist ways of life that constitute much of the world of higher education. It does, however, come with the potential for the real joy that emerges from the full experience of the world, of good company, and of the satisfaction of going to bed at night exhausted, but knowing that there are indeed other possibilities besides those currently leading us toward an unnecessarily bleak future.

A version of this article was originally published in the journal Open Rivers *(Winter/Spring 2025).*

ENDNOTES

1 Donna Haraway, *Staying with the Trouble: Making Kin in the Chthulucene* (Duke University Press, 2016); José Esteban Muñoz, *Cruising Utopia: The Then and There of Queer Futurity* (New York University Press, 2009); Anna Tsing, *The Mushroom at the End of the World: On the Possibility of Life in Capitalist Ruins* (Princeton University Press, 2017); Cleo Wölfle Hazard, *Underflows: Queer Trans Ecologies and River Justice* (University of Washington Press, 2022).

2 Michael Pollan, *Food Rules: An Eater's Manual* (Penguin, 2009).

3 Paul Crutzen and Eugene Stoermer, "The 'Anthropocene,'" *IGBP Newsletter* 41 (May 2000): 17–18.

4 Joseph Underhill, "Navigating the Anthropocene River: A Traveler's Guide to the (Dis)comforts of Being at Home-in-the-World," *Anthropocene Curriculum: Evidence and Experiment*, July 27, 2020, https://www.anthropocene-curriculum.org/contribution/navigating-the-anthropocene-river.

5 Virginia Iglesias, Jennifer Balch, and William Travis. "U.S. Fires Became Larger, More Frequent, and More Widespread in the 2000s," *Science Advances* 8, no. 11 (2022), https://doi.org/10.1126/sciadv.abc0020.

6 "Prison population rate," Our World in Data, accessed October 10, 2025, https://ourworldindata.org/grapher/prison-population-rate?tab=table.

7 For data on these and a range of other current issues, see Our World in Data, accessed October 13, 2025, https://ourworldindata.org.

8 bell hooks, *Teaching to Transgress: Education as a Practice of Freedom* (Routledge, 1994); Parker Palmer, *The Courage to Teach: Exploring the Inner Landscape of a Teacher's Life*, 20th anniversary ed. (Jossey-Bass, 2017).

9 Dennis Lien, "Influential director of Audubon's Upper Mississippi River Initiative is retiring," *Pioneer Press*, November 13, 2015, https://www.twincities.com/2008/05/28/influential-director-of-audubons-upper-mississippi-river-initiative-is-retiring-2/.

10 Michael Bastedo, Philip Altbach, and Patricia Gumport, eds., *American Higher Education in the Twenty-First Century: Social, Political, and Economic Challenges*, 4th ed. (Johns Hopkins University Press, 2016); Harold Perkin, "History of Universities," in *The History of Higher Education*, ed. Harold Wechsler, Lester F. Goodchild, and Linda Eisenmann (Pearson Learning Solutions, 2007); John Thelin, *A History of American Higher Education*, 3rd ed. (Johns Hopkins University Press, 2019).

11 Octavia Butler, *The Parable of the Sower* (Grand Central Publishing, 2019).

12 Muñoz, *Cruising Utopia*.

13 adrienne maree brown, *Emergent Strategy: Shaping Change, Changing Worlds* (AK Press, 2017).

14 David Graeber, *Pirate Enlightenment, or the Real Libertalia* (Macmillan Publishers, 2023); Marcus Rediker, *Outlaws of the Atlantic: Sailors, Pirates, and Motley Crews in the Age of Sail* (Beacon Press, 2015).

15 Ivan Illich, *Energy and Equity* (Marion Boyars, 2009).

16 Kevin Williams, "Student Housing Has a New Mantra: Bigger Is Better," *The New York Times*, February 13, 2024, https://www.nytimes.com/2024/02/13/business/student-housing-off-campus-real-estate.html.

17 la paperson, *A Third University Is Possible* (University of Minnesota Press, 2017).

18 Elizabeth Kolbert, *The Sixth Extinction: An Unnatural History* (Henry Holt & Co., 2014); David Wallace-Wells, *The Uninhabitable Earth: Life After Warming* (Tim Duggan Books, 2019).

19 David Gruenewald, "The Best of Both Worlds: A Critical Pedagogy of Place," *Educational Researcher* 32, no. 4 (2003): 3–12; bell hooks, *Teaching to Transgress*.

20 Haraway, *Staying with the Trouble*.

21 Tsing, *The Mushroom at the End of the World*.

22 Sarah Evans and Harry Boyte, *Free Spaces: The Sources of Democratic Change in America* (University of Chicago Press, 1997).

23 Hazard, *Underflows*.

24 Laurence Smith, *Rivers of Power: How a Natural Force Raised Kingdoms, Destroyed Civilizations, and Shapes Our World* (Little, Brown, 2020).

25 James Scott, *Seeing like a State: How Certain Schemes To Improve the Human Condition Have Failed* (Yale University Press, 1998).

26 Michel Foucault, "Des Espaces Autres (Of Other Spaces)," trans. Jay Miskowiec, *Architecture/Mouvement/Continuité* (October 1984).

27 "Facility Rules and Policies," Upper Mississippi River National Wildlife and Fish Refuge, accessed October 10, 2025, https://ourworldindata.org/grapher/prison-population-rate?tab=table.

28 Lee Sandlin, *Wicked River: The Mississippi When It Last Ran Wild* (Vintage, 2011).

29 Jay Feldman, *When the Mississippi Ran Backward: Empire, Intrigue, Murder, and the New Madrid Earthquakes of 1811–12* (Free Press, 2012).

30 "Wettest 12 Months in U.S. History," Weather Underground, accessed October 10, 2025, https://www.wunderground.com/cat6/Wettest-12-Months-US-History.

31 Raymond Moose Jackson, *Dreaming in the Bone Boat* (University of New Orleans Press, 2022).

32 Raymond Moose Jackson, *The Loup Garou: A Lunar Cycle* (Lavender Ink, 2010).

33 Xander Peters, "In New Orleans, a 'Black Beach' Is Being Rescued From the Ruins," *The New York Times*, September 24, 2024, https://www.nytimes.com/2024/09/24/travel/lincoln-beach-new-orleans.html.

34 Catherine Brown and William Morrish, "The Fourth Coast: An Expedition on the Mississippi River," *Design Quarterly* 150 (1990): 1–29, 32, http://www.jstor.org/stable/4091279.

35 Wes Modes, "The Shantyboat," A Secret History of American River People, last modified 2023, https://peoplesriverhistory.us/.

36 Kyle Whyte, "Way Beyond the Lifeboat: An Indigenous Allegory for Climate Justice," in *Climate Futures: Reimagining Global Climate Justice*, ed. K.-K. Bhavnani, J. Foran, P. A. Kurian, and D. Munshi (Zed Books, 2019).

Wild Rice: The Three Sisters

A recipe from the River Semester by MORGAN PIPER CORDOVA

Written for the Mississippi River Open School, this recipe is an excerpt of Mississippi Mud Book of Recipes, *a collection of stories, reflections, and recipes that Morgan Piper Cordova assembled while an undergraduate student on the Fall 2023 River Semester. Cordova traces connections between food sovereignty, environmental justice, and resistance, offering both practical recipes and deeper meditations on how "everything you need to live is around you" along the Mississippi River.*

Ricing began the night before we went out on the lake. We sat around the second fire, carving wood knockers from cedar branches that Justin had cut earlier that day. He sat across the fire from me, not speaking except when asked for advice, when he would say a brief, assuring remark about how good our knockers looked so far. There wasn't much instruction except watching him and others around us who had started before we did. We borrowed knives from each other and from Justin, swatted mosquitoes and talked. He might comment on a particularly bent branch and we would laugh, or we might listen to a hilariously bawdy story told by his Aunt Betsy, as she sat on her walker near the fire. "Didn't you show them how to do this?" she would ask Justin, who would glance around at us and say, "Looks like they've got it figured out for themselves!" with a knowing smile.

Once the strong wood knockers were smooth and balanced in our hands, we placed them all in a basket for everyone to share and use. Everything made at the Welcome Water Protector Center in Northern Minnesota was for everyone to share and use. The place was run by two principles: "Be a good relative" and "Many hands make easy work"—it did not need to be spoken, it was enough to know the history of the place as a shelter for pipeline fighters, land stewards, and water lovers.

The process of gathering rice is ceremony, and acknowledging these principles is the first precept. On the morning we went to the lake, we gathered on the shore by the Big Sandy Lake's boat ramp with tobacco in our left hands and gave gratitude for the land, and the innumerable relatives that brought us to this day and this opportunity to harvest the rice to eat. Aileen, Justin's sister, said a quiet blessing in Lakota and we gave our tobacco to the lake. Rory, Justin's brother, told me at one point "you can tell the story of the Dakota people simply through telling stories of their food." The ceremony looks forward and backwards. The collection and harvest of food is both a means for remembrance and self-care and the beginning of a new time for creation and memory making.

Ricing works this way: two people are in a canoe, aluminum in our case, one standing with a push pole and one sitting with a knocker in each hand. I held the push pole—and though we started early in the morning, the sun baked my flesh and my tendons ached about a half-hour into the two and a half hour process. The push pole was a 20 foot long maple wood trunk, whittled down to a smooth pole about five inches in diameter. The pole makes the canoe easier to maneuver in the dense rice paddies. I would get us stuck above the water on stalks of purple rice as my sweat dripped into my eyes and blinded me. This would require the even more physical challenge of going in reverse and finding a more passable route.

The knocker (the person holding the knockers) sits in the belly of the canoe and pulls the stalks into the boat, beating them with the other knocker to loosen the rice. It is also hard work, and the process often leaves the canoe full of spiders and earwigs amongst the hair-like rice casings. We collected about 10 pounds as a group in two and a half hours, a small amount compared to how much our experienced friends from the Welcome Center had gotten the day before, but not meager.

Back at camp, we dug a hole for the fire and began to parch, a multiple-day process of mixing the rice in a large metal cauldron over a hot flame. This hardens the rice, separating it from its casings and lightly toasting the grain. After that came dancing on the rice, separating the black and white grains from the now parched brown casings. It was described by some of the people there as processing the rice, but it's a different form of processing grain than that known by American flour mills and sugar refineries.

I have Native American heritage through my mother and my grandfather. My grandfather was of the Mimbrenos band of the Chiricahua Apache in what is now southern New Mexico, and my mother and her side of the family were largely the inspiration for this foodways project. They are all cooks or lovers of good food in some capacity, and meals at our house are binding for our family. Meals are feasts with us, where everyone is responsible for bringing something and critiquing everything. Chef and food writer Michael W. Twitty writes "in memory there is resurrection, and thus the end goal of my cooking is just that—resurrection."[1] Twitty writes of his memory in relation to a cooking life that is dependent on the importance and necessity of cooking in the lives of enslaved people and their descendents, but it speaks to an intrinsic remembering that lies in food, cooking, and that loaded term "foodways."

Foodways describes the strength and cunning of Indigenous and Black people in preserving and revitalizing their cultural knowledge. A paleobotanist at Cahokia, Illinois may use "foodways" to describe an antiquated process for harvesting and preparing ancient grains or beans. Ultimately process and memory cannot be separated and in memory lies a unique knowledge of self, place, and ancestry. My family gathers in the week between Christmas and New Years to make tamales, and the process of making the chile and masa is a solemn and celebratory ceremony of my grandparents and a tradition that has largely been lost to time and systemic erasure.

The reason why I mention this ceremony and the indistinguishable strength of process, Indigeneity and home is because rice—the staple of this dish—cannot be confined to a single family or culture. Like many things that thrive in water, defining it takes more than just encountering it in a few places. As Twitty writes, "Rice connects me to every other person, southern and global, who is nourished by rice traditions and customs."[2] We witnessed unfathomable acres of rice grown over the levee in Arkansas by white farmers. When we visited Whitney Plantation, Dr. Ibrahima Seck spoke of rice's influence in southern cuisine. Jambalaya, he said, is the way rice is traditionally prepared by the Jolof people in Senegal. Only two variations of rice have ever been domesticated, yet other varieties of rice exist as staples in Indigenous communities worldwide. Rice is to culture as process is to indigeneity, a way of exploring self and people as nuance and indigeneity are largely becoming more difficult things to practice and rediscover.

The Lakota people (and most all native folk) live with the precept of being a good relative. This was not lost on us visitors. I said that the ricing ceremony began the night before we went out on the lake, but it began long before that. It began when the rice took root in the muddy bottom of a river or lake. It began when that water began flowing, or when sediment began to form. Defining beginnings and rice is a vague, muddy task, as are defining most things that live alongside and in water. Where we end and our relatives begin is equally as challenging to define, especially along the banks of a river.

The evening we ate this three sisters soup was the end of our first rainy day on the river. We built our kitchen on the muddy bank as the torrential day turned into a misty evening. The sky broke through the dense floodplain forest as an apology towards our silent, damp-clothed bodies—John worked alone in the small patch of bank that could support his weight, and the boats sank into the earth only a few feet from his heels. We collected wild mint. No tows passed, and the river introduced its wilderness for the first time in our young trip. Toni Morrison wrote: "'Floods' is the word they use, but in fact the river is not flooding; it is remembering." We had encountered water above and below us, a subtle but bone-chilling deluge. We were beginning to get to know the fertile valley that produced and sustained the three sisters, and the river's muddy, unseen ceremonial process.

Photographs by Morgan Piper Cordova

ENDNOTES

1 Michael W. Twitty, *The Cooking Gene: A Journey Through African American Culinary History in the Old South* (Amistad, an imprint of Harper Collins Publishers, 2020).

2 Ibid.

John Kim's Three Sisters Soup

INGREDIENTS:

Squash
Wild Rice
Chicken Bouillon
Onion
Fennel Seed
Paprika
White Vinegar
Scarlet Runner Beans
Wild Mint (as a garnish)

INSTRUCTIONS:

HEAT BOUILLON IN A POT WITH OIL. SAUTE ONIONS. DEGLAZE POT WITH WATER + START SIMMERING BROTH, ADDING SQUASH, WILD RICE, + SOAKED BEANS. ALLOW TO SIMMER, ADDING EACH INGREDIENT WHEN CIRCUMSTANCE CALLS FOR, FINISHING WITH WHITE VINEGAR SPLASHES. BEST SERVED AFTER A LONG, COLD DAY & WITH AVAILABLE INGREDIENTS.

Action Camps Everywhere by John Kim, page 30.
Photograph by John Kim

Upper Mississippi

The Upper Mississippi River is roughly the portion of the river upstream of St. Louis, Missouri. Major tributaries include the Minnesota, St. Croix, Chippewa, Black, and Wisconsin Rivers. The Upper Mississippi River hub foregrounds Indigenous and Black perspectives and histories around southeast Minnesota and southwest Wisconsin.

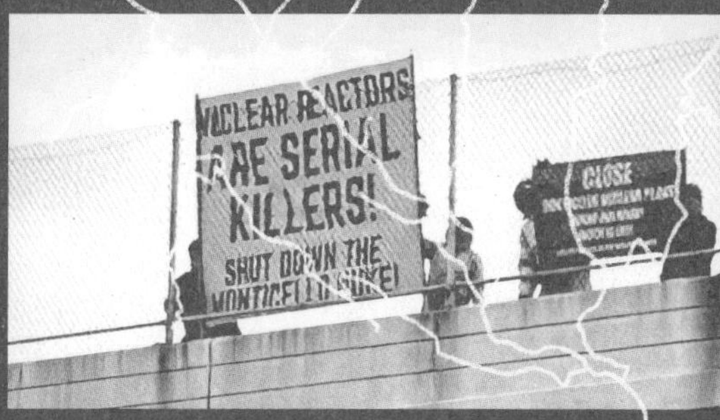

The Mississippi River Is the Opposite of the Anthropocene

Andrea Carlson

In an essay that draws from the deep Indigenous history of the Mississippi, artist Andrea Carlson challenges its characterization as an "Anthropocene River." Doing so, she argues, contributes to the erasure of Native philosophies about water and place and reaffirms a necropolitical vision of progress and temporality.

The title of this piece is a bold statement within the context of the Mississippi. An Anthropocene River project. The superimposition of the Anthropocene on specific colonized places may be further characteristic of abstracting Indigenous places into theoretical unoccupied zones. This is why the Indigenous histories of the region and our teachings about water that rely on relationships rather than on human domination are so valuable. Perhaps the Anthropocene could be better associated with the Danube or Volga rivers, but the Mississippi River is an inappropriate mascot for the Anthropocene because this association forecloses on Native philosophies about water and place that implicate us as part of the river. We must consider the settler erasures of the histories, relationships, and Indigenous bodies that have existed in the area we are defining as Field Station 1* to better understand the nature of the Anthropocene.

* Field Stations were the name used to refer to the regional groups that convened as part of Mississippi. An Anthropocene River. The term "river hubs" came to replace it in the Mississippi River Open School.

The Dakota people call the area of the confluence of the Minnesota and Mississippi rivers Bdote. According to the Bdewakanton—the first Dakota—the Dakota people originated in Bdote and this is why it is called Maka Cokayaki (Center of the Earth). Many Dakota were forcibly removed and exiled from Mnisóta (Minnesota) in the years following 1862. The Dakota who stayed behind kept a low profile, but remembered their Nation, their teachings, and their homes as they once were. The Twin Cities of Minneapolis and St. Paul industrialized over the years, and many once-exiled Dakota people found their way back home.

In 2006 a Dakota artist and media producer/director, Mona Smith, grew frustrated living in cities that were so proud of their settler histories. She created an installation titled City Indian at All My Relations Gallery (then, Ancient Traders Gallery) in Minneapolis. The installation was about a genesis for the Dakota people, and the irony of relocating Dakota people to their original homeland during urban relocation. Central to Smith's installation was the trunk of a police car. A video of Native folks talking about how their families came to the city was projected into the trunk. Smith states that the trunk referred to "the time Minneapolis police put Native men in their trunk to transport them." The installation also included another video about the Bdote area, its role in Dakota history, and a fine art map of the region created by Paul Durand with Anishinaabemowin (Ojibwe) and Dakota place

Installation images of the video "The Uncompromising Hand" (2017) by Andrea Carlson. Photograph by Rik Sferra

names. The installation was the impetus for other interventions that followed. Smith teamed up with the Minnesota Humanities Center to create the Bdote Memory Map, an online presence that collects Dakota memories associated with the extended Bdote area. Smith leads tours of selected Dakota sites in the Bdote area. She shares memories and produces interactive maps of significant Dakota places and place names, makes audio recordings of elders' stories, and founded an Indigenous artist-led non-profit called the Healing Place Collaborative. Mona Smith and her collaborative efforts about a place aren't field stations, aren't anthropological or remote forts, but are homes and places of belonging.

Sometime in the terrible aftermath of the Dakota–U.S. War of 1862, the war that led to the exile of many Dakota people, a Dakota woman named Wiyaka Sinte Win (Tailfeather Woman) hid for several days in a swamp among the reeds as U.S. soldiers attacked her community. Wiyaka Sinte Win dove under the water at times to stay out of sight, and she breathed through a hollow reed. She suffered, and she prayed for survival. Toward the end of her ordeal, Wiyaka Sinte Win received a vision instructing her how to construct the Big Drum. She was told to give these drums to the Ojibwe (Anishinaabe) people. When Wiyaka Sinte Win came out of hiding she did what the vision told her to do and established treaties between the Dakota and Ojibwe people through the gift of the Bwanni Dewe'igan (Anishinaabemowin for "Dakota drum") or the Chi Dewe'igan (Ojibwemowin for "Big Drum").[1] The Ojibwe, and many other nations, practice Big Drum ceremonies and the story of Wiyaka

Sinte Win is often cited as the origin of the contemporary powwow. The Dakota and Ojibwe people will remain allies for as long as we uphold our treaties with each other, as long as we dance to the sound of a heartbeat given to us by Dakota people.

Although the Dakota and Ojibwe people have gained from each other's friendship, Ojibwe people do not cite Bdote as our place of origin. A long time ago, the Ojibwe people lived around the mouth of what is now called the St. Lawrence Gulf. Sometime prior to the European invasion, an elder prophesied about the arrival of death from across the ocean. The elder's vision linked our survival with migrating west until we reached "the food that grows on water," which turned out to be minoomin (wild rice). The Ojibwe people followed the chain of Great Lakes through land where many other Anishinaabe and related Nations lived. We encircled Gichigami (Lake Superior), and moved onto Dakota land. The Dakota and Ojibwe are different Nations, and serious conflict between us was followed by learning about each other's medicine and healing each other. The word Mississippi is the Ojibwe word Misi-ziibi (Great River). The Dakota knew it as Ȟaȟáwakpa (River of the Waterfalls). The Ojibwe were brought to Mnisóta by water, and it is central to our cosmology.

WOMEN ARE OFTEN DESCRIBED AS THE WATER CARRIERS WITHIN OJIBWE CULTURE, BUT WE HAVE NOW BEEN FORCED TO BECOME WATER PROTECTORS WHEN CONFRONTED WITH SETTLER ENVIRONMENTAL DOMINANCE.

Our teachings about water are often described as traditional beliefs, but this is not an accurate description. Water is ancient, but we cannot propel any life into the future without it. A phrase from a ceremony made popular by the Dakota Access Pipeline protests is Mni Wiconi (Dakota for "Water is Life"), but the phrase Mitákuye Oyás'iŋ (Dakota for "We are all Related") further connects us to our environments, animal and plant life, and one another. For Dakota, Ho-Chunk, Ojibwe, and other Native people living in Bdote, our relationship to water is not something held in a river alone but something kept inside our bodies. Women are often described as the water carriers within Ojibwe culture, but we have now been forced to become water warriors and water protectors when confronted with settler environmental dominance.

In the spring of 2003, Josephine Mandamin of Wikwemikong First Nation began a 1,555-mile-long walk around Lake Superior while carrying a bowl of water. This beautiful act brought awareness to water pollution and led to the creation of the Water Walkers Movement. On February 22, 2019, Mandamin passed away leaving behind a legacy of inspired water activism. One year before she passed, Mandamin's 13-year-old niece, Autumn Peltier, addressed world leaders at the United Nations about the importance of protecting water. On the significance of water to Anishinaabe people, she said:

> We believe our water is sacred because we are born of water and live in water for 9 months. When the water breaks, new life comes. But even deeper than that, we come from our mother's water, and her mother's water and so on. All the original water flows through us from the beginning and all around us.[2]

The water within our living bodies is an ancient river. The poem "Water," by Ojibwe poet Al Hunter, states, "It is said that the amount of water that covers the earth's surface directly correlates to the amount of water that makes up the human body. / We are the same. / The earth is mostly water. / We are mostly water."[3]

THE WATER WITHIN OUR LIVING BODIES IS AN ANCIENT RIVER.

All waters connect, just as all living things are connected to one another, and should be maintained without dominance—without human dominance. With these few teachings about the water and histories of Bdote, which do not even begin to scratch the surface of Indigenous knowledge about the Mississippi River, I want to consider the Anthropocene.

What is meant by the term Anthropocene?

I cannot answer this question in a way that satisfies my philosophical views of animal interdependency, time, and place. It is not a term meant to satisfy my worldview. The Anthropocene is simply the name of a theoretical geological epoch defined by significant human impact on the Earth. Some scholars want to place the beginning of the Anthropocene on June 16, 1945 with the world's first atomic-bomb detonation test in the Jornada del Muerto desert in New Mexico. What could be more ominous than giving an entire epoch an exact start date centered on such violence? Others have suggested that the Industrial Revolution or the onset of colonization should be where the epoch begins. All of these proposed beginnings share the feature of being disastrous to human survival. They all locate power in what Édouard Glissant would call the "project" of the West.[4] Beyond the doomsday implications of placing the Anthropocene's origins within these contexts, are the extended implications of naming the current epoch. We aren't leaving it to future generations to look back and decide what distinguishing parameters characterize this epoch. We aren't surrendering to the judgement of future generations to make these evaluations. We aren't waiting for them to name the current epoch, because we don't believe that these future humans will exist.

The Anthropocene is the final epoch that will see humans through to the end of our impactful existence on Earth. No matter where we put its beginning we know that any beginning implies an end. A human-centered beginning infers a human-centered end, and perhaps, the end of humanity itself. But no one knows how humans will meet our collective end. We make predictions with science and observations, visions and prophecy, and we apply what we learn from histories passed down from time immemorial. We've generated many speculative ends for humanity. Unfortunately, for many Indigenous people, our past and continuing genocides are ever-present. It should come as no surprise that adjacent to popular speculations about humanity's end are art movements like Indigenous Futurism and Afrofuturism, and more and more artists are citing healing as a motivation for the creation of art. It isn't coincidental that when the end of humanity is imagined so robustly some of us envisage our survival in rich, glittery ways. Perhaps we are hoping to undermine or curtail the Anthropocene in order to simply survive. We have been forced to contemplate our annihilation since the arrival of Europeans; we are trying to imagine the end of ongoing efforts to disappear us.

THE ANTHROPOCENE IS THE FINAL EPOCH THAT WILL SEE HUMANS THROUGH TO THE END OF OUR EXISTENCE ON EARTH. NO MATTER WHERE WE PUT ITS BEGINNING WE KNOW THAT ANY BEGINNING IMPLIES AN END.

A version of this article was originally published on the website Anthropocene Curriculum (Winter/Spring 2020).

ENDNOTES

1 Thomas Vennum Jr., "Ojibwe Drum Decor: Sources and Variations of Ritual Design," in *Circles of Tradition* (Minnesota Historical Press, 1989), 60–62.

2 CBC News, "Autumn Peltier, 13-year-old water advocate, addresses the UN," streamed live on March 22, 2018, YouTube, https://www.youtube.com/watch?v=zg60sr38oic.

3 Al Hunter, "Water," in *Days of Obsidian Days of Grace*, ed. Patrick McKinnon, Andrea McKinnon, and Ellie Schoenfeld (Poetry Harbor, 1994), 30.

4 Edouard Glissant, *Caribbean Discourse: Selected Essays* (University of Virginia Press, 1989), 2.

Meeker Dam

Bruce Braun

Bruce Braun draws upon the hauntological qualities of a post-industrial, Mississippi ghost: Meeker Dam, Minneapolis, taking the now largely underwater ruin as a lens through which to examine other histories–and presents–long-submerged: the dispossession of land and denial of Indigenous sovereignty as a result of settler colonialism.

Submerged ruins of Meeker Dam. Photograph by Dio Cramer

If you walk south from the Franklin Bridge in Minneapolis along the east bank of the Mississippi, you can pick up a rough trail that takes you under the towering Short Line Bridge, past stormwater outlets, to a small historic park. Here, if you are fortunate, you might see the remains of a long-forgotten lock and dam. I say "fortunate" because the dam is a ghostly presence. Completed in 1907, abandoned and largely destroyed in 1912, its remains lurk just beneath the surface. When water levels fall, often toward the end of summer, it seems to rise from the river, an apparition that disappears just as silently as it arrived.

"Ghostly" may be the wrong term. Or, if it is to be the right term, we will have to understand better what it is that returns. For ghosts return; they haunt. They must be attended to, be come to terms with. Which is to say that the Meeker Dam, as it is commonly known, is not just a ruin that occasionally presents itself to those who walk along the river's shore or to those who descend a wagon road from St. Paul, restored not long after the dam was placed on the National Register of Historic Places in 2003. Nor is it merely a quaint reminder of the engineering feats of settlers or a charming remnant from past struggles between Minneapolis and St. Paul—mediated far away in Washington, D.C.—over which city could rightly claim to be the head of navigation on the river.[1]

Rather, it represents the historical emergence of a new paradigm, a particular way of thinking about the Mississippi and its social and political futures, one that remains submerged in settler consciousness today, in the same way that the dam is submerged in the river—as an absent presence that we see only poorly, refracted from beneath the surface of a now-placid river. For the Meeker Dam represents a settler vision and a settler spatiotemporality: the river imagined and remade as infrastructure on which the development of a settler society and the fortunes of an emerging industrial capitalism would rest. This is a vision that turns the river into a problem of engineering, fluid mechanics, geology, and hydrology. It makes of it a puzzle to be solved: how to channel water, hold it back, let it flow at the right times and through the right spaces; how to move boats up a river that is too shallow, its drop too steep; how to regulate flows so that commodities can be moved to markets, investments realized, speculations in land made profitable. The river was remade within a spatiotemporal imagination that linked northern forests and farmer fields to distant markets that no logger or farmer had ever seen.

Yet, if the remains of the Meeker Dam haunt us, it is perhaps for other reasons. For when the Meeker Dam was first proposed in 1852, the ink on the Treaty of Traverse des Sioux[2] had not yet dried, the Dakota Uprising was still a decade in the future, and the concentration camps established in the winter of 1862/63 at the confluence of Mnisóta Wakpá and Ȟaȟáwakpa—a sacred site for the Dakota—existed only as a latent potential within the violent expansion of settler colonialism. The Meeker Dam haunts us for what it embodies. Not just as the projection of an infrastructural vision, but the projection of such a vision when other territorialities, temporalities, and ontologies—Dakota, Ho-Chunk, and Anishinaabe—were present all around. Rising from its watery grave, the Meeker Dam forces us to ask what made it possible to imagine the river then as an industrial river, part of an emerging industrial capitalism that had only recently taken hold further to the east? What erasures were necessary, what ontologies, territorialities, and temporalities had to be willfully ignored, for the river to become the "nation's river," subsumed within the taken-for-granted temporalities of a settler nation and its political and legal institutions? How was a settler futurity set in place and Indigenous futures rendered unimaginable? And what might it mean to reflect on this moment today, when the future of the river is again in play?

I am drawn to this site because it requires me to consider what remains in and what returns from the past. The dam was abandoned in 1912 because a much larger dam—what is now known as Lock and Dam No. 1—was built a few miles downstream, large enough to allow for navigation upriver to just below St. Anthony Falls, and with sufficient head to generate energy for the Ford Motors assembly plant that relocated there in 1925. In the following decades, almost 30 locks and dams would be built on the Upper Mississippi. Together with levees and dredging to control floods and enable larger barges, they produced an engineered river linked to industry and agriculture from Minneapolis all the way to the Gulf of Mexico, one which conformed to a geopolitical imagination that had no place for, or even consideration of, other temporalities and territorialities, other relations to water and land that did not follow the logic of settler law and property.[3] Today, managed as an integrated system, the locks and dams capture and channel the energy of water toward particular ends rather than others, creating new social and ecological relations, subtending settler society and its industrial ecologies, and, in their day-to-day operations, obscuring and continuing the work of dispossession, oblivious to those or that which have been displaced. Indeed, what remains of the Meeker Dam is less the physical ruins of the dam itself than a political, economic, and ecological rationality that presupposes nation and state, one that imagines capitalist markets to be as natural as rivers, and one that projects and assumes a settler future as a matter of course, much as Meeker and his associates already did 167 years ago.

HOW WAS A SETTLER FUTURITY SET IN PLACE AND INDIGENOUS FUTURES RENDERED UNIMAGINABLE? AND WHAT MIGHT IT MEAN TO REFLECT ON THIS MOMENT TODAY, WHEN THE FUTURE OF THE RIVER IS AGAIN IN PLAY?

The story of the Meeker Dam is thus not just about a dam and a river, but a world created around it, a bustling city built on the fruits of primitive accumulation and the depletion and degradation of northern forests, soils, and water. As residents of the Twin Cities, we inherit this river and its worlds, albeit in radically different and unequal ways. During periods of low water, when the Meeker Dam appears to rise from its watery grave, it reminds us that the urban worlds we take for granted are built upon and carry forward these settler temporalities, spatialities, and ecologies.

But what does it mean to say that we inherit the Meeker Dam, when this "we" is defined by the benefits derived from Indigenous dispossession? What responsibilities does this demand? We might begin by noting that benefits are derived unevenly, that in the context of forced migration, immigrant exclusion, relocation, and chattel slavery, not all non-Indigenous residents are settlers in the same way.[4] We might continue, as Potawatomi scholar Kyle Whyte proposes, by refusing to deny that as settlers, we live in what our ancestors could have only seen as fantasy times. Whyte notes that for centuries, European colonists and settlers were unable to dominate the Native alliances in the region, and "would have relished the very idea that they could advance whatever business interests they wanted without facing threats of empowered resistance and diplomacy. They would have delighted in the idea that their legal orders would not have had to bend to or accommodate Indigenous legal orders."[5] Even for Meeker, confidently projecting a future of river commerce and white settlement, the world we inhabit today would have seemed a fictional utopia. Dakota resistance had not ended and would only become more vigorous. Settler law and property were far from settled, and the river did not bend easily to the desires of investors and engineers. When construction of Meeker's dam was finally begun, long after Meeker himself was dead, engineers struggled to control the force of the river, resulting in cycles of destruction, redesign, and repair. Whyte asks us to see our present as continuous with this past, indeed, founded on it. Borrowing his language, we might say that infrastructures built in the past "were constructed to provide privileges to the builder's descendants. They were gifts of a troubling sort."[6] Draw up a list of Minnesota's Fortune 500 companies, its many co-ops, or its public institutions like the University of Minnesota, where I teach and write, perched above the river gorge. Built on past and present dispossession, these institutions—private, cooperative, and public alike—presuppose and often extend the displacements of settler law and violence, quietly folding past appropriations into the present, benefitting from the "natural" workings of property and market and the infrastructural and institutional environments that today appear as nothing more than sites and effects of "good governance."

DURING PERIODS OF LOW WATER, WHEN THE MEEKER DAM APPEARS TO RISE FROM ITS WATERY GRAVE, IT REMINDS US THAT THE URBAN WORLDS WE TAKE FOR GRANTED ARE BUILT UPON AND CARRY FORWARD THESE SETTLER TEMPORALITIES, SPATIALITIES, AND ECOLOGIES.

Meeker Lock and Dam under construction Sept. 27, 1905.
Photograph by the U.S. Army Corps of Engineers

This is what Whyte asks us to consider. If the Meeker Dam haunts, it is not only because it reminds us about a past where the future was not assured, but because when it rises from its watery grave, it brings that past into the present, it reminds us that if we look beneath the surface and allow ourselves to see what remains, we see that we are still fully within this history as an ongoing process. The Meeker Dam is (in) our present.[7]

Today, as the U.S. Army Corps of Engineers considers the disposition of the locks and dams in the Twin Cities, and as proposals to "rewild" the river gain traction, we do well to reflect on what remains and what returns from this past. But it is also critical that as settlers we refuse to assign Indigenous sovereignty and resistance to the past. As Jean O'Brien, scholar of the White Earth Band of Ojibwe, notes,

> the view that settler colonialism has an eliminatory nature may be correct, but it problematically "pulls toward the notion of extinction," when what is needed is an understanding of "the continuance and survival of Indigenous sovereignty."[8] Just

INDIGENOUS FUTURITIES ARE MULTIPLE & EXIST IN THE NOW, WHILE SETTLER FUTURES ARE NOT AS ASSURED AS THEY MAY SEEM.

as Dakota resistance had not ended when Meeker proposed his dam, it has not ended today. Whether through the construction of the Bdote Memory Map, the work of the Healing Place

Collaborative, demands to remove Sam Durant's gallows sculpture from the Walker Art Center's sculpture garden, the insistence on remembering Indigenous sites like Spirit Island, or the work of Water Protectors along the route of the Line 3 pipeline in Northern Minnesota, Indigenous futurities are multiple and exist in the now, while settler futures are not as assured as they may seem.

Perhaps this is what the ruins of the Meeker Dam surface tell us: not only that we inherit its troubling gift, albeit in different ways, but that the river we inherit—this Anthropocene River that is also a settler-colonial river—is not the only river or the last river. Other rivers, other sovereignties, other futures are already here, have been all along, and are still to be invented.

A version of this article was originally published on the website Anthropocene Curriculum (Winter/Spring 2020).

ENDNOTES

1 Bradley B. Meeker was a settler, property owner, and judge who served on the Minnesota Territorial Supreme Court from 1849 to '53. Eager to establish Minneapolis as the head of navigation on the Mississippi River and capture the site's potential hydropower, Meeker and a number of Minneapolis businessmen proposed building the dam at a site owned by Meeker. Accounts of the Meeker Dam can be found in John Anfinson, "The Secret History of the Mississippi's Earliest Locks and Dams," *Minnesota History* 54, no. 6 (1998): 254–67. See also the Meeker Dam application form to the National Register of Historic Places (2003), https://npgallery.nps.gov/NRHP/GetAsset/0564d3e0-d32b-4483-bbdc-23408bebf357/?branding=NRHP.

2 The Treaty of Traverse des Sioux of 1851—between the Sisseton and Wahpeton bands of Dakota and the U.S. Government—ceded large tracts of Sioux territory along the Minnesota River to the U.S. Government in exchange for annuities of cash and goods. Deception in the treaty negotiations, along with subsequent broken promises, contributed to the Dakota Uprising of 1862.

3 Audra Simpson notes that settler colonialism proceeds without regard for "other life forms, other sovereignties, other forms of political will." Audra Simpson, "The State is a Man: Theresa Spence, Loretta Saunders and the Gender of Settler Sovereignty," *Theory & Event* 19, no. 4 (2016): para. 17, https://muse-jhu-edu.ezp2.lib.umn.edu/article/633280.

4 See Iyko Day, "Being or Nothingness: Indigeneity, Antiblackness, and Settler Colonial Critique," *Critical Ethnic Studies* 1, no. 2 (2015): 102–21.

5 Kyle Whyte, "Indigenous Science (Fiction) for the Anthropocene: Ancestral Dystopias and Fantasies of Climate Change Crises," *Environment and Planning E: Nature and Space* 1, no. 1–2 (2018): 224–42.

6 Whyte, "Indigenous Science (Fiction) for the Anthropocene," 237.

7 Audra Simpson reminds us that "structures move through time and place and if you pay close attention, you can actually see structural activity." Simpson, "The State is a Man," para. 20.

8 Jean O'Brien, "Tracing Settler Colonialism's Eliminatory Logic in Traces of History," *American Quarterly* 69, no. 2 (2017): 249–55.

Submerged ruins of Meeker Dam. Photographs by Dio Cramer

Real Estate River: The Mississippi as Amenity

Morgan Adamson

Morgan Adamson chronicles the historical mechanisms that have led to the Mississippi's transformation from an industrial river to what she terms a "real estate river." Deindustrialization seems to hold the promise of a more desirable ecological future, but leaving past violence and injustices unacknowledged will serve only to continue the long history of extraction along the Mississippi.

In the summer of 1997, Mayor Norm Coleman's office published a document entitled "Saint Paul on the Mississippi: Development Framework." The detailed report describes a "profound transformation" underway in the city of St. Paul, as Coleman puts it: "not only a physical transformation, but a transformation of the very spirit of the Capital City."[1] At the heart of this transformation was, in the words of the report, the "retreat of the industrial glacier," which had revealed a "vast terrain of opportunity in the river valley." In the era of climate change, the phrase "retreat of the industrial glacier," coined by urban designer Ken Greenberg, unwittingly evokes images of glacial retreat, but more on that later. What concerned city planners and developers in the 1990s was that industry's "retreat" would mean substantial landholdings along the river's edge being vacated, leaving new spaces from which the city could conjure its postindustrial future.[2] The "development framework" detailed by the report includes a combination of environmental and infrastructural improvements aimed at giving the city of St. Paul a "competitive advantage in an increasingly globalized world." The "new spirit" of the city projected by Mayor Coleman, then, was one that fully integrated the Mississippi into the urban fabric of St. Paul, understanding it as a crucial amenity for urban life and a propeller of economic development in a postindustrial era. St. Paul—like cities across the U.S. wrestling with deindustrialization—had been developing plans for "urban revitalization" along its waterfront since the 1980s, commissioning the Riverfront Development Corporation in 1984 to connect public assets with private interests to oversee investment along the Mississippi.

In what might be seen as the culmination of the city's efforts over the past 40 years, the RiversEdge development, approved by the Ramsey County Board in July of 2019, completes St. Paul's postindustrial makeover. Composed of four towering glass structures, like those on the waterfronts of cities from Singapore to Miami, the 788-million U.S. dollars RiversEdge project includes a luxury hotel, condos, and apartments, one million square feet of Class A office space, and a public walkway that connects them to the river. RiversEdge will be constructed atop land owned by the city, formerly home to West Publishing Company headquarters and printing facilities, refrigerated storage, and a county jail. The project was proposed by AECOM, a multinational engineering and architectural firm that has worked on a number of high-profile projects, including the 2016 Olympic Games in Rio de Janeiro, the World

Proposed redevelopment of St. Paul. Image by AECOM Properties

Trade Center, Dubai Health Care City, and numerous international airports. AECOM is asking for $80 million from the city to subsidize the project, which Ramsey County hopes to partially cover through a $40 million State bonding bill. This is on top of the $11 million the city has already invested in anticipation of a large-scale development of the site, having demolished the existing remnants of industrial infrastructure in 2015 in order to attract developers.

The transformation of St. Paul's orientation to the river in the past decades exemplifies what we might understand as the shift from the industrial river to what I am calling the real estate river. In *Capital City*, Samuel Stein argues that the deindustrialization of U.S. cities has given rise to the "real estate state" in which "real estate capital has inordinate influence over the shape of our cities, the parameters of our politics, and the lives we lead."[3]

With the decline of industrial capitalism, real estate development has become a primary economic driver in cities, dictating the terms through which space is organized and land use is determined. In the Twin Cities, the Mississippi's diminishing importance as an industrial river has given rise to a situation in which the river now serves as an amenity that augments the value of real estate capital. In this context, decisions made about the river's future as it flows through the Twin Cities are intimately wrapped up in considerations of the immense value of the land adjacent to it. Even positive social and ecological interventions that reimagine the postindustrial river often unwittingly dovetail with the interests of real estate capital and developers.[4] In other words, deindustrialization is a process that is not necessarily about "liberating" the river but subjecting it to the new necessities of capital accumulation.

Take, for example, the Upper Harbor Terminal (UHT) in Minneapolis: the longest contiguous stretch of real estate on the upper Mississippi, which served as the river's northernmost port until it closed in 2014. Located in the historically African American neighborhood of North Minneapolis, the UHT was built atop of the demolished homes of residents in the 1960s and has since barred the neighborhood access to the riverfront. Like the proposed site of the RiversEdge development in St. Paul, the UHT sits on land owned by the city, and, like the St. Paul redevelopment, this land is being offered to the private sector to build for-profit developments, heavily subsidized by taxpayers. The proposed redevelopment of the UHT looks strikingly similar to the kinds of redevelopment projects that have been taking place in deindustrialized spaces across the U.S. since the 1980s. Geographer David Harvey describes this process in the city of Baltimore, where throughout the 1960s deindustrialization and racial turmoil led to white flight and a declining tax base.[5] The city's solution to this crisis was to finance massive waterfront developments, such as the Inner Harbor Project, in order to attract capital back to the city center. Through bonding bills that served as giveaways to the finance and real estate industries, the developments created low-wage service jobs in place of the industry jobs that had been lost, whilst fueling the gentrification of historically African American neighborhoods.

This kind of neoliberal city management fueled the rise of the real estate state in the 1980s and 1990s, where public resources were given over to private developers to fulfill the promise of economic revitalization. The current redevelopment of the Minneapolis and St. Paul riverfronts follow strikingly similar patterns. The original proposal for the UHT redevelopment by United Properties and Thor Companies—which included a "destination" music amphitheater, a hotel, retail space, housing (the majority of which is market rate), and parkland—was sold to the neighborhood and the city through the language of economic revitalization while simultaneously offering only low-wage, service-sector jobs to the already marginalized neighborhood in which it was planned. Against the backdrop of intense community pressure,

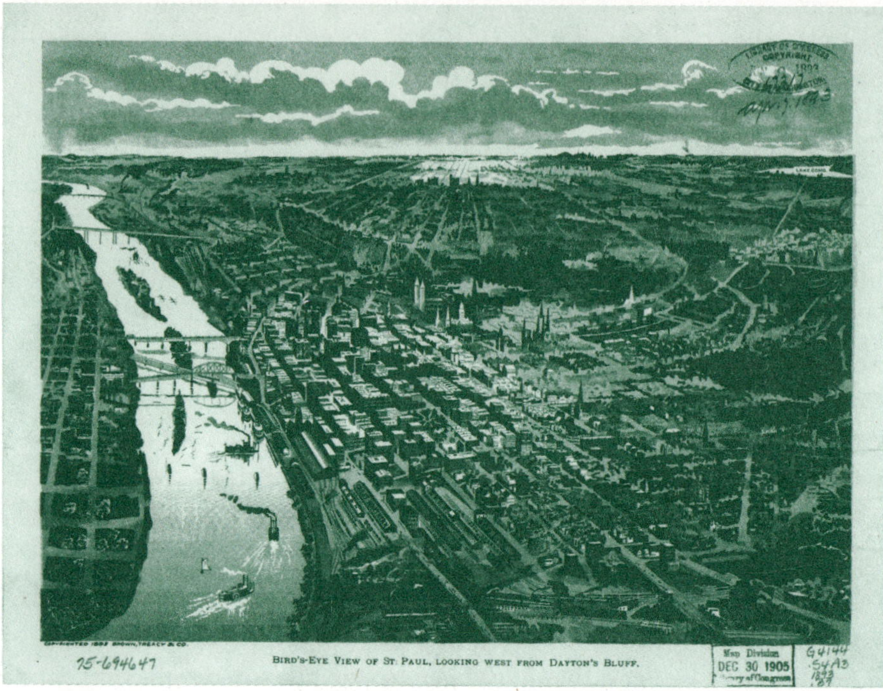

Bird's-eye view of St. Paul, 1893. Image courtesy of the Geography and Map Division, Library of Congress

before it was approved by the city council the developers offered some concessions, removing the hotel from the concept plan and adding a commitment to "community ownership models" for some of the retail space. With the formation of a Community Planning and Engagement Committee, the developers and the city offered only a muted hope that the core issues of racial and environmental justice would be addressed as the redevelopment is pushed through. Already, property values around the site are spiking, accelerating the ongoing processes of speculation and displacement taking place in North Minneapolis.

The story of the UHT reflects the ways that the river remains a site of extraction, where publicly held land is mined by the forces of financial speculation, and where city governments facilitate the flow of capital to and from these extractive spaces. Beneath the talk of "economic revitalization" and the boosterism of city officials lies a deep impotence of advocacy for a just social ecology and a feeble interest in mitigating the transfer of public wealth into private hands. These dynamics come into stark relief when we examine the RiversEdge development in St. Paul. In a metropolitan area currently in the midst of one of the worst affordable housing crises in its history—like many cities across the country in the grips of the real estate state—the proposed RiversEdge development in St. Paul contains no affordable housing units. Instead, AECOM has proposed to "give" the city a paltry $5 million to be spent on affordable housing elsewhere (a mere fraction of the $80 million it is demanding from the city to build the project). Like with the UHT, small concessions are offered to appease the public while largely excluding it from the enormous wealth to be generated from this publicly owned land. While cities are desperate to increase their tax revenue through projects like RiversEdge, as Harvey and many others point out, there is little evidence that public subsidies of real estate developments actually benefit everyday citizens. In its stark reproduction of economic and spatial inequality, RiversEdge exemplifies the vision of the river as a site of consumption and luxury, where public access to and interaction with the river functions as an amenity that increases land values and land speculation.

As it flows through the Twin Cities, the transformation of the Mississippi into a real estate river typifies the grip that real estate capital—and the neoliberal civic-management strategies that facilitate it—have on our collective imagination of the river's future. While civic leaders looked at the "retreat of the industrial glacier" with a sense of possibility at the close of the twentieth century, in the present we should approach any such enthusiasm with suspicion. As the industrial glacier retreats in places like Minneapolis and St. Paul, it leaves in its wake not a tabula rasa ready for new development, but deep layers of sedimented violence. Indeed, as we face the reality of actual glacial retreat and the possibility of the end of life on the planet as we know it, the deep wounds of colonial conquest and the industrial era confront us like never before. In the case of the Twin Cities and the Mississippi, the story of industrialization is inseparable from the expropriation of land from the Dakota people, their displacement and attempted genocide throughout the nineteenth century, and the ongoing legacies of settler colonialism today. Likewise, as the story of the UHT lays bare, the histories of racial violence and the displacement of African Americans, which have been constitutive of the industrial Mississippi since the time of slavery, still haunt it today. To say the Mississippi is an Anthropocene River, to emphasize human impact and

AS IT FLOWS THROUGH THE TWIN CITIES, THE TRANSFORMATION OF THE MISSISSIPPI INTO A REAL ESTATE RIVER TYPIFIES THE GRIP THAT REAL ESTATE CAPITAL HAS ON OUR COLLECTIVE IMAGINATION OF THE RIVER'S FUTURE.

to imagine its different futures, is also to contend with the colonial and racial violence that took place alongside the massive infrastructural interventions into the river's flow and its attendant ecological degradation. In significant ways, the retreat of the industrial glacier is not the harbinger of Mayor Coleman's imagined "new spirit"; it marks not a break from extractive processes but a continuation of them. The real estate river reimagines the river and its shores, employing a similar settler imagination to the one that shaped it at the beginning of the industrial era. By failing to truly confront the myriad violences of that era, it threatens to repeat them.

TO SAY THE MISSISSIPPI IS AN ANTHROPOCENE RIVER, TO EMPHASIZE HUMAN IMPACT AND TO IMAGINE ITS DIFFERENT FUTURES, IS ALSO TO CONTEND WITH THE COLONIAL AND RACIAL VIOLENCE THAT TOOK PLACE ALONGSIDE THE MASSIVE INFRASTRUCTURAL INTERVENTIONS INTO THE RIVER'S FLOW AND ITS ATTENDANT ECOLOGICAL DEGRADATION.

How do we understand the river's value beyond that of an amenity for real estate capital or an entity that provides ecological or other "services" to the public at large? How might the values of reconciliation and reparation drive our approach to the river's future? Whose voices should be foregrounded, including non-human actors? As we witness the intensive land grab currently taking place on the Mississippi's shores, let us form a radical imagination that looks beyond, and struggles against, the terms set by the real estate state.

A version of this article was originally published on the website Anthropocene Curriculum (Winter/Spring 2020).

ENDNOTES

1 Berridge Lewinberg Greenberg and Dark Gabor Limited, "Saint Paul on the Mississippi: Development Framework," Ramsey County Historical Society, posted 1997, https://rchs.com/wp-content/uploads/2017/09/St.-Paul-on-the-Mississippi-Development-Framework_1997.pdf.

2 For more on deindustrialization along the river's shores in the Twin Cities see Patrick Nunnally, "Mapping the 'Retreat of the Industrial Glacier,'" *River Life* (May 21, 2019): https://riverlife.umn.edu/rivertalk/21may2019.

3 Samuel Stein, *Capital City: Gentrification and the Real Estate State* (Verso, 2019), 5.

4 For example, see Patrick Nunnally, "One Place, Many Names," Anthropocene Commons, February 10, 2020, https://www.anthropocene-curriculum.org/contribution/one-place-many-names.

5 David Harvey, "A View from Federal Hill," in *The Baltimore Book: New Views of Local History*, ed. Elizabeth Fee, Linda Shopes, and Linda Zeidman (Temple University Press, 1992).

Real Estate River: The Mississippi as Amenity
by Morgan Adamson, page 76.
Photograph by Joachim Mueller Jung

Blackhawk Park Is Indigenous Land (Beyond Acknowledgment)

Nicholas Brown, Ryan Griffis, and Sarah Kanouse

The effects of the Anthropocene are not experienced evenly, with certain regions and their communities harder hit than others. The seminar *Over the Levee, Under the Plow* took as its starting point one of these spaces: Blackhawk Park, a "wounded place" where the colonial ties of the Anthropocene are palpable. As with any place in the U.S., uncovering its contested history troubles narratives of the present.

Arriving in cars, vans, pickups, and canoes, a group slowly assembled under an overcast sky on the banks of the Mississippi in a place called Blackhawk Park, near the small town of De Soto, Wisconsin. As organizers of Anthropocene Drift,* we believed it was necessary to acknowledge that we were gathering on Indigenous land. On Ho-Chunk land. However, we chose not to begin our program, *Over the Levee, Under the Plow,* with a formal land acknowledgment. Rather, we viewed the five-day seminar—itself building on eighteen months of focused research and planning—as a *prolonged* land acknowledgment, and also a concerted attempt to move *beyond* acknowledgment. That is to say, we need to move from words to actions as we grapple with what it means to live and work as settlers on Indigenous land. On Ho-Chunk land, in this case.

* Anthropocene Drift (or Over the Levee, Under the Plow) was a five-day traveling seminar through the Driftless Region. Part of Mississippi. An Anthropocene River, the seminar focused on settler colonialism, industrial agriculture, Indigenous resurgence, and food sovereignty along the Mississippi River and its tributaries in the Upper Midwest.

Land acknowledgments are necessary but insufficient gestures of accountability to Indigenous peoples in the colonial present. Chelsea Vowel, a Métis writer and teacher from manitow-sâkahikan (Lac Ste. Anne) in Alberta, Canada, invites us "to start imagining a constellation of relationships that must be entered into beyond territorial acknowledgments."[1] She encourages settlers to "start learning about [their] obligations as a guest in this territory." One of the very first obligations as a guest is to know the names of your hosts, and to listen closely to them. In the case of our seminar, doing so elevated homelands and places of belonging instead of field stations, a perspectival shift suggested by Ojibwe artist Andrea Carlson.[2]

ONE OF THE VERY FIRST OBLIGATIONS AS A GUEST IS TO KNOW THE NAMES OF YOUR HOSTS, AND TO LISTEN CLOSELY TO THEM.

"Moving beyond territorial acknowledgments," Vowell continues, "means asking hard questions about what needs to be done once we're 'aware of Indigenous presence.' It requires that we remain uncomfortable, and it means making concrete, disruptive change." Acknowledgment is therefore not an end itself but a provocation to disrupt, to "unsettle"—figuratively and literally—our relationships to the land, to history, and to one another. As three white settlers, artists, and academics, we welcomed participants to lands that are not rightfully ours and spoke with voices authorized and amplified by white supremacy. Ours is the white, middle-class subjectivity—already a complicated assemblage of varying identities—that the anthropologist Heather Anne Swanson describes as "predicated on not noticing. [...] on structural blindness: on a refusal to acknowledge the histories we inherit."[3] So we began *Over the Levee, Under the Plow* by unsettling the very land on which we gathered—acknowledging our complicity in the violence that secured our place there.

HERE AND NOW

Anthropocene Drift began in a place usually marked as an ending.

Not far from where we gathered in Blackhawk Park, a massacre took place. On the first and second days of August 1832, the U.S. Army and Illinois militia fired on a group of starving, exhausted Native Americans—mostly Sauk and Meskwaki, but also Kickapoo, Ho-Chunk, and Potawatomi—as they tried to cross the Mississippi River to safety. Their leader, Black Hawk, had already tried to surrender several times during the so-called war that bears his name, and the massacre began even after he once again waved a flag of truce. When soldiers began firing, Black Hawk's band had little choice but to provide cover for those trying to cross. Soldiers on the bluffs streamed down to shoot at closer range, while a military riverboat fired on retreating families with cannons. Although some made it to safety, many of those who crossed the river were soon captured by the U.S.-allied Dakota. Militiamen gleefully mutilated corpses; sharpshooters deliberately targeted babies. When reproached for these actions, one volunteer soldier coldly replied, "Kill the nits, and you'll have no lice."[4]

Banners from Dylan Miner's project "The Land is Always" installed on the banks of the Mississippi River at the opening event programming for Anthropocene Drift, September 25, 2019. Photograph by Katie Netti/Meredith Dallas

Officially called the Battle of Bad Axe, the event produced carnage so one-sided that it has been described as a massacre since the 1850s. Of the nearly 2,000 people who had joined Black Hawk in April to contest the terms of a fraudulent treaty and return to their ancestral village of Saukenuk to farm, only thirty-nine survivors were captured at the conclusion of the massacre. Many had died on the journey before reaching the Mississippi, while others no doubt managed to escape during the fighting. Black Hawk surrendered himself to American authorities a few days after the massacre and was imprisoned just down the river in Prairie du Chien.

The Black Hawk War inaugurated an era of massive change to physical, cultural, and political landscapes throughout the region. A newsletter from the Dane County Historical Society summed it up: "Without an Indian war threat, Wisconsin Territory was created just four years later and rapid settlement produced statehood in 1848."[5] The genocidal war unleashed a new phase of regional settler colonization and justified an aggressive campaign of removal of the northern Indigenous peoples, including the Ho-Chunk, Meskwaki, Iowa, and Kickapoo Nations. Historian Jeffrey Ostler argues, "After the Bad Axe Massacre, federal officials seized the moment to separate Indians from their lands. Whether they had supported Black Hawk, remained neutral, or assisted the United States government made no difference."[6] Beginning in 1832, the Ho-Chunk suffered multiple removals—from Wisconsin to Iowa, Minnesota, Dakota Territory, and Nebraska. Of course, some Ho-Chunk refused to be removed, and remained in or returned to each of these places.

The Bad Axe Massacre has a prehistory, a context. A land cession treaty had been signed in St. Louis in 1804 by a Sauk delegation that did not expect to enter into land negotiations and lacked the authority to do so, leading many members of the Sauk Nation to regard the treaty as invalid and to resist American attempts to enforce it. This fraudulent treaty and increasing squatter incursions into their traditional territories prompted the Sauk, Meskwaki, Ho-Chunk, and Potawatomi to support the British during the War of 1812. Black Hawk himself fought in that war and incorporated British insignia into his wardrobe for the rest of his life. Under the terms of the Treaty of Ghent of 1814, the U.S. assumed actual, rather than nominal, control over the so-called Northwest Territory, and settlers began arriving en masse. At the conclusion of that war, Saukenuk, the Sauk capital where *Over the Levee, Under the Plow* ended, was the largest city in what would soon become Illinois. Occupied mostly during the growing season when the Sauk returned from their winter hunting grounds in what is now Iowa, Saukenuk's log houses were surrounded by vegetable and corn fields. The lead deposits of northwestern Illinois and southwestern Wisconsin were mined seasonally by Ho-Chunk, Sauk, and Meskwaki women. These well-stewarded resources were extremely attractive to settlers, and from the 1820s both Sauk and Meskwaki leaders began to complain of finding white squatters living in their Saukenuk homes, stealing their corn, and mining the ore with people they had enslaved.

In this historical context, we can understand Blackhawk Park, the nearby town of Victory, and the Black Hawk Trail, which we followed over five days, as "environmental fantasies" of our "settler ancestors." As Potawatomi scholar Kyle Powys Whyte asserts:

> Many Indigenous peoples in North America [...] are already living in what our ancestors would have understood as dystopian or post-apocalyptic times. In a cataclysmically short period, the capitalist-colonialist partnership has destroyed our relationships with thousands of species and ecosystems. [...]
>
> Settler ancestors wanted today's world. They would have relished the possibility that some of their descendants could freely commit extractive violence on Indigenous lands and then feel, with no doubts, that they are ethical people."[7]

We must acknowledge this environmental fantasy/dystopia, too, and sit with the discomfort acknowledgment arouses. We gathered at Blackhawk Park because of the massacre that took place on August 1 and 2, 1832. But that is obviously not all that has happened there, and those who survived the massacre have relationships to this place that cannot be reduced to a simple narrative of domination and extermination. As George Thurman, a direct descendent of Black Hawk and the former Principal Chief of the Sac and Fox Nation in Oklahoma, explains:

"Battle of Bad Ax," 1857 engraving by Henry Lewis. Image courtesy of the Library of Congress Online Catalog

> To say that Black Hawk still has relevance to the Sac and Fox implies a hold to the past, and that's true because we are all connected, a part of those who came before and holding on to what they taught us for those yet to come. However, our past is not a fixed point that grows farther away with each new generation; instead, our past is like a bloodline, living, breathing, and growing as we grow. [...]
>
> As a descendant, my perspective about Black Hawk is more personal. He is a very real part of what I bring to the Sac and Fox Nation as its chief and who I am as Sac and Fox. I have visited the places where he walked and could place my own footsteps where his had been. I stood on the banks of the Mississippi River at Bad Axe where 179 years ago I would have been a target for the guns and cannon just for being Sauk.
>
> So many of our people died there. The massacre still echoes within us. It was a tragic ending. But I, a member of that same tribe, stood there at the place of "ending" and saw my people of today make offerings at the riverside. Black Hawk fought so his people could live, and there, where one might think it all ended for us, we stood, remembering our people in the way they left to us and that is uniquely ours.[8]

Blackhawk Park can also be understood as a "wounded place," which geographer Karen Till describes as "present to the pain of others and [embodying] difficult

Commemorative marker to the Treaty of 1804 installed by the Sac and Fox Nation of Oklahoma and the Meskwaki Tribe/Sac and Fox of the Mississippi in Iowa.
Photograph by Ryan Griffis

Flooding at Blackhawk Park, May 2019.
Photograph by Sarah Kanouse

social pasts."[9] In this sense, the confluence of the Bad Axe River with the Mississippi is not unlike Bdote, the confluence of the Minnesota and Mississippi Rivers, which has been the focus of Dakota artist Mona Smith's ongoing healing work.[10] In places such as these, we must challenge ourselves to understand, following historian Christine DeLucia, "how memories of devastation exist relationally alongside those of regeneration."[11] If the Mississippi Valley can be understood, in part, by tracing Indigenous removals and land cessions, it can also be understood in terms of refusals and returns, particularly among the Ho-Chunk and Meskwaki Nations. The effects of removals are felt today and every day, and shape what Lakota historian Nick Estes calls "the Indigenous political practice of return, restoration, and reclamation of belonging and place."[12] As the ecological devastation initiated by the wounding of places like Bdote and Bad Axe spreads across the planet, how to remember, care for, and address sites of intergenerational and profoundly uneven trauma become ever more urgent questions.

HERE AND *NOW*

We began our public program forty-one hours after an equinox; six days into the student-led Global Climate Strike; a few months after the water that covered Blackhawk Park for much of the spring and early summer receded; and at the end of the hottest decade in human history.

We all followed different paths to arrive at Blackhawk Park that September afternoon.

Some of us drove to the park from South Central Wisconsin and Central Illinois, the middle of the so-called Corn Belt, where rivers with names like the Rock, Vermilion, Platte, Mackinaw, Menominee, Embarras, Wisconsin, Kaskaskia, and Sangamon—along with many drainage ditches and canals—connect, eventually, to the Mississippi River. The dominant plants found in that territory for most of the year—genetically modified yellow dent #2 corn and soybeans—require vast amounts of energy and chemical inputs. When discussing the Anthropocene, this landscape is a seemingly easy case study as a totally transformed ecosystem, as environmental historian William Cronon described years ago in *Nature's Metropolis*.[13]

Shortly after massacres like Bad Axe secured U.S. ownership over the Midwest, the series of Swamp Land Acts passed between 1849 and 1860 "gave" lands considered swamps and wetlands to states so that these ecosystems could be converted into private property and made "productive." This federal legislation did not result directly and immediately in what geographers like Michael Urban have argued is, for all intents and purposes, the permanent transformation of the region's hydrological and ecological composition.[14] Rather, the policies were only one step that prefigured the work that speculators and farmers would undertake to remake the land in their own image through drainage ditches and subsurface tile drainage systems. The near total elimination

Monument to the last Wisconsin passenger pigeon, shot at Babcock in September 1899 adjacent to an effigy mound of the Woodland culture, ca. 350-1350 CE. Wyalusing State Park. Photograph by Sarah Kanouse

Okjökull memorial plaque. Photograph by Dominic Boyer (CC BY-SA 4.0)

of wetlands and grasslands in this region was also a colonial war—this time against what anthropologist James C. Scott has referred to as the ungovernable spaces of wetlands and mud, and, of course, against the lifeways that were sustained by them.[15] The vast fields of corn and soy that we see today are local instantiations of the colonial and capitalist land use and plantation economies that exist around the world. This model is, in fact, one that has been exported at an enormous scale to Brazil and Argentina. Like all plantation economies, the conceptualization of the land as a storehouse of resources waiting to be extracted also includes the conceptualization of bodies, both human and otherwise, as expendable forms of capital.

The effects of this physical transformation are reverberating across the biosphere. A week before the launch of our seminar, the *New York Times* reported on an article in the journal *Science* that shows "the number of birds in the United States and Canada has fallen by 29 percent since 1970. [...] There are 2.9 *billion* fewer birds taking wing now than there were 50 years ago."[16] Blackhawk Park lies within the Mississippi Flyway, a vital migration corridor for more than 325 bird species, which pass by there twice a year en route from breeding grounds in Canada and the northern United States to wintering grounds along the Gulf of Mexico and in Central and South America.

Two weeks before the launch, the *New York Times* reported that "this year's flooding across the Midwest and the South affected nearly 14 million people." The article noted: "The year through May 2019 was the wettest 12-month period on record in the United States, according to the National Oceanic and Atmospheric Administration. Edward Clark, director of NOAA's National Water Center, said, 'This is a year that will remain in our cultural memory, in our history.'"[17] The year continued to be very wet into fall. The Midwest witnessed—and was unevenly impacted by—historic flooding along the Mississippi and Missouri Rivers and many of their tributaries. "The fields are washing away," Missouri farmer Kate Glastetter told *Pacific Standard* magazine in June, a month when Blackhawk Park was submerged beneath the swollen Mississippi.[18] The silt left by receding floodwaters added to the layer—already several meters thick in many places—of what scientists call "post-settlement alluvium," or "legacy sediment," the result of nineteenth-century Euro-American agricultural practices that initiated widespread erosion and washed upland sediment into the region's valleys. The economic stress posed by the most recent floods may exacerbate the epidemic of depression among American farmers, whose suicide rate in 2018 was already twice that of combat veterans.[19] And although words like "Anthropocene" and "climate crisis" are controversial or even unknown in many rural communities, it is possible to identify within them what environmental researchers Ashlee Cunsolo and Neville Ellis call ecological grief: "the grief felt in relation to experienced or anticipated ecological losses, including the loss of species, ecosystems and meaningful landscapes due to acute or chronic environmental change."[20]

MOURNING NATURE IN THE (COLONIAL) ANTHROPOCENE

Seventy-two years and forty miles from where we gathered at Blackhawk Park, ecologist Aldo Leopold dedicated a monument to the last Wisconsin passenger pigeon, which was shot dead in September 1899. In his speech at the unveiling, Leopold reflected: "We have erected a monument to commemorate the funeral of a species. It symbolizes our sorrow. We grieve because no living man will see again the onrushing phalanx of victorious birds, sweeping a path for spring across the March skies, chasing the defeated winter from all the woods and prairies of Wisconsin." In dedicating what was perhaps the first monument to extinction, Leopold called out the actions of previous generations—"Our grandfathers," he declared, "[believed it was] more important to multiply people and comforts than to cherish the beauty of the land in which they live"—while also reserving his greatest grief not for the birds themselves but for the loss of cultural and aesthetic relationships that mainstream settler American culture had developed with that species.[21]

Leopold's elegiac warning foreshadowed the recent rash of extinction-related monuments, both physical and virtual. These monuments, like the one initiated by Cymene Howe and Dominic Boyer to Iceland's vanishing Okjökull glacier or Maya Lin's multimedia biodiversity memorial *What Is Missing?* (2009–), frequently employ a non-specific, present-day human "we." Billed as a "global memorial to the planet," Lin's artwork is dedicated to:

> The species that have gone extinct.
>
> The species that will go extinct in our lifetime.
>
> The species that we will never know because we destroyed their habitats before we could ever know them.[22]

The glacier memorial's text, written by prominent Icelandic author Andri Snaer Magnason and unveiled in July 2019 to much fanfare, similarly addresses a future human reader: "This monument is to acknowledge that *we* know what is happening and what needs to be done. Only *you* know if *we* did it." Leopold's pigeon plaque is more explicit in its accusation: "This species became extinct through the avarice of and thoughtlessness of *man*."[23]

These monuments are significant because they point to an ongoing shift toward considering longer, multigenerational timespans and finding "nature" and cultural relationships with the natural world grievable. Yet in invoking an undifferentiated "we," they risk reinforcing the already widespread narrative—epitomized in Leopold's plaque—that humanity writ large is responsible for these losses. However, as Kyle Powys Whyte reminds us, some humans have long benefited from the very forces that generated the losses that we now grieve or find "ourselves" suddenly vulnerable to.

The very real grief that climate change can and should engender—and that creative projects are uniquely suited to hold space for—risks becoming an eco-variant of what Renato Rosaldo called "imperialist nostalgia [which] uses a pose of 'innocent yearning' both to capture people's imaginations and to conceal its complicity with often brutal domination."[24] Those of us who have inherited the structural blindness endemic to white, middle-class American culture must insistently recognize the staggering ecological costs already born by Indigenous peoples long before the last passenger pigeon fell from the sky.

THE COLONIAL ANTHROPOCENE

In starting our seminar at Blackhawk Park on September 25, 2019, we were making two implicit propositions. The first is that what has been called the Anthropocene—the intensification and industrialization of land and resource use that has led us to the brink of ecological collapse—is not the inevitable product of humanity writ large but rather the consequence of Euro-American colonialism and the capitalist economic systems it built. Anthropocene Drift (Field Station 2) tried to

Community member testifies at an Illinois EPA Public Hearing for 401 Water Quality Certification, Danville Area Community College, March 26, 2019. Photograph by Ryan Griffis

make visible not just the Anthropocene but also the *colonial Anthropocene*, which is to say it sought to reveal how ongoing processes of colonization are transforming the Earth. The (colonial) Anthropocene is everywhere, of course, but it is particularly palpable in places like Blackhawk Park, Indian Lake, and the former site of the Badger Army Ammunition Plant in Wisconsin, where our field station programming took place.

Our second proposition is that the Anthropocene is an uneven spatial phenomenon. Debates about the start of the Anthropocene are usually framed in temporal rather than spatial terms. *When* did it begin, we ask, not *where* did it start? Dates are singular rather than plural. The Anthropocene started in either 1492, 1610, 1619, *or* 1950. It didn't start in all these, plus a million other times and places. We contend that the Anthropocene is both a world geo-historical event and a highly variegated and textured condition that is experienced unevenly and very specifically across space, species, gender, race, and class. Anthropocene Drift asked not *when* did the (colonial) Anthropocene begin, but, instead, *where* is it most visible? And where, how, and by whom is it felt most intensely? Part of our interest in the Driftless Area was thus pragmatic, insofar as it ties the Anthropocene to colonialism in *place(s)*.

It's ironic to think about the Anthropocene in terms of temporal golden spikes. Spikes are, after all, driven into space, not time. They are staples connecting one thing with another, an attempt to bridge a gap. According to historian Manu Karuka, that other famous golden spike—the one that connected the First Transcontinental Railroad—"did not suture the Union after the Civil War; it symbolically finalized the industrial infrastructure of a continental empire where none had existed before."[25] But if you wanted to place a spatiotemporal golden spike to mark the start of the Anthropocene in the Upper Midwest (or, as it was known from 1787 to 1803, the Northwest Territory), the confluence of the Bad Axe and Mississippi Rivers—that is to say, Blackhawk Park—would be an ideal location.

Yet framing the "quotidian Anthropocene" as starting here risks reducing this place to the Bad Axe Massacre and reinforcing what literary scholar Mark Rifkin calls "settler time," a temporality that consigns Indigenous people to the past while selectively admitting them to a present defined entirely in settler terms. Only within settler time could the Black Hawk conflict be described as the "last Indian war east of the Mississippi." This designation is another instance of the "phenomenon of lasting," which Ojibwe historian Jean O'Brien identifies as a "rhetorical strategy that asserts as a fact the claim that Indians can never be modern."[26] The Black Hawk War was obviously not the "last Indian war," nor was it the last conflict over settlement or sovereignty in the Midwest—or anywhere else. It wasn't even the last Black Hawk war. The longest and most destructive conflict between so-called pioneer immigrants and Native Americans in Utah history, which occurred thirty-three years *after* the conflict in Illinois, is also commonly referred to as the Black Hawk War.

Similarly, calling the Anthropocene a new geologic time that "we" are all in only makes sense in the framework of settler time. If we adopt the Anthropocene as a useful analytic framework, we must take care that it not become a totalizing, teleological narrative, an extension of Rifkin's "settler time" to which Indigenous people might be admitted, but only on terms that ultimately undermine the heterogeneous temporalities that are forms of sovereignty existing beyond settler recognition.[27] For this reason, our Field Station largely did not engage the Anthropocene as a definitional project, whether by establishing its temporality or locating exemplary anthropocenic phenomena. We were most interested in how the Anthropocene is to be survivable and, crucially, for whom. We must remember that the colonial project that undergirds the Anthropocene was never fully successful: there still exist biocultural *and* temporal "refuges," sustained by the descendants of the people colonization failed to exterminate. Anthropocene Drift (Field Station 2) was a protracted effort to learn about what novelist and essayist Gerald Vizenor calls "survivance" ("survival" plus "resistance") in the face of extended, violent ecosocial trauma.[28] While we sought to listen to and learn from Indigenous people, we do not hold up Indigenous "resilience" as a model for settler society, such that the refusal to be eliminated becomes yet another resource for Euro-Americans to plunder. Rather, we sought to strengthen relationships with and between Indigenous individuals and groups and among settler descendants, out of which we aimed to build practices of survivability that foreground both difference and justice in the (colonial) Anthropocene. Clint Carroll, a citizen of the Cherokee Nation, professor at the University of Colorado Boulder, and the seminar's concluding speaker, describes this as "relational activism," explaining:

> For Indigenous peoples, the political is environmental—our struggles are most fundamentally about and for the land. This is not a liberal stance, not an environmentalist stance, not a Marxist class-struggle stance. It is an Indigenous stance that may touch on points within the above positions yet offers the world something distinct, something fundamentally different that seeks to benefit all those who have a right to life, that is, all things living—and this includes plants, animals, landforms, waterways, and the many other beings with which humans must maintain respectful relations.[29]

Recognizing fundamental differences between Indigenous and progressive Euro-American political traditions is essential for any meaningful exchange. In the especially fraught context of settler-Indigenous contact—which has long mixed violent conquest with romanticized celebration, and forced assimilation with cultural appropriation—we must treat concepts of "reconciliation" and "understanding" with caution, lest they become yet another settler "move to innocence."[30] Rather, by highlighting both what is relational and what is incommensurable, we hope to live a better, more responsive, and inescapably Earth-bound life *in place*, whether Indigenous, settler, "arrivant," or all three.[31]

WE CONTEND THAT THE ANTHROPOCENE IS BOTH A WORLD GEO-HISTORICAL EVENT AND A HIGHLY VARIEGATED AND TEXTURED CONDITION THAT IS EXPERIENCED UNEVENLY AND VERY SPECIFICALLY ACROSS SPACE, SPECIES, GENDER, RACE, AND CLASS.

GROUNDED RELATIONALITIES

In the Vermilion River watershed near the border of Illinois and Indiana, there has been something of a successful campaign against the unregulated impacts of waste from coal-burning power plants, which

BY HIGHLIGHTING BOTH WHAT IS RELATIONAL AND WHAT IS INCOMMENSURABLE, WE HOPE TO LIVE A BETTER, MORE RESPONSIVE, AND INESCAPABLY EARTH-BOUND LIFE IN PLACE, WHETHER INDIGENOUS, SETTLER, "ARRIVANT," OR ALL THREE.

of course are always located alongside rivers. A coalition of urban and rural organizations—including the Prairie Rivers Network, Faith in Place, Eco-Justice Collaborative, and Earthjustice—mobilized a large, politically diverse population to pressure the Illinois government to force power companies to deal with the problems posed by mountains of coal ash. At one Illinois Environmental Protection Agency hearing, residents packed a gym at Danville Area Community College to argue that the river needs to be understood as a living thing that cannot be legislated or controlled by engineering solutions. These residents represented the largely white, rural, working-class population that voted for Donald Trump in 2016, and we have no illusions that they—whether individually liberal or conservative—were representing anything other than their own interests, in the form of maintaining their property claims and protecting the health of their families and friends. But we could also choose to hear at least some recognition of what one of our participants, the historian Alyosha Goldstein (along with his coauthors Jodi Byrd, Jodi Melamed, and Chandan Reddy) has called "grounded relationalities": "If the grounded relationalities of Indigenous philosophies might tell us anything, then, they remind us that knowledge must always remain grounded as the land calls to us and for us to find our place within the ongoing acts of interconnectivity that surround us."[32]

How might the experience of these testifying Illinois residents, as settlers in the (colonial) Anthropocene, be mobilized toward living within it differently? Goldstein and his coauthors ask for a consideration of how land, "understood not as property or territory but as a source of relation with an agency of its own," might make other possibilities available, possibilities that recognize the racialized and embodied histories that we have inherited and continue to create.

Although our Field Station research and public program centered Indigenous voices, the opening of the seminar did not include the visible participation of Native Americans in the spiritually, historically, and ecologically charged site of the Bad Axe Massacre. Early in our planning, we spent several weeks asking individuals we know in the Sauk, Meskwaki, Ho-Chunk, and Kickapoo Nations about the value of meeting there to address this history. Several of these people joined us for portions of the seminar but did not respond to or declined the invitation to meet us at Bad Axe. Bill Quackenbush, Tribal Historic Preservation Officer for the Ho-Chunk Nation, who led a four-hour tour with the group on the seminar's second day, explained his reluctance: "Our internal perspectives, stories, and histories of this and many other traumatic events are only intended to stay within our tribal communities."

Quackenbush helped us understand that an invitation to perform or narrate at this site of trauma is inappropriate. It is only within settler time that this "history" needs to be specifically addressed as such, since it is being actively lived in Indigenous communities every day. If the (colonial) Anthropocene is to be survivable, Indigenous people and settlers will have different roles. As Dakota medicine gardener Francis Bettelyoun explains in artist Corinne Teed's booklet for the Field Station: "We [the Dakota people] are Indigenizing. We are not decolonizing. Your work is decolonizing."[33] Anthropocene Drift (Field Station 2) was our humble contribution to that ongoing work.

As we assemble these reflections a few months after the conclusion of the seminar, we continue to be mindful of the here and now, and how shifting places and times assert themselves and inflect our understandings of the (colonial) Anthropocene. The end of the year—the end of the decade—witnessed another UN Climate Change Conference (COP25), and teenage environmental activist Greta Thunberg is in the news again. This time it is not because of what she said, but because of what she didn't say, and how she used her platform to center other voices, especially Indigenous voices. "Our stories have been told over and over again," Thunberg said to delegates at COP25. "There is no need to listen to us anymore." She continued, "It is people especially from the global south, especially from Indigenous communities, who need to tell their stories."[34]

A version of this article was originally published on the website Anthropocene Curriculum (Summer 2020).

ENDNOTES

1 Chelsea Vowel, "Beyond Territorial Acknowledgments," *âpihtawikosisân*, September 23, 2016, https://apihtawikosisan.com/2016/09/beyond-territorial-acknowledgments/.

2 Andrea Carlson, "The Mississippi River Is the Opposite of the Anthropocene," *Anthropocene Curriculum*, February 10, 2020, https://www.anthropocene-curriculum.org/contribution/the-mississippi-river-is-the-opposite-of-the-anthropocene.

3 Heather Anne Swanson, "The Banality of the Anthropocene," *Society for Cultural Anthropology*, February 22, 2017, https://www.culanth.org/fieldsights/the-banality-of-the-anthropocene.

4 William Henry Perrin, *History of Crawford and Clark Counties, Illinois* (O. L. Baskin, 1883), 232.

5 *Dane County Historical Society Newsletter*, Summer 2007, 2.

6 Jeffrey Ostler, *Surviving Genocide: Native Nations and the United States from the American Revolution to Bleeding Kansas* (Yale University Press, 2019), 307.

7 Kyle Powys Whyte, "White Allies, Let's Be Honest about Decolonization," *Yes!*, April 3, 2018, http://www.yesmagazine.org/issues/decolonize/white-allies-lets-be-honest-about-decolonization-20180403.

8 George Thurman, "We Are Still Here to Tell Their Stories and to Add Our Own," in *Re-Collecting Black Hawk: Landscape, Memory, and Power in the American Midwest*, ed. Nicholas Brown and Sarah Kanouse (University of Pittsburgh Press, 2015), 20–21.

9 Karen Till, "Artistic and Activist Memory-Work: Approaching Place-Based Practice," *Memory Studies* 1, no. 1 (2008): 108.

10 See Mona Smith, "Learning from the Dakota: Water and Place," *Open Rivers*, no. 11 (Summer 2018): https://editions.lib.umn.edu/openrivers/article/learning-from-the-dakota-water-and-place/.

11 Christine M. DeLucia, *Memory Lands: King Philip's War and the Place of Violence in the Northeast* (Yale University Press, 2018), 22.

12 Nick Estes, *Our History Is the Future: Standing Rock versus the Dakota Access Pipeline, and the Long Tradition of Indigenous Resistance* (Verso, 2019), 248.

13 William Cronon, *Nature's Metropolis: Chicago and the Great West* (W. W. Norton, 1991).

14 Michael Urban, "Catastrophic Human-Induced Change in Stream-Channel Planform and Geometry in an Agricultural Watershed, Illinois, USA," *Annals of the Association of American Geographers* 93, no. 4 (2003).

15 James C. Scott, *Seeing Like a State: How Certain Schemes to Improve the Human Condition Have Failed* (Yale University Press, 1998), 56.

16 This summary of the *Science* article comes from Carl Zimmer, "Birds Are Vanishing from North America," *New York Times*, September 19, 2019, https://www.nytimes.com/2019/09/19/science/bird-populations-america-canada.html.

17 Sarah Almukhtar, Blacki Migliozzi, John Schwartz, and Josh Williams, "The Great Flood of 2019: A Complete Picture of a Slow-Motion Disaster," *The New York Times*, September 11, 2019, https://www.nytimes.com/interactive/2019/09/11/us/midwest-flooding.html.

18 Emily Moon, "'The Fields Are Washing Away:' Midwest Flooding Is Wreaking Havoc on Farmers," *Pacific Standard*, June 6, 2019, https://psmag.com/environment/the-fields-are-washing-away-midwest-flooding-is-wreaking-havoc-on-farmers.

19 Debbie Weingarten, "Why Are America's Farmers Killing Themselves?," *Guardian*, December 11, 2018, https://www.theguardian.com/us-news/2017/dec/06/why-are-americas-farmers-killing-themselves-in-record-numbers.

20 Ashlee Cunsolo and Neville R. Ellis, "Ecological Grief as a Mental Health Response to Climate Change-Related Loss," *Nature Climate Change* 8, no. 4 (2018): 275.

21 Aldo Leopold, quoted in Kelly Enright, "Exhibiting Extinction: Martha and the Monument, Two Modes of Remembering Nature," *Cultural Studies Review* 25, no. 1 (2019): 151–71.

22 Maya Lin, *What is Missing?* (2009), https://www.whatismissing.net/.

23 Emphases added to both quotations.

24 Renato Rosaldo, "Imperialist Nostalgia," *Representations*, no. 26 (1989): 108.

25 Manu Karuka, *Empire's Tracks: Indigenous Nations, Chinese Workers, and the Transcontinental Railroad* (University of California Press, 2019), xiv.

26 Jean O'Brien, *Firsting and Lasting: Writing Indians Out of Existence in New England* (University of Minnesota Press, 2010), 107.

27 Mark Rifkin, *Beyond Settler Time: Temporal Sovereignty and Indigenous Self-Determination* (Duke University Press, 2017).

28 Gerald Vizenor, *Manifest Manners: Narratives on Postindian Survivance* (University of Nebraska Press, 1999).

29 Clint Carroll, "Relational Activism and Indigenous Futures," *World Literature Today*, October 10, 2019, https://www.worldliteraturetoday.org/blog/cultural-cross-sections/relational-activism-and-indigenous-futures-clint-carroll.

30 Eve Tuck and K. Wayne Yang, "Decolonization Is Not a Metaphor," *Decolonization: Indigeneity, Education & Society* 1, no. 1 (2012): 1–40.

31 Literary scholar Jodi Byrd disrupts the Indigenous/settler binary by inserting a third category of arrivant. Borrowed from the African Caribbean poet Kamau Brathwaite, the term "arrivant" describes "those people forced into the Americas through the violence of European and Anglo-American colonialism and imperialism around the globe." See Jodi A. Byrd, *The Transit of Empire: Indigenous Critiques of Colonialism* (University of Minnesota Press, 2011), xix.

32 Jodi A. Byrd, Alyosha Goldstein, Jodi Melamed, and Chandan Reddy, "Predatory Value: Economies of Dispossession and Disturbed Relationalities," *Social Text* 36, no. 2 (2018): 11–14.

33 Corinne Teed, with Francis Bettelyoun, Rhonda Funmaker, and Jodee Smith, *Amongst Relatives*, Field Guides to the Anthropocene Drift. Berlin: Haus der Kulturen der Welt; Munich: Goethe-Institut, 2019, https://regionalrelationships.org/anthrodrift/bookletPDFs/AmongstRelatives.pdf.

34 Associated Press, "Greta Asks Media to Focus on Other Young Climate Activists," *Voice of America*, December 9, 2019, https://www.voanews.com/europe/greta-asks-media-focus-other-young-climate-activists. In response to Thunberg's action, Hartman Deetz, an environmental activist and member of the Mashpee Wampanoag Tribe, wrote on Facebook: "see...I like Greta. She gets it, what privilege is and how to use it. Create a platform and give it to the people who need it. Thank you Greta." Hartman Deetz, "see...I like Greta," Facebook, December 14, 2019, https://www.facebook.com/hartman.deetz/posts/10156754200397267.

Fort Snelling's Deep Time Stories

Roopali Phadke

The stories that we tell of a place can contain numerous errors and omissions. The recent renovation of Fort Snelling in Minnesota is an opportunity for Roopali Phadke to reflect on its stories. The confluence of the Mississippi and Minnesota Rivers has been a place of birth, death, origin, and genocide. What histories get to be told in this place? Will telling its "deep time" stories begin to correct these errors and omissions?

"Distant View of Fort Snelling" (1847-49) by Seth Eastman.
Image courtesy of the Minnesota Historical Society

My past visits to Historic Fort Snelling have felt like ghostly encounters. The Fort occupies a 300 acre site high above the confluence of the Mississippi and Minnesota Rivers in Minnesota. It was built in 1820 by the U.S. Army to serve as a vantage point for protecting the American fur trade. This site has had many lives over its 125 years. It has served as military barracks, the enslaved home of Harriet and Dred Scott, a forced internment camp for over 1,600 Dakota men, women, and children during the U.S.-Dakota War, and the location of a secret Military Intelligence Service language school during World War II. Today, the Fort Snelling National Cemetery holds the remains of soldiers from each of the wars that the U.S. engaged in throughout its history; a total of 170,000 servicemen and servicewomen.

To commemorate its bicentennial in 2020, the Minnesota Historical Society invested $34.5 million to renovate the site guided by a vision statement titled "Many stories—still untold." They removed a failing 1980s underground visitor center and created a new Plank Museum & Visitor Center inside the rehabilitated 1904 cavalry barracks. The new center includes exhibit spaces, galleries, meeting rooms and classrooms.

When I first learned about Fort Snelling's "revitalization," it raised many questions for me about storytelling. Who gets to write and tell those "still untold" stories? How will the Historical Society determine which stories are the ones that need to be told now? And, as a site of important ecological as well as cultural relevance, how might those stories go "deep time" and open up new vantage points on the site and its intertwined physical, material, and social histories? Writing a deep time story of Fort Snelling is an unenviable challenge. There are clear stakes in telling some stories, and not others, as well as telling stories in one way rather than another.

THERE ARE CLEAR STAKES IN TELLING SOME STORIES, AND NOT OTHERS, AS WELL AS TELLING STORIES IN ONE WAY RATHER THAN ANOTHER.

At the same time, Fort Snelling is a place so steeped in painful histories that it feels like only some people should have license to tell its stories; its Dakota stories, its black slave stories, its military stories. Yet, it is also one of our most public places, where families and schoolchildren come daily to learn about Minnesota's early history—nearly everyone in Minnesota knows where Fort Snelling is and what they think it is about.

Fort Snelling's most important feature to many is that it sits on Bdote. Bdote is a Dakota word, meaning where two waters meet, that refers to the confluence of the Minnesota and Mississippi Rivers. Many Dakota people consider this location as a sacred place of creation, identifying themselves as the Wicahpi Oyate (Star Nation) who originated in the sky and came into being on this land.

I visited the "revitalized" Fort Snelling site with some hesitation in 2025. I was joined by four yellow school buses filled with elementary school children. I was pleasantly surprised to see that visitors are now immediately grounded in the site's history as Dakota homeland. A welcome plaza imprinted with sinuous rivers etched in concrete mark Bdote as the confluence of the Mississippi and Minnesota rivers.

A sign above reminds visitors that "This has been a site of diplomacy and conflict; pride and tragedy; service and sacrifice. We invite you to experience, find connections, and further understand this often complicated and contradictory place." The old visitor center has been removed and replaced with a river overlook, an expansive prairie

This reflective space is called a "Place to Remember." Photograph by Roopali Phadke

restoration and pathways that wind toward and away from the river. Interpretive signage, in English and Dakota, signal native plant and animal histories. Visitors who meander the trail are lead to "A place to remember," captured in the above photograph. According to the Historical Society, the circular stone seating was designed to be a place to "pay tribute, reflect on, and honor the diverse people and generations who shaped the history of Fort Snelling."

The Historical Society writes on its website that it worked with community partners to design a "new interpretive plan for the site that brings more depth to the cultural understanding and features more histories of the many people who have been part of its remarkable history, including Dakota, Ojibwe and other Native Americans, African Americans, Japanese Americans, women, soldiers, veterans." Matthew Keenan, one of the designers from the architecture firm Leo A. Daly, stated that their goal was to connect visitors with the landscape. "You can stand in one room and experience the military story, the river story, and the new story: that we're trying to bring this prairie back to what it used to look like 5,500 years ago." Maura Rockcastle, principal and cofounder of the contracted landscape design firm Ten x Ten, said, "What we hope comes through is the complexity of the multilayering of stories—the good, the bad, and the difficult—that happened on this site over time. Hopefully, the truths of those tensions and layers are coming out in ways that help people understand them more fully."[1]

Children climb up to the iconic fortress tower. Photograph by Roopali Phadke

While the Visitor Center and its grounds have been "revitalized," the Fort buildings have not. Children on school fieldtrips weave in and out of the fort buildings visiting the Commander's House, the blacksmith and enslaved quarters. In the above photo, a group of school children climb up to the iconic fortress tower. They heckle their friends who pass below while an American flag waves in the grass beside them.

My visit to the Historic Fort on a Fall day in 2025 was a special ticketed occasion. Yet, I see Fort Snelling regularly on my meanderings. I bicycle near it on the river parkway. I glance puzzlingly at the stone tower nearly every time I cross the Highway 5 Fort Road Bridge over the Mississippi driving west. I hike through the Fort to cross the bridge that leads to Pike Island so I can pause at the confluence. Because of its everyday presence in my own life, I need to be reminded of its importance as a site of political conflagration over how we remember and reckon with to whom it belongs. I also never know where to start when I use stories to encapsulate the history of this place to my students, neighbors, friends, and family.

The new Plank Visitor Center begins with the Dakota story. One placard reminds us that the "story of this place is always in motion." Following the Dakota oral history and homeland stories, visitors follow along a chronological telling of the site's past, from the eruption of the Civil War in 1861, the U.S.-Dakota War in 1862, through to World War I and II. What's missing are the more recent protests about the site's symbolism and fights over representation.

In 2008, a Minnesota Statehood Sesquicentennial Wagon Train rolled its way toward Fort Snelling as part of a 100-mile, week long journey. In all, eighty-five people in period dress traveled by horseback in covered wagons, buggies, surreys, and one stagecoach. When they reached Fort Snelling, they were met with indigenous protestors who were drumming, burning sage, and carrying signs that read: "I am not invisible." Some protesters laid on the ground in front of a squad car with a pair of signs reading: "If we get in your way"..."Will you kill us again?"[2] Eventually, 13 different law enforcement vehicles arrived on the scene to carry away the disruptors. When you research stories about the Sesquicentennial Wagon Train, it takes some digging to find mention of the protests. Instead, most news stories revel in the fireworks and celebrity speeches that marked Minnesota's hardscrabble Little House on the Prairie history.

A decade later, Fort Snelling was still a flashpoint of controversy. In May 2019, the signs that read "Fort Snelling Historic Site" were replaced with newer signs that read "Historic Fort Snelling at Bdote."[3] Those newer signs were then taken down because of public confusion and outrage at "historical revisionism." As part of the Fort's revitalization project, the Historical Society conducted a state wide study and public comment period over a potential renaming of the site. The MN Historical Society's governing board unanimously approved on June 24, 2022, to keep the name "Historic Fort Snelling," concluding there was no "conclusive" public support for a name change. For many, this was a further erasure of the larger Dakota story.

By contrast, the Bdote Memory Map is a living history of Dakota lands and culture. The project asserts the Dakota occupied the land for nearly 10,000 years before the onset of settler colonialism in 1860, and they continue to exist. Through oral history plotted on the map, we learn why Fort Snelling is sacred land, and how the bluffs provide an ideal vantage point for seeing Wita Tanka (Pike Island) and the burial area that is now Pilot Knob. The memory map also tells the painful stories of Fort Snelling as the site of a Dakota concentration camp from 1862–63. Here, 1,700 people, primarily women, children, and elders, were imprisoned during the winter of 1862–63. For many Bdewakantunwan Dakota members, Bdote is the center of the earth for them, and as such it is now both a site of genesis and genocide.

I have been a Minnesota resident for over twenty years, and on most days I feel like a newcomer. Yet, I mostly feel comfortable teaching about the Mississippi River and its history. When it comes to Fort Snelling though, I shudder at the thought of attempting to represent all this site means. Part of my hesitation is that Fort Snelling deserves an Anthropocenic reckoning; a deep time analysis that layers human and non-human histories together.

It is meaningful that this Fort Snelling's bicentennial renovation was called a "revitalization project." Breathing life into the Fort means listening to its ghosts. The Bdote Memory Map provides some of these stories. A deep time history of the site could also juxtapose and intertwine many stories across time and space. It could render visible how enslaved peoples, including Harriet and Dred Scott, may have interacted with Dakota peoples before, during, and after they were held in captivity at the Fort. In 1857, U.S. Supreme Court Chief Justice Taney wrote that Black people, free or enslaved, could not be citizens and had no rights the white man was bound to respect. It is well known that this decision influenced the nomination of Abraham Lincoln—who opposed the Dred Scott decision—for the presidential election in 1860. Lincoln went on to sign the Homestead Act in 1862, creating the broader context for the Dakota War of 1862 and internment at Fort Snelling. What visions or nightmares of the United States of America did both African Americans and Dakota enslaved at Fort Snelling and beyond share?

WHEN WE TALK DEEP TIME ON THE UPPER MISSISSIPPI, IT IS AT ONCE HUMAN AND NATURAL HISTORY.

Go even deeper in time and we can imagine stories of human and geological agency woven together. Native peoples have inhabited the region since the Ice Age ended. The petroglyphs in Waḳaŋ Ṭípi (Carver's Cave), which used to be called Bruce Vento Nature Sanctuary, are interpreted to be a premodern planetarium. At the time those were drawn, St. Anthony Falls was located just outside Waḳaŋ Ṭípi in today's downtown St. Paul. The waterfall scoured the sandstone and limestone bluffs, essentially eroding its way upriver to Minneapolis. When we talk deep time on the upper Mississippi, it is at once human and natural history. Fort Snelling then appears as an important and bloody chapter, though still only a brief one in telling the stories of Bdote.

As I encounter the Historical Society's reimagined stories of and at the Fort, I look forward to growing into a different relationship with this place. As a resident of the river, however long my roots grow, I want a renewed experience not only when I visit the site but also when I think about representing its stories to others. I simply want to know more and know more deeply. The Minnesota History Society has begun the process of using Fort Snelling to teach us about the past beyond cannon firings and blacksmith demonstrations. It is the place where so much of the history that shapes our deeply fraught modern Minnesota experience begins.

Seth Eastman, an Army officer stationed at Fort Snelling, painted a series between 1847–1855 that are often used by the Minnesota Historical Society in their galleries and publications. Eastman's "Distant View of Fort Snelling" tells a visual story of daily Dakota life during the brutal period of conquest and settlement. The bucolic scene of Dakota life near the Fort belies the cultural devastation being experienced at the time. These paintings tell not only different stories, but perhaps even fabricated ones.

A version of this article was originally published on the website Anthropocene Curriculum (Fall 2025).

ENDNOTES

1 Both quotes are derived from Ann Mayhew, "The Revitalization of Historic Fort Snelling," *ENTER*, January 12, 2023, https://www.entermn.com/articles/the-revitalization-of-historic-fort-snelling

2 Scott Russell, "Dakota protesters meet sesquicentennial wagon train," *Twin Cities Daily Planet*, May 11, 2008, https://www.tcdailyplanet.net/dakota-protesters-meet-sesquicentennial-wagon-train/.

3 "Controversy Arises over New Signs at Fort Snelling," *KSTP*, May 21, 2019.

Nuclear Free World Making Along the Mississippi River

Kirisitina Sailiata

A proposed marker of the Anthropocene is the radioactive contamination released into Earth systems by atmospheric nuclear weapons testing starting in the 1940s. Connecting Oceania–where significant amounts of this testing took place–to the Mississippi River, Kirisitina Sailiata reads the epoch's colonial history in global movements for Indigenous sovereignty, independence, and a nuclear free world.

In late November 2025, protestors gathered at an overpass of Interstate 94 and Highway 25 in the Twin Cities Metro area holding up bright fluorescent yellow banners with black bold text—"Nuclear Reactors Are Serial Killers! Shut Down the Monticello Nuke!"[1] Just three years prior, the Monticello Nuclear Generating Plant leaked hundreds of thousands of gallons of tritium into the Mississippi River. Soon after the leak the Coalition for a Nuclear Free Mississippi formed vocalizing concerns about both the health of the community and the health of the river. A relative newcomer to a rich and storied history of antinuclear activism in Minnesota, The Coalition for a Nuclear Free Mississippi (CNFM) joins a range of local antinuclear and more broadly environmental advocacy collectives from earlier decades such as the Northern Sun Alliance, the Prairie Island Coalition Against Nuclear, Friends of the Mississippi River, the Indigenous Environmental Network, Honor the Earth, and the North American Water Office. Through gatherings, protests and petitions, CNFM organizers have focused their demands around the Monticello plant and the 2022 tritium leak pressuring Minnesota lawmakers to deny extensions to the licensing agreement for the plant and close it down for good by 2030.

Across the Midwest region, more antinuclear collectives like CNFM were forming and or reawakening. The Nuclear Free America movement in the United States gained traction in the 1970s and 1980s and has since waned both nationally and locally in the late 1990s. Why are these collectives forming again? What is their relationship to this previous movement? What lessons can we glean from this prior movement? Some of these answers may seem self-evident with the aging infrastructure of nuclear plants and their proximity to residential communities and major sources of water like the Mississippi River. Since the 2011 Fukushima nuclear disaster, there has certainly been renewed alarm about the safety of nuclear energy plants. However, if we follow the lead of Indigenous-led environmental advocacy groups and consider the relationship between nuclear weapons and energy as part of a larger structural formation of nuclear colonialism then we arrive at a different understanding of our present moment and movement work.

Over the past couple of years, I have developed a course, *American Culture in the Atomic Age*, in conversation with the Mississippi River Open School for Kinship and Social Exchange. Framed around Cold War cultural history and antimilitarization movements, we examine

Photograph courtesy of Nuclear Free Mississippi River Collective

local and global scales of nuclear history and policy that have been shaped by sustained antinuclear grassroots organizing. Alongside this political history, we unpack cultural texts of nuclearism examining film, media, poetry, theater, and art. Cultural and multimedia modes of expression and communication have been essential in translating not only the complexities of nuclear science including policy briefs and memos but their impact on everyday people. This course, *American Culture in the Atomic Age*, has also been a way for me to draw active connections between the Pacific Islands and the Midwest regions through Indigenous and transnational feminist organizing practices and also frameworks around radical relationality, cultural histories of nuclearism, and tracing transnational coalitions for protection of water and the making of nuclear free worlds.

In this essay, as in my American cultural studies course, I consider the Mississippi River as a frontline for nuclear politics through social movement organizing and cultural texts making transnational connections to movements and places elsewhere, but especially, Oceania. Through contemporary policies and energy publications, I examine the American cultural imaginary of the future as nuclear and the Mississippi River as a significant frontline of that vision. Mapping the global movements and histories of antinuclear organizing and activism for a nuclear free world, I contextualize the significance of this emergent Coalition for a Nuclear Free Mississippi within a much older trajectory and movement of organizing by looking at the Nuclear Free America and the Nuclear Free and Independent Pacific movements as a form of Indigenous futurism and world making. With a brief tracing of contemporary antinuclear and Indigenous cultural resurgence work in Minnesota, I conclude with cultural modes of antinuclearism and futurism to consider the range and stakes of these struggles.

NUCLEAR FRONTLINES

Nuclearism has returned to center stage again in global politics. Over the past few years, there has been more pressure to meet increasing energy demands with the rise of data centers as well as public pressure to phase out fossil fuels and meet international and local commitments to decarbonization. At COP28 in Dubai, a multinational compact was signed as part of the Atoms 4 Net Zero initiative of the International Atomic Energy Agency.[2] In December 2023, as part of COP28, the Declaration to Triple Nuclear Energy multinational compact was launched with the backing of countries, special interest nuclear groups and financial institutions.[3] These recent global initiatives and agreements have made it clear that the answer to climate mitigation and the future of the world rests with the return to nuclear power.

In this global push towards expanding nuclear energy outputs, the United States remains at the center. Both the Atoms for Net Zero and Atoms 4 Climate IAEA campaigns are direct references to President Eisenhower's 1953 speech Atoms for Peace at the United Nations seventy years prior.[4] The Atoms for Peace initiative also led to the formation of the International Atomic Energy Agency (IAEA) in addition to multiple cultural programs and campaigns to domesticate nuclearism and distance its association with mass death and destruction in the wake of the 1945 U.S. bombing of Hiroshima and Nagasaki at the close of World War II. In a parallel move to the IAEA campaign, domestic nuclear policy in the United States is also shifting. President Donald Trump in collaboration with the Department of Energy is once again attempting to "make nuclear energy cool again."[5]

Through multiple executive orders in 2025, President Trump has made nuclear expansion a cornerstone of his second administration as part of their Make Nuclear Great Again campaign.[6] Both the Trump administration and the IAEA are drawing on rhetorical inspiration from the 1940s ideological formations of American exceptionalism in their efforts to champion the supremacy of American culture and progress. Promoted by Department of Energy Secretary Chris Wright:

> For too long, America's nuclear energy industry has been stymied by red tape and outdated government policies but thanks to President Trump, the American nuclear renaissance is finally here. With the emergence of AI and President Trump's pro-American manufacturing policies at work, American civil nuclear energy is being unleashed at the perfect time.[7]

The policies aim to "reinvigorate" nuclear defense strategies and "reform" nuclear energy capacities with the overall goal of "re-establishing the United States as the global leader in nuclear energy." The plans include upgrading existing nuclear reactors and to start construction on ten new reactors over the next five years. Additionally, reorganization of the Nuclear Regulatory Commission is underway to shorten the time for licensing, construction and operations of new nuclear reactors to just a couple of years. On November 24, 2025, the White House launched the Genesis Mission to use artificial intelligence (AI) to advance scientific discoveries.[8] Led by the Department of Energy, nuclear energy and nuclear security are at the core of this project. Similar to Nixon's Project Independence, Trump's Genesis Mission seeks to restore America's greatness through scientific advancement with explicit comparisons to the Manhattan Project made by Chris Wright, Secretary of Energy and head of Genesis Mission.[9] In these efforts to expand nuclearism, the Trump administration oversimplifies the problem. These policies rely on a deeply flawed historical narrative that the rise and fall of nuclear energy from the 1960s to the present has primarily been an issue with government bureaucracy and inefficiency. These narratives omit the role of mass social mobilizations and demonstrations against nuclearism.

From the 1940s to 1990s, communities across America mobilized en masse to protest nuclear weapons and energy. This movement merged previously single-issue organizations into larger coalitional formations for a robust global antiwar, peace and disarmament movement. By the 1980s and 1990s, those peace and disarmament movements coalesced with Black and Indigenous-led environmental justice movements organizing for a nuclear free world. This work was deeply transnational with a focus both on global connections but also hyperlocal policies and impact.

In considering the Mississippi River as a frontline for antinuclear resistance, we should consider important terms and frames around nuclear colonialism, waste and water regulations as well as the local and regional narratives of place and the role of nuclear in that storytelling process. The Mississippi River as a frontline of nuclear colonialism facilitates conversations across distinct regions including the upper Midwest, the Great Lakes, the southern Midwest, the South and the Gulf South. Linking disparate geographies from deserts to oceans to riverways, nuclearism has come to define the health and wellbeing of places and communities around the world. Nuclear colonialism is a central conceptual frame shared by Indigenous organizers and scholars around the world to describe the entire system of nuclear technology from the mining of critical ores to waste disposal. Nuclear colonialism includes a vast global network of mines, secret cities, labs, weapons storage facilities, testing sites and dumps. The nuclear frontline for many Indigenous communities is about sovereignty and for many this form of colonial violence was quite intimate as in the case of Mdwekantaon Prairie Island community in Minnesota, just 700 yards away from the Prairie Island Nuclear Generating Plant as well as the Navajo Nation. Traci Brynne Voyles, an environmental historian, has traced this history and culture of nuclear colonialism in the southwest, poignantly describing this confluence of extractive violence and infrastructural abandonment as "wastelanding."[10] Even with the abandoning of over five hundred "zombie" mines on or near the Navajo Nation, this continual not-so-slow violence is a form of ecocide that is also by extension a genocide, prematurely killing nearby communities through high rates of cancer. Nuclear colonialism along the Mississippi River and elsewhere is not just a frontline but a fenceline struggle.

Nuclear reactors along the Mississippi River corridor are not only united by geography but by shared narratives about American history and progress. Along the Mississippi River, there are six nuclear facilities. Three are located on the Upper Mississippi River with two in

Minnesota and one in Illinois. The remaining three are located in the Gulf South, two in Louisiana and one in Mississippi. In her forthcoming book, *Radioactive Dixie*, environmental historian Caroline Peyton traces the history of how the South became a major center for nuclear energy in the United States—where much of the nation's nuclear reactors and waste are located—and how that has shaped debates and cultures around nuclearism.[11] One of the major sites of environmental injustice along the Mississippi River is the Grand Gulf Station. The slogan for Entergy Energy is "We power life." In a short advertisement campaign by Entergy Energy from 2010 celebrating the 25th anniversary of the Grand Gulf Station, the Mississippi River is described as a palimpsest, a historical document or brochure filled with unique markers.[12] It gestures towards ancestral or ancient history with Indian burial mounds to modernity with the founding of the nation and connections to the founding figures of the United States and this project of American exceptionalism. If the Indigenous burial mounds define the Mississippi River's past, then Grand Gulf Nuclear Station is promoted as the American future. "Helping Power Mississippi's Future" sells a future that is green and clean, and offers jobs and injects surplus tax dollars into the Mississippi economy. It is also a point of national pride as one of the largest facilities in the nation. The advertisement is both a celebration of nuclear energy as the future for the state of Mississippi as well as the United States. It also masks the uneven burdens and impact of nuclearism. The siting of the Grand Gulf Nuclear Station and its impacts upon the Black majority community in Port Gibson and the larger Claiborne County has been a major case study of environmental racism and injustice. In addition to high rates of cancer locally, much of the perceived energy and tax benefits of the local nuclear plant were diverted to bolster and power communities elsewhere.[13]

NUCLEAR COLONIALISM IS A CENTRAL CONCEPTUAL FRAME SHARED BY INDIGENOUS ORGANIZERS AND SCHOLARS AROUND THE WORLD TO DESCRIBE THE ENTIRE SYSTEM OF NUCLEAR TECHNOLOGY FROM THE MINING OF CRITICAL ORES TO WASTE DISPOSAL.

Similar to the Grand Gulf Station in the northern corridor of the Mississippi River, the Prairie Island Nuclear Generating Station is situated on the front door step of the Prairie Island Community. When the plant first formed in the late 1960s, Northern Sun Power began publishing books, comics, and graphic pamphlets to educate the public and celebrate its work. One of those publications was a book entitled

Prairie Island: from Antiquity to Atoms. Similar to the Grand Gulf Station promotional materials in the 2000s, this 1970s book illustrated this shared narrative of an American modernity of scientific progress juxtaposed against "the primitive" Indigenous past. On the front cover of the book, the title is framed by symbols of Indigenous architecture in opposition to American architecture with the teepee opposite the atomic symbol. The nuclear power plant sprawled across the front cover of the book signifies modernity in contrast to the much smaller portrait of an unnamed Indigenous leader in the bottom left corner. The book goes on to detail the building of the power plant including archeological surveys of the area for burial mounds. While decades apart, these energy campaigns share common strategies: the wastelanding of nearby mostly Black and Indigenous communities and the discursive promotion of nuclearism as America's future in contrast to its primitive past. At no point in this book is there an acknowledgement that the Prairie Island Community exists not only in the present but just a few hundred feet away from the plant. Similar to the Grand Gulf Station, the Prairie Island Nuclear Generating Station has also been a major case study in environmental racism, nuclear colonialism and antinuclear movement organizing.

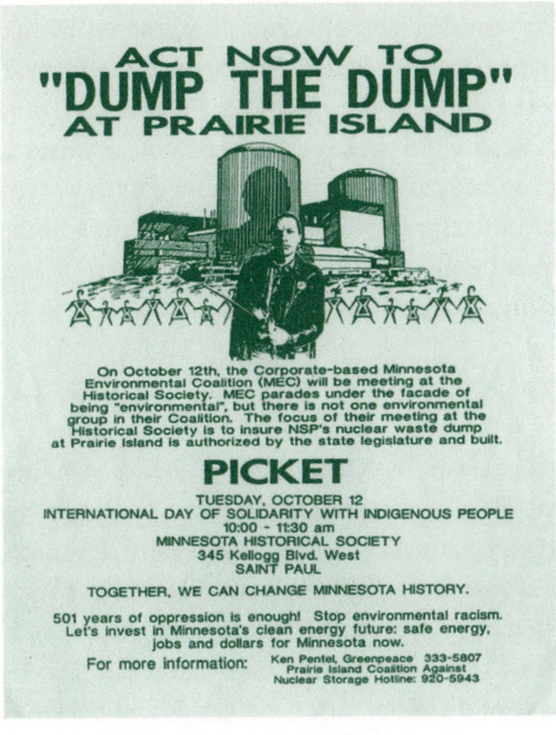

Image courtesy of Nuclear Free Mississippi River Collective

In addition to issues of siting nuclear facilities in predominantly poor and Black and Indigenous communities, one of the major shared issues between antinuclear organizing along the Mississippi River as well as Oceania centers environmental policies that regulate waste in waterways. Interdisciplinary scholar and artist, Max Liboiron, who specializes in Indigenous Studies as well as waste and discard studies, examines the impact of western approaches to environmental science in their book *Pollution Is Colonialism*.[14] These approaches are grounded in colonial values and perspectives around water and land as resources in the service of capitalism. Using the Streeter-Phelps equation as an example, Liboiron argues that the allowable thresholds for pollution are a form of ongoing colonial violence. Liboiron argues that the science propping up even progressive water policies and regulations still enables colonial violence through the permitting threshold of allowable pollution and this perception of water and waterways as an infinite sink. Along the Mississippi River, the impact of these theories and policies are clearly evident through the siting of nuclear and manufacturing facilities along its banks and the creation of the delta dead zone as the river pours into the Gulf of Mexico. Similar to the Mississippi River, Oceania is perceived to be a sink, internationally, for nuclear waste from nuclear energy plants to weapons testing. Just recently, Japan initiated a thirty year discharge project dumping millions of gallons of tritium waste, radioactive water, from one of the biggest nuclear disasters in recent global history, the 2011 Fukushima Daiichi accident, into the Pacific Ocean.[15] In these examples, nuclear waste siting and management proposals are deeply intertwined with water policymaking both along the Mississippi River and across Oceania. Both water and waste management policies have been a major point of contention for Indigenous led organizing for a nuclear free world.

MAPPING NUCLEAR FREE STRUGGLES ACROSS TIME

Antinuclear struggles across Oceania have always been interwoven with Indigenous struggles for national and regional independence. Since the 1940s, France, Britain and the United States have detonated over 300 nuclear bombs across Oceania.[16] The majority of these tests were focused in two areas: French Polynesia and Micronesia. After the close of World War II and the mass withdrawal of troops from the "Pacific front," there was the first wave of decolonization struggles and national independent movements. Nuclear politics and organizing remained core to these conversations and movements. By the early 1970s transnational political networks mostly led by young women, theologians and college students from across the region began to emerge in Fiji.[17] In 1973, A.T.O.M. (Against Nuclear Testing on Moruroa), an emergent organization, hosted a panel discussion around nuclear zones and whether a nuclear free Pacific was possible and what that could look like. This momentum led to a conference a few years later for a Nuclear Free Pacific that would include representatives from eighty-five countries from all across the region. The Nuclear Free Pacific movement eventually transformed into the Nuclear Free and Independent Pacific movement. By 1981, the Republic of Palau would ratify the first nuclear free constitution in the world. And a few short years later, in 1985, the Pacific Islands Forum would pass the Treaty of Rarotonga declaring the South Pacific officially a nuclear free zone.[18] These were hard won efforts by Pacific activists and organizers. Many of them in the case of the nuclear free constitution led by Indigenous women in Palau were intimidated and harassed for decades into concessions and compliance with United States defense interests and the Compact of Free Association.[19] This suppression further intensified antinuclear organizing across the Pacific to develop stronger coalitions with other communities and places around the world.

To date, the United States has conducted over a thousand nuclear tests. Between 1945 and the 1990s, the United States conducted over 900 tests across Turtle Island, mostly concentrated in Nevada.[20] Across the United States in the 1980s, as part of the larger nuclear disarmament movement during the Cold War, small, hyperlocal collectives pressured non-federal forms of governance—cities, towns, states, tribal governments—to pass nuclear free ordinances. Over the next two to three decades, over 200 ordinances were passed as part of this broader movement to stall the acceleration of nuclear power across the United States.[21] While the movement for a Nuclear Free America was formally organized in the early 1980s, the movement for nuclear free zones began much earlier in the late 1950s in central Europe at the close of World War II. Nearly a decade later in the 1960s the first regional nuclear free zone agreement was passed in Latin America with the Treaty of Tlatelolco.[22] In the United States, momentum for a Nuclear Free America had been growing for some time, but the accident on Three Mile Island in 1979 was a major turning point in public opinion. By 1982, a massive Nuclear Freeze march for disarmament infamously mobilized massive demonstrations through the streets of New York City.[23] Where the Nuclear Freeze and Nuclear Free America movements focused mostly on disarmament as part of a larger peace movement, they emphasized hyperlocal organizing.

Nuclear Free America was formally organized out of Boston in coordination with many other hyperlocal and regional coalitions. As part of this movement, there was a proliferation of local ordinances with nearly 15,000 entities, including cities, counties, states and tribal nations, enacting nuclear free zones through the 1990s. These policies, while non-binding in international law as federal and tribal governments are still the only governments that can enter into foreign policy agreements, had a major impact in halting the growth of nuclear industries. These policies targeted weaknesses in the nuclear manufacturing process focusing on facility shutdowns, weapons testing areas, waste storage, and the permitting of the transport of radioactive materials through public roadways and ports. As part of this movement, there still remain a number of states that have nuclear bans and moratoria in place. In Minnesota, the moratorium against the construction of new nuclear power plants was passed by the state legislature in 1994 and continues to be challenged in legislative sessions as local pro-nuclear energy groups pursue its repeal.[24] Through hyperlocal organizing, movements against nuclear energy coalesced with the disarmament movement primarily around both the beginning and end of the nuclear cycle. This is largely credited to the work of Black and Indigenous feminist-led antinuclear resistance formations that were rapidly making connections between environmental racism and colonialism across global and local scales. Through their work issues like uranium mining as well as the siting and transportation of nuclear waste became a central part of the work of Nuclear Free regional organizing in thc Midwest and Oceania.

Around the world, transnational feminist networks have led the push for denuclearization, demilitarization and de-occupation. These formations have been led mainly by Indigenous women organizers and leaders like Darlene Keju-Johnson, Grace Thorpe, Winona "No Nukes" LaDuke, Mililani Trask and many others who have challenged the ways in which nuclear colonialism has targeted Indigenous communities as sacrificial zones. In describing Oceania as the most nuclearized region in the world, Haunani-Kay Trask interprets nuclearization as a unique kind of racism, a form of eugenics and genocide.[25] In *The Militarization of Indian Country*, LaDuke maintains that the majority of uranium ore in the world is located on or near Indigenous communities and lands. She expands on the connections between nuclearism and Indigenous struggles:

> You know, we have been, from the beginning, heavily impacted by radiation exposure from the U.S. military, you know, continuing on to nuclear testing, whether in the Pacific or whether the 1,100 nuclear weapons that were detonated over Western Shoshone territory. You know, our peoples have been heavily impacted by radiation, let alone nerve gas testing. You've got nerve gas dumps at Umatilla. You've got a nerve gas dump at the Skull Valley Goshute Reservation. You have, you know, weapons bases, and the military is the largest polluter in the world. And a lot of that pollution, in what is known as the United States, or some of us would refer to as occupied Indian Country, is in fact all heavily impacting Indian people or Indigenous communities still.[26]

In her 1983 address at the World Council of Churches Assembly in Vancouver, Canada, Darlene Keju-Johnson talked about the legacy of U.S. nuclearism in the Marshall Islands. She made direct connections between nuclear testing and the contamination of both the environment and the people, describing issues with cancer and reproductive struggles with many women experiencing serial miscarriages because of severe radioactive poisoning. Keju-Johnson concluded her speech by saying:

> The Marshallese are dying out now. My island that is up in the north is also contaminated. I too have three tumors in me. I am about to have surgery. And I am frightened...All we know is that we must travel throughout the world and share this kind of experience from the bombs so that we must stop it before it gets to you. Remember we are the victims of the nuclear age. Don't become a victim.[27]

Since the first wave of nuclear testing, across the region, Micronesians have experienced high rates of cancer, in particular, issues with thyroid and throat cancers as well as reproductive health issues. Indigenous women across Turtle Island and Oceania have been especially impacted by nuclearism through health, family, environmental labor, and work. The organizing for nuclear free zones has brought these communities into conversation and coalition even across disparate geographies.

VISIONS OF A NUCLEAR FREE MISSISSIPPI

Between the two existing nuclear energy plants in Minnesota, the Prairie Island site has been the main focal point of antinuclear resistance since its operation. That there were controversies over its siting would be an understatement. "Just 700 feet away" from residential neighborhoods and a childcare center, the environmental disparities are stark. The siting is so close that all traffic in and out of the nuclear energy plant runs straight through the community using tribal roadways. And while the plant contributes to the tax base of the city of Red Wing, like Port Gibson and many other communities living in close proximity to nuclear facilities, little to no benefits either through energy or tax incentives were negotiated for the Prairie Island community.

In the 1970s and 1980s, seventeen tribes were solicited by the Department of Energy to participate in the Monitored Retrievable Storage (MRS) survey. Of the twenty locations for potential storage of additional locations, seventeen tribes were offered a $100,000 grant to participate in this program. In her 1996 essay, "Our Homes are not Dumps: Creating Nuclear-Free Zones," Sac and Fox elder, Grace Thorpe, reflects on nuclear struggles across Indian country, especially the MRS struggle:

> The government and nuclear power industry attempt to flatter us about our abilities as "earth stewards." Yet as I declared to the National Congress of American Indians in 1993, "It is a perversion of our beliefs and an insult to our intelligence to say that we are 'natural stewards' of these wastes." The real intent of the government and the utilities is to rid themselves of this extremely hazardous garbage on Indian lands so they are free to generate more of it.[28]

Of the seventeen tribes solicited, one was Sac and Fox and another was Prairie Island. Upon learning of this initiative in her community, Grace Thorpe came out of retirement, so to speak, to fight nuclearism. She went on to co-found the National Environmental Coalition of Native

Americans (NECONA) and partnered with Nuclear Free America to coordinate a movement for Nuclear Free Indian Lands. Through this organizing, she was able to pressure all but two tribes to drop out of the program. She also visited Prairie Island and many other tribal nations to coordinate antinuclear strategies and pass ordinances to declare Indian Country nuclear free.

In 1991, the Prairie Island nation passed the Nuclear Radiation Control Ordinance in coordination with the nuclear free movement and began regulating and charging fees to the Northern Sun Power company for the use of tribal roadways in everyday operations of the facility, including the transportation of nuclear waste. In response, the lawsuit *Northern States Power Co. v. Prairie Island Mdewakanton Sioux Indian Community* was initiated to repeal the tribal ordinance. Because the Prairie Island Nuclear Generating Plant was built in such close proximity to the Prairie Island reservation, all of the roads surrounding the plant fall under tribal jurisdiction. Lea Foushee, the director of the Indigenous Women's Network and North American Water Office, described some of the struggles with coalitional organizing with the Prairie Island Coalition Against Nuclear: "Sovereignty was a really big thing in this...Most non-Native groups don't have a clue about it, and they need some front-line education about what it means."[29] These alliances were uneasy and at times fractious. However, they mobilized marches and mass protest demonstrations.

A really prime example of local mobilization and protest occurred against the corporate aligned Minnesota Environmental Coalition (MEC) lobbying for nuclear waste siting at the Prairie Island nuclear waste plant. Many local grassroots antinuclear collectives, including the Prairie Island Coalition, declared October 12 an international day of solidarity with Indigenous People to "Dump the Dump" at Prairie Island and protest the MEC meeting at the Minnesota Historical Society. The flier for the protest graphically opposes the visual grammar of the Northern Sun Power cover of *From Antiquity to Atoms.* A contemporary Indigenous organizer is centered and surrounded by symbolic pictograph representations of their ancestors past, present and future. The figure's gaze is direct and cutting while their shadow is cast upon the nuclear power plant on the hill. The poster does more than illustrate an opposition to the Prairie Island Nuclear Generating Plant and the debates around an expansion of nuclear waste siting.

It opposes Northern Sun's repeated attempts to epistemically erase the Prairie Island Community from the present and future by relegating them to "antiquity." The poster graphically opposes the visual grammar of the 1970s cover by intentionally remixing all of the visual elements to empower and center Dakota sovereignty and activism. Historical narrative and visual aesthetics were and still remain a powerful terrain of antinuclear struggle especially in Indigenous and hyperlocal movement work.

These local and tribal ordinances, as well as regional treaties and constitutions, often fell short of their initial vision. They were challenged in courts as in the case of *Northern States Power Co. v. Prairie Island* where they challenged the tribal ordinance and ruled in favor of Northern Sun. They were repealed in the case of Palau. And they often revised out key commitments in their passage as happened with the Treaty of Rarotonga. However, all of these efforts continued to create pockets of resistance, to challenge and slow the expansion and growth of nuclearism around the world. These coalitions also continued to advocate for the health and wellbeing of water and communities in the push for a nuclear free world.

THESE PREDICTIONS OF FUTURE TECHNOLOGICAL ADVANCEMENTS ARE NOT BASED ON CURRENT WORK BUT ON PURE FAITH IN AMERICAN SCIENTIFIC SUPERIORITY AND PROGRESS.

In August 2025, the Minnesota Public Utilities Commission approved Xcel Energy's request to extend the operations of the Prairie Island Nuclear Generating Plant through the early 2050s. This would extend the license of the plant by another twenty years and expand its local onsite storage of nuclear wastes in dry casks. There are currently 50 dry casks of waste on site, but with the extension the facility will likely increase to upwards of 98. American Studies scholar, Jessica Hurley, in her book, *Infrastructures of Apocalypse*, examines nuclear policy and legal texts as speculative fiction.[30] She considers the planning and design around security and potential risk to be a form of world making where lawmakers prophesy the advancement of science in the future where nuclear waste can be solved despite the lack of supporting research and technology. These predictions of future technological advancements are not based on current work but on pure faith in American scientific superiority and progress. As evidenced by the Monticello and Prairie Island Nuclear Generating Plants, no such technology exists even after thirty years of operation.

In Fall 2022, the restored *Golden Rule* sailboat began its most recent voyage as the Veterans for Peace Golden Rule Sailboat for Peace project for nuclear disarmament in Saint Paul, Minnesota. The Great Loop is a route that runs over 6,000 miles. The route runs through freshwater lakes and rivers as well as local seas and the Atlantic Ocean. The sailboat is stewarded by Helen Jaccard and Captain Kiko Johnston-Kitazawa, a Kanaka Maoli canoe builder and educator. Jaccard expands on the significance of the voyage:

> From 1958 to today, the *Golden Rule* challenges the apathy and complacency that have settled over a world teetering on the brink of nuclear destruction. Its aim was—and is—not just to protest, but to awaken the slumbering collective conscience of humanity, to kindle a flame of awareness and resistance against the devastating potential of weapons of mass destruction.[31]

The *Golden Rule* sailboat was originally built in the late 1950s by four peace activists working with the Committee for Non-Violent Action (CNVA) with the intention of sailing from Hawai'i to the Marshall Islands to disrupt military weapons testing. During the ten year period from 1947 to 1958—when the United States detonated over 67 nuclear bombs in the Marshall Islands, 23 near Bikini Atoll and 44 near Enewetak Atoll—many were outraged. The activists organized protests and sent petitions to President Eisenhower claiming that if he did not cease testing they would bring their protest to the nuclear testing frontlines in the Marshall Islands, specifically the Enewatak "Proving Grounds."[32] This prompted the Atomic Energy Commission to preemptively ban sailing into these waters. The *Golden Rule* was eventually seized by the Coast Guard and never made it to the Marshall Islands, however, the voyage made a symbolic impact. It inspired the launch of a second ship, the *Phoenix of Hiroshima*, which did make it to the Proving Grounds. Before being seized by the Coast Guard, the *Phoenix of Hiroshima* inspired hundreds of thousands of protestors across the United States and around the world. Nearly four hundred people petitioned for their own arrest at the San Francisco District Attorney's office in support of the *Golden Rule*. This work has been largely credited as the precursor and inspiration for the emergence of the Don't Make a Wave Committee and later Greenpeace.

The *Golden Rule* eventually fell out of memory and into great disrepair. In 2010, it was fished out of Humboldt Bay and restored through community fundraising efforts. For the past decade, the *Golden Rule* has revived its name and mission, sailing over 22,000 miles, docking at over 150 ports including those along the Mississippi River and in Oceania for conversations and events raising awareness of nuclear colonialism, and promoting the movement for a nuclear free world.[33] In these efforts by international and national policymakers to reframe history, it is more vital and important than ever for a nuclear free world to document and tell these histories of antinuclear resistance, civil disobedience, and solidarity.

> FOR INDIGENOUS PEOPLE, ANTINUCLEAR AND ENVIRONMENTAL JUSTICE ORGANIZING IS DEEPLY EMBEDDED IN CULTURAL RESURGENCE WORK AND LIFEWAYS, AND THESE TRANSNATIONAL PRACTICES OF KNOWLEDGE SHARING AND RADICAL RELATIONALITY BETWEEN OCEANIA AND THE MIDWEST ARE PART OF THIS LARGER WORK OF NUCLEAR FREE WORLD MAKING.

As part of his ongoing work around Native Canoe resurgence, "Navigating Indigenous Futures With the Mississippi River," Indigenous Studies scholar, Vicente Diaz, works with knowledge keepers from Chuuk, the Carolinians, Oceti Sakowin and Anishinaabe nations in Micronesia and the Midwest.[34] A basis for these exchanges has been around Indigenous science and technology through cultural resurgence practices in voyaging and birthing work, in particular, as well as shared notions of relationality and kinship with water and land and more-than-human beings. Many Micronesians have migrated to the Midwest, specifically from the islands of Chuuk in the Federated States of Micronesia. The Federated States of Micronesia are one of the Compact of Free Association States along with the Marshall Islands and the Republic of Palau. Comparatively more attention has been paid to the impact of nuclear testing in the Marshall Islands, but all of these islands and local seas have been affected by nuclearism. In Milan, Minnesota, near the border of South Dakota, the Chuukese community has flourished to such an extent that people now refer to the town as "Milanesia."[35] As part of this coalitional cultural resurgence work, Christine DeLisle, Katie Johnston-Goodstar, Autumn Cavendar, and many others have gathered formally to create kinship and exchange between Chamorro and Dakota birthworkers around traditional reproductive practices that intimately link community health to environmental health and wellness. For Indigenous people, antinuclear and environmental justice organizing is deeply embedded in cultural resurgence work and lifeways, and these transnational practices of knowledge sharing and radical relationality between Oceania and the Midwest are part of this larger work of nuclear free world making.

Indigenous philosophies and cultural practices animate and give life to antinuclear resistance work and struggle. “Breathe Deep and Sing,” a poem by Gwen Westerman (Sisseton Wahpeton), describes the people and more-than-human kin—the otter, frog, dragonfly, beaver and more—singing a song for the Mississippi River, for the mussels, the lungs of the river, for the sacred which has existed long before any of us and will continue long after.[36] In this poem, she describes how the River has been polluted, which we can extrapolate through feats of American engineering and also through speculative water policy that treats water as an eternal environmental sink for waste. Westerman proclaims that through these actions and thinking that have run “through the heart of us,” the Mississippi River has become “banked by the edge of destruction.” In conversation with Westerman’s poem, artist Cole Redhorse Taylor (Prairie Island), as part of the Red Wing Arts Poet and Artist Collaboration, created a piece of ledger art entitled “Our River: NSP.” In ledger art, Plains Indian portraits and scenes of life are drawn over old banking records, certificates, stocks and bonds. This is a form of storytelling that maps stories of relationality and kinship atop documents of colonial and capitalist dispossession. In “Our River: NSP,” a nuclear power plant looms over the top half of a pen and ink drawing reinforced by the clear and crisp lines of the ledger against a backdrop of stars and dragonflies. Along the bottom half of the drawing, a feminine figure is suspended facing downwards towards the bottom of the river bed. All around her flowing through the lines of ledger are songbirds, fish, otter, turtle, and beaver—teeming with life. The figure of the suspended woman between worlds is a strong visual echo to the 2018 animated short, *Biidaaban (The Dawn Comes)*, a collaboration between Amanda Strong and Leanne Simpson. The story centers the eponymous two-spirit sugarer, Biidaaban, as they move between urban and rural worlds in their journey through the practices of sugarbush, including the harvesting of sap. Through the living force, the energy, the spiritual connection between all living beings, the trees and the people, Biidaaban is able to move between worlds past, present and future, visually represented in the grammar of bodily suspension. In reflecting on their inspiration for this piece, Cole Redhorse Taylor offers: “I often think about the river and our tiny reservation and wonder maybe what it would be like without the nuclear power plant only about a mile from my grandma's front door step."[37]

A vital part of antinuclear struggle and abolitionist movements more largely has been the role of artists, poets, knowledge keepers, musicians, visionaries. Many have characterized the Mississippi River as a palimpsest, as a many storied text. Historical and visual narratives and truth telling projects along the River are a major part of this work. In her poem against nuclearism, "From Sea to Shining Sea," June Jordan reframes the ongoing relentless dispiriting violence of everyday life in the United States as the best time to gather. Anishinaabe transdisciplinary artist and scholar, Leanne Simpson, in her new book *Theory of Water: Nishnaabe Maps to the Times Ahead* expands on the importance and centrality of forms of water kinship and also transnational solidarity movements or what she has called "constellations of co-resistance" to build worlds of radical relationality for liberatory futures.[38] This tracing of the Nuclear Free visions and world making along the Mississippi River and Oceania offers important insights to current movements for sovereignty, abolition, and environmental justice.

ENDNOTES

1 "Nuclear Coalition Holds Banner Protest Over I-94," *Monticello Times*, accessed November 23, 2025, https://www.hometownsource.com/monticello_times/nuclear-coalition-holds-banner-protest-over-i-94/article_a1497da0-9d29-4e86-9c16-772566b8cbb3.html.

2 International Atomic Energy Agency, "Climate Change and the Role of Nuclear Power: Atoms4NetZero," accessed November 23, 2025, https://www.iaea.org/atoms4netzero.

3 "Declaration to Triple Nuclear Energy," World Nuclear Association, accessed November 23, 2025, https://world-nuclear.org/net-zero-nuclear/tripling-pledges/declaration-to-triple-nuclear-energy.

4 "Atoms for Peace," Eisenhower Presidential Library, accessed November 23, 2025, https://www.eisenhowerlibrary.gov/research/online-documents/atoms-peace.

5 Nuclear Energy Institute, "Trump Puts Nuclear First on America's Energy Agenda," NEI, June 29, 2017.

6 "President Trump Signs 4 Executive Orders to Deploy New Nuclear Reactors, Strengthen Supply Chain," *Holland & Knight*, May 2025, accessed November 23, 2025; The White House, "Ordering the Reform of the Nuclear Regulatory Commission," May 23, 2025, https://www.whitehouse.gov/presidential-actions/2025/05/ordering-the-reform-of-the-nuclear-regulatory-commission/; The White House, "Reforming Nuclear Reactor Testing at the Department of Energy," May 23, 2025, https://www.whitehouse.gov/presidential-actions/2025/05/reforming-nuclear-reactor-testing-at-the-department-of-energy/; The White House, "Deploying Advanced Nuclear Reactor Technologies for National Security," May 23, 2025, https://www.whitehouse.gov/presidential-actions/2025/05/deploying-advanced-nuclear-reactor-technologies-for-national-security/; and The White House, "Reinvigorating the Nuclear Industrial Base," May 23, 2025, https://www.whitehouse.gov/presidential-actions/2025/05/reinvigorating-the-nuclear-industrial-base/.

7 "ICYMI: President Trump Signs Executive Orders to Usher in a Nuclear Renaissance, Restore Gold Standard Science," U.S. Department of Energy, May 23, 2025.

8 The White House, "Fact Sheet: President Donald J. Trump Unveils the Genesis Mission to Accelerate AI for Scientific Discovery," The

White House, November 24, 2025, https://www.whitehouse.gov/fact-sheets/2025/11/fact-sheet-president-donald-j-trump-unveils-the-genesis-missionto-accelerate-ai-for-scientific-discovery/.

9 Princeton Plasma Physics Laboratory, "Energy Department Launches 'Genesis Mission' to Transform American Science and Innovation Through the AI Computing Revolution," *PPPL News*, November 24, 2025.

10 Traci Brynne Voyles, *Wastelanding: Legacies of Uranium Mining in Navajo Country* (University of Minnesota Press, 2015).

11 Caroline Peyton, *Radioactive Dixie: A Nuclear History of the American South* (University of Georgia Press, 2025).

12 Grand Gulf Nuclear Station, "25 Years of Grand Gulf: Helping Power Mississippi's Future," YouTube, June 22, 2023, video, 5:01, https://www.youtube.com/watch?v=K5ImEqOjcXo.

13 Public Citizen, "The Nuclear Burden on Mississippi," Public Citizen, 2004, accessed November 23, 2025, https://www.citizen.org/wp-content/uploads/ggfactsheet.pdf. Mary Alldred and Kristin Shrader-Frechette, "Environmental Injustice in Siting Nuclear Plants," *Environmental Justice* 2, no. 2 (2009): 85–96; Caroline Peyton, *Radioactive Dixie: A Nuclear History of the American South* (University of Georgia Press, 2025).

14 Max Liboiron, *Pollution Is Colonialism* (Duke University Press, 2021).

15 Maria F. Ferreira, Andrew Turner, and Awadhesh N. Jha, "Controlled Release of Radioactive Water from the Fukushima Daiichi Nuclear Power Plant: Should We Be Concerned?," *Environmental Science & Technology* 58, no. 11 (2024): 4840–4843.

16 Nic Maclellan, "Introduction: Resistance and Survival – The Nuclear Era in the Pacific," *The Journal of Pacific History* 59, no. 1 (2024): 1–16.

17 Kirisitina Sailiata and Stephanie Nohelani Teves, "The Pacific," in *The Routledge Global History of Feminism* (Routledge, 2022), 151–162.

18 Dimity Hawkins, "'We Will Not Relax Our Efforts': The Anti-Nuclear Stance of Civil Society and Government in Post-Independence Fiji," *The Journal of Pacific History* 59, no. 1 (2024): 17–36.

19 Teresia K. Teaiwa, "Microwomen: U.S. Colonialism and Micronesian Women Activists," in *Pacific History: Papers from the 8th Pacific History Association Conference*, ed. Donald H. Rubinstein (University of Guam Press, 1992), 125–141.

20 Winona LaDuke and Sean Aaron Cruz, *The Militarization of Indian Country*, 3rd ed. (Honor the Earth, 2017).

21 Nuclear Free America Records, 1945–2003, MSS NFA, Special Collections and Archives Research Center, Oregon State University Libraries, Corvallis, OR.

22 William Epstein, "Nuclear-Free Zones," *Scientific American* 233, no. 5 (1975): 25–35.

23 Henry Richard Maar, *Freeze!: The Grassroots Movement to Halt the Arms Race and End the Cold War* (Cornell University Press, 2021).

24 Minnesota House of Representatives, "Legislation Lifting State's Nuclear Moratorium Clears House Energy Committee," *Session Daily*, March 13, 2025, https://www.house.mn.gov/sessiondaily/Story/18602.

25 Haunani-Kay Trask, "The Color of Violence," in *Color of Violence: The INCITE! Anthology*, ed. INCITE! Women of Color Against Violence (Duke University Press, 2006), 81–87.

26 Winona LaDuke, "Native American Activist, Author Winona LaDuke on *The Militarization of Indian Country* and Obama Admin's 'Lip Service' to Indigenous Rights," interview, *Democracy Now!*, May 6, 2011.

27 Darlene Keju, speech to the World Council of Churches (Vancouver, Canada, 1983), YouTube, accessed November 23, 2025, https://www.youtube.com/watch?v=1hxCGlA5oJQ.

28 Grace Thorpe, "Our Homes Are Not Dumps: Creating Nuclear-Free Zones," *Natural Resources Journal* 36, no. 1 (1996): 955–963.

29 Monika Bauerlein, "Prairie Island Revisited: A Minnesota Reservation Fights for a Nuclear-Free Future," *Native Americas*, June 30, 1995, 26.

30 Jessica Hurley, *Infrastructures of Apocalypse: American Literature and the Nuclear Complex* (University of Minnesota Press, 2020).

31 Nuclear Energy Information Service, "Golden Rule Ends 11,000 Mile Journey for Peace in Chicago," press release, September 13, 2023.

32 "The Golden Rule and Phoenix Voyages in Protest of U.S. Nuclear Testing in the Marshall Islands, 1958," Global Nonviolent Action Database, accessed November 23, 2025.

33 Veterans For Peace, "Historic Golden Rule Sailboat to Lead Peace Flotilla Around Alcatraz," August 20, 2025.

34 Vicente M. Diaz et al., "Navigating Indigenous Futures with the Mississippi River," *Open Rivers: Rethinking Water, Place & Community*, no. 17 (2020).

35 Vicente M. Diaz, "Oceania in the Plains: The Politics and Analytics of Transindigenous Resurgence in Chuukese Voyaging of Dakota Lands, Waters, and Skies in Miní Sóta Makhóčhe," *Pacific Studies Journal* 42, no. 1 (2019): 1.

36 Gwen Westerman, "Wakpa Definition," Public Art Saint Paul, September 30, 2022, https://publicartstpaul.org/wakpa-definition/.

37 Cole Redhorse Taylor, "Our River: NSP—Collaged ledger paper on handmade water color paper and ink," Instagram, April 6, 2022, https://www.instagram.com/p/CcB6h-Lrbt7/.

38 Leanne Betasamosake Simpson, *Theory of Water: Nishnaabe Maps to the Times Ahead* (Haymarket Books, 2025).

Moving Spirits Through Water Together

Stephanie Lindquist

In reflections on frozen Minnesota mornings, the dying Salton Sea, and the damaged landscapes of the Mississippi River, artist Stephanie Lindquist writes about moving and creating in the face of overwhelming grief. She reflects on the power of water as healer and connector while advocating for liquid rituals of care that align communities toward mutual respect and sustainable resistance.

The Mississippi River at night near Sunshine, Louisiana, with a faint glow from distant industrial lights reflecting on the water. Photograph by Stephanie Lindquist

FROZEN

On mornings when it is seventeen degrees below zero Fahrenheit, it is hard to crawl out from my warm sheets. I see the frost on the window panes, and I feel the cold draft radiate from my home's walls. The water in my backyard chicken coop is undoubtedly freezing. If the water is not frozen solid yet and the chickens are desperate, they will peck through the slushy top layer for a few precious sips before it hardens entirely. If I don't tend to them soon, I will hear them clucking. Or, worse, I risk their health and production of fresh eggs. If I don't bundle up before going out, my body will freeze and lose sensation. If I don't weatherproof the chicken coop, they will suffer. Numbness to the elements may be a protective mechanism in the short run, but in the long run it leads to death.

And so I get up, get dressed, and start moving to take care of them and me. My chickens keep me grounded in a daily rhythm of feeding them treats of mealworms, kitchen scraps, and their own egg shells, and, most importantly, changing their water.

It is even more painful to tune in to what is going on around us when the news is hard to weather and we lack any protective gear. We are sensitive creatures after all. I wonder how to confront these daily traumas. Listening to current news of the U.S. executive branch's relentless dismantling of our society's broad social supports for the enrichment of a few, I often feel incapacitated and numb with depression, frozen by the feeling that I can't change anything around me, and sometimes even reluctant to feel my own sorrow. While freezing, like running or fighting, may be an instinctive response, if endured for too long it removes my agency.

I fear that my numbness may be a dissociation not only with current events, but with the natural world, the universe to which I belong and am a small part. So how do I keep feeling and moving while confronting my own and others' grief in hard times? How might I ground myself in something unchanging or at least seasonal? I'm not seeking a quick high, fix, or distraction, but something that satiates my deep desire for connection, beauty, and meaning while also acknowledging the world's pain.

When I first moved to Minnesota, the frozen lakes in the winter looked impenetrable and dead to me. But deep below, the water is still moving with life. The first time I walked onto a frozen lake with my nephew, we were scared of the sound that ice makes when it is being made. We dropped and rolled off the ice as quickly as possible. Now, dressed in layers on warmer winter days after a hard freeze, I have learned to trust the lake to be my ground. This, only after manually drilling 2 feet deep holes through the ice to catch black crappies lurking thirty feet below. Even the frozen lakes support and connect me to the world.

Thousands of miles southwest of this water that reflects the clouds—Mni Sota Makoce—is a sea believed to be dead by some, cut off from restorative sources with nowhere to flow. And while many are incapacitated by the toxic sediments discharged there and widely dispersed in the air, others continue to flock to its shores made of bird and fish bones.

FLOWING

Three years ago, I visited the Salton Sea in Southern California. While driving around the sea I was struck by dystopian scenes of spray-painted furniture amongst collapsed structures being reclaimed by desert sand. Over hundreds of thousands of years, this body of water has intermittently been filled by the Colorado River, where water remained for many years, then evaporated into the desert. Before this place was settled by Europeans, the much larger, biologically vibrant Ancient Lake Cahuilla and its lava domes thrived. Last filled around 1400 and drying in the late 1500s, the lake held and still holds great significance to the Cahuilla people.[1] In less than two centuries, the river was dammed and canalled, cutting off the sea's replenishing flow. In the 1950s and 1960s, the remaining Salton Sea briefly became a tourist destination for Hollywood celebrities. The rich soil to the south in the Salton Trough was inundated with massive farms that sent their salty discharge to the sea. Despite this causing massive die-offs of birds, whose finely ground bones line the southern beach, the Salton Sea remains a critical stop in bird migration. And, with little water to replenish this place, the dusty dry seabed is picked up by wind storms, becoming a far reaching asthma attack.[2]

In the face of windstorms that spread dangerous pollutants for miles, I was surprised to watch people visit, camp, and walk along the Salton Sea's shores, a place where some scientists recommend wearing an N95 mask. I was perplexed and impressed. I had never seen anything like this. Whether they were tourists from far away or local Cahuilla people celebrating this sacred site, to my eyes, they confronted this sacrificial zone with love.

Abandoned buildings covered in graffiti at Bombay Beach near the Salton Sea. Photograph by Stephanie Lindquist

The people there reminded me of Anishinaabe nibi (water) walkers closer to my present home in the Midwest, people like Nokomis Josephine Mandamin or Sharon Day who physically confront man-made trauma on the land and water by walking immense distances around the Great Lakes and along the full length of the Mississippi River. Over a Zoom call, Day told me that while they walk with prayer and ceremony in each footstep to heal the water, they are in turn being healed by the water.

Two years ago in the fall, I had the opportunity to sail down the Mississippi River with a group of college students, professors, activists, and artists on Augsburg's River Semester organized by Joe Underhill. I was excited and also full of trepidation to face this riverscape and travel to the South for the first time as a person of color. There would be no reasonable way for me to hide or close my eyes from the pain humans have carved along the river's banks, or dumped and trafficked up and down its currents. I joined the crew in Greenville, Mississippi for the last eight weeks of their journey. I quickly integrated into their daily rhythms of early rising, group discussion, watching the wind in our sails while singing

A desolate landscape near the Salton Sea, with scattered vehicles and sparse vegetation under a cloudy sky. Photograph by Stephanie Lindquist

shanties, carrying supplies off the boats for the evening, setting up tents, collecting firewood, rinsing our dishes with the river water and sand, and generally checking in with one another. On sunny layovers, I would watch the students swim in the river. The further south we meandered, the more overwhelmed I felt. The entirety of the river was surrounded by old plantations now converted to industry, prisons, or wedding rentals except for the Whitney Plantation, the only site dedicated to retelling its history. One afternoon we happened to camp across from the Louisiana State Penitentiary, known for holding three wrongfully accused Black Panther Party members—Robert King, Albert Woodfox, and Herman Wallace, known as the Angola 3—in solitary confinement for 29 to 44 years each.[3] The next day, some of us visited the prison's museum. There was no mention of these three men who organized prisoners across racial lines to advocate for prison reform to improve the abysmal conditions in what was known as "The Last Slave Plantation."[4] Instead we looked upon displays about famous escapes, the prisoners' tradition of making handmade coffins for those on death row, and the longest-running prison rodeo to entertain locals, and merchandise, including reused license plates and hot sauce made by prisoners. Nearing Baton Rouge, the start of Louisiana's chemical corridor that extends south to New Orleans and is also known as cancer alley to some, we were told to no longer swim in the water.[5] We even stopped using the river

Tents set up under an abandoned structure at Lincoln Beach, Louisiana, during a rainy day. Photograph by Stephanie Lindquist

water to wash our dishes. Confronted by this tragic landscape of refineries, smokestacks, discharge sites, old plantations, and prisons, I lost all feeling.

Not knowing any rituals to ground me, I found solace in coming together as a group in ceremony through weekly water blessings, a format we adopted from Sharon Day. When alone, I meandered the batture—this land of seasonal flux between the river and the levee, where the water beats the land (stemming from the French word battre). There I greeted the plants—invasive, native, and naturalized alike. There was still unexpected beauty to be cherished as we drifted and sailed in two homemade catamarans between informal campsites. Thankfully, the river carefully carried our bodies safely to the Gulf. And the river connected us with a wide swath of people—activists, gardeners, educators, naturalists, residents, fishermen, partygoers, even the prisoners laboring on tugs who were looking to trade white bread for oreos. Despite all of the wounds settlers have inflicted upon this place in recent history, water continues to nurture us spiritually and physically.

Sometimes these lessons of facing pain with love are years and months in the making from California to Louisiana, and sometimes they are sitting right in front of you in your backyard and experienced in the intimacy of an epsom salt bath. I nearly panicked one evening this winter when I came home to find one of my chickens was egg-bound. Who knows how long poor Chanteclair was standing on the roost with an egg stuck halfway out of her. Watching the other

Ingredients and tools for the first herbal sauna, including sage, apples, and cedar tips, arranged for a community workshop in St. Paul, Minnesota. Photograph by Stephanie Lindquist

chickens begin to peck at her, I became terribly worried that the egg might break in her and possibly cause an infection. Unsure what to do, I called my partner, then some local vets, and eventually consulted Google. That night, we prepared two warm, thirty-minute epsom salt baths to put Chanteclair in. As we held her bottom calmly in the water, we massaged her belly downwards, and I sang to her while her muscles began to relax. After about three hours, she finally released the egg. It was soft, a mark of calcium deficiency. The next night we performed the same warm water treatment to help her pass another soft egg. For the next few days, we continued to bathe her bottom with a little soap to keep her clean. Acknowledging her pain and the healing power of water, I am glad to report she has safely rejoined the flock and is healthy and laying hard eggs again.

All thanks to water, the great connector, cleaning and caressing our bodies and souls—the chicken's, mine, and everyone on river, sea, and lake.

STEAMY

I'll never forget listening to Nick Tilsen, founder of the NDN Collective, speak at the 2022 National Tribal and Indigenous Climate Conference.[6] He spoke about the importance of ritual, and not just that of his ancestors. He reflected that while his ancestors could predict future events, they never knew what it was like to actually live today like us. Because of that truth, it is imperative for all people today to not only continue their traditions, but also invent new rituals born from the present reality to create the future they want. I can't say that I have ever been taught any rituals to manifest a joyful collective future, but I felt inspired by this invitation to create new rituals for myself that might nourish my joyful future with others. At the time I didn't know what they might be.

DESPITE ALL OF THE WOUNDS SETTLERS HAVE INFLICTED UPON THIS PLACE IN RECENT HISTORY, WATER CONTINUES TO NURTURE US SPIRITUALLY AND PHYSICALLY.

Late that summer, I gained an appreciation for how warriors recoup their strength between fights, individually and together, at the former Welcome Water Protector Center (WWPC) in Palisade, Minnesota. Upon meeting this group of activists and water protectors for the first time, I could feel, see, and hear their exhaustion even months after their battle against Enbridge ended in the rerouting of the Line 3 oil pipeline from Alberta, Canada to Wisconsin, passing under rivers like the Mississippi. Given Enbridge's culpability for the largest inland oil spill in U.S. history in 1991, which was along Line 3, this group of water protectors, along with hundreds of other people, had organized to try to prevent this from happening again.[7] The weekend I visited, WWPC was hosting a cultural camp led by Anishinaabe cultural specialist Jim Northrup and his brother, Jeff. The two of them instructed twenty-two of us in building and participating in a sweat lodge. For a few hours after sunset, we sat in a dark, canvas-covered lodge supported by Ironwood saplings, sweating and singing together. Our firekeeper carefully brought in red-hot stones that Jeff then sprinkled with a special decoction he prepared. When we finally reemerged into the light of the night, it felt like a rebirth into the world! This was a beautiful experience that promoted the spiritual, mental, emotional, and physical health of all of its participants, and it used a minimal amount of water.

As I later learned from Mikkel Aaland's book *Sweat*, sweating together is an ancient activity from all over the world that maintains public health.[8] This ritual has taken on different meanings for different people and cultures. For some, it may simply be a water efficient bath; for others, it may have social, spiritual, and medicinal significance. On a biological level, when we sweat our bodies remove toxins through our sweat glands that we have collected in our trashed environments.[9]

Deeply inspired by my first sweat at WWPC, I, too, wanted to practice both pleasurable and sustainable ways of interacting with water. After this experience, and still inspired by Tilsen's call to ritual, I decided to host an experimental herbal sauna series that honored water and considered how participants might take their health into their own hands. I had started studying herbalism under Erica Fargione at Minneapolis Community and Technical College, so I was very intentional about the infusions, decoctions, lotions, and scrubs I prepared for these gatherings.

WHAT EACH OF THESE PRACTICES HAS IN COMMON IS A DEEPENING OF OUR INTERNAL FEELINGS AND EXTERNAL AWARENESS. THIS TUNES US TO THE WORLD, EMPOWERS US TO ACT WITH MUTUAL RESPECT, AND FOSTERS BALANCE AROUND US.

My partner learned where to find clay from her ceramics professor and brought me to the banks of the Mississippi River to gather some. Under the white sand, she touched a vein of clay. We each gave thanks for the clay which would become a small soap dish shaped like the river's current and a scrub for our bodies in the sauna. We each then filled a small container with the clay. The first sauna I hosted was behind an auto shop in St. Paul, Minnesota and involved mostly artists. Later I hosted students, teachers, nonprofit workers, activists, community members on the northside of Minneapolis, and even environmental studies classes with their instructors, all in mobile, wood-burning saunas that I rented with the support of Second Shift Studio Space and Macalester College.

Collective rituals like this, ones that promote profound feeling and mindfulness, are powerful tools. I would argue that they not only benefit our health as a society, but also slow us down and tune our spirits to the world around us—cooling our ravenous urges to selfishly extract, hoard, or steal without considering our environment and other living beings. These rituals are diverse, as are people. They may be as personal as a prayer or poem, as sensual as a sweat or sauna, as expansive as traditional plant knowledge diligently passed through the generations, or as simple as intentional breathing, body movements, and drinking tea (an act of inviting plants to heal different parts of our body and spirit). For me, these rituals may be playing cards and listening to jazz with my partner while sitting on a frozen lake waiting for the crappies to bite thirty feet below the ice, changing the chicken's water, or collecting their eggs to boil for sandwiches. What each of these practices has in common is a deepening of our internal feelings and our external awareness. This tunes us to the world, empowers us to act with mutual respect, and fosters balance around us. In her essay *Uses of the Erotic: The Erotic as Power*, Audre Lorde says that "once we begin to feel deeply all of the aspects of our lives, we begin to demand from ourselves and from all our life's pursuits that they feel in accordance with the joy we know ourselves to be capable of."[10] When we share these experiences and feelings together, Lorde tells us that these activities may lead us to genuine change.

Discovering our collective fulfillment—what genuinely satisfies the needs of you, me, the water, the land, and everyone that lives there—will lead us to our strongest political solutions. Imagine how regularly slowing down together with others, sharing fresh eggs, a sauna, tea, a swim, walk, or paddle along the river, may begin to shift and align our values together. Imagine how collective rituals can then attune and inspire us to move together toward a common goal. Discovering our collective fulfillment requires time together and respect for one another's limits. Overharvesting, or extracting each other's gifts without permission or thanks, isn't mutually pleasurable. There is beauty in recognizing the natural limits of what each of us can offer. There is honor in recognizing the natural laws of interdependence and our delicate position within the world.[11] Whether or not our institutions can successfully move towards recognizing these laws, I believe that individually and collectively we can shift our own cultures. We can be in the flow. Authentic collective practices of care, inherently beautiful and pleasurable, can slowly build a passionate consensus. Our shared values will support our ability to commit over the long term to sustainable solutions. Our collective depth of feeling is reparative for us and all those around us.

A version of this article was originally published in the journal Open Rivers *(Winter/Spring 2025).*

ENDNOTES

1 Juan Valencia, "Imperial Valley's Torres-Martinez Desert Cahuilla Tribe Shares Creation Story," *Calexico Chronicle*, November 17, 2024, https://calexicochronicle.com/2024/11/17/imperial-valleys-torres-martinez-desert-cahuilla-tribe-shares-creation-story/; "What Lake Cahuilla Once Was," UC Riverside Palm Desert Center, January 13, 2021, https://palmdesert.ucr.edu/calnatblog/2021/01/13/what-lake-cahuilla-once-was; "The Troubled Salton Sea. A Tribal Perspective. Sean Milanovich (Cahuilla), Gathering Fire," produced by Robert Lundahl and Tracker Ginamarie Rangel Quinone, posted October 15, 2023, by Agence RLA, LLC, YouTube, 21 min., 9 sec., https://www.youtube.com/watch?v=TvagSPqvTWg.

2 Fletcher Reveley, "At the Salton Sea, Uncovering the Culprit of Lung Disease," *Undark*, August 19, 2024, https://undark.org/2024/08/19/salton-sea-uncovering-lung-disease/.

3 Jimmy O'Halligan, *The Angola 3: Black Panthers and the Last Slave Plantation*, PM Press, (2008), 109 minutes; Angad Singh Bhalla, "Herman's House," POV, *PBS*, season 26, aired on July 8, 2013, https://www.pbs.org/pov/films/hermanshouse/.

4 O'Halligan, "The Angola 3."

5 Al Shaw and Lylla Younes, "The Most Detailed Map of Cancer-Causing Industrial Air Pollution in the U.S.," ProPublica, last modified August 28, 2023, https://projects.propublica.org/toxmap/; "Cancer Alley," Wikipedia, last modified March 26, 2025, https://en.wikipedia.org/wiki/Cancer_Alley.

6 Melanie Lenart, "Indigenous Climate Conference Offers Hopeful Message," *Native Science Report*, September 9, 2022, https://nativesciencereport.org/2022/09/indigenous-climate-conference-offers-hopeful-message/.

7 Dan Kraker and Kristi Marohn, "30 Years Later, Echoes of Largest Inland Oil Spill Remain in Line 3 Fight," *MPR News*, March 3, 2021, https://www.mprnews.org/story/2021/03/03/30-years-ago-grand-rapids-oil-spill.

8 Mikkel Aaland, *Sweat, The Illustrated History and Description of the Finnish Sauna, Russian Bania, Islamic Hammam, Japanese Mushi-Boro, Mexican Temescal and American Indian & Eskimo Sweatlodge* (Capra Press, 1978).

9 Aaland, *Sweat*.

10 Audre Lorde, "Audre Lorde Reads Uses of the Erotic: The Erotic as Power (FULL Updated)," posted August 1, 2019, by growbean, YouTube, 23 min., 25 sec., https://www.youtube.com/watch?v=aWmq9gw4Rq0.

11 Gregory Cajete, *Native Science* (Clear Light Publishers, 2000).

Moving Spirits Through Water Together
by Stephanie Lindquist, page 124.
Photograph by Neli Wagner

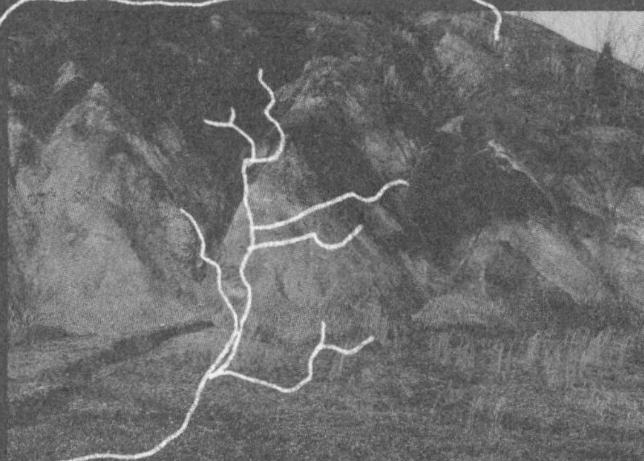

Middle Mississippi

The Middle Mississippi River is the portion of the river around St. Louis, Missouri. Major tributaries include the Illinois, Missouri and Ohio Rivers. The Field School of the Middle Mississippi River has examined and developed collective narratives about the river's construction as a colonial divide between the East and West, the freed and enslaved, settler and Indigenous.

Pokelore: How a Common Weed Leads Us to Kinship with Our Mid-River Landscape

Lynn Peemoeller

A weed or a relative? Drawing on botany, everyday stories, and African American and Indigenous foodways, Lynn Peemoeller looks to pokeweed—a hardy, native plant frequently vilified as a weed—to find kinship in the marginal space between the levee and the river, the Middle Mississippi's batture.

> "A weed is a plant growing in a place where we don't want it, and I have seldom seen a poke plant that I wanted removed."
> —Euell Gibbons, *Stalking the Wild Asparagus*[1]

Poke in the space between the levee and the river. Photograph by Jennifer Colten

It's certainly not the primary defining characteristic of St. Louis, Missouri, nor is it the secondary, but if you are looking, it's hard to miss. Phytolaccaceae, otherwise known as the pokeweed family of plants, runs wild in this part of the middle waters just south of the confluence of the Missouri and Mississippi Rivers. To some who look through empty spaces, these weeds are just the backdrop to a prosaic landscape here in the river city. But for others, who are drawn to the botanical lives that share our ruderal spaces, poke is a beacon of kinship.[2]

Weeds, often considered the outlaws of the plant family, are widely maligned today; the deep-rooted desire to conquer and eradicate is culturally pervasive. The idea of a weed is a human construct; there is no biological equivalent. Ralph Waldo Emerson formulated the famous adage "What is a weed? A plant whose virtues have not yet been discovered"—an optimistic view that reflects how humans have been assigning a hierarchy of value to plants for thousands of years and coaxing them into productive relationships with humans by selective breeding.[3] Yet the cultural emphasis on weeds as "a plant in the wrong place" eliminates the ecological attributes of plants and is rife with human bias on what qualities are wanted and unwanted.

WEEDS, OFTEN CONSIDERED THE OUTLAWS OF THE PLANT FAMILY, ARE WIDELY MALIGNED TODAY; THE DEEP ROOTED DESIRE TO CONQUER AND ERADICATE IS CULTURALLY PERVASIVE.

What we pay attention to grows, and ironically, so does the idea of a weed. We can't get rid of weeds. They follow us everywhere in response to human footprints, they compete for ecological resources with crops, and they thrive in disturbed areas. *Plantago major*, known as broadleaf plantain, was named "white man's footsteps" because it grew widely around European settlements in North America. Today it is commonly seen in cracks of sidewalks. Weeds—aggressive, invasive, toxic, ugly, useless, unloved saboteurs—are the plants that haven't quite made it as chosen human companions, and yet, we're stuck with them. The kindest thing we might be able to say is that weeds are simply plants in the wrong place. But what is the right place for a weed? Is there such a thing?

One could say that poke is a paradox. On the one hand it embodies the spontaneous vegetative ethos of a weed, and on the other hand, unlike Emerson's limited view, we have proof that it is a plant whose virtues *have* historically been explored. According to Jonathan Sauer, botanist and plant geographer who extensively researched *Phytolacca americana* (the scientific name for poke also known as pokeweed), the plant's native area includes North America, specifically southeastern Canada and the entire eastern half of the United States, and a small area in the northeast of Mexico.[4] Poke acts in ways that are often characterized as weed-like, even though it is a native plant. Prehuman evidence shows that poke aggressively colonized streambanks and disturbed ground and then gave way to plant (or rather, ecological) succession in due course. Human activity in the landscape creates disturbances in the ground that lead to increased poke colonization. Grazing animals left it alone and so its spread was vigorous. Today, it seems to occupy a niche, much more comfortable inhabiting disturbed areas and thriving in ditches, railroad embankments, floodplains, roadsides, fence rows, hedges, old fields, old orchards, gardens, pastures, dumps, clearings, and spaces of general human habitation. "Poke's success as a weed of the cultural landscape appears to be based, not on selective modification during human times, but on previous adaptation to disturbed habitats."[5] Although poke has coexisted with humans in North America and has spread to other continents, it has only had moderate success as a cultivated plant and has never quite reached full integration into agricultural practice.

Botanist and agronomist Jack R. Harlan explains, "one man's weed is another man's crop and vice versa...Plants drift in and out of cultivation, are domesticated, abandoned, ennobled, and may degenerate again: they escape, become naturalized, migrate, retreat, build hybrid swarms, and evolve new races."[6] Weeds can tell us a lot about ourselves and our relationship with the land—what we see and don't see, what we value and what we don't—and how we currently completely outsource our food procurement to a select few farmers and increasingly industrialized food systems. Is it any wonder that the term plant blindness—the ability of humans to ignore the plants around us—has become a common and widespread condition? Yet, there are people who maintain botanical knowledge and relations with the land. Today, poke maintains a robust vernacular identity in the United States. The name itself, poke, is derived from the Virginia Indian or Algonquin word *pokan*, referring to plants used for red or yellow dye. Other names of Indigenous origin include scoke, cunicum, coakum, and cokan. More common names referring to the red stem and berries include redweed, redberry, inkberry, pigeonberry, crow berry, shoe button plant, bear's grape, red nightshade, and American nightshade.[7] But the most common name throughout the United States vernacular is poke sallet, also spelled sallit, salat, and salad, and it is colloquially known as "poor man's greens." Poke leaves and stems are never eaten raw

Phytolacca decandra (American Pokeweed) (1806). Image via "The Botanical Magazine or Flower Garden Displayed" by Francis Sansom. Courtesy of The Cleveland Museum of Art

and are cooked as a potherb. The leaves and stems need to be carefully prepared through multiple rounds of boiling and rinsing to remove toxins. This knowledge has been carefully passed down through countless generations of people who depended on the land for survival. Jack Harlan, in his influential work *Crops and Man*, examines the deep connection between crops and human civilization, highlighting the botanical expertise of hunter-gatherer societies.[8]

He addresses their remarkable understanding of how to use plants that are otherwise poisonous, stating, "detoxification is required for a considerable number of plants used by the North American Indians... Gatherers knew how to make plants safe."[9]

Only in the last 10,000 years have humans begun to domesticate plants and animals. All human life before that, in a period known as the Golden Age, subsisted using hunter-gatherer strategies. At the time of European contact in the Americas, while many

Allens canned poke.

Indigenous societies were hunter-gatherers, there were others that were agriculturally based.[10] Since then, the practice has been declining in relation to the development and dominance of selectively breeding plants and animals for food. It was only after agricultural systems had been adopted that weeds became more conspicuous. Agrarian adopters bore prejudice against hunter-gatherers and their practices. The stereotype of hunter-gatherers was that they were lazy people always on the verge of starvation and did not apply their time and energy to the pursuit of cultivation.[11] The 1966 symposium *Man the Hunter* held at the University of Chicago was a groundbreaking exploration of ethnographic research on hunter-gatherers, which has led to hundreds of subsequent research papers and critiques that have expanded the understanding of the so-called Golden Age. Yet the question remains: why do people who have access to agricultural knowledge systems still continue to forage?

In recent times, poke has largely been associated with hardscrabble survival in the American South, and it has a strong connection to Indigenous American and African American foodways that were also adopted by white settlers. Folk stories of poke parallel those of human subsistence, land dispossession, and migration in North America. As one of the first spring greens, it served to provide relief from a poor winter diet. Those who knew the landscape and followed the rivers found what they could use to survive. It wasn't the first choice for eating, but if it was the only plant available, it was supper.[12]

The legendary forager Euell Gibbons grew up in the Dust Bowl era and once subsisted exclusively on wild foods for five consecutive years. In *Stalking the Wild Asparagus*, which Gibbons wrote in 1962, he calls poke "a wild potherb par excellence."[13]

He writes that poke (at that time)

> is probably the best known and most widely used wild vegetable in America... it is a favorite green vegetable with many country people and the tender young sprouts, gathered from wild plant often appear in vegetable markets especially in the South...Settlers carried seeds back to Europe and the plant spread as a cultivated plant throughout the southern Europe and North Africa.[14]

It's hard to believe that not so long ago poke occupied a quasi-cultivated status as a market vegetable not so different from wild gathered watercress, lamb's quarters, or purslane that are sometimes seen at farmers markets today.

In fact, poke almost reached the mainstream in the mid-twentieth century. According to the University of Arkansas Division of Agriculture, Research and Extension, in the 1950s "Dr. John Bowers, a former colleague in the horticulture department, made efforts to turn pokeweed into a legitimate 'vegetable' presumably through breeding efforts that never quite took off."[15] However, two vegetable processing plants—Bush Brothers of Tennessee and Allen of Siloam Springs, Arkansas—produced canned poke salat that were distributed in supermarkets widely throughout the South. Allen's was also famous for the iconic Popeye (canned) spinach. Unlike spinach, which was cultivated by farmers and sold to the cannery, the poke was wild harvested and sold to the cannery. According to John Williams, the canning supervisor at Allen Canning,

> as the generation of people who grew knowing poke sallet began to pass, the demand for the item dried up. Allen Canning packed its last batch of poke sallet greens in the spring of 2000...The decision to stop processing poke was primarily because of the difficulty of finding people interested in picking poke

Harvesting poke. Photograph by Jennifer Colten

> and bringing it to our buying locations. Also, poke processing was never a significant item in the multimillion-dollar enterprise, so it just became more bother than it was worth.[16]

The loss of canned poke is felt in the twenty-first century as botanical and culinary knowledge slip away through generations. Canned poke represented a cultural bridge between generations who carried relationships with the landscape and the shift to upwardly mobile mid-century lifestyles which traded plant relations for the convenience of a safely prepared, shelf-stabilized foodstuff. The fact that it had nutritional value and regional cultural identity to boot was a bonus. With a canned product, you could have your poke in minutes without all the effort to identify, harvest, and prepare it. You didn't even have to call mama or grandma to get the recipe. Yet unlike other modern food conveniences of the twentieth century, like Spam, the demand for canned poke faded. It could never surpass the stigma of being attached to a poor Southern identity.

Today, the suggestion of eating poke strikes a chord of fear among those who have not learned from tradition and are not confident about identifying or preparing it. Some simply see it as too much trouble. Many wild plant guides cite a responsible warning with poke that root, seeds, and mature stems and leaves are dangerous: "Be very careful not to include part of the root when collecting the shoots, and peel or discard any shoots tinged with red."[17] Its edibility can be confusing territory to navigate for the uninitiated. A wild foods blog, *Eat the Weeds*, explains how to approach the harvest:

> When I go collecting poke weed, I take a ruler with me. It's called my hand. From the tip of my middle finger to my wrist is about six inches. If the shoot is six inches or under, into the pot it will go, taller I leave it be. The second rule is, pick nothing with red stems, but that's not so hard and fast because even two-inch shoots can sometimes be pink to red. And when I gather it, I don't pull it up, I cut it to avoid the possibility of getting any root. And do not handle raw poke weed if you have any cuts or abrasion on your hands.[18]

In Michele Lee's comprehensive collection of traditional African American folk healing practices, *Working the Roots*, she calls poke

> the Jedi of the plant world. Why? Because it has a wide range of beneficial applications from use as food, medicine, ink, dye, paint and as a solar absorbent (to generate solar power). And like the

Woman preparing "poke-salad" near Marshall, Texas in March 1939. Photograph by Russell Lee

> Jedi, poke has both a light side and a dark side. As a medicine, it is a potent and concentrated substance that, like the light side of "the Force," can effect a powerful healing. However, like the dark side of "the Force," if used incorrectly, it can harm, even kill.[19]

The toxins in pokeweed range from deadly to mild. They are usually concentrated in the roots, berries, and seeds and include an alkaloid (phytolaccine), a resin (phytolaccatoxin), and a saponin (phytolaccigenin).[20] Medicinally and culturally, the roots and berries of the plant have several applications. It's emetic, which means that its toxic qualities can cause vomiting if ingested. Many applications are topical in the form of tincture or salve. The berries contain abundant red pigment (anthocyanin) which has been used as dye on fabric, on paper, and in foods. Some recipes use poke berries to make wine or color foods. The seeds are completely toxic and should be avoided. Traditional healers like Lee who worked with poke knew that using any part of the poke plant for medicine should be done with caution.

Alexis Nikole Nelson, known as the Black Forager, has posted about poke on TikTok several times. "Poison or soul food?" she asks, "This plant is both!"[21] What a good reminder that we should hold nonbinary thinking as a possibility. Yes, two things can be true. We don't have to live in worlds of absolutes. She encourages people to learn the history of eating poke because the knowledge and tradition of how to prepare it correctly is passed down through generations. "If people don't know how to do it, that knowledge will be lost," she cautions.[22] Once the old ways are forgotten, how quickly a culture can dissolve if we don't practice it into being.

A post on Facebook in the spring of 2021 shared a photo from the Library of Congress of an African American woman preparing poke in 1939.[23] There were over 7,000 likes and more than 1,200 comments such as: "It is a very Southern thing. I have aunts and great aunts that share stories about how to eat it," and, "I still eat it if I can find it. It's not hard to fix. You need to drain the water from it at least 3 times." "I'm 63 and learned from my Grandmother. We ate it every Spring." "My parents ate it a lot in the depression. It was an equal opportunity food." "Love poke and can spot it anywhere!! Boil three times changing the water, add fat back green onions, with a bowl of pintos and cornbread...Man, I miss my Mom and Gma!! Good eatn'." These comments not only reflect nostalgia but also the value of intergenerational knowledge and some hope that points toward a desire to reclaim these traditions.

To this day, there are several parts of the regional south that hold poke festivals: Arab, Alabama; Blanchard, Louisiana; Gainesboro, Tennessee; Harlan, Kentucky, which celebrated its seventieth anniversary in 2025; and Toccoa, Georgia. The Poke Sallit festival in Toccoa has been led by community historian Larry Gholston for over 30 years, emphasizing Black self-reliance. He is quoted in *The New York Times* saying, "The festival is meant to maintain our heritage. A lot of Black folk will tell you, 'I don't eat that mess, man. It has connotations of poorness and rural.'"[24]

Take for example, the 1968 song "Polk Salad Annie," a slice of Americana written and performed by Tony Joe White (and later Elvis.) It's a swampy rock country ode to the poor Southern lifestyle of presumably white folks in Louisiana:

Summer poke. Photograph by Jennifer Colten

"My folks raised cotton and corn. There were lotsa times when there weren't too much to eat, and I ain't ashamed to admit that we've often whipped up a mess of poke sallet. Tastes alright too—a bit like spinach…Poke salad Annie…the gators got your Granny."[25] That may have been half a century ago, but the idea of resilience is in high circulation these days.

Upriver from Louisiana, resilience is a subject of study in St. Louis, a city that is no stranger to hardship. A small but dynamic group of mostly female artists, healers, historians, and plant people have been meeting regularly since 2021 as part of the Mid-River Field School. The field school explores synergies of our contemporary landscape on both sides of the river, emphasizing kinship with the nonhuman world and collective deinstitutionalized knowledge building. Thematically, the idea of crossings guides project-based work that is anchored in the practice of how to be in relation with a place that is at odds with itself. Both valued and abandoned, vibrant and suffering, St. Louis is not unlike many other American cities. Yet it straddles American history in particular ways. It has been described as the northernmost southern city and the westernmost eastern city and "the right place for all the wrong reasons" according to George Lipsitz, a Black scholar at the University of California, Santa Barbara.[26] It is primarily a river city, and we use that as our guide. The water connects us to relatives both upriver and downriver. We are the middle waters.

It is along the banks of the Mississippi River, the muddy gap of rushing water that divides St. Louis city and its eastern counterpart, East St. Louis, in an area that artist Jennifer Colten calls "the space between the levee and the river," otherwise known as the batture, that the pokeweed grows most majestically.[27] Poke is a subject of field study for our group. Physically, the plant is hard to ignore. Its stature is large, growing 6 to 10 feet tall and like something out of a Dr. Seuss book, the white summer blossoms give way to a dense peduncle or stalk holding a cluster of shiny dark purple berries that are very attractive to birds and irresistible to children's play. Historically, it was noted that "leaves of pokeberry were worn on the lapels of supporters of the first dark-horse candidate for president, James Polk who served from 1845 to 1849 and for whom Polk County is named."[28] Today it is not uncommon for flowers and berries to make their way into wildcrafted bouquets. We can't seem to get this second-rate, toxic plant out of our minds or our landscapes.

Compared with aggressors like kudzu or Japanese knotweed, poke is not an aggressive invasive species. It is more of an opportunist with a perambulatory relationship with the landscape. It moves slowly to stake its claim by power of root and seed. Poke roots are thick, yellow gnarls resembling a giant mandrake. They are deep and strong, keeping the plants rooted in place year after year. It is the berries that are the travelers, attracting birds who eat them untouched by the toxins. If there is a poke plant, it is sure to be there year after year unless it is forcefully removed. All bits of the root need to be carefully combed from the soil. Like a worm, if there are any pieces left, they can easily regenerate. This strong hold in the ground demands high labor relations with humans. Poke is not easily removed once it has become established. Perhaps this is why it has become so unloved. In most highly controlled areas, poke, like other weeds, is eradicated by all means necessary. But St. Louis is just wild enough that poke finds its way to root in place, living side by side with human relations.

As a weed, poke is very successful. Its functionality is based on adaptation. Unlike cultivated plants, weeds thrive in the company of humans in ruderal ways by following our footsteps in the upheaval of the stirred-up human landscape. Plants and people share similar stories. Whether we choose to engage with it or not, it is a human companion plant. Could it live without us? Probably. Would it thrive? It's hard to know. Many hopeful signs of resilience can be found in attention to relational multispecies behaviors. Indigenous knowledge recognizes "a genealogic ancestry that binds humans and non-humans including plants in a web of intertwining kinship connections."[29] Environmental philosopher Matthew Hall writes about kinship with plants as a kind of mutuality of being, a reciprocity of being in relation.[30] Perhaps it is because the mature poke meets us at eye level that it draws our attention. On a winter's walk, the dry skeletons of poke stand rigid in the landscape as an inescapable brush-force encounter for those who stray off the pavement. Along river walks, through abandoned lots, or in cobbled alleyways, poke can be seen as markers for wayfinding, as architecture of the cultural landscape. Notice: how does it steer us? Does it bend, point toward, or seed our relationship with the place? More often than not, it points back to us. St. Louis, like many river cities, offers liminal spaces that have stories buried in the rubble. We are so tied to our humanity that we often forget the significance of our relationship with the nonhuman world, especially those living creatures that are unfortunate enough to dwell in ecosystems that are literally out of our sight. Out of sight, out of mind. But poke has the advantage of being very present in the landscape. In sight, in mind, and in body, it holds memory for us.

Plants can hold memory in the landscape in different ways than people. Another reason for poke's success is its relationship with time. A 1946 study showed that poke seeds buried in 1902 at depths too great for germination gave 80 to 90 percent germination after being unearthed in 1941.[31] The soil holds innumerable seeds underground in seedbanks. Generationally speaking, these seeds have patience built into them, waiting for the serendipity of conditions to activate them—the claw of an excavator, the channel of a flooding river, the slow steady erosion of time. Much of this activation is in relation to human activity. If we continue to look at the world through settler colonial logic, we consume landscapes as a tabula rasa with no historical or ecological underpinnings. How can we escape these cycles?

PLANTS CAN HOLD MEMORY IN THE LANDSCAPE IN DIFFERENT WAYS THAN PEOPLE.

Perhaps if we view weeds as partners in place more than invaders in space, we can move closer to kinship with our landscape. When we engage in field observations our attention expands to see interspecies worlds that are bigger than us. We can see weeds not necessarily as invaders, but rather the evidence of our legacy on the landscape. They reflect a deep ancestral presence of the lineage of time connected to places. Plants help us locate ourselves, they are rooted to the ground and cannot float so easily off in the river. Yet, when we move, the weeds move with us. When we control, the weeds are suppressed. When we crumble, the weeds reemerge. We are in relation with them. That is kinship. They respond to our present with ancestral knowledge of resilience and survival. Weeds are artifacts of plant intelligence and embedded memory. If we are able to accept weeds as our plantcestors, they can offer us a way of partnering in place beyond the normative platform of exploitation through which many of us view the land and its resources. Writer and cultural geographer Lucy Lippard seeks historical narratives as they are written in the landscape at the intersection of nature, culture, history, and ideology.[32] From the ground on which we stand comes our place: the local. We share the ground upon which we stand with poke.

PERHAPS IF WE VIEW WEEDS AS PARTNERS IN PLACE MORE THAN INVADERS IN SPACE, WE CAN MOVE CLOSER TO KINSHIP WITH OUR LANDSCAPE.

The warm weather wakes up new shoots of poke from perennial taproots. This is the best time to collect the tender young greens for eating. Spring activates the life around us. All seasons are charged with memory and emotion for those who carry legacy. In tune with the clockwork of the phenological calendar, we come to expect the cycles by how we see poke. Poke offers itself to these relations in all seasons. The Mid-River Field School asks us to notice how the outer landscape mirrors the inner landscape. How can we see our place for what it is and not what we want it to be? Lippard says that "artists can make the connections visible. They can guide us through the sensuous kinesthetic response to topography... They can expose social agendas that have formed on the land, [and] bring out multiple readings of places."[33] By providing space for encounter, observation, and community, the study of poke becomes a practice of resilience in how we view and represent our relations with the landscape. It gives us a material agent to practice collective learning and unlearning about our place. It offers us a lens to look into the past and toward futures. We take these parts to weave narratives of our truths which we present to the world as heterogeneous collective memories.[34] These are the offerings of the Mid-River Field School.

Nimble weeds are most likely to survive the upheaval of time. Nature writer Richard Mabey calls weeds "a time-biding genetic bank over which our buildings and tinkerings are just an ephemeral carapace."[35] Weeds remind us that the built environment is merely a temporary event. It seems the plants are saying, "we were here before you and we will be here when you are gone." In our effort to control life, wildness is a quality we have lost touch with. Weeds are embedded with a wild spirit and a reassurance that life goes on. Poke helps us appreciate how we can partner with the wild, how we can see beauty in the greening over of the dereliction of human activity. Poke has always been here. It has so much to teach us. The weeds belong; we are the outlaws.

A version of this article was originally published in the journal Open Rivers *(Winter/Spring 2025).*

ENDNOTES

1 Euell Gibbons, *Stalking the Wild Asparagus* (D. McKay Co., 1962), 174.

2 Ruderal refers to a plant that grows in waste places or requires soil disturbance to become established. From Latin rudera, "ruins" or "rubbish," plural of rudus, "broken stone." In botanical parlance, a disturbance-adapted species. See Peter Del Tredici, *Wild Urban Plants of the Northeast: A Field Guide* (Cornell University Press, 2020).

3 Ralph Waldo Emerson, "Fortune of the Republic," in *The Later Lectures of Ralph Waldo Emerson 1834–1871*, Vol. 2: 1855–1871, eds. Ronald A. Bosco and Joel Myerson (University of Georgia Press, 2001 [1863]), 321.

4 Jonathan D. Sauer, "A Geography of Pokeweed." *Annals of the Missouri Botanical Garden* 39, no. 2 (1952): 113–25, https://doi.org/10.2307/2394507; Jonathan Deininger Sauer, "Poke (Phytolacca americana L.): Biology and Geography of a Weed," (master's thesis, Washington University, 1948).

5 Sauer, "A Geography of Pokeweed," 113.

6 H. Thomas Stalker, Marilyn L. Warburton, and Jack R. Harlan, *Harlan's Crops and Man: People, Plants and Their Domestication*, 3rd ed. (American Society of Agronomy, Crop Science Society of America, and Wiley, 2021), 116.

7 Jack R. Harlan, *Crops & Man* (American Society of Agronomy, Crop Science Society of America, 1992).

8 Harlan, *Crops & Man.*

9 Harlan, *Crops & Man*, 20.

10 Harlan, *Crops & Man.*

11 Harlan, *Crops & Man*, 4.

12 The City Wire Staff, "Allens, Poke Sallet and Change," Talk Business, January 12, 2014, https://talkbusiness.net/2014/01/allens-poke-sallet-and-change/; Gerald Klingman, "Plant of the Week: Pokeweed (Pokeberry)," University of Arkansas System Division of Agriculture Cooperative Extension Service, accessed June 1, 2025, https://www.uaex.uada.edu/yard-garden/resource-library/plant-week/pokeweed.aspx.

13 Gibbons, *Stalking the Wild Asparagus*, 174.

14 Gibbons, *Stalking the Wild Asparagus*, 174.

15 Klingman, "Plant of the Week: Pokeweed (Pokeberry)."

16 Klingman, "Plant of the Week: Pokeweed (Pokeberry)."

17 Lee Peterson, *A Field Guide to Edible Wild Plants of Eastern and Central North America* (Houghton Mifflin Harcourt, 1978), 46; Allison O. Adams, "A Mess of Poke," *Southern Spaces*, October 11, 2011, https://southernspaces.org/2011/mess-poke/.

18 "Allen Canning Company: Pokeweed: Prime Potherb," Eat the Weeds and Other Things, Too, accessed June 1, 2024, https://www.eattheweeds.com/tag/allen-canning-company/.

19 Michele Elizabeth Lee, *Working the Roots: Over 400 Years of Traditional African American Healing* (Wadastick, 2017).

20 "Pokeweed, American (Phytolacca Americana): The Jekyll and Hyde Plant," Nadia's Backyard, accessed June 1, 2025, https://nadiasyard.com/our-native-plants/american-pokeweed/.

21 blackforager, "LOL, one day I'll be good at social media but until then have some American food history! Poison! Culture! Dolly Parton! This video has a lot!" Instagram, May 18, 2022, https://www.instagram.com/tv/CdthHyUj4xp.

22 blackforager, "LOL."

23 Eating History, "Preparing 'poke-sallet' (or poke salat) made from the pokeweed. This is a green which grows wild in the South and if not prepared properly can be deadly, Marshall, Texas in 1939. From the Library of Congress," Facebook, May 27, 2021, https://www.facebook.com/share/p/17bNCyvU8q/.

24 Cynthia Greenlee, "How Black Foragers Find Freedom in the Natural World," *The New York Times*, July 30, 2021, https://www.nytimes.com/2021/07/30/dining/black-foragers-nature-alexis-nelson.html.

25 Rick Moore, "Behind the Song: Tony Joe White, 'Poke Salad Annie,'" American Songwriter, updated November 11, 2019, https://americansongwriter.com/tony-joe-white-polk-salad-annie/.

26 Attributed to George Lipsitz in Walter Johnson, *The Broken Heart of America: St. Louis and the Violent History of the United States* (Basic Books, 2020).

27 Jennifer Colten, "Between the Levee and the River," Jennifer Colten, 2024, https://www.jennifercolten.com/between-the-levee-and-the-river.

28 Klingman, "Plant of the Week: Pokeweed (Pokeberry)."

29 Matthew Hall, "Kinship with Plants," in *Kinship: Belonging in a World of Relations* 5, eds. Gavin Van Horn, Robin Wall-Kimmerer, and John Hausdorffer, Practice (Center for Humans and Nature, 2021), 39.

30 Hall, "Kinship with Plants."

31 Sauer, "Poke (Phytolacca americana L.): Biology and Geography of a Weed."

32 Lucy R. Lippard, *The Lure of the Local: Senses of Place in a Multicentered Society* (New Press, 1997).

33 Lippard, *The Lure of the Local*, 19.

34 This framework is generally attributed to Donna Haraway; see Donna Haraway, "Situated Knowledges: The Science Question in Feminism and the Privilege of Partial Perspective," *Feminist Studies* 14, no. 3 (Autumn, 1998): 575–599.

35 Richard Mabey, *Weeds: In Defense of Nature's Most Unloved Plants* (Harper Collins, 2011).

Persimmon Pudding; Wild Persimmon

A recipe from the River Semester by MORGAN PIPER CORDOVA

Written for the Mississippi River Open School, this recipe is an excerpt of Mississippi Mud Book of Recipes, *a collection of stories, reflections and recipes that Morgan Piper Cordova assembled while an undergraduate student on the Fall 2023 River Semester.*

An empty marble pedestal sleeps conspicuously at the entrance to Southwest St. Louis's Tower Grove Park. Flanking it are enormous green sycamore, oak, and sweet gum, a small sampling of the arboretum that surrounds us. We met Lynn Peemoeller in the shade of these trees, near the empty marble block, a welcome refuge from the hot day. Peemoeller is a food systems planner, working as a facilitator between St. Louis and farmers with the goal of making food more accessible to those in cities. She lives in one of the tall brick townhouses that borders the park, and remembers the morning when she noticed that the Christopher Columbus statue had been removed from the marble pedestal—she was walking her dog. "Now my kids climb all over the block...pretending to be statues themselves."

About 400 feet from this false monument is a trickling stream bed, filled with round river rocks baking in one of the rare sunny patches of this park. Peemoeller explains that this creek was recently "daylighted" by the Osage Tribal Nation Historic Preservation Office after a century of subsurface flow. It's been named Nee Kee Nee, or "revived water" in Osage, and was used as a gathering place for the Osage people in the midst of their former hunting grounds. The dedication ceremony in November of 2022 included members of the Osage nation and city engineers and officials. Tower Grove Park is one of the only parks managed by an independent Board of Commissioners, and the removal of the Columbus statue and daylighting of Nee Kee Nee are related efforts started in collaboration with the Osage nation. Both are significant in a city known for its monuments to European nostalgia exemplified by the St. Louis white capitalist elite throughout the history of the city.

The treaties of 1808 and 1825, along with the convincing of the Superintendent of Indian Affairs William Clark, forced the Osage to the plains via the Trail of Tears. The United States Government sold the Tower Grove Park land to Henry Shaw, an amateur botanist and slave owner who had secured his fortune merchanting iron goods to settlers traveling westward on the Missouri River. A retired Shaw sold the land back to the city in 1866 with the requirement that it "shall be used as a park forever," and that an "annual appropriation" be made by the city "for its maintenance." He had already established the Missouri Botanical Gardens on the park's grounds. Tower Grove Park was made to be controlled and monitored, to serve as a monument to the exotic riches of a city that has done nothing but take. Still in the midst of this park, by the banks of Nee Kee Nee, two native trees persist: an Osage orange and a wild persimmon.

Wild persimmon is unlike its domesticated varieties that are more commonly known. It is a squishy orange ball when ripe, and the whole fruit is edible (minus its distinctive green crown). The so-called oriental persimmon, of the varietal Fuyu, is common on the Pacific Coast of the United States and originated in Japan. It has a tough skin that is inedible raw. The name persimmon is of Algonquin origin, and the fruit have been a staple of Indigenous groups all along the Mississippi River. When we visited Andeab and Mila Berhane's Greenhand Nursery outside of Baton Rouge, Louisiana, an enormous wild persimmon tree greeted us as we entered their driveway.

Before colonization, southern Missouri was a rich repository of persimmons, paw paws, mushrooms, and wild grapes. These fruits were so hearty that Missouri wild grapes were spliced with French grape varietals to save the French grapes from blight in the 1800s. Today, the greatest abundance of wild persimmon trees in the world is in the Mississippi River Valley, and Native populations have used the fruit, bark, and leaves of persimmon trees for medicine and food. Early African American populations would use persimmons to make cakes, candy, and pudding, which is a staple on many Midwestern and Southern tables. Cherokee would chew the bark as a gastrointestinal aid, and prepare it in steam baths for indigestion. Many Indigenous groups—including Rappahannock, Comanche, and Cherokee—would use the inner bark as a wash for hemorrhoids, thrash, and sore throats (if the inner bark is from the north side of the tree). The Rappahannock would also roll the fruits in corn meal, brew in water, drain, and bake and mix with hot water to make a beer.

Rice, pecans, soybeans and corn have overshadowed the native edible fruits grown in Southern Missouri in the 20th century. As we walk through the Tower Grove Park Farmers' Market, Peemoeller tells us, "Truth is on the price tag here...Cheap food is cheap because it's subsidized." I didn't see wild persimmons utilized in the farmers' market, granted they don't travel well, but to make this market lucrative to farmers, they need to follow the price tag. Peemoeller's work focuses on the question, "How will we feed ourselves in the future?" She studies the complex role of food in urban systems, and the size and business of this farmers' market speaks to how engagement with food is monumentally important in a city like St. Louis, surrounded by some of the most fertile agricultural land in the world. For rural farmers, farmers' markets are not an economic boon, but traveling to town to sell at a farmers' market is a way of selling direct to consumers, avoiding intermediary costs from packers and food agents. But for these often small family farms, the amount of work to pack and travel to a park that was once lush farming and hunting lands for the Osage is not the best possible sale option.

The unassuming marble block at the entrance to the park is only a small testament to what once was considered monumental in the creation of this city. Now, there is a creek and native plant garden that not only serves as a monument to the Osage, but to the scarcity of shade and greenery amidst this city, especially in the redlined neighborhoods north of the infamous Delmar Divide.

Daylighting is not only an effort of "rewilding," it's also an act of uncovering truth—usually that has been long hidden by those who wish to control a place or population. As Andrea Hunter, director of the Osage Tribal Nation Historic Preservation Office said, "We [the Osage] have a longtime history of being here and taking care of the landscape, taking care of the plants, the animals in the water, and that was a mission that we held in common with the Tower Grove Parks folks." Keeping in mind the ostentatious Victorian architecture of the park's gazebos and arcades, the park is beginning to return to a less European-idyll state, and asking questions like, "What kinds of plants are going to grow along this streambed?" and "How do we show the history of this land through natural processes?" I'm often discouraged by daylighting efforts that highlight symbolism over consideration of use. A monument is one thing, but how does that monument interact with the world around it? Is that interaction practical to those who have been oppressed or removed? Is it the job of city and park officials to shepherd land that isn't theirs? This stream shows an acknowledgement of land stewardship that is essential to the Osage—and Indigenous-lifeway.

Joe made this persimmon pudding in a dutch oven at our little KOA campsite outside of St. Louis. After heating the coals for an hour or so, he placed the dutch oven directly onto the fire, scooping coals from the fire and placing them on top of the oven. Cooking directly over a fire connects the cook with the alchemy of cooking. Anybody can turn on a stove or an oven, but the interplay of heat energy and knowledge of the ingredients speaks to a deep-seated, ancestral intuition. Persimmon pudding is one thing that can be easily made over an open flame, approaching the bruisable fruit with care as we consider how Indigenous and Black folk have used this fruit as a dessert or treat or ceremony. A fire is a memorial. For the Ojibwe, the fire is called grandfather, built in the center of a group to allow for stories and food on any cold night. We daylighted the hallowed grounds with the delicate art of dessert—in our case, persimmon pudding.

ENDNOTES

1 Lee Peemoeller, "About," Food Systems Planning, https://www.foodsystemsplanning.com/about/.

2 Tower Grove Park, "Our History," Tower Grove Park, November 9, 2023, https://www.towergrovepark.org/our-history-1.

3 Slow Food Foundation, "American Wild Persimmon—Arca del Gusto," Slow Food Foundation, last modified December 8, 2018, https://www.fondazioneslowfood.com/en/ark-of-taste-slow-food/american-persimmon-2/.

4 Myra Jean Perry, "Food Use of 'Wild' Plants by Cherokee Indians" (M.S. thesis, University of Tennessee, 1975), 38.

5 Frank Speck, Richard Hassrick, and Edmund Carpenter, "Rappahannock Herbals, Folk-Lore and Science of Cures," Proceedings of the Delaware County Institute of Science 10 (1942): 7–55.

6 Valerie Schremp Hahn, "A Stream Ran Underground in Tower Grove Park for 100 Years, Now It's Seen Again," St. Louis Post-Dispatch, November 3, 2022.

Photograph by Morgan Piper Cordova

Professor Joe Underhill's Prodigious Persimmon Puddin' Cake

This persimmon "pudding" looked more like bread, but cooked like a sheet cake. It wasn't pudding like you make from a package (milk, eggs, chocolate, etc.) but a moist cake.

We didn't have all the ingredients, so Joe winged it.

He took the flesh off the pits of the wild persimmon (they are mostly pits so this was a messy procedure). There wasn't much pulp. so Joe added some fig preserves that he had bought from a stand at Tower Grove Park Farmers' Market, along with eggs, sugar, melted butter, enough flour to make a very loose batter, and some baking powder & soda for leavening.

We cooked it in the oven until firm to the touch. When it springs back in the middle after being pushed down with your finger, it is finished. Joe says that the trick to cooking over the fire was getting the right amount of heat - not too much or too little. You need a good supply of hot coals, and a way to move them around so you can regulate the heat by piling coals on the lid of the dutch oven. It's a delicate process, he says, and he's still working on improving this technique while baking things at camp.

Thank you Joe!

Imagining Life-as-Place: Harm Reduction for the Soft Anthropocene by Sarah Lewison, page 182. Photo of "Lounging Through the Flood" (2019) by Jeremy Bolen and Jenny Kendler

HOW COULD WE TAKE BETTER CARE OF EACH OTHER THROUGH ATTENTION TO OUR REGIONAL SPECIFICITIES?

Significant and Insignificant Mounds

Jennifer Colten and Jesse Vogler

Mountains of waste and mounds of slag may be the enduring landscapes humans are building today. In the distant future will these be interpreted as monuments to the Anthropocene or traces of an unknowable civilization? East of St. Louis, Missouri, the Cahokia Mounds are the remains of arguably the most sophisticated pre-contact Indigenous civilization in North America which inspire Jennifer Colten and Jesse Vogler to consider how landscape radiates an overabundance of human meaning.

Mound [7009], 2018. Photograph by Jennifer Colten and Jesse Vogler

Once we would have looked to the natural ecology of place for meaning, and subsequently to systems of land division and settlement. However, it is in the landscape typology of the mound that the American Bottom most clearly enters the field of legibility. This region is celebrated quite rightly as the center of a vast civilization that had as its central architectural and urban expression the construction of mounds. Mound complexes from the well-known Cahokia Mounds to the lesser-known Pulcher and Grassy Lake sites remain the defining signifiers of a long and advanced era of North American settlement.

Yet the construction of mounds continues. Mound building if anything has even increased. While the civic and cosmic ordering that apparently animated so many of the Mississippian-era mound builders in this new era of mound building has been sidelined for the logistical and the proximate, our contemporary mounds index a way of being no less profoundly than the artifacts of the mound builders of prehistory. Slag heap, salt dome, aggregate piles, landfill, mulch mound—these are the forms of our cosmologies.

Which is to say, in landscape, it all matters. It all has meaning.

This is an itinerary of the Significant and Insignificant Mounds of the American Bottom.

Mound [9397], 2016. Photograph by Jennifer Colten and Jesse Vogler

It is oriented toward an intentional flattening of signification—where meaning mingles uneasily with form. It puts us in proximity to meaning, without being identical to it. The value judgments suggested in our title do not cut along easy lines. For, in the end, each of these mounds is, on its own terms, both significant and insignificant. They are all markers to a way of being, a way of seeing the world. Our interest in the pairing of text and image, and in the pairing of so-called meaning-filled and meaning-less subjects, is to bring the process of signification itself to the surface, in order to complicate the received value judgments that so often attend landscape photography and description.

The American Bottom is a particularly prolix landscape—with an archive of written description that stands in marked contrast to its relatively unknown status today. From the early notebooks of French Canadian explorer Louis Jolliet and those of the French American Jesuit missionary Father Marquette, to the French Jesuit monks who set up parishes in the region, through the Early Republic notebooks of both William and George Rogers Clark, and going forward, throughout the nineteenth-century expeditions—this is a landscape that has been cast within the net of language for centuries. Yet we are also keenly aware that it is only since European settlement that this landscape has been made to "speak." And it is here where our photographs put forward an

Mound [9182], 2018. Photograph by Jennifer Colten and Jesse Vogler

argument for artifacts as evidence—artifacts that index a way of being and which carry meaning and value across discursive registers. Indeed, it is through a measured approach of adesignation—the intentional misalignment of image and referent—that Significant and Insignificant Mounds frames an irreducible landscape form—subject to neither appropriative reverence nor declinist narratives.

Among the many voices coaxing this irreducible landscape into the order of language, we might look to Edmund Flagg for one of the earliest and most comprehensive descriptions. Writing from the edge of Monks Mound in 1837, Flagg gives voice to the mingling of cultural and natural landscapes that define the American Bottom:

> The view from the southern extremity of the mound, which is free from trees and underbrush, is extremely beautiful. Away to the south sweeps off the broad river-bottom, at this place about seven miles in width, its waving surface variegated by all the magnificent hues of the summer flora of the prairies. At intervals, from the deep herbage is flung back the flashing sheen of a silvery lake to the oblique sunlight; while dense groves of the crab-apple and other indigenous wild fruits are sprinkled about like islets in the verdant sea. To the left, at a distance of

Mound [1699], 2020. Photograph by Jennifer Colten and Jesse Vogler

Mound [9614], 2014. Photograph by Jennifer Colten and Jesse Vogler

three or four miles, stretches away the long line of bluffs, now presenting a surface marked and rounded by groups of mounds, and now wooded to their summits, while a glimpse at times may be caught of the humble farmhouses at their base. On the right meanders the Cantine Creek, which gives the name to the group of mounds, betraying at intervals its bright surface through the belt of forest by which it is margined. In this direction, far away in blue distance, rising through the mist and forest, may be caught a glimpse of the spires and cupolas of the city, glancing gayly in the rich summer sun. The base of the mound is circled upon every side by lesser elevations of every form and at various distances. Of these, some lie in the heart of the extensive maize-fields, which constitute the farm of the proprietor of the

> principal mound, presenting a beautiful exhibition of light and shade, shrouded as they are in the dark, twinkling leaves. The most remarkable are two standing directly opposite the southern extremity of the principal one, at a distance some hundred yards, in close proximity to each other and which never fail to arrest the eye. There are also several large square mounds covered with forests along the margin of the creek to the right, and groups are caught rising from the declivities of the distant bluffs.[1]

Today, standing atop the visitor-worn surface of Monks Mound, we might be more likely to take note of the hulking mass of Milam Landfill directly to the west, or the brown smoke-filled horizon of U.S. Steel to the north, or, until very recently, the twin stacks of the former Armour Meatpacking Plant of National City. Look hard enough, and we might be able to retrain our eye to see the meander scars and lowland forests that still define the creek margins of Flagg's description. Even though those creeks no longer flow, and canals and ditches over the past century have channelized them, the floodplain of the American Bottom retains traces of its lacustrine past. Similarly, the array of mounds, now sharply delimited by the lawn-mowing regime of the State Park maintenance staff, remind us that, despite the destruction of a large number of mounds in the period of industrial and infrastructural growth, markers to prior inhabitation remain numerous.

Yet the provenance of precontact mounds has not always been so unambiguous. Up until the early twentieth century, it was common enough to find in scholarly reviews and articles suggestions and arguments as to the natural origins of the mounds. It was as if the ideological barriers to accepting the creative and constructive capacity of pre-contact Native Americans was too great an intellectual burden for anthropologists to bear. As only one example, we might cite the paper given in Philadelphia at the 1914 Geological Society of America meeting by Dr. A. R. Crook, titled "Origin of Monks Mound," in which he writes: "It may be well to inquire if all so-called mounds in the Mississippi Valley are not natural topographic forms."[2] And where, eight years later, he recapitulates—in no less an authority than the celebrated journal *Science*—the position that a recent study "establishes, beyond doubt, that [Monks Mound] is not of artificial origin, as has been so generally held but that it is a remnant remaining after the erosion of the alluvial deposits, which at one time filled the valley of the Mississippi, in the locality known as the 'Great American Bottoms.'"[3] Windblown piles of loess; aggregated sediment from eddying currents of the river; or simply the remainder of even larger mounds eroded by the regular flooding of the Mississippi—the theories of the mounds' origins seem to more easily imagine a natural world full of creative agency than a native people's summoning of order and meaning.

Alternatively, alongside this topographic framing, a parallel narrative emerged further divesting the agency of contemporaneous Native American predecessors—the Mound-builder myth. In 1788, one no less influential than Noah Webster described the Ohio River Mounds as the work of "Carthaginians or other Mediterranean nations." With this, archaeologist John Kelly writes how "the beginnings of the 'Mound-builder' myth were carefully being sown in the fertile minds of the American Public."[4] This broader attitude can perhaps be understood as a symptom of the so-called Theory of Two Civilizations—the theory that, prior to exploration and inhabitation by Europeans in historic time, there must have been two distinct epochs of human habitation of the Continent. The inability of a European-settler consciousness to imagine and accept the mounds as a product of the indigenous peoples or their immediate forebears led not a few to posit an "Extinct Race"[5] of people who inhabited the territory and left these material traces of their civilization. For others, however, the mounds display little more than an innate animal consciousness. Lucien Carr, for example, was a significant figure in turn-of-the-century archaeology and assistant curator of the Peabody Museum of Archeology and Ethnology. He somewhat apologetically writes, "as a matter of fact, the ant hills of Africa, in point of relative size, and in the architectural knowledge and engineering skill displayed in their construction, are quite equal to any earth-work in the Ohio Valley."[6]

Mound [0814], 2015. Photograph by Jennifer Colten and Jesse Vogler

Where, then, is the threshold for mound-ness to be found? As an early geologist of the Mound groups of the American Bottom noted in 1922: "Practically all of the mounds which are large enough to attract attention have a distinct artificiality in their regularity of form and steepness of slope."[7] Which is to say, in the eye's catalog of forms, it is a particular angle of repose, a ratio of figuration, which enters a mound into the field of the remarkable. However, when compared to the complexes that enliven a kind of global pyramid consciousness, what distinguish the Cahokian Mound group are its blunt, earthen edges. Rather than the sharp stonework of the Temple of the Sun and Moon, Monks Mound is constructed entirely of dirt and is currently covered in a wooly sheet of grass and weeds. The mounds surrounding the main ceremonial center likewise are carpeted in turf and most distinctly enter the field of legibility immediately following their biweekly lawn mowing. It is in this bright line of demarcation, in the contour and mowing decision of the maintenance crew, that Cahokia reaches its architectural apotheosis.

What do we gain by following the piles, by attending to this base ordering of matter? It is my belief that there is a counter historiography that could be written, which traces the mound as the originary architectural gesture. A mark with meaning. An alternate tectonic myth grounded in the recognition of earth out-of-place. Adolf Loos, in recognizing the unadorned, psychological power of the mound, writes:

> "When walking through a wood, you find a rise in the ground, six foot long and three foot wide, heaped up in a rough pyramid shape, then you turn serious, and something inside you says: someone lies buried here. That is architecture."[8]

Architecture as a recognition of matter out-of-place; of matter in particular arrangement; of an affective register of arrangement. Although, as for every pile there is a pit, we would do well not to let the formal legibility of the mound distract us from the fundamental transactional economy in this (dis) ordering of matter. Lewis Mumford, that scion of urban meta-narratives, reminds us that the quarry pit is characteristic of the process of Abbau, or un-building: "What is taken out of the quarry or pithead cannot be replaced."[9] And so, with the borrow pits that form a ring around Cahokia Mounds State Park, the regular, rectangular water bodies that lie adjacent to highway construction, and the hundreds of mines and quarries that lie out of eyeshot, we must be attentive to the reordering of earth that gives us all of our mounds. In this, we can read the mound as a transitional object. As the becoming-city. For it is in the hundreds of unremarked piles of limestone, earth, mulch, and sand, and their parallel constellation of pits, that our roads, buildings, sidewalks, and parks are aggregated and extracted.

THERE IS A COUNTER HISTORIOGRAPHY THAT COULD BE WRITTEN, WHICH TRACES THE MOUND AS THE ORIGINARY ARCHITECTURAL GESTURE.

But perhaps our mounds are no less enigmatic. After all, who, really, can account for the otherworldly, colorful mound sitting across the river just south of the Gateway Arch? That reliable sources tell me it is a heap of residue left over after the cleaning of coal does not explain the range of reds, browns, blues, and yellows that marble its surface—let alone begin to answer what it is doing in the floodable part of the floodplain. I have revisited this mound dozens of times, and each visit reveals a new silhouette, a new stratum, a new rent carved by the most recent rain or flood.

I know all the constituent parts of this mound—the Fe, the C, the O, the N, the Pb—but I will never understand this mound.

It eludes me in its significance.

A version of this article was originally published on the website Anthropocene Curriculum (Summer 2019).

ENDNOTES

1 Edmund Flagg, *The Far West; or, A Tour Beyond the Mountains: Embracing Outlines of Western Life and Scenery; Sketches of the Prairies Rivers, Ancient Mounds, Early Settlements of the French, Etc.* 1 (Harper & Brothers, 1838), 166–67.

2 A. R. Crook, "Origin of Monks Mound," paper presented at the Geological Society of America, Philadelphia, 1914.

3 A. R. Crook, "Cahokia or Monks Mound Not of Artificial Origin," *Science* 40, no. 1026 (1922): 312.

4 John E. Kelly, "The Grassy Lake Site: An Historical and Archeological Overview," in *Mounds, Modoc, and Mesoamerica: Papers in Honor of Melvin L. Fowler*, ed. Steve R. Ahler, Illinois State Museum Scientific Papers 28 (n.d.), 469–510.

5 Ephraim G. Squier and Edwin H. Davis, *Monuments of the Mississippi Valley* (Smithsonian Classics of Anthropology, 1988).

6 Lucien Carr, *The Mounds of the Mississippi Valley, Historically Considered* (Yeoman Press, 1883).

7 Morris M. Leighton, "The Cahokia Mounds: Part II: Some Geological Aspects," *University of Illinois Bulletin* (October 1923).

8 Adolf Loos, "Architecture," *Der Andere* (1909), quoted in Joseph Rykwert, *On Adam's House in Paradise: The Idea of the Primitive Hut in Architectural History* (The Museum of Modern Art, 1972).

9 Lewis Mumford, *The City in History: Its Origins, Its Transformations, and Its Prospects* (Harcourt Brace International, 1968).

Inheritance: A Guided Meditation with Coal Miners and Paleontologists

with KAYLA ANDERSON, SARA BLACK, AMBER GINSBURG, SARAH LEWISON, and CLAIRE PENTECOST

Beneath the rolling hills of Southern Illinois lies a fossilized forest concealed within the heart of the Illinois Basin coal seam. It stretches over one hundred miles along both sides of an ancient river as wide as the Mississippi. This fossil forest was formed by the inundation and compression of multitudes of giant fern-like trees (Arborescent Lycopods) which anchored their roots along the banks of that river over 300 million years ago.

While it took millions of years to sequester the carbon of these trees into the form of coal, it has taken a mere 200 years to extract the carbon that fuels the lifestyle that defines our inheritance. Coal miners are the front line. They are witness to the remnants of the fossil forest that remains hidden to those above ground. They are also the first to experience the costs of the industry.

Inheritance was an art exhibit, part of Confluence Ecologies, held at the Southern Illinois University Museum. Stepping through a curtain, viewers entered complete darkness to hear the voices of miners and paleogeologists describing their encounters with the fossilized forest while laboring in the mines. Here are excerpts of this recording:

...

DURING THIS MEDITATION, YOU WILL HEAR MY VOICE AND THE VOICES OF OTHERS, CONNECTING YOUR BREATH TO DEEP TIME.

IF YOU CAN, FIND A PLACE WHERE YOU CAN SIT DIRECTLY ON GRASS OR SOIL. HOW DOES IT FEEL TO REST? TAKE A DEEP BREATH IN AND OUT.

SEND YOUR AWARENESS TO THE POINTS OF YOUR BODY THAT FEEL TENSION, STARTING AT THE TOP OF YOUR HEAD, SLOWLY TRAVELING DOWNWARDS.

IMAGINE EXTENDING YOUR FINGERS INTO THE EARTH.

SLOWER.

REALLY SLOW.

YOU HAVE ALL THE TIME IN THE WORLD. NOW EXTEND YOUR AWARENESS BACKWARDS IN TIME.

WHERE WERE YOU A YEAR AGO?

10 YEARS AGO?

MAYBE 15?

THIS IS HUMAN TIME. NOW FEEL YOUR BREATH.

IMAGINE EACH BREATH IS A MILLION YEARS. WE ARE MOVING PAST THE SCALE OF YOUR LIFETIME, PAST THE SCALE OF HUMAN CIVILIZATION.

BREATHE IN OUT IN OUT IN OUT IN

WE ARE GOING BACK 300 MILLION YEARS...

300 million. Well, what does that mean? How do you even come to terms with that?

WE ARE ENTERING

A TIME WITHOUT HUMANS.

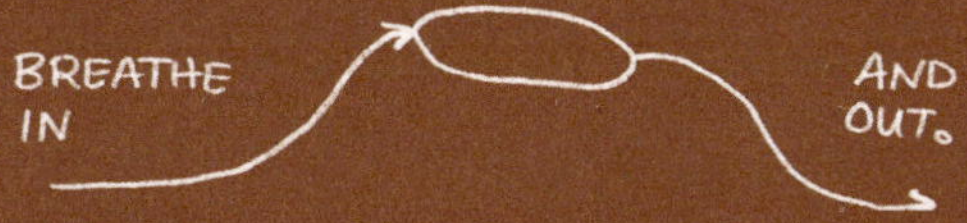

We were at the equator. And the landscape was extremely flat. We were fairly close to sea level.

First thing you would notice is that there weren't any large mammals, because mammals aren't around yet. There aren't really that many large animals to speak of. There are some large amphibians, and some rather large insects in the forests. But probably the biggest thing that you'd notice is that there were huge stands of these trees, called lycopod trees.

They have a very interesting bark pattern on the outside. Sometimes they're called scale trees, because they look like scales.

THE OXYGEN YOU EXPIRE IS FILLING THE ATMOSPHERE.

THERE'S A COOL SENSATION TICKLING YOUR FEET. SLOWLY, WATER BEGINS TO TRICKLE IN AROUND YOUR EDGES. AS THE WATER LEVEL RISES, SILT ENVELOPS YOU.

IT FITS PERFECTLY INTO THIS EMPTY SPACE AROUND YOUR BODY. IT FILLS IN ALL OF YOUR CREVICES.

YOU ARE BEING HELD BY THE EARTH AT THIS PRECISE MOMENT IN TIME.

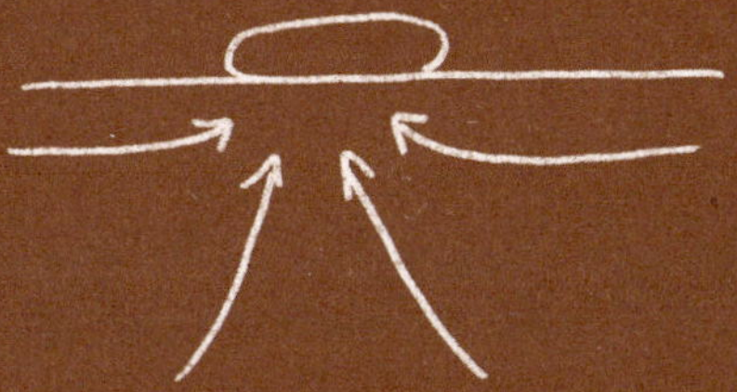

IT'S LIKE THIS FOR A FEW BREATHS.

ANOTHER FEW MILLION YEARS.

Key to taking organic material and preserving it in the rock record is that you have to protect it somehow from being eroded or oxidized away.

AND THAT MEANS YOU NEED TO BURY IT. TAKE A MOMENT TO FEEL YOUR EDGES.

NOTICE THE SPACE THAT YOUR BODY TAKES UP.

FEEL YOURSELF BEGIN TO COMPRESS. YOU'RE BECOMING SOLID, HEAVY, AS THE TIME MOVES ON AROUND YOU.

THE WATER IS RISING.

YOU START TO SINK.
ALLOW YOURSELF TO SLUMP A LITTLE.
IF YOU CAN, LAY DOWN HERE – YOU'RE SINKING INTO THE GROUND.

WITH EACH BREATH,
ALLOW YOURSELF TO SINK
A LITTLE DEEPER INTO THE EARTH.

The first trip down, we had a cage, which is the elevator. It's called the cage, and it had an expanded metal bottom, so you could see right through it.

WITH EACH BREATH, IMAGINE YOURSELF DROPPING DOWN EVEN FARTHER. YOU ARE MAKING YOUR DESCENT DEEP DOWN INTO THE EARTH.

BREATHE IN,

AND OUT...

That was a little disconcerting the first time when you realize that you're going down 400 feet. Roughly 50 people to a cage.

And I'm going to say roughly five minutes, and you're going down 1,000 feet over here at Inland II. Sometimes our ears would pop.

AS YOU SINK DOWN,
FEEL YOURSELF
GETTING HEAVIER.
YOU AND THE TREES
AROUND YOU
ARE
COMPRESSING.

FEEL YOUR BODY
BECOMING DENSE,
FLAT,

FORMING A HARD SEAM
THAT STRETCHES ACROSS
THE EARTH.

FEEL THE WEIGHT OF TIME
ABOVE YOU HOLDING YOU
FIRMLY IN PLACE. AS YOU
EXHALE, LET YOURSELF
FEEL
THAT
WEIGHT.

You have trees that are in the swamp, and as they age and die and fall over, they start collapsing in on themselves.

And as that collapses in, what you have is both sides of the actual bark or outer area gets collapsed all the way down. To flat, vitreous layers, you know, and that is how you get one tree upon another tree. Doing that, you get the stacking of the coal.

YOU ARE STILL
AND SHINY
AND HARD.

Here in this basin, it's all bituminous coal, and it has, you know, these vitreous layers, which are really the trees. That's the vitrein.

And it looks like glass. If you look at coal, you'll see real glassy-like layers, and then duller layers, and glassy-like layers, and duller layers. Well, that is the actual, you know, part of the tree that's been imploded and totally turned to carbon.

YOUR LEAF HAS LEFT
A STAMP IN THE SILT.

You know, again, being the first person to see it, it's just like, I don't know, it's weird. Shells and trees and leaves all laying in the same place, and we're just dirty coal miners, you know? We don't get to do anything exciting.

But, you know, I've laid my hands on things that nobody's ever seen.

Oh, yeah. Yeah, because, I mean, coal is nothing but fossils.

And I do remember walking around and going, oh, my gosh, this stuff is millions of years old. So you do have a sense of awe.

YOU'RE IN A PLACE OF
DEEP SLUMBER
LET THE DARKNESS BECOME
EXPANSIVE.

YOU ARE IN STASIS.

YOU ARE PART OF A VAST LAYER HELD IN TIME.

YOU ARE NOT ALONE IN THIS UNIVERSE UNDERGROUND,

IN THE IMPOSSIBLE COMPRESSION OF TIME...

YOU SHARE THIS SPACE-TIME UNDERWORLD

WITH AGENTS OF EXTRACTION.

YOUR BODY IS PART OF A LARGER BODY.

YOU CAN SENSE THINGS FAR AND WIDE. SIMPLY BY SENDING YOUR AWARENESS INTO THE GROUND BENEATH YOU.

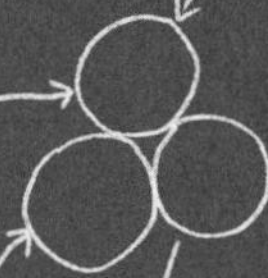

YOUR BODY IS FRACTURING.

YOU ARE IN PIECES.

CONTINUE TO BREATHE.

You would roof vault your way in, then they would set up along that 600-foot face. The face is what you call the active mining place. And you set this huge piece of equipment with all these hydraulic jacks, and you would mine under the jacks and slowly walk the jacks as you mined out the coal.

Walk the whole thing backwards till you get out to the main line again. If I'm on the return side of that miner when it first starts cutting and it does a blow through, there is this smell of coal. And it's like, when you smell it, you're like, oh, we're cutting coal now.

I mean, it's amazing. It's a certain smell too. That coal, I mean, when you actually get to the good bituminous coal, I mean, that stuff is the prime stuff that the power plant loves to eat.

AS YOU BREATHE, OTHERS BREATHE WITH YOU.

I've had a guy that had, I think he had a heart attack as soon as we got underground and I had to do CPR on the whole way out. That 25 minute ride out was a long ride out.

The vascular bundles in the cellulose, really tough. It doesn't really go away, the pith and the inner part.

But the actual live xylem and phloem in the vascular bundles in the trees, cellulose is incredibly tough.

It doesn't really go anywhere. So that's why you get the preservation because cellulose is very strong.

YOU ARE STILL HERE.

YOU'RE STRONG WHEN YOU'RE CONNECTED.

TOGETHER, YOU CONTRACT AND EXPAND WITH EACH BREATH.

Freeman Three shut down. Brushy Creek shut down. Kerr-McGee turned into American Coal. The union died.

I think the people that are working at American Coal now are making about the same amount of money I was making 30 years ago because they didn't have any unions around to raise wages. If you have a union around, they try to pay, non-union businesses try to pay union wages or close to it. But once the union in Illinois kind of got really, really weak, wages stopped rising.

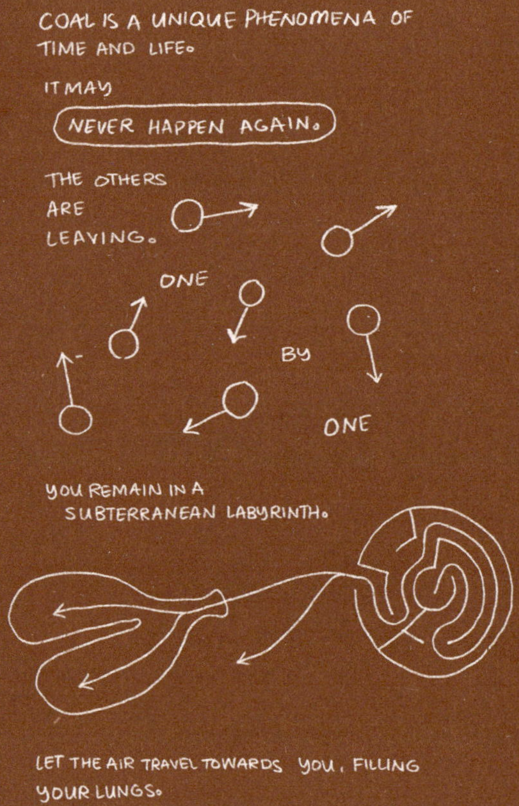

When you had a mine explosion, naively I thought it just blew up and that was it.

It doesn't.

It chases you.

You have your initial explosion and if you have methane and dust, the explosion will blow the methane and the coal dust up in the air. It might be too much methane to explode when initially it explodes and it pushes it and it could be in a higher concentration some on down the tunnel. But when it blows it, it makes it the perfect explosive range, five to 15%. So it blows up again and it travels up and down the tunnels.

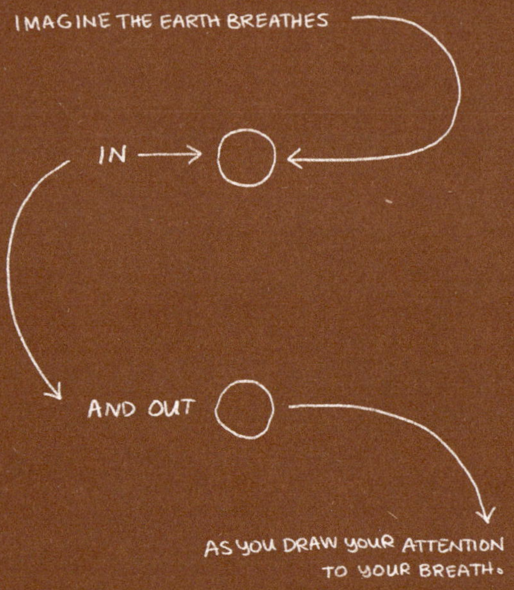

For a place over, it was over, it was like 7,000 by 7,000 square feet and it actually went down the return, up the belt line, out the travel way and followed all those tunnels, entries, until it basically killed everyone in there, blew them to bits. And the ones that were just on the edge of the explosion, that continuous, of it continuously propagating itself, they suffocated.

To make a long story short about 10 different lung tests and x-rays later, I do have black lung lightly. I have particles of it. But the doctor told me, he said, I'll be honest with you, I don't think you have a bad enough case to receive any benefits.

I fought it for two and a half years and I kept staying in the running. It was iffy all this way, all this way. So I tend to get bronchitis very easy.

And I think it's just torn my immune system down even further. So I do have a little black lung but not enough doing anything about it. But he said, you better hope it just stays a little and you have a good long life.

BREATHE IN DEEPLY.

FEEL YOUR LUNGS EXPANDING IN YOUR CHEST.

BREATHE OUT SLOWLY.

FEEL THE AIR TOUCHING YOUR SKIN.

BEGIN TO OPEN YOUR EYES.

SLOWLY LETTING LIGHT IN.

Since I'm getting this knee redone, I haven't put a regular garden out. My doctor, I've had my back fused and my doctor told me I could have a small garden. So anyway, I've just got four peppers and two tomatoes but I bought some beautiful wisteria plants and I put some of them out and built a couple of trellises for them.

Those are beautiful. Yeah, these are re-bloomers too.

YOU ARE A PRODUCT OF TIME.

But every once in a while, it dawns on you, it's like, I'm down here and this stuff is old and it was all alive once. Yeah. Yeah, it was a forest.

LET YOUR PALM BRUSH AGAINST THE GROUND BENEATH YOU.

START TO PULL YOURSELF UP FROM THE GROUND,

STACKING YOUR VERTABRAE,

ONE
ON
TOP
OF
ANOTHER.

YOU CAN DO THIS SLOWLY. YOU HAVE ALL THE TIME OF THE WORLD.

Data Flow

Tahani Nadim

Travelling down the Mississippi River by canoe, Tahani Nadim witnesses monocultural landscapes where humans have terraformed nature for extraction. From industrial agriculture to maize's datafication, humans translate biotic and abiotic life into governable units. However, nature cannot be subjected so easily to human control. Reflecting on a genome's transposable elements, or "jumping genes," Nadim discovers an apt metaphor for reckoning with the inhuman timescale of the Anthropocene.

How does it feel to flow? I think of frictionless, liquid movement, of moving onward without effort, my limbs melting into the surrounding momentum, my body fluently aligning with the bodies next to me as we are carried along. Flowing seems to be not so much an act as a state of being, a state that requires some surrender to another energy, like nature, collectivity, or gravity. Some things are compelled to flow, like blood, time, oxygen, rivers, tears. But while some things appear to flow naturally, flowing is never straightforward. Its ease rests on labors, past and present; its current contains fractures and frictions in the form of turbulences. Take the Mississippi River, for example. It flows in specific ways because of geological formations, weather events, and ongoing interventions by the U.S. Army Corps of Engineers, including dredging and damming, that have altered the river's basin. The flow continues among eddies and interventions, but all the time it changes, too.

I fell into this journey and went with the flow. I had wanted to write about maize—maize as a "model" organism for industrial agriculture as well as genomic sciences and, more generally, for data-intensive evidence practices. I think it makes for an opportune companion for thinking about this time that some are calling the Anthropocene, because maize has developed with people and lands, and these lands and people have developed with maize. Enormous swaths of land in the Midwestern United States along the Mississippi River have been reconfigured to accommodate the industrial production of maize. This region known as the Corn Belt comprises 150 million acres that are almost exclusively planted in a corn-soybean rotation. Depending on one's viewpoint, it can be a devastating sight. One of the world's most diverse plants reduced to a handful of varieties planted in monocultured row after row after row. Not much lives in these fields apart from the cultivated plant. Landscapes without insects, without nematodes, spiders, poppies, grasses, people.

Monocultured Corn Belt and seemingly endless landscape of maize "clean fields." Film by Tahani Nadim

Food activist and journalist Michael Pollan calls these landscapes "clean fields."[1] During my trips to view various parts of the Mississippi River Basin, at times all I could see out the window of the van was corn stretching all the way to the horizon. This sight could be read as "food security" and perhaps induce a sense of comfort. For the local farmers, it's equally existential. But it's not that they have a choice. The image of white smallholding farmers living and working the land in ecological harmony perpetuated by popular imagery and Big Agriculture belies the reality of an extractive and punishing industry that saps the life out of people and plants alike. Rising demand for food, fuel, and feed is forcing farmers to maximize productivity, which is increasingly tied to data: measuring and quantifying nutrients, seed viability, weather conditions, planting depth or disease history are meant to ensure the most precise and economic distribution of input, be it seeds, water, fertilizer or other chemicals. A flow of data guides a flow of matter that secures the flow of food.

SOME THINGS ARE COMPELLED TO FLOW, LIKE BLOOD, TIME, OXYGEN, RIVERS, TEARS.

My interest in maize stems from my fascination with the plant geneticist Barbara McClintock, or more precisely, from reading Evelyn Fox Keller's biography of McClintock, *A Feeling for the Organism*.[2] Keller, a feminist historian of biology, has pioneered a critical history of genetics in the twentieth century, attending to how social and cultural aspects have shaped (and in turn were shaped by) the "century of the gene." McClintock revolutionized genetics. She showed that there is more to the genome than just genes. Rather, she figured out, the genome contains so called transposable elements (TEs)—"jumping genes"—which make up 50 percent of the human genome, 75 percent of the maize genome, and 98 percent of the iris genome, to name just a few.[3]

TEs are vital for generating diversity, as their actions increase the frequency of mutations. Human geographer Kathryn Yusoff deems the jump to be a good model of movement for reckoning with the inhuman timescales of the Anthropocene.[4] Though genes are us, there is something equally inhuman about their scale. So jumping as an epistemic move works well in both directions—upstream and downstream, backward and forward. Jumping is flowing with turbulences. It lets me connect maize, the Mississippi, friends, and data.

McClintock figured all of this out by asking why the kernels of flint maize, also known as "Indian corn," are spotted. She planted maize in her experimental fields in Upstate New York near Cold Spring Harbor Laboratory and Cornell University, the two research institutions that would (barely) tolerate a woman scientist in the 1940s. Keller's account, which is partly based on interviews with McClintock, describes the systemic discrimination McClintock had to face every step of the way. She also documents her principled resolve and her extraordinary understanding and intimate connection with her plants, her "feeling for the organism." It took forty years for her research to be validated and recognized—because she was a woman, but also because no one could quite replicate her technique of "seeing" chromosomes, the entities in the cell nucleus that contain the genes.

Historian of science Bruno J. Strasser has argued that the corn genetics community that was established in the early twentieth century at Harvard University laid the foundation of what would become data-driven biology.[5] Its data practices, recoding practices, observing practices, collecting and archiving practices, as well as exchange of seeds and data created not only lasting protocols and infrastructures but data science. I like to think that the colorful kernels of flint corn are the beginning of big data. They are nonbinary, carrying many shades of color. I hadn't quite realized just how many until Michael Swierz, poet, translator and "participant ecologist," while clearing the back seat of his car to make room for journalist and author Fritz Habekuß, MPI research scholar Christoph Rosol, and me, handed me an enormous mason jar filled with flint corn kernels. It was beautiful—small pebbles of magnolias, violets, yellows, whites, and blues. At first, I didn't really know what I was looking at.

What would it mean to think about data through maize, to think about maize through data? For one, it'd make data more tangible and material, add a temporal, developmental dimension to its analysis. Concurrently, diffracting maize through data can render visible how variant forms of maize, like patented hybrids, are structured through heterogenous networks involving copyright and patent laws, international development policies, population statistics, and logistical standards. In my work as a sociologist and sociocultural anthropologist, I'm concerned with the datafication of nature and its social, political, and cultural ramifications. To me, the datafication of nature refers to a wide-ranging project that seeks to translate biotic and abiotic life into governable measures and values. It involves diverse practices, from digitizing natural-history specimens, to sequencing and barcoding environmental samples, to modeling vegetation types using remote sensing. Despite their obvious differences, all these practices represent attempts to abstract and reduce complex organisms and interactions into discrete data points. Yet, these processes are shot through with turbulences that don't reduce but displace complexity. In going on this journey to trace flows of data and maize along the Mississippi, I wanted to recover some of this complexity.

With the help of McClintock, maize initiated a radical shift in Western science in thinking about the relation between bodies and their environments. According to Darwinian evolutionary theory, adaptions (evolution) of organisms occur over extremely long periods of time and no rapid mutations happen in "nature." To be sure, this point has been a long-standing battleground in natural history as well as its successor sciences. The issue was settled when McClintock's work, which found the genome to be much more responsive than previously thought, became accepted. This motivated the development of epigenetics, which proved that environmental factors can lead to changes on the genetic level, thus returning scientific consensus to the previously discredited idea of inheritance of acquired traits. So, flint maize kernels changed the understanding of interaction between bodies and environments, making bodies coextensive with their environments.

What I like about the story of McClintock seeing chromosomes that transform into jumping genes that fuel data-driven genomics is what it says about data. Data are the product of embodied labors, sometimes far away, but never entirely absent. In my work, I'm concerned with recovering or figuring these labors that make data work, that make data global, and, possibly, that make data accountable. My colleague at the Museum für Naturkunde Berlin, Christian Bölling, recently stressed the importance of "metadata provenance" for ensuring responsible sharing and reuse of data as well as the longevity of the resource. Whereas metadata describe the properties of an object, such as its size, language, or title, provenance metadata relates to an object's creation and gestation: when it was made, modified, issued and who created it, contributed to it and retains the rights and ownership. This means that data models—the structures that determine the entities that data describes and how they relate—need to provide for data histories or,

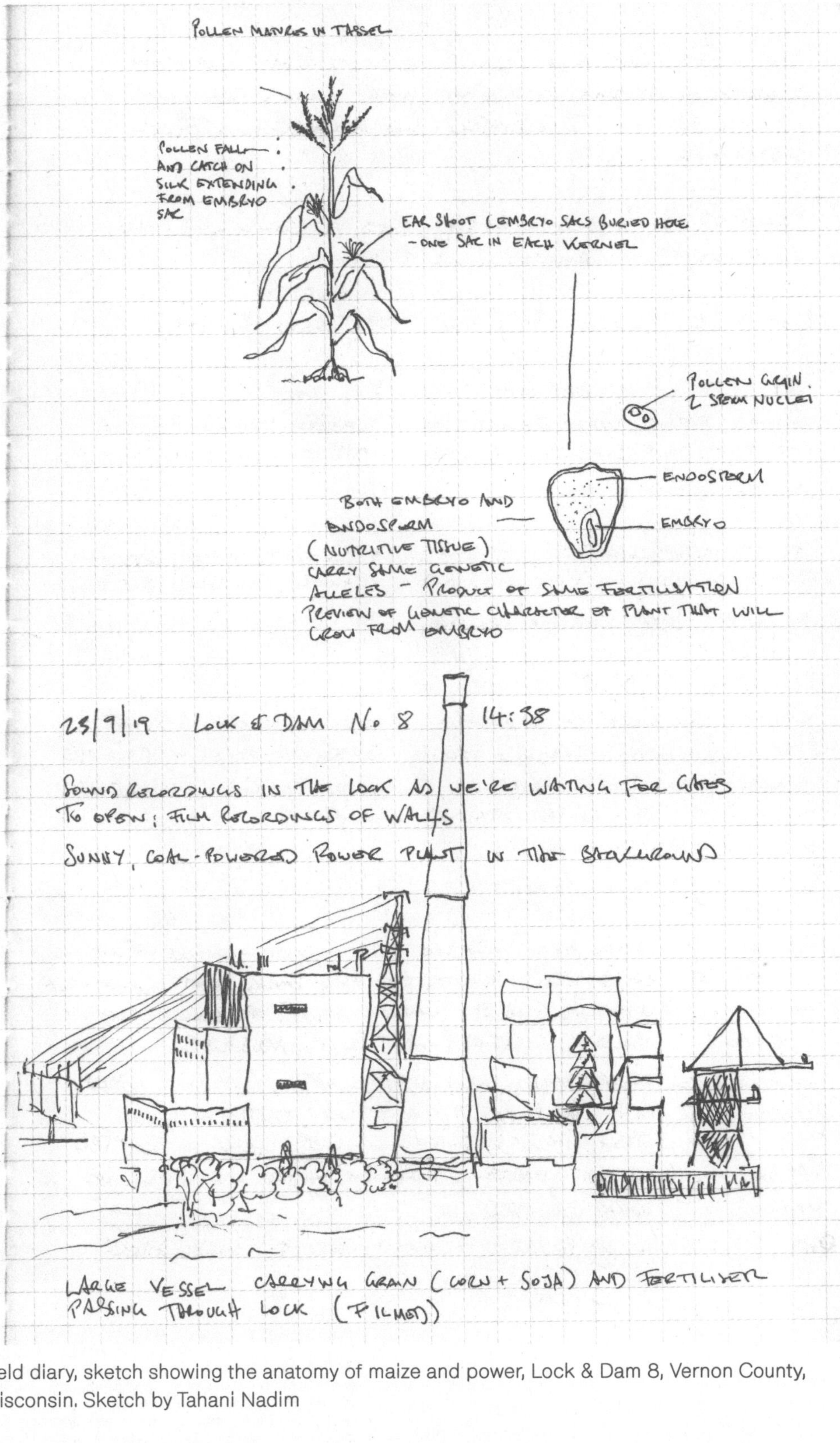

Field diary, sketch showing the anatomy of maize and power, Lock & Dam 8, Vernon County, Wisconsin. Sketch by Tahani Nadim

602

GUATEMALA
Dept. Huehuetenango

ZEA MAYS L. ssp. MEXICANA (Schrad.) Iltis
Huehuetenango Race.

Maize fields and abandoned old maize fields with la
populations of _Zea m. mexicana_ and many (ca. 5% or
more) F_1 hybrids, on steep slopes along road to
Jacaltenango, ca. 1.5-2.5 km. ENE of SAN ANTONIO HU
(Region of subtropical dry forest).
Alt. 1300-1400 m. (15°40';91°45')

Plant 4

Hugh H. Iltis G-120
Karen Lind Negative G-
Alejandro Barrios Jan. 9 1

ISOTYPE OF

Zea mays L. ssp. _parviglumis_ Iltis & Doebley
var. _huehuetenangensis_ Iltis & Doebley

more precisely, genealogies. If we, for example, digitize a herbarium sheet containing (parts of) a pressed and dried maize plant, then we include relevant metadata concerning not just the physical object—its scientific name, where and when it was collected, by whom—but also concerning the entities and processes that contributed to its creation as a resource and digital object. But, naturally, there will always be data missing because they were lost or deemed not relevant or because the interface didn't allow for their capture. Data provenance makes evident the many steps and protagonists involved in making data. It also points to the decisions behind systems and infrastructures, decisions that often manifest as gaps and absences.

Corn and soy constitute our planet's most important grain crops, used for human food, animal feed, and ethanol production (biofuel). Eating constitutes an interesting flow between bodies and environments, where mutual ingestions eat away at species boundaries. Eating, my colleague Filippo Bertoni writes, is an "ecological relationship."[6] On my journey along the Mississippi, which took me from Minneapolis to just south of St. Louis, we did many kinds of eating. We ate processed bread and processed cheese as part of a parking-lot picnic in front of a bleak supermarket in a desolate-looking part of Hannibal, Missouri. We learned later from Faye Dant, founder of Jim's Journey: The Huck Finn Freedom Center, that this had been a thriving African American community that was destroyed in the course of the racist "urban renewal" policies of the 1950s and '60s. Later that day back at our camp site, we ate a delicious hot pot cooked by our resident chefs and fellow River Travelers John Kim and Steven Diehl, made inside an enormous pumpkin procured by HKW's Neli Wagner from a petrol station somewhere near the Quad Cities. They stuffed the decorative Halloween pumpkin with mushrooms, pumpkin flesh, and cheese and placed it on a log fire, where we watched it blubber for hours. In Burlington, Illinois, we were treated to a collective feast by the members of the Aldo Leopold Foundation, who kindly and generously shared their delicious dishes with us. I ate mac and cheese for the first time.

As Bertoni writes, "eating does not occur alone," meaning that it always involves others, even if only distant and microscopic ones—the gut bacteria that help digestion and all the human and nonhuman participants of the food chain that deliver produce. Nowhere was the flow of relations that eating enacts as present as at the dinner that was

Maize plant collected on the steep slope along the road to Jacaltenango in the Western Highlands of Guatemala in 1976 and now residing in the Herbarium of the Royal Botanic Gardens, Kew in London. The Herbarium Catalogue, Royal Botanic Gardens, Kew, © The Board of Trustees of the RBG, Kew prepared and shared at the Black Hawk Museum and Lodge in Rock Island, Illinois. The women who cooked the food described how their dishes combined food traditions from the local First Nations and from Indigenous Peoples in Brazil who have been fighting to protect their lands and right to nourishment. Traces of maize have been found in the remains of ceramic vessels in Ecuador, Peru, Brazil, and the Caribbean, some dating back to 8000 BCE. Imagine the social relationships that have all this time been flowing through the sharing of food and drink.

In relation to food production, food security has come to be linked to ensuring a contiguous data flow with no gaps. Here, the provenance of foodstuff is secured through establishing traceability. This means issuing unique identifications to elements in the supply chain, from farm to storage location, suppliers, logistical units, and companies. I started thinking about traceability after fellow traveller, John Kim, mentioned its impact on small-scale organic farming. We were driving through the Driftless Area of Wisconsin, which is home to many organic farms, including the biggest producer in the U.S., Organic Valley. Traceability becomes an existential issue once it is seen as a prerequisite for entering markets or, indeed, for being considered "organic." One problem for small-scale operations is the time and effort spent on record-keeping and data management, which becomes all the more complex the greater the diversity of plants

EATING CONSTITUTES AN INTERESTING FLOW BETWEEN BODIES AND ENVIRONMENTS, WHERE MUTUAL INGESTIONS EAT AWAY AT SPECIES BOUNDARIES.

Observing maize; barges transporting maize along the Mississippi; lake sturgeon fingerlings at Genoa National Fish Hatchery in Wisconsin. Film by Tahani Nadim

a farm grows. I imagine that tracing and tracking heirloom varieties and seeds that have been kept and circulated in communities across generations is quite an impossible task. Yet, like all life, maize retains traces of its close and distant relatives in its genome:[7] of the wild grass (teosintes) in Mexico, Guatemala, Honduras, and Nicaragua; of rice, from which it diverged 50 million years ago; and of sorghum, with which it parted ways only 9 million years ago.

At the Genoa National Fish Hatchery in Wisconsin, we were able to bear witness to how traceability is being integrated into restoration efforts. Lake sturgeon populations in North America (some scientists estimate globally) have been declining due to overfishing and habitat destruction, and so the hatchery is producing sturgeon to restock the populations in lakes around the country.[8] We arrived on a sunny day and entered a low building crammed with big plastic vats, each teeming with thousands of lake sturgeon fingerlings. They were no bigger than twelve centimeters but they looked their age: somewhere between 208 and 245 million years old. At the back of the building, a school class had gathered around an assembly line of volunteers who were tagging each fish using coded wire micro-tags. This is done so that, once released into the wild, hatchery-reared fish can be distinguished from wild populations (for the calculation of survival rates and population trends) and to distinguish between different lots of fish. At Genoa, they tag about 60,000 to 80,000 fingerlings per summer.

The spectacle upset me. The ancientness of the sturgeon, so present and visible in its astonishing body, was affecting, especially in contrast to the plastic-based hubris of the breeding program. Like maize, sturgeons

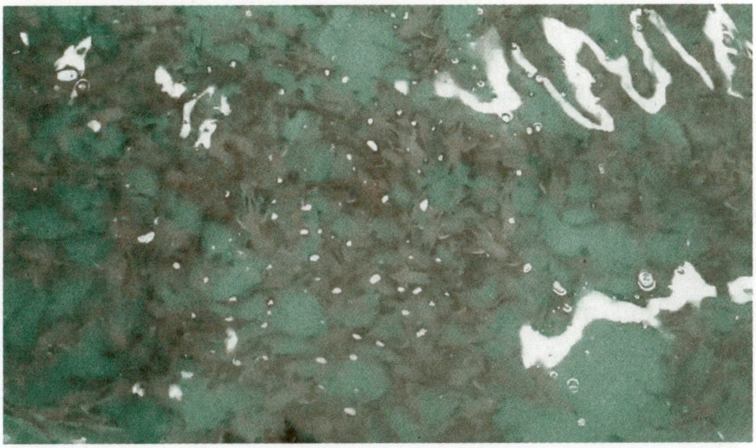

have come a long way. In fact, they are almost 200 million years older than corn. Like all living organisms, they are "of all times."[9] It's just that, with sturgeon, you can really *see* this. I've joined fellow paddlers Audrey Buturian Larson and Steven Diehl in the sun outside the shed where the lake sturgeons are being tagged. We are in a somber mood, somewhat upset by the goings-on in the building behind us. A long conversation spins out that weaves our discomfort about the industrial hatching of fish in the name of conservation with our dismay at the "industrial production" of students that sees them reduced to standardized assets on the balance sheets of corporate education. To our minds, fish and human bodies become abstract, commodified objects in the calculative logic geared toward the optimization of stocks.

Field diary, looking across the Mississippi River from our camp site on 24 September 2019. Sketch by Tahani Nadim

A couple of days later, we amble around the John Deere Pavilion in Moline, Illinois. A large display is making the moral case for John Deere-powered industrial agriculture by bellowing exploding population statistics. Large percentages are printed all over the wall, an LED ticker provides the current number of humans on Earth, and a see-through plastic box is fed with a steady trickle of maize kernels. Each emits a click as it lands in an already vast sea of kernels, reminding visitors that another hundred, another thousand, another ten thousand humans have joined the planet, threatening its limited resources. KERNEL PANIC!

The data that are imagined to reside in maize are vast indeed. With its turn to big data, Big Ag has set its sights on data as a new cash crop. The movement of crops, from farms to silos, barges, and processing plants to plates and troughs is nowadays accompanied by a thick data flow that is feeding more and more distributaries. Farm machinery is equipped with sensors that continuously send soil, land, and weather data and numbers on fertilizer use and water levels. These data can be aggregated to set crop prices or predict insurance claims or develop fertilizer. They can also be combined with data on land registration and credit use to drive the dispossession and privatization of common lands. Geographer Alistair Fraser argues that data-based precision agriculture changes the production of food, altering agrarian relations—our relations, really, since we are never not inside the flow.[10] This is hard to see, although I was looking out for it from the canoe, from the window of the van, from the airplane flying over the Corn Belt. It remains a challenge, to see (the work of) data, to see organisms and (in) human history.

THE DATA THAT ARE IMAGINED TO RESIDE IN MAIZE ARE VAST INDEED. WITH ITS TURN TO BIG DATA, BIG AG HAS SET ITS SIGHTS ON DATA AS A NEW CASH CROP.

Data keep flowing from and through maize. And as they move, infrastructures emerge, equipment and humans transform, lands change—and so does maize, because the plant is engineered in response to the models that are predicted out of data streams. Many labors remain. Stories, too. They're right there, in the code, even though splicing and cutting have left their marks. But the ghosts of teosintes, of Cahokia, of the Mississippi River, and of the sturgeons are patient. They are waiting for their moment to jump. McClintock has told us already.

To maintain matters in a state of flow.

A version of this article was originally published on the website Anthropocene Curriculum (Summer 2020).

ENDNOTES

1 Michael Pollan, "Playing God in the Garden," *The New York Times Magazine*, October 26, 1998, https://www.nytimes.com/1998/10/25/magazine/playing-god-in-the-garden.html.

2 Evelyn Fox Keller, *A Feeling for the Organism: The Life and Work of Barbara McClintock* (W. H. Freeman, 1983).

3 See, for example, Barbara McClintock, "The Origin and Behavior of Mutable Loci in Maize," *Proceedings of the National Academy of Sciences* 36, no. 6 (June 1950): 344–55, https://doi.org/10.1073/pnas.36.6.344.

4 Kathryn Yusoff, "Geologic Subjects: Nonhuman Origins, Geomorphic Aesthetics and the Art of Becoming Inhuman," *Cultural Geographies* 22, no. 3 (2015): 383–407, https://doi.org/10.1177/1474474014545301.

5 Bruno Strasser, *Collecting Experiments: Making Big Data Biology* (University of Chicago Press, 2019).

6 Filippo Bertoni, "Soil and Worm: On Eating as Relating," *Science as Culture* 22, no. 1 (March 2013): 61–85, https://doi.org/10.1080/09505431.2013.776365.

7 Susan Bostwick et al., "Lost Crops Conversation," Anthropocene Curriculum, accessed October 10, 2025, https://www.anthropocene-curriculum.org/contribution/lost-crops-conversation.

8 Tim Haxton and Mike Friday, "Are We Overestimating Recovery of Sturgeon Populations Using Mark/Recapture Surveys?" *Journal of Applied Ichthyology* (2018), https://doi.org/10.1111/jai.13795.

9 Michel Serres, "The Origin of Language: Biology, Information Theory, and Thermodynamics," in *Hermes: Literature, Science, Philosophy*, ed. Josué V. Harari und David F. Bell (Johns Hopkins University Press, 1982), 75.

10 Alistair Fraser, "Land Grab/Data Grab: Precision Agriculture and Its New Horizons," *Journal of Peasant Studies* 46, no. 5 (2019): 893–912, https://doi.org/10.1080/03066150.2017.1415887.

Lower Mississippi

The Lower Mississippi River is roughly the portion of the Mississippi River downstream of Cairo, Illinois. Major tributaries include the White, Arkansas, Yazoo, and Red Rivers. Along this vast midsection of the Mississippi's meander, a constellation of people work on issues of race, ecology, and place.

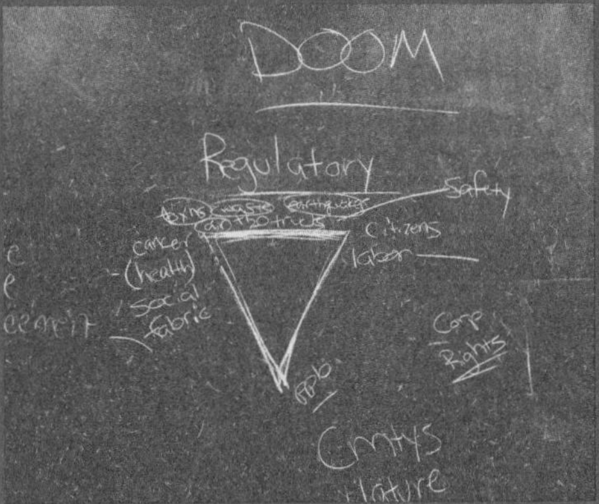

Imagining Life-as-Place: Harm Reduction for the Soft Anthropocene

Sarah Lewison

Sarah Lewison diagnoses the need to exercise control and mastery over other than human worlds as a historic trauma in our relationship with nature. Lewison defends the concept of the "bioregional" as key to unlocking a therapeutic process of healing this social and ecological rupture through the application of creativity, compassion, and direct action.

Bison and Stars reinhabitation ceremony with Jim Rock at the Waḳaŋ Ṭipi site in St. Paul, Minnesota, 2023. Photograph by Sarah Lewison

During the summer of 2023, at a conference of the Mississippi River Open School, an experimental learning group I belong to, the brilliant Dakota astronomer Jim Rock invited us to enact a performance of reinhabitation. We met near the site of Waḳaŋ Ṭipi Cave in St. Paul, Minnesota, a place sacred to the Dakota people. Upon gathering, each participant in our group was asked to name and express gratitude toward a river or body of water that connected to their lives in a meaningful way. Rock then invited us to join him in honoring the bison people, Tataŋka Oyate, from whom he is descended. To do so, he guided us in a somatic understanding of the Dakota Sky-Earth mirror symbol through a ceremonial personification of a bison.[1] Under his instruction, we become bearers of stars and bison, connecting land and sky through embodied actions that made our connections and responsibilities to each other and the lands and waters we live with apparent. Through his storytelling, Rock drew us into an awareness of being part of something bigger than our individual selves, melting away our modern alienation. He effectively showed us how we twenty-first-century technological humans might reinhabit the earthbound place where we live with a sense of care, attention, and belonging. Rock transported us by bringing together our individual histories and our bodies in movement with ancient stories from the Dakoka people. Although many of us were not part of the rich Indigenous cosmologies that Rock exposed us to, he briefly composed a connection for us. This transporting experience has led me to think about the incremental nature of healing and to wonder about pathways for addressing our anthropocenic human loss of place.

In this essay I meditate on society's separation from nature as a key underlying characteristic of the Anthropocene. I suggest here that alongside a physical, or "hard" Anthropocene of human-made infrastructures, objects, and practices, is a "soft" Anthropocene of the consciousness which normalizes human overreach of the planet's capacity and its subsequent impact. In this thought experiment,

I pursue the perspectives of two distinct modalities for fostering the transformation of human consciousness in relation to the environment. I compare some principles from harm reduction, which aspires to balance the psychosocial ecosystem of an individual, to the affective language of bioregionalism, an eco-cultural movement intended to reintegrate humans within a territorial ecosystem.[2] I begin by defining both harm reduction and bioregionalism, before introducing the latter's creative and interventionist approach toward opening new pathways of imagination regarding placemaking. I compare the analytical practices of harm reduction with those of a bioregionalist understanding of place to frame ways of helping humans cope and heal from trauma and to highlight the role of creativity, compassion, and direct action in addressing social and ecological disconnection. Finally, I'll share some of my own interpretations of bioregional pedagogies that align with harm reduction's analytical frameworks. In so doing, I conjure harm reduction as a provocation for conducting ecological healing in the human social terrain of the Anthropocene.

Still captured from "Naxilandia," a feature documentary about rural development in Yunnan, China.

THE MATERIAL ANTHROPOCENE AND THE ANTHROPOCENE OF THE MIND

The Anthropocene is so called to mark the pervasive material ways humans have altered our planet. As a complex of cascading impacts by human technologies upon Earth and its atmosphere, the Anthropocene works through layered violences of colonization and systematic subjugation, a globalized and totalizing agent of trauma and addiction. The Anthropocene operates on embodied agents, human and beyond-human, changing consistencies and possibilities, not unlike substance addiction and unwanted pregnancies. Anchored in the principle of turning life into property, and then producing profit off this property, anthropocenic techne also harms human people by alienating them from the planet as the place which sustains their lives. This happens without our awareness. It could be considered that our everyday fossil-fueled human existence in the developed world both speeds up experience and changes our sense of time to an extent that it becomes hard to find out how we feel and where we are. As Jim Rock reminded us at the Wakaŋ Ṭípi site, our connections to place, environment, and to our own social histories need to be actively recalled. It could be said that we become addicted to the accelerations that capitalism and fossil-fueled markets expose us to; witness the difficulty people have in turning away from their screens

AS A COMPLEX OF CASCADING IMPACTS BY HUMAN TECHNOLOGIES UPON EARTH AND ITS ATMOSPHERE, THE ANTHROPOCENE WORKS THROUGH LAYERED VIOLENCES OF COLONIZATION & SYSTEMIC SUBJUGATION, A GLOBALIZED & TOTALIZING AGENT OF TRAUMA AND ADDICTION.

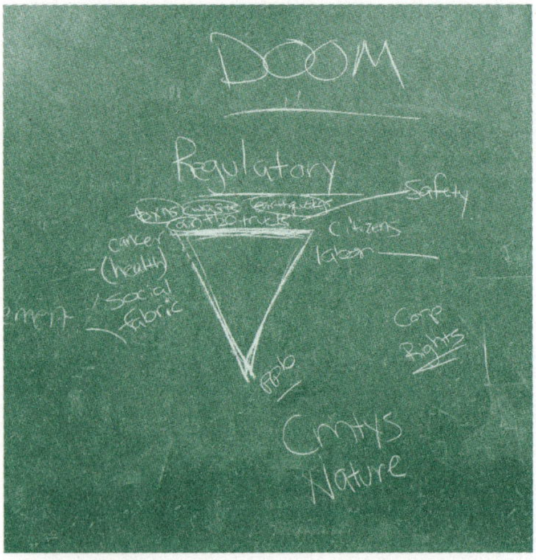

Doom Diagram: diagramming corporate capture on the chalkboard. From the 2017 Media and the Environment class "Storytelling in the Anthropocene" at Southern Illinois University, Carbondale.

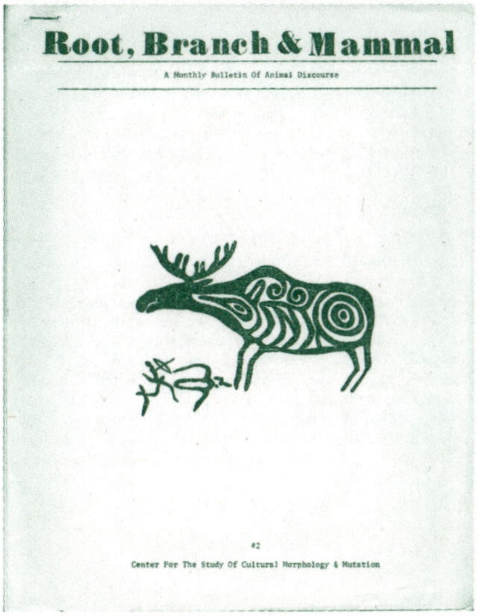

"Root, Branch & Mammal" by the Center For The Study Of Cultural Morphology and Mutation.

and devices. I propose that this addictive behavior alienates us from connecting to an environment, and all the more so, from the capacity to even imagine alternative futures for ourselves within an environment.

UNDOING HARM THROUGH THE DEVOLUTION OF POWER

Harm reduction is an activist approach to public health that mitigates the negative consequences of substance addiction and disease transmission by giving people the material and psychological assistance they need without judgement.[3] Harm reduction can also be seen as an interpretive device which enlists attention, acceptance, and dialogue to clear pathways for change in complex circumstances.

Harm reduction takes different forms. It is tailored to local human-social ecologies to effect a drawing down of trauma-coping behaviors that have destructive or negative outcomes. It may mean providing condoms to high school students or clean syringes to substance-addicted people. According to the National Harm Reduction Coalition, the approach offers dignity for vulnerable people coping with extremes of injustice, deprivation, and grief, allowing time for healing without stigma. Harm reduction in the United States draws its transformative inspiration from earlier models of public health activism, such as the Young Lords' provision of acupuncture to treat addiction in New York City in the 1970s.[4]

I am most interested in how harm reduction strategies respond to the human-centered ecological specificities of a place. As an example, clean needles for substance-dependent people are distributed in the neighborhoods where people buy and use. Although such actions might be imitated as models elsewhere, they are devised and conducted on a local level by community volunteers with insight into that location. It is an activist approach that devolves power wherein amateur practitioners step in with safety measures not otherwise available. Sometimes harm reduction activists operate outside of the law (as with needle provision), autonomously addressing a lack of policy. Thus, harm reduction becomes an interpretive and analytical tool for understanding healing and struggle in an ecosocial context.

BIOREGIONS AS A BASIS OF COMMUNITY

Bioregionalism may be familiar to some as an eco-cultural movement that arose in the 1970s to address the ecological and psychological damage of human disconnection from ecological place.[5] The 1970s artists, writers, ecologists, activists, and poets who conceptualized bioregionalism were already addressing capitalism, violence, and commodification in the urban sphere, concerns which were incorporated into their environmental turn. A bioregion was defined as "a distinct area with coherent and interconnected plant and animal communities, and natural systems, often defined by a watershed, a whole 'life-place' with unique requirements for human inhabitation so that it will not be disrupted and injured."[6]

In contrast to mainstream environmental approaches that are premised upon a nature outside of humans to be identified, repaired, replenished, or conserved, bioregionalism sees humans as integral to an ecobiotic mesh. Bioregional writers used concepts and metaphors promoting the idea of humans as a species among other species within specific places, offering practical, affective,

Diggers distributing free food, courtesy of the Digger Archives

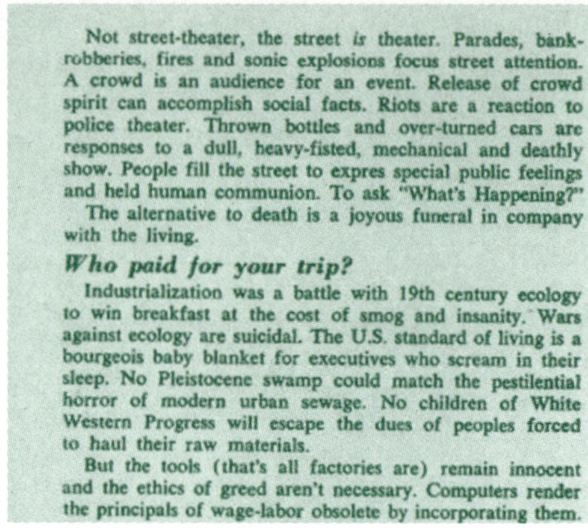

Not street-theater, the street *is* theater. Parades, bank-robberies, fires and sonic explosions focus street attention. A crowd is an audience for an event. Release of crowd spirit can accomplish social facts. Riots are a reaction to police theater. Thrown bottles and over-turned cars are responses to a dull, heavy-fisted, mechanical and deathly show. People fill the street to expres special public feelings and held human communion. To ask "What's Happening?"

The alternative to death is a joyous funeral in company with the living.

Who paid for your trip?

Industrialization was a battle with 19th century ecology to win breakfast at the cost of smog and insanity. Wars against ecology are suicidal. The U.S. standard of living is a bourgeois baby blanket for executives who scream in their sleep. No Pleistocene swamp could match the pestilential horror of modern urban sewage. No children of White Western Progress will escape the dues of peoples forced to haul their raw materials.

But the tools (that's all factories are) remain innocent and the ethics of greed aren't necessary. Computers render the principals of wage-labor obsolete by incorporating them.

"Trip Without a Ticket" by Peter Berg, courtesy of the Digger Archives

and somatic experiments in repairing the rift between humans and beyond-human ecosystems.

This essay mostly highlights concepts developed by California-based writer and environmental activist Peter Berg. His ideas, however, were forged in dialogue with many other writers, activists, scientists, and artists, including well-known ecological poet Gary Snyder, conservation biologist Raymond Dassmann, and writers Stephanie Mills and Kirkpatrick Sale. The use of the word bioregion to define a territory by qualities other than human distinctions was coined by surrealist poet and publisher Allen Van Newkirk in his independent journal *Root, Branch and Mammal*.[7] Newkirk sought "models guided by less arbitrary scales of human activity—in relation to the biological realities of the natural landscape."[8] Adopting Newkirk's term, Snyder, Dasmann, and Berg added humans back into the conception of a bioregion, investing them with a responsibility "both to geographical terrain and a terrain of consciousness—to a place and ideas that have developed about how to live in that place."[9] In a 1976 talk given at the University of California, Berkeley, Raymond Dassman described peoples who "lived in communities that were dependent upon and in harmony with their local ecosystems as 'ecosystems people,' who 'did not consider themselves apart from nature.'"[10] Stressing the concomitant destruction of Indigenous people and their cultures with the destruction of the natural world, he called for an end to "dependence on the exploitation of other people, places, and living communities."[11]

Peter Berg's environmental insights evolved in the rich matrix of creativity, resistance, and activism of 1960s-era San Francisco where he was a performer and writer with The San Francisco Mime Troup, an alternative theater project which held performances in the city parks. San Francisco in the 1960s swelled with youth seeking alternatives to mainstream U.S. culture, and Berg and a small crew of artists started to use everyday spaces of the city for provocations that reframed social relations outside of the commodity. Calling themselves Diggers after the seventeenth-century radical protestants who planted on the enclosed land of wealthy estates to meet their subsistence needs, the San Francisco activists took the practice of liberating property into a twentieth-century context with free concerts, festivals, housing, and food.[12] They distributed pamphlets extolling a philosophy of abundance, and used guerrilla theater to interrupt traffic and business-as-usual on San Francisco's Haight Street.[13] Berg wrote prolifically about the consequences of converting life into property, elevating the liberatory, communitarian, and libidinal potential of human relationship and existence once freed from service to the abstraction of an economy:

> First free the space, goods and services. Let theories of economics follow social facts. Once a free store is assumed, human wanting and giving, needing and taking, become wide open to improvisation.

Death of a Hippie Procession, courtesy of the Digger Archives

Image from "Reinhabiting a Separate Country" (1978) by Judi Quick, courtesy of the Planet Drum Foundation

> A sign: If Someone Asks to See the Manager Tell Him He's the Manager.
>
> Someone asked how much a book cost. How much did he think it was worth? 75 cents. The money was taken and held out for anyone. "Who wants 75 cents?" A girl who had just walked in came over and took it.[14]

Berg's broadsides and essays were poetic provocations to resist the commodification of consciousness, or what I am calling a Soft Anthropocene that works upon people's desires, perceptions, and expectations. His polemics called out the alienating effects of putting a price on everything and offered propositions for positively transforming relations between people and environment.

In 1973, Berg and his partner, dancer Judy Goldhaft, founded the Planet Drum Foundation as a forum for imagining codependence between people and the biosphere through the bioregion concept. Publishing was, and continues to be, central to this project, beginning with a series of letterpress broadsides focused on and authored by people in specific bioregions, with titles such as "The Pacific Rim Alive." These were distributed as bundles by mail to subscribers.[15] The basis of a bioregion was not prescriptive. It was, on the contrary, up for participatory debate based on group studies of geographical features, cultural motifs, historic dwelling patterns, economies, and practices. Eschewing colonizing and extractive patterns such as homesteading, where people bring foreign cultures and building styles to reproduce an image of a former homeland, the goal of bioregionalism was to consider how to contribute to the biodiversity of place. Bioregionalism wrapped together environmental philosophy, social critique, and evolving practice. The core idea of "living-in-place" would thus always look different, a coevolution of biodiverse habitation. The introduction from Planet Drum Foundation's collection of essays, art, research, and maps titled *Reinhabiting a Separate Country* set out the motifs for what Berg called living-in-place, or reinhabitation:

> Reinhabitation means developing bioregional identity. It means learning to live-in-place in an area that has been disrupted and injured through past exploitation. It involves becoming native to a place through becoming aware of the particular ecological relationships that operate within it. Simply stated, it involves becoming fully alive in and with such a place. It involves applying for membership of a biotic community and ceasing to be its exploiter.[16]

Reinhabiting a Separate Country featured regional authors from scientists, poets, naturalists, and storytellers reflecting on a "natural country" formed by the geographic boundaries and ecological uniquenesses of Northern California. These specificities extend beyond physical features to encompass social and economic customs, including those of the Indigenous humans and beyond-human denizens.

REINHABITORY THEATER

To reinhabit is to begin with the premise that you, a human, are a species among

Image from "Reinhabiting a Separate Country" (1978) by Eric Weber, courtesy of the Planet Drum Foundation

many other species. Reinhabitation is an incitement to cultivate sensitivity, creativity, dialogue, observation, and study as a way to care for an inclusive community. Community membership is defined by the inhabitants in the region; reinhabitation asks, "how will all members live better in this place?" Reinhabitation counters the force of the Soft Anthropocene we carry within, that lets us hallucinate a separation between humans and nature or territory. Demolishing dams, for example, is a practical act that reclaims the river for the good of the salmon. The destruction of dams, however, must be preceded by the potential of humans to imagine the needs of salmon. Reinhabitation can include more conventional practices of conservation or restoration but also exceeds these approaches by queering relationships to place and the other inhabitants. The human is encouraged to imagine themselves within an ecological matrix, to learn who else lives there, and to ask questions about how to share the abundance of that place with all species within a territory. What is the spirit that drives people to make paintings in caves? What would that look like today? What are appropriate technologies? What do the animals want? Questions like these gave rise to research on animal behavior and ecosystems. Sparked by her dance background, Judy Goldhaft studied ways of miming animals to create an emergent kind of ecological theater. Working alongside Berg, they incorporated ideas from Indigenous stories to illustrate reinhabitation as dialogue and physical play. Joined by other actors to form the Reinhabitory Theater as a performing troupe, players imagined and invoked the territories and behaviors of beyond-human dwellers while also modeling ways for humans to share space with beyond-humans within a territorial boundary.[17]

REINHABITATION CAN INCLUDE MORE CONVENTIONAL PRACTICES OF CONSERVATION OR RESTORATION BUT ALSO EXCEEDS THESE APPROACHES BY QUEERING RELATIONSHIPS TO PLACE AND THE OTHER INHABITANTS.

FIGURES OF REGULATION

Coexistence is not an easy proposition in our society! How can humans develop self-regulation through nonauthoritarian and non-proscriptive constraints? In his essay "Figures of Regulation: Guides for Rebalancing Society with the Biosphere," Berg enlists the dialogic imagination to concoct what he alludes to as a dance with place.[18] He hypothesizes what he called "the new equivalents to customs that we need to learn."[19] Regulation, he explains, can be understood biologically in terms of resource distribution, while the figure is a tentative iconic or symbolic move rather than a hardline rule—something to be tested incrementally as if it was a game. In proposing a figure as a unit of action to be executed in a serial, dialectic and experimental fashion, he breaks systems-within-place into fragments to be articulated and tested variously as a kind of analog cybernetic system. His examples include the drawing and redrawing of lines, dance steps, and other series of movements that respond to force, friction, or wobble, the physical means by which one organism performs a regulatory effect upon another by the impact of its actions.

As an example, a flowing river repeats itself in patterns and variations, producing figures in the sense of dance steps coming one after another, extending or opposing the last one. A figure, like a seasonal flood, is only partial—partially decided or described—and there are other parts still undetermined and changing. Think about how undulating tango dancers share the weight of each other, reacting and compensating. Alternatively, consider the attitude of reciprocity toward gifts of strawberries from the land, described by Robin Wall Kimmerer in *Braiding Sweetgrass*.[20] Strawberries grow, and humans and animals eat them. In this way, we humans interact with nonhuman others. How shall we acknowledge these interactions? This exchange between human desires and the capacity of the land to give can be seen as a dialogic flow of human action and ecosystemic response. For Berg, the weight of impacts between humans and beyond-human entities can be observed in incremental steps that cultivate sensitivity to the patterns and scales of human action, seasonal changes, the movement of animals, soundscapes of hurricanes, glaciers, rising waters, and other substantial processes of nonhuman assemblages, past and present, in relation to human activity.
This incrementalism can be seen as a kind of harm reduction for both earth and humans.

The *figure of regulation* preemptively critiques how environmental regulations are often not enacted until after ecological harm occurs in the United States.
Berg experiments with an unfolding precautionary principle as practice, as opposed to the use of mitigating regulations enacted after environmental damage has occurred. Figures break down regulation as rules by patterning changes into increments that can be taught, observed, and listened to, a call and response. For Berg, figuring becomes a process of evolving new social customs by incrementally incorporating complexity.[21] If practices of figuring within a community are dedicated to imagining a built environment that harmonizes and rescales human lives, habits, and infrastructures, they could present new challenges to the anthropocenic discourses of individual rights that hold legislated regulations such as the Clean Water Act hostage.

One of the ways that humans learn is by observing difference and change. The figure of regulation, based in the observation of change, charts a path for creating customs as pedagogical practice. It also bears a resemblance to the healing processes conducted through harm reduction, as a prefigurative and diagnostic process of exploring the potential for human dignity and transformative healing through association to place. In the Argentinian La Plata watershed, Brian Holmes and Alejandro Meitin use the term "bioculturalism" with the same intention as a figure of regulation, "as both something autonomously real, and as idealizations or imaginaries that can guide collective behavior and action."[22] Much like Berg and Dasmann's framing of bioregionalism as both geographical terrain and a terrain of consciousness, bioculturalism expresses the consciousness of a terrain's people as much as its biological character.

DEVOLUTION

In 1981, Anishinaabe organizer and economist Winona LaDuke spent her summer studying European secessionist movements where distinct regional language and culture groups were resisting state policy and control as a form of internal occupation. Tracing between these movements and the jurisdictional status of Indigenous lands in

Washington Street Garden, Carbondale, Illinois. Photograph by Sarah Lewison

the United States, her article for *CoEvolution Quarterly*'s Bioregions issue, "Indian Land Claims and Treaty Areas of North America: Succeeding into Native North America," made a case for Indigenous treaty rights—the right of Indian governments to hold regulatory and enforcement power over traditional lands. She wrote, "It means the land which is currently taxed, regulated, strip mined, militarized, drowned by overirrigation and nuked by and or with the blessing of the U.S. and Canadian governments would not be under their jurisdiction anymore."[23]

Landback movements and purchases for the reclamation of ancestral lands for Indigenous people in the U.S. are slowly, albeit unevenly, facilitating a reversal, or devolution of power from the state back to what Raymond Dasmann, in 1976 called "ecosystems people" who wish to manage the land ethically. For LaDuke, to "relocalize economies" is to harmonize human economic and social systems with a region's capacity for sustenance for all who live there through the elevation of traditional cultural practices. [24] Devolution is a form of resistance to colonialization and economic occupation by monocultures of all kinds. In the United States, devolution might correlate to an expansive municipalism in which state decision-making power over the living and geological entities called natural resources in a management context are handed to bioregional governance systems. Devolution entails imagining a future for a place that is not reinvented with every new political wind. LaDuke uses the Ojibwe phrase ji-misawaanvaming to describe "something like positive window shopping for your future," adding that "we need to ask what our community is going to look like 50 or 100 years from now."[25] Such future thinking would entail individual and social transformations that seem impossible given the present level of alienation and polarization in our current society; transformation can only happen through a series of adjustments that will predispose people to change. What might those adjustments look like? How could they be achieved?

COUNTER-CARTOGRAPHIES

Collective mapping plays a key role in creating a bioregional consciousness; such counter-cartographic exercises bring together the experience and knowledge of those who live in a region. These perspectives are rarely represented in maps developed for navigation or for extraction of materials such as coal, oil, or wood. Resource maps reduce regional and ecological uniquenesses to what can be grown, manufactured, or mined. Imagine instead a group of people of different ages around a table with pens and paper, old maps, hand-drawn directions, ecological studies, and naturalist observations. Meeting monthly over the period of a year, they draw and discuss, slowly determining the boundaries of their bioregion by defining its unique characteristics.[26] Such a map is a powerful visual counter to the flattening gaze of state and industrial maps. Mapmaking workshops bring people together to share their knowledge of home, including its human and beyond-human inhabitants, its histories, needs and cultures, and its anthropocenic spoilage. Bioregional mapping also affects urban policies and development by addressing social inequities around urban and exurban sustainability as well as access to natural surroundings.

My own work as an artist, teacher, and proponent of the "river as an open school" began with mapping exercises like those described above. These were first done with a group of people in my university's library. Together, we identified trees, creeks, beaver dams, and early sightings of northward migrating armadillos. We also mapped spaces where people felt safe or unsafe or

Sankofa Series director Sharifa Stewart. Understory Center Kitchen for Subsistence Research, Carbondale, Illinois, circa 2017. Photograph by Sarah Lewison

more likely to be stopped by police. Through this sharing of perspectives, we blended our attention to local ecosystems together with the unique experiences of humans in our mapping group.

BIOREGION AS A SITE FOR SUBSISTENCE

Tamil eco-literary critic Nirmal Selvamony stresses that bioregional praxis "cannot be anything other than communitarian," writing that

> Living-in-place is possible only in a land area in which the agent (the one who practices it) can have face-to-face contact with all of the members of the community of the agent, not in an Andersonian imagined community where such contact is not possible.[27]

In 2015, I got to use an old restaurant as a space for collective community research into subsistence, a practice often stigmatized as a marginal form of food provision. In their 1999 book *The Subsistence Perspective*, sociologists Maria Mies and Veronika Bennholdt-Thomsen tackle this stigma, recharacterizing subsistence as labor that directly satisfies human life and reproductive needs within the limits of place.[28] *The Subsistence Perspective* brings feminist theories of labor to bioregionalism by recognizing the labor of social reproduction, from childbearing to growing a garden. For Mies and Bennholdt-Thomsen, a subsistence perspective entails the withdrawal of one's energies from commodity production in order to compose a post-commodity culture that restores what Mies describes as the "diversity, or symbiosis between various forms of life—animals, plants, and people—all living together in a certain area, all with their livelihood and good life."[29]

The Understory Center Kitchen for Subsistence Research (also known as the Subsistence Kitchen), was named for the layer of trees and foliage waiting in the shadow of taller branches until a clearing is made for them to shoot up. The project was framed by the question of what subsistence might look like in our current technological era and our specific place. How could we take better care of each other through attention to our regional specificities? This question was asked again and again across different activities, including a weekly meal that was open to all. Each Saturday, people came to pick vegetables, herbs, and flowers from the urban garden across the street to be used to plan and prepare a free public lunch. During and after lunch we held cultural, practical, and theoretical workshops, teach-ins, and meetings. Some days we cooked or preserved food together or tried to reverse engineer branded prepared foods, such as salad dressings and cookies, that people's families favored.

Other weeks, local and visiting activists, organizers, and artists gave presentations that were followed by discussion or group action, such as letter writing campaigns. Materials were gathered for Standing Rock, where thousands were camping to demonstrate opposition to the Dakota Access pipeline.[30] There were also closer pipelines to learn about and oppose, and questions about the management of the Shawnee National Forest, one of the largest forested areas remaining in Illinois. Someone painted an iceberg model on the wall to illustrate how 90 percent of the factors controlling a situation are concealed beneath the surface. We used this model in discussions to get a better understanding of how underlying factors determined how people thought they should live. Using the kitchen as a common learning space was empowering, and it was a joy to engage with our small mission of gathering food to feed as many as possible. Each week, new people joined an already diverse group of townies and students willing to spend time reflecting about how we live.

In *The Dawn of Everything*, David Graeber and David Wengrow's reframing of early human social organization, the authors problematize a long-accepted hypothesis about the role of agriculture in the formation of civilizations. Citing Plato's Gardens of Adonis, which they call "a sort of festive speed farming which produced no food," they point out that serious concerns and skills evolve from play and social experiment.[31] The Subsistence Kitchen was such a space of material and imaginative play, a place to plant seeds for the future.

Imagining bioregional autonomy is audacious. Kirkpatrick Sale writes that "bioregional diversity...does not mean that every region of the Northeast or of North America or of the globe will build upon the values of democracy, equality, liberty, freedom, justice or other suchlike 'desiderata.' There's a risk that truly autonomous bioregions will go 'their own way.'"[32]

Brian Holmes, writing about bioregionalist governance in the Pacific Northwest clarifies which entities should lead: "A bioregional state is emergent whenever the survival and flourishing of non-human actors becomes an issue in formal political negotiations over land-use within a given territory."[33]

In places that have gathered enough political or social momentum, bioregionalism is expressed in fragments through, for example, local foodsheds, species protection, transition initiatives and the elimination of dams. There are places where inhabitants have become frustrated enough with extractivism by outside interests that they have thrown out external governance and created new governments guided by principles of mutual respect between humans and the natural environment. In the Michoacán, Mexico village of Cherán, the Indigenous Purépecha people drove out loggers, politicians, and outsiders profiting from and destroying their lands and water sources. Returning to traditional forms of self-governance, they banned the unsustainable cultivation of avocados and are developing an economy that protects regional biodiversity.[34] In Southern Illinois, it seems ridiculous to dream about regional autonomy as long as coal companies own much of the land, or while the U.S. Forest Service serves lumber industries instead of protecting our woody carbon sinks.[35] We don't know yet how to transform the consciousness of our region on the scale necessary to stop the hungry ghosts of capitalism, but we can practice, or play farm, around the edges. We can develop sensitivity toward each other, toward one another as a collectivity, and toward place as region and territory for the plenitude of diverse beings. We can explore ways of making these practices contagious.

The Subsistence Kitchen eased lives in small ways, producing new relationships for people between humans and the beyond-human, and offered a dance step—a glimpse of place as life. We exchanged experiences across differences and learned each other's concerns in a time when the resources that sustain are being withdrawn faster than ever. We reactivated customs of sharing resources, food, and time, which, for some people, had been suppressed or never experienced. Here, we could acknowledge and understand specific ways that oppression is locked into the built environment, and how the energies of the human within environment can be released. It is in this sense that I began to imagine the Soft Anthropocene as a way to characterize the psychic and emotional injuries to humans and other life forms that occur as a result of Anthropocene techne and the disconnection of humans from the natural world. This is the unseen bottom of the iceberg.

WE DON'T KNOW YET HOW TO TRANSFORM THE CONSCIOUSNESS OF OUR REGION ON THE SCALE NECESSARY TO STOP THE HUNGRY GHOSTS OF CAPITALISM, BUT WE CAN PRACTICE, OR PLAY FARM, AROUND THE EDGES.

The Subsistence Kitchen hosted conversations about things like isolation, childcare needs, neighborhood solar and internet networks, and the lack of essential skills among people, such as cooking. The socially isolated experiences of so many

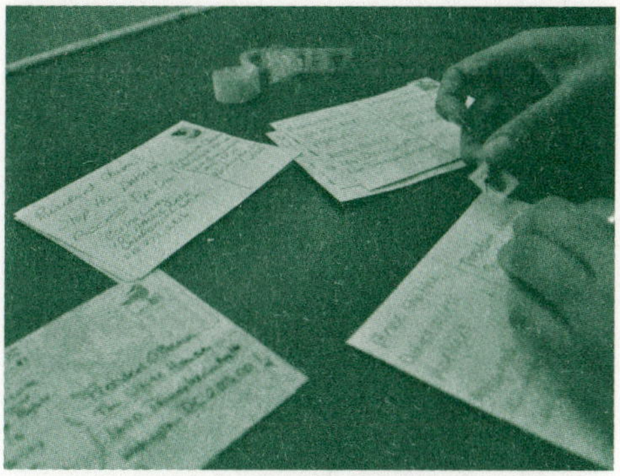

"Stop the Pipeline" letter-writing campaign. Understory Center Kitchen for Subsistence Research, Carbondale, Illinois, circa 2017. Photograph by Sarah Lewison

begin, under the lens of harm reduction, to look like a public health issue even before the pandemic. Enlisting harm reduction principles might entail first acknowledging the isolation people experience and then finding ways to fill gaps in social services that address psychological dissociation. As a beginning, the Understory Center Kitchen for Subsistence Research opened a portal for acknowledgement, cooperation, and reconnection.

What other figures or tools might reduce the malaise of these disassociations and disconnects? Although restoring the integrity of an ecosystem and devising ways for humans to contribute to that is foundational, there are many layers of human activity that divorce humans from place that might be investigated and reconnected. We live in places that are so fragmented that perhaps forging new connections between life and place can start by following the threads of the anthropocenic practices that first interrupted life-place connections. Whilst pondering the multidimensional scales of these complexities, I encountered Free Soil, a project presented in St. Louis by artist jackie sumell and curator Risa Puleo.[36] A pamphlet describes it as a "three-part material intervention in conversation with three moments in the city's history."[37] The project asks us to imagine the city's initial construction, from clay taken from the ground to forming and firing the clay to make bricks for houses. A map marks the quarries where clay was removed and acknowledges the low-paid or enslaved quarry and kiln workers. By the 1970s, legions of buildings made with these bricks sat dilapidated owing to redlining policies that denied their black inhabitants sufficient money for rehabilitation. As the houses fell apart, the bricks were purloined and sold downriver for neo-plantation-style new construction in Louisiana. For Free Soil, sumell, who dedicates her practice to the abolition of prison, retrieves bricks from New Orleans, Louisiana, returning them to St. Louis, Missouri. She invites people to smash them back into dust so they may be "rematriated into the soil" from where they first came.[38] A planting mix was made with the brick dust, sand, soil, and wildflower seeds gathered from the ancient mounds of the early Mississippian people. The seeds will grow out into flowers favored by wild bees for pollination.

sumell's reinhabitory project relates to harm reduction principles through the acknowledgement of harm and the initiation of a reconciliation or reparative process. It begins with recognizing and linking the destructive acts toward environment and people over time that includes the extraction of clay, the peonage of workers, and the destruction of housing. sumell and Puleo trace this damage for others to see and participate in acts of repair and connective restoration, both physical and symbolic, by returning the bricks to a soil medium for new life. Mapping out complexities of damage makes openings for incremental steps and encounters, much as Berg describes in "Figures of Regulation." Bioregional indicators are always present in our research about place in the Mississippi River Open School; they share a forensic impulse to track human interventions in the land, carrying the question of what can come next. Bioregional principles can serve as a guide both to inoculate against technologies that sever us even further from natural systems and to move us from economics to "ecologics."

Even though we find our contemporary selves mired in the time of the Anthropocene, there have always been pathways toward reconnection with the natural world. As I reach an end, I feel moved to note the resonances between bioregionalist concepts such as Figures of Regulation, and even Berg's early writing about the commodification of life, that are present in sources I've just mentioned in passing. Toward the end of her essay called "The Gift of Strawberries," Robin Wall Kimmerer acknowledges the challenge of acquiring the self-restraint to wait for berries to ripen to sweetness rather than rushing to eat unripe white ones. It occurs to me that our haste to eat the sour berries is the Soft Anthropocene at work in our consciousness. Kimmerer writes, "Now I am old, and I know that transformation is slow. The commodity economy has been here on Turtle Island for four hundred years, eating up the white strawberries and everything else. But people have grown weary of the sour taste in their mouths."[39] We can hope that Kimmerer is right, but in these passages, she also summarizes our ambivalences and the difficulty of changing. Humans are not simple and addictions are, by their very nature, intractable. Treating addiction requires incremental steps, repetition, and a great deal of forgiveness.

In this essay addressing the Anthropocene through harm reduction practices and a set of poetic and symbolic concepts drawn from bioregionalism, I've drawn together fields and concepts that might seem to jump between subjects or to lean on suppositions about the human consciousness. It is my sense that it is necessary to include poetry, contradiction, and leaps of understanding in order to discover the forms of imagination that make it possible to set such a difficult task as transformation in motion. This is a trying time, one when our capacities to care for our human selves and our beyond-human kin within the context of place are terribly stretched. This makes it even more important that we do not disconnect from the matrix of the earth and of human fellowship. Bioregionalist philosophies opened paths of imagination through social critique and creative practices that addressed this kind of alienation, and it is our turn to carry them forward. As we learned from Jim Rock's ceremony of reinhabitation at the start of this essay, we must declare our affinities out loud and bring them into a shared space with other humans. We must seek community with those who are not human and who have occupied spaces upon the earth for much longer than we humans have. To conjure harm reduction as a path for ecological healing in the human social terrain of the Anthropocene is to acknowledge there is no easy route for finding coexistence within the planetary biosphere. It is also to acknowledge there is no other option than to step, swim, and crawl, humans and beyond-humans alike, into an unpredictable journey toward bioregional belonging.

A version of this article was originally published in the journal Open Rivers *(Winter/Spring 2025).*

ENDNOTES

1 Jim Rock, "Sky Watchers, Earth Watchers, and Guardians of the Former and Future Garden," *Open Rivers: Rethinking Water, Place & Community*, no. 17 (2020), https://openrivers.lib.umn.edu/article/sky-watchers-earth-watchers-guardians/.

2 For introductions to bioregionalism, see Phil Lane, Jr.'s recent blog posting, "The Emergence of the Bioregional Movement: Remapping Mother Earth as Bioregions," *Bioregional Earth*, January 13, 2025, https://www.bioregionalearth.org/blog/bioregional-movement; or, Kirkpatrick Sale, *Dwellers in the Earth: The Bioregional Vision* (Random House, 1985); or Peter Berg and Raymond Dasmann, "Reinhabiting California," in *The Biosphere and the Bioregion*, ed. Cheryll Glotfelty and Eve Quesnel (Routledge, 2014).

3 G. Alan Marlatt, "Harm Reduction: Come as You Are," *Addictive Behaviors* 21, no. 6, (1996): 779–788, https://openlab.citytech.cuny.edu/nehhealth2013/files/2013/11/G-Alan-Marlatt-Harm-Reduction-Come-As-You-Are.pdf.

4 "Harm Reduction Movement," National Harm Reduction Coalition, accessed December 1, 2024, https://harmreduction.org/movement/evolution/.

5 Discussion of bioregionalism and spirituality in Bron Taylor, *Encyclopedia of Religion and Nature* (Continuum, 2005), http://religionandnature.com/ern/sample/Taylor%2CBron–Snyder.pdf.

6 Peter Berg, "Bioregionalism: An Introduction (2002)," Planet Drum Foundation, 2002, https://planetdrum.org/bioregionalism-an-introduction/.

7 Alan Van Newkirk, *Root, Branch and Mammal Bulletin #1*, Center for Study Cultural Morphology & Mutation (1970).

8 Allen Van Newkirk, "Bioregions: Towards Bioregional Strategy for Human Cultures," *Environmental Conservation* 2, no. 2 (July

1975): 108, https://www.cambridge.org/core/journals/environmental-conservation/article/abs/bioregions-towards-bioregional-strategy-for-human-cultures/B85A50F189EDCDB2F80283055173A986.

9 Nirmal Selvamony, "From Bioregion to Kuṭi, a Prologue," in *Bioregion and Indigeneity in Literary Imagination*, ed. Aleena Manoharan (Cambridge Scholars Publishing, 2023), https://www.cambridgescholars.com/resources/pdfs/978-1-5275-1519-2-sample.pdf.

10 Raymond Dassman, "The Threatened World of Nature," Horace M. Albright Lecture in Conservation at the University of California, 1976, https://nature.berkeley.edu/albright/1976.

11 Dassman, "The Threatened World of Nature."

12 Gail Dolgin, Vincente Franco, and Peter Berg, "Peter Berg Interviewed about the Summer of Love for the American Experience," Planet Drum Foundation, April 19, 2006, https://planet-drum.net/2017/12/10/peter-berg-interviewed-about-the-summer-of-love-for-the-american-experience/.

13 The Digger Archives houses many artifacts concerning this period. Digger free stores are credited with inspiring the Black Panther Party for Self Defense's Breakfast for Children program. Find an anecdotal interview available here: https://anarchyinaction.org/index.php?title=San_Francisco_Diggers.

14 Peter Berg, "Trip Without A Ticket," *The Digger Papers* (August, 1968), The Digger Archives, accessed December 1, 2024, https://www.diggers.org/digpaps68/twatdp.html.

15 "Planet Drum Bundles," Planet Drum Foundation, accessed December 1, 2024, https://planetdrum.org/planet-drum-bundles/.

16 Peter Berg, ed., *Reinhabiting a Separate Country: A Bioregional Anthology of Northern California* (Planet Drum Foundation, 1978).

17 Judith Helfand, "The Reinhabitory Theater," Planet Drum Foundation, January 4, 2023, https://planetdrum.org/the-reinhabitory-theater/; Yeshe Salz, "Reinhabitory Theater: A Legacy of Inspiring Bioregionalism Through Storytelling," Found SF, accessed March 1, 2025, https://www.foundsf.org/Reinhabitory_Theater:_A_Legacy_of_Inspiring_Bioregionalism_Through_Storytelling.

18 Peter Berg, "Figures of Regulation: Guides for Rebalancing Society with the Biosphere," in *Planet Drum Bundle #8*, 1982, republished in *The Biosphere and the Bioregion: Essential Writings of Peter Berg*, ed. Cheryll Glotfelty and Eve Quesnel (Routledge, 2015).

19 Berg, "Figures of Regulation."

20 Robin Wall Kimmerer, *Braiding Sweetgrass: Indigenous Wisdom, Scientific Knowledge, and the Teachings of Plants* (Milkweed Editions, 2015), 22–32.

21 Berg, "Figures of Regulation."

22 Brian Holmes, correspondence with author, June 13, 2023.

23 Winona LaDuke, "Indian Land Claims and Treaty Areas of North America: Succeeding into Native North America," *CoEvolution Quarterly*, Bioregions Issue, no. 32 (Winter 1981): 65.

24 Sarah Van Gelder, "An Interview with Winona LaDuke," *YES! Magazine*, June 18, 2008, https://www.yesmagazine.org/issue/just-foreign-policy/2008/06/18/an-interview-with-winona-laduke.

25 Van Gelder, "An Interview with Winona LaDuke."

26 See Doug Aberley, ed., *Boundaries of Home: Mapping for Local Empowerment* (New Society Publishers, July 1998).

27 Selvamony, "From Bioregion to Kuti, a Prologue."

28 Veronika Bennholdt-Thomsen and Maria Mies, *The Subsistence Perspective: Beyond the Globalised Economy* (Zed Books, 1999).

29 Bennholdt-Thomsen and Mies, *The Subsistence Perspective*.

30 "On Standing Rock," Stand with Standing Rock, accessed December 1, 2024, https://standwithstandingrock.net/.

31 David Graeber and David Wengrow, *The Dawn of Everything: A New History of Humanity* (Farrar, Straus and Giroux, 2021), 210.

32 Kirkpatrick Sale, "Mother of All: An Introduction to Bioregionalism," E. F. Schumacher Center Lecture, Mount Holyoke College, October 1983, South Hadley, MA, https://centerforneweconomics.org/publications/mother-of-all-an-introduction-to-bioregionalism/.

33 Brian Holmes, "After Chimerica: Bioregionalism for the City of Ashes," boundary 2 (2020), https://www.boundary2.org/2020/07/brian-holmes-after-chimerica-bioregionalism-for-the-city-of-ashes/.

34 Alejandra González Hernández and Victor Alfonzo Zertuche Cobos, "Cherán. 5 Years of Self-Government in an Indigenous Community in Mexico," *Open Democracy*, December 2, 2016, https://www.opendemocracy.net/en/cher-n-5-years-of-self-government-in-indi/.

35 "Coal Mines in Illinois Viewer," Coal Mine Viewer, accessed December 1, 2024, https://ilmineswiki.web.illinois.edu/wiki/ILMINES.

36 jackie sumell and Risa Puleo, "Free Soil Party Pamphlet," Counterpublic, 2023.

37 sumell and Puleo, Free Soil Party.

38 sumell and Puleo, Free Soil Party.

39 Kimmerer, *Braiding Sweetgrass*, 32.

Bioculture Now! The Paraná Talking with the Mississippi

Brian Holmes

In comparing the Mississippi River to the Paraguay-Paraná in Latin America, Brian Holmes discovers two different models for imagining river systems today: one, a heavily engineered industrial canal, an Anthropocene river; the other, a living biocultural corridor that teaches with its flood pulse a new-old way of inhabiting the water and the land.

From the 1930s onward, the Mississippi has been a globally touted model of industrial river management. On its upper reaches, 27 lock and dam structures maintain a nine-foot channel throughout the year, permitting continuous navigation from Minneapolis to the Gulf of Mexico. On the Lower Mississippi, south of Cairo, Illinois, a vast levee system provides flood protection for the cities and towns along its banks, and for all those who farm its alluvial soils. From north to south, innumerable dikes, chevrons, and weirs serve to channel the surging current, reducing the need for dredging, while reinforced concrete revetments hold the river in its place, arresting its natural tendency to carve meander loops that would ultimately be cut off and cast aside as oxbow lakes. The Mississippi has been extensively tutored by its human masters and overwhelmed by their powerful machines. It has been almost entirely disconnected from the surrounding wetlands to which it was formerly joined by the flood pulse. For these and many other reasons it has rightly been called an "Anthropocene River"—that is, a river dominated and profoundly damaged by human beings.[1] At every hour of the day or night, its forested islands reverberate with the roar of diesel engines pushing barges full of grain, coal, chemicals, and industrial products toward domestic ports and the high seas.

Wandering across the meticulously farmed floodplains or camping on the wild forested islands beneath the searchlights of passing tows, I have often been carried away in reverie to another river: the Paraguay-Paraná in Latin America, which also flows through endless corn and soybean fields and which also serves as an artery of commerce for the nations along its banks. It's the serpentine twin of our great Midwestern stream—the same in so many ways yet so profoundly different. Like the Mississippi from the Bird's Foot delta to Baton Rouge, the Paraná serves ocean-going freighters all the way up to the Argentinean cities of Rosario and Santa Fe. Like the Midwestern waterway, it has been the object of endless engineering schemes aimed both at deepening the main channel and improving barge traffic along the upper reaches. Yet unlike the Mississippi, the Paraguay-Paraná is still entirely free of dams across its entire 2,500-mile length, and equally free of levees and revetments outside the major urban areas. Its immense floodplains have remained, if not intact, at least broadly open to the river's seasonal pulse. At its headwaters lies the tropical twin of the Mississippi's graceful Anishinaabe rice lakes: the Pantanal, the largest and most biodiverse wetland on Earth.

The Paraguay-Paraná, with its integrally floodable banks, has rightly been called a "living river." Such intricate lifeforms are deeply intertwined with our own, as Indigenous teachings, Gaia theory, and Earth system science have shown in their own ways. For this reason, friends and defenders of rivers have begun to speak not only of biological diversity but, more importantly, of *biocultural diversity*, recognizing the regionally specific relations between humans and nonhumans that are needed to sustain a river's way of life in the present.[2] Yet human beings, especially those of the "wild capitalist" variety, also represent a tremendous threat to living rivers. How has the Paraguay-Paraná escaped the fate of the Mississippi? And how can both of them survive as rivers, not canals, in the present epoch?

HOW HAS THE PARAGUAY-PARANÁ ESCAPED THE FATE OF THE MISSISSIPPI? AND HOW CAN BOTH OF THEM SURVIVE AS RIVERS, NOT CANALS, IN THE PRESENT EPOCH?

As a member of the eco/art group Casa Río in Argentina, I have had multiple occasions to meet the Paraguay-Paraná and to converse with it through its allies, gathered in the Wetlands Without Borders[3] network. Encounters with activists, scientists, and inhabitants of the La Plata Basin have sparked both my imagination and my scholarly interest. Yet I am primarily an artist and activist moved by the urgency of global ecological change. In this article, I'll try to let the Paraná and the voices of its defenders speak through me to engage a conversation with the Mississippi. Of course, this kind of ventriloquism is against all the academic rules—but how exactly shall we learn what a river can teach?

Fisherfolk on the Paraná bluffs near Rosario, Argentina, 2011. Photograph by Claire Pentecost

BABBLING BASINS

On the map, rivers appear to branch as they go up. But that's a backwards human view. In the river's reality, multiple tributaries converge as they flow downstream. The personality of a great river emerges from myriad convergences, tracing a catchment or drainage basin at subcontinental scale. Just as a sturdy tree draws its sustenance from its delicate foliage, so does a great river live from the dendritic tangle of its upper reaches. The deepest current of the mainstem—the invisible thalweg—can be understood as an intricate sensory system registering the day-to-day experience of distant forests and waterfalls. It's wonderful that in human languages, a delta is often called a "mouth." If a river could talk, it would speak of its basin.

The Mississippi and La Plata basins are among the most industrialized in the world. Yet accidents of geography and culture, along with the deeds of certain human beings, have left the Paraná mainstem and its northern tributary, the Paraguay, relatively free to express what they sense from the surrounding territory. The most dramatic of these free expressions is called a flood—much in the news these days since the rains have started radically changing in intensity. For humans, floods are mainly known through the cities and infrastructures they destroy with increasing force. For rivers, seasonally oscillating pulses are a way of communicating distant raindrops and snowmelts to nearby floodplain ecologies. In wide valleys like those of the Mississippi and the Paraná, even relatively small river rises can have extensive effects, turning grasslands or farmers' fields into glittering prairies with incursions of spawning fish, crustaceans, birds, and reptiles. Along the Paraná where there are no levees to hold back the rising water, human populations adopt boats, rafts, and even floating schools in a seasonal round. Scientists now understand that the flood pulse is key to the reproduction of many species—it's the lifeblood of fluvial ecologies.[4] In contemporary times, it's striking to see the machinery of everyday affairs suddenly overtaken by muddy brown swirls and great streamers of water hyacinth, known in Spanish as *camalote*. Of course, some of the swollen pools never quite dry out; they are always a kind of slow-moving river in the earth, better known as wetlands. It's paradoxical that these drowned environments provide a valuable "sponge effect": wetlands are what slow the deluge through pooling and absorption, unlike levees that channel and accelerate it. These unstable, mutating ecologies, where the land frequently crumbles and fissures before your eyes, deliver what Casa Río calls "the teachings of the flood."[5]

Stills from "Alejandra, Eva y Fátima. Poéticas del Delta" by Casa Rio

Everything in a spoken language depends on the way the listener interprets it. It's no different with talking rivers. In the Mississippi Valley, the flood pulse was interpreted as an assault on human affairs and the United States went to war. In response to the great flood of 1927, which was already exacerbated by an excess of levees, the U.S. Army Corps of Engineers went on to build a series of gigantic walls around the Lower Mississippi, definitively curtailing its ability to share the accumulated waters of the basin with the surrounding alluvial plains. This decade-long construction program, known as the Mississippi River and Tributaries Project, completed the work of deforesting, ditching, draining, and planting that had already been underway in the floodplains since the late nineteenth century, notably in the Delta and Bootheel regions of the states of Mississippi and Missouri.[6] There, and throughout the Mississippi River valley, an orthogonal grid of functional ditches and canals gradually replaced intricate cypress swamps. Because it was the Great Depression and so many people needed a job, commercial interests along the Upper River engaged the Army Corps in the construction, at government expense, of the lock-and-dam system and the nine-foot channel, permanently inundating huge swathes of territory in the process.[7] After World War II and the development of ever more powerful technology, it was a small matter to devastate the Mississippi's greatest tributary, the Missouri, with a series of largely useless dams that are now aging dangerously and accumulating unsustainable loads of sediment. In this way, the Lakota/Dakota peoples who lived along the Missouri became early members of a growing global population: people displaced by dams.[8]

A similar dam-building frenzy played out on the Upper Paraná in Brazil above its confluence with the Paraguay. In the 1980s, another major enclosure, Yacyretá, was built on the Argentina-Paraguay border. Industrialization also overtook the Uruguay River, the third major artery of the La Plata basin. Only the Paraguay and the Lower Paraná have escaped. This is why Casa Río, like the wider network Wetlands Without Borders, attends primarily to the natural and human expressions of the uninterrupted fluvial corridor running from the Pantanal to the Río de la Plata estuary.

From Casa Río's location on the southern shore of the estuary, just outside the university town of La Plata, it is only a short excursion through the Buenos Aires megalopolis to reach the 200-mile-long, 40-mile-wide Paraná delta with its intricate tapestry of forested islands and grasslands open to the flood pulse. Despite the presence of artificially elevated gated communities near the cities and the encroachment of diked tree plantations and soybean fields everywhere else, the Paraná delta can still give you a sense of what the Mississippi may have been like before the walls arrived. Here, the river is not a calibrated channel but an expansive, mutating world of sinuous veins draped in fractal patterns of vegetation. Sparse but resilient islanders (*isleños*) earn a living by fishing and small-scale forestry, maintaining homes on stilts and transiting by wooden boats to the mainland. Rural towns on bluffs far from the main channel look out over seasonal pastures that regularly disappear beneath vast sheets of water. Closer to Buenos Aires, a riot of cabin dwellers expose themselves both to the floods and the estuary's tides, creating an ebullient reserve of socio-ecological sensitivity right alongside the mechanized press of urban life. This texture of lived experiences and culturally transmitted imaginaries extends throughout the delta and into the Middle Paraná, with its diverging channels and sleeping wetlands. Further north, the Paraguay converges, fed by the flood pulse of the Pantanal.

Traditions, inventions, and songs flow downstream, along with plants, seeds, sediments, and giant barge tows. Bioculturalism considers everything

Biocultural Dialogue. Photograph courtesy of Casa Río

together, in both directions. The river's intrinsic connection to its far-flung basin is doubled by the knowledge and desire of its human denizens, gesturing across the gap between the delta and the headwaters. The specific role of biocultural art (Casa Río's vocation) is to transmit and amplify these gestures. As experience shows, the human conversation with and about the river, marginal and intermittent though it may be in contemporary society, proves nonetheless essential to the maintenance of the river's own expressivity, as we shall see.

ANCIENT ENEMY

When the Venetian explorer Sebastian Cabot entered the estuary and traveled up the river in 1527, he gave it a name that perfectly expressed the colonial dream: Río de la Plata, "the River of Silver."[9] This was the dream of a watery highway to the legendary mines of Potosí in the high Andean mountains of what is now Bolivia, where the Spanish later established their mint. However, it turned out that the river did not really lead to Potosí but instead to an impassable swamp, so the colonizers adopted a heavily guarded mule train over the Andes as an escape route for

the loot. Still the colonial dream never faded; only the color changed. Across succeeding centuries, the Paraná-Paraguay became a river of golden grain: first wheat and corn, grown in the Pampas for export from river ports such as Rosario and Santa Fe, then genetically modified soybeans and their processed derivatives, grown from the 1990s onward in Argentina, Paraguay, Bolivia, and the Brazilian states of Matto Grosso and Matto Grosso del Sur.[10] The drive to export these profitable commodities has made the great river into an object of sublime desire for the industrial bourgeoisies of South America. Thus, at the close of the twentieth century, the ancient dream of the River of Silver was reborn under the auspices of the Paraguay-Paraná "Hidrovía": an international plan to turn the river into a logistics corridor for the transport of gasoline, agricultural chemicals, corn, and soybeans.

The 1990s were a dangerous decade for Latin American rivers. In 1989, Argentina, Bolivia, Brazil, Paraguay, and Uruguay created the Intergovernmental Committee on the Paraguay-Paraná Waterway.[11] Its aim was to carve out a navigable channel 2,140 miles long, stretching from Cáceres in Brazil to Nueva Palmira on the Uruguayan side of the Río de La Plata estuary.[12] The proposed river corridor, promising a minimum nine-foot channel for barge traffic through the

Excerpt from Pedro de Cieza de León, Parte primera de la Chronica del Peru, 1581. Courtesy of Library of Congress

upper reaches, would soon be conceived as the logistics backbone of Mercosur, a transnational economic bloc launched in 1991. As in the case of the Mississippi, the Hidrovía project entailed dredging the Upper Paraguay River, installing dikes to raise water levels, straightening five curves, and dynamiting eight rocky outcrops that constrict the river's flow. These interventions would have led to the shrinking of the Pantanal, gravely damaging its wetland ecology and curtailing its "sponge effect" on downstream flood pulses.[13] Flawed feasibility studies and a nearly complete disregard for the project's consequences led to widespread denunciation by biologists and river defenders, culminating in the formation of the activist coalition Ríos Vivos, or "Living Rivers," in 1994. In that same year, the newly constructed Yacyretá reservoir began to be filled with water, provoking the displacement of some fifteen thousand people in the initial phase alone. Now it became obvious that the drive toward an integrated South American economy would exact a devastating non-monetary cost: the transformation of the Paraguay-Paraná river system along the lines that had already been traced in cement across the Mississippi River basin.[14]

Ríos Vivos marked an extraordinary moment in Latin American social history.[15] The coalition gathered over 300 groups and movements from the five-nation La Plata basin; but it acted nonhierarchically, serving as an information gathering system and open strategy center whose deliberations and conclusions could be drawn upon, or not, by each of the member organizations in their local struggles. The aim was to render regional governments politically accountable for their technocratic planning processes through the power of Indigenous agency, grassroots pressure, scientific expertise, and international law, the latter of which was binding for international financial institutions (IFIs) such as the World Bank and the Inter-American Development Bank. Support was also provided from outside the region by International Rivers,[16] a U.S.-based network that could draw on the hydrological engineering expertise of the environmental consulting firm Philip Williams & Associates, and by the Dutch ecological organization Both Ends, which has continuously assisted with strategy and fundraising while generating critical information on the role of the IFIs and the European Union. Within this open and agile coalition, scientific and environmentalist interventions could coexist with local and Indigenous modes of organizing. Resisting top-down control, the coalition developed the ecological sensitivity of a vast river basin populated by humans since time immemorial and connected atmospherically to the emergent ecology of global river activism. As a Ríos Vivos publication declared some years later:

> The peoples and indigenous communities that have joined the organizations forming the Ríos Vivos Coalition seek to build a society founded on sustainability and equity. These peoples have a long history of struggles for the defense of their territories, for the legitimate right to preserve and enrich their customs, beliefs and cultural traditions. We share a common dream but each Organization, Community and People in the Coalition has its own pathway, traced by its own demands. Ríos Vivos is the mainstem where the actions of over 300 organizations, communities and peoples converge and overflow.[17]

Even as controversy over the Hidrovía plan grew, Argentina's neoliberal president Carlos Menem revived a Soviet-designed hydroelectric plan from the 1970s that had been shelved in the face of Cold War opposition from the United States.[18] The new Paraná Medio Dam involved the construction of a five-mile-wide barrier spanning the river, plus a 145-mile-long levee running along the western bank between the cities of Sante Fe and Goya to create

Sidney A. Murray Jr. Dam, Mississippi River, Louisiana. Photograph by Brian Holmes

a deep pool for Panamax-class freighters. The plan included a possible extension for a second deep pool to the north, which would have been another major step toward the canalization and industrialization of the entire river. Its designer was a North American consortium called Energy Developers International (EDI), based in Metairie, Louisiana, which proposed to supply a $5 billion capital investment in exchange for 50 years' worth of electricity revenue plus 30 years of tariffs on bridges, locks, and similar structures. The consortium included the engineering mega-firm Brown & Root, but its hydroelectric technology was to be furnished by a smaller military contractor, New Orleans, Louisiana based Avondale Industries, whose blueprint for the giant installation on the Paraná was founded on a transportable steel-encased powerhouse that it had previously supplied for the comparatively tiny Sidney A. Murray Jr. Dam at Old River Control on the Mississippi.[19]

Menem approved the EDI offer by decree in December 1996, bypassing the democratic process. For Argentines who had only recently emerged from dictatorship, this was yet another abuse of power under Yankee influence. As filmmaker and activist Glenn Switkes of International Rivers noted a year later:

> To secure the Argentine government's support for the project, the consortium has employed high-level officials of the Bush administration, according to Argentine press reports.
>
> Among the consortium's lobbyists: former Treasury Secretary Nicholas Brady, now chair of Dillon Read, which would coordinate financing for the project; former Defense Secretary Richard Cheney, chair of the board of Halliburton, Brown and Root's parent company; and the ex-president's son, Texas Governor George Bush, Jr.[20]

Rivers have mortal enemies. But their ability to fight back flows through those who know them most intimately. In early 1996 when the Paraná Medio project was first publicly announced, two fishermen, Luis "Cosita" Romero and Raúl Rocco, began wondering what they could do to save the river and their own way of life from millions of tons of compacted earth and reinforced concrete. Romero was convinced that resistance was an absolute necessity, but Rocco had the audacious idea: they'd put a fishing skiff on the back of a truck, travel upstream to Yacyretá, and row 600 miles downstream to their home port of Paraná where the dam was to be built.[21] At every town along the way they'd stop to rally the river defenders, debate the authorities, and steal the public's hearts with a rendition of Rocco's poem, "The Fisherman's Pride." So, like a pair of Davids in a cockleshell boat, they set off to confront Goliath Incorporated: a recklessly ambitious Argentinean president, a group of immensely powerful Gulf Coast engineering firms, and the whole George H.W. Bush gang in action. Despite all the promises of modernization coming from the incorporated powers, a multiscalar civil society coalition would rather listen to the river.

Some twenty years after the fact, I'll never forget a wild night on a Casa Río trip in a half-ruined house on a bluff in Paraná city overlooking the immense dark river, drinking staunch red wine and listening to Cosita Romero tell his hilarious tale.[22] After writing NEVER AGAIN in chalk letters on the wall of the Yacyretá dam, the two began their journey, meeting allies in one port and adversaries in the next, taking sides with the generous and confronting the indifference of the majority. Every day their oars bit into the powerful brown current. And slowly the balance began to tremble. In the town of La Paz 3,000 people came out to greet them. And in Santa Elena the next day they heard drums over the water. Then a fire engine arrived at the dock to parade them through the city, where municipal authorities were shaking their hands and reporters were lining up for interviews. Back home in Paraná, the port and the streets were theirs, and on September 25, 1997, the province of Entre Ríos asserted its hard-won democratic rights by legislating that the large rivers under its jurisdiction would forever flow free of impoundments.[23]

The First International Meeting of People Affected by Dams was held in Curitiba, Brazil on March 14, 1997.[24] In that same year, the presidential decree authorizing the Paraná Medio dam was declared unconstitutional by the Supreme Court of Argentina. Negotiations over the Hidrovía came to a halt in the year 2000 when Brazil suspended its collaboration over concerns about the environmental integrity of the Pantanal.[25] In 1999, Carlos Menem's presidency ended under clouds of scandal, and two years later his successor, Fernando de la Rúa, had to flee the presidential palace in a helicopter. The river had spoken, the Argentine popular uprising of December 2001 had begun, and for a few years no further steps were taken toward the draining of the Paraguay-Paraná wetlands.

BIOCULTURAL VISION

After the victories of the century's close, some of the Ríos Vivos organizations took advantage of Latin America's leftward turn (the "Pink Tide") to formulate a socio-environmental strategy that would enable local inhabitants and river activists to work jointly with regional governments. Like the North American bioregionalists of the 1970s, they envisaged their territory not in terms of national boundaries but as a watershed: the La Plata basin, containing parts of Argentina, Bolivia, Brazil, Uruguay, and Paraguay.[26] Here they saw a field of experimentation on the scale of contemporary ecological issues, focusing not only on conservation but also on questions of survival and cultural flourishing for both Indigenous and campesino populations. A series of founding acts led to a new collaborative framework in 2007, the Alliance for the Paraná-Paraguay Wetlands System ("Alianza Sistema"[27]). The alliance aimed to create a feedback loop, using bottom-up practices to generate environmental policies that would simultaneously protect the wetlands corridor and restore popular access to the river-based lifeways sustaining the social movement. Alianza Sistema proposed that it was not the technocratic state but the actions of local inhabitants that maintained the dynamic equilibrium of the La Plata River basin.

Centro de Saberes, Itaipú Dam, 2011. Photograph by Alejandro Meitin

From their grassroots positions, alliance members reached into regional governments, creating a transnational "Center for Socio-Environmental Knowledge and Care of the La Plata Basin" which brought river defenders *inside* the gargantuan Itaipú dam on the Upper Paraná beginning in 2006. With the support of Brazilian environmental minister Marina Silva, the Center for Socio-Environmental Knowledge and Care sought to oppose and supplant the Intergovernmental Committee on the Paraguay-Paraná Waterway. Claiming the ecological rights of a bioregion, this watershed-scale institution proposed biocultural restoration in place of accelerated industrial development. Its five principles distill an astounding clarity:

1. Water as integrative theme.
2. The basin as operational territory.
3. Environmental thinking as the conceptual framework for action.
4. Environmental education as social mobilizer.
5. The collective construction of knowledge, action and organization.[28]

A period of utopian thinking opened up in Latin America in the mid 2000s. It spread internationally through global-scale projects like the World Social Forum, launched in Brazil in the wake of 1990s antiglobalization activism. Ríos Vivos and its inheritors participated intensively in this utopian upsurge, as did many campesino and Indigenous movements.[29] All of this inspiration has remained alive to the present day. Yet across the years of social and environmental progress, logistical planning continued in the vaults of power.

In 1998, the Andean Development Corporation (one of the major banks behind the Hidrovía) published a collectively authored volume under an enigmatic title: "The Rivers Unite Us: Fluvial Integration in South America."[30] The book, replete with maps, proposed a series of canal infrastructures creating linkages between all the continent's major river systems. The aim was to create an integrated maritime transport corridor on a north-south axis, running all the way from Buenos Aires through the Pantanal and the Amazon basin to the Amacuro delta of the Orinoco River, with additional east-west road and rail connections. Two years later, in August 2000 at a Summit of South American Presidents held in Brasília, a similar but even more extensive set of plans was adopted as the Initiative for the Integration of Regional Infrastructure in South America (IIRSA, now COSIPLAN).

In this iteration, the Hidrovía concept for the regional integration of the Mercosur economies was extended to the entire continent, with a plethora of east-west multimodal corridors boosting Asian trade.[31] Meanwhile, the expansion of the "soy frontier" continued, reaching far beyond the La Plata basin into distant Amazonia. It is hard to overstate the sweeping changes that the golden bean, and the worldwide appetite for meat that it feeds, have brought to Latin America since the early 1990s.[32] The "technological package" (genetically modified seeds, no-till farm equipment, and glyphosate pesticide raining down from small planes) has been applied to vast acreages using the financial strategy of "planters' pools" (*pools de siembra*) to put together the mega-farms required for industrial agriculture. In the worst and most profitable cases, notably in Argentina's northwestern Gran Chaco region, local inhabitants are expelled or killed, primary forest is summarily burnt, globally significant quantities of CO2 are released to the atmosphere, the soil food web is seriously degraded, and the hydrological cycle is gravely damaged.[33] In the same process, the new class fraction of the corporatized "countryside" (*el Campo*) emerges as a powerful political actor, pressing for trade liberalization and currency convertibility to fuel yet more frontier expansion.[34]

Fishermen, Paraná River.
Photograph by Alejandro Meitin

Land use change of these proportions has Earth system consequences. It disrupts biogeochemical cycles, effecting "metabolic rifts" at multiple scales.[35] An example of such transformations of terrestrial metabolism is the continental-scale disruption of the hydrological cycle by deforestation. For the last 30 years in Brazil, there have been studies suggesting that the atmospheric rivers arising from evapotranspiration in the Amazonian jungle and transporting water to the Southern Cone of Latin America might substantially dry up as the forest is converted to savanna. In fact, they recently did so during the severe drought that affected the Argentinean Pampa in 2019–20 and then again in 2023–24.[36] This is an apocalyptic prospect for the Paraná-Paraguay fluvial corridor, whose wetlands, forests, and verdant grasslands depend on rain wafting down from the neighboring basin. How do we live with the foreknowledge of disaster? How can grassroots groups respond to the all-pervasive phenomena of global ecological mutations?

In 2017, the organizations of Alianza Sistema again reformulated their endeavors, this time under the name Humedales sin Fronteras (Wetlands Without Borders). A look at the online map[37] Casa Río has created to illustrate the Wetlands Without Borders program reveals a philosophy that has taken form over three decades of experience. Entitled *Corridors*, the map offers a double vision of the La Plata basin. One view depicts it in textured black like a gigantic burnt-out cinder, with a sinuous blue line studded with red dots running north to south. This is the *extractive corridor*, marking the Hidrovía and its industrial ports. Additional layers represent the ecological damage of soybean expansion, deforestation, and ever-worsening fires (often deliberately set to clear away native trees for soybeans or cattle). By contrast, the other view of the basin is composed in tropical tones of brown, green, yellow, and magenta, inspired by the colors of water hyacinth floating on muddy streams. This is an emergent collaborative map of *biocultural corridors*, which are conceived not as the entire sweep of the river valley but as localized patches declared and cared for by specific groups.

Often located near urban areas, these projects emerge from local efforts at consciousness raising, land defense, restoration, and continuing stewardship. In Argentina, member organizations of Humedales sin Fronteras have created biocultural festivals while at the same time attempting to inscribe the corridors into national and provincial law.[38] The aim is "learning from the flood" by multiplying the opportunities for fluvial reconnection to human beings. As one reads in the sidebar text of the map:

> It is vital that biological corridors remain interconnected, to allow the continuity of ecological processes such as genetic exchange, evolution, migration and repopulation. Yet the idea of biocultural corridors also involves human knowledge, beliefs and practices that bring a symbolic-biotic fabric into play, where cosmovision, myth and ritual, history, memory and cultural expression all act as dimensions of the territory.[39]

Bioculturalism emerges from the meeting of Indigenous and traditional lifeways and contemporary ecological science, particularly Gaia theory. One of the latter's crucial insights is this: life creates the conditions of habitability for life.[40] This is explicitly the case when a river floods a wetland, opening it to the flourishing of insects, fish, birds, and mammals. It's also the case when Amazonian trees exhale water vapor that falls as rain on the La Plata basin. And isn't some very similar principle at work when Indigenous social forms act to sustain rather than destroy their surrounding environments?[41] Bioculturalism suggests that a range of actors, both human and nonhuman, can take on such sustaining roles together, exercising a steering function not by means of any centralized plan or design but instead through generalized sensory feedbacks that allow each part to fit more intricately into the whole.[42] This reciprocal fitness is also relatively easy to recognize and, therefore, to intensify. Bioculturalism is a mode of inhabitation that contributes to the habitability of a territory.

Biocultural relations can be experienced among the Guaraní peoples of Paraguay, with whom the Wetlands Without Borders member organization Sobrevivencia[43] does much of its work. They can be found in the lives of the traditional mestizo communities practicing hunting, fishing, and seasonal cattle grazing in the flooded Pantanal wetlands close to another member organization, Instituto Gaia.[44] But they can also be encountered in the more densely colonized and heavily industrialized regions of the Paraná delta and the Río de La Plata estuary, where member organizations including FARN,[45] CAUCE,[46] and Taller Ecologista[47] are located. In these regions the artisanal agriculture inherited from impoverished Italian immigrants coexists with contemporary agro-ecological farming, land-defender conservationists, organic gardeners, and urban green-space movements.[48] The question asked by Humedales sin Fronteras is how to recover, develop, and share an old/new cosmovision whose sources ultimately lie in the capacity of rivers to sustain the territories through which they flow. The aesthetic that seems to move everyone involved is not any particular image or sacred representation but something more like an overflow of singular gestures through place and time, expressing a trans-regional and trans-species perception.

On the Mississippi south of Carbondale, Illinois, there's a place called Dogtooth Bend that speaks to me more clearly on each visit. In 2019, the overtopping river ripped out a lengthy section of farmer-built levee, depositing many tons of sand on the fields along with a number of hulking barges that eventually had to be cut up with welding torches and hauled away. Here the deep current wants to fulfill a fundamental river desire, to cut off a constrictive bend and rediscover its own uninhibited flow on the other side. Amazingly, the Army Corps did not choose to build a higher levee at the breach, but instead chose to follow the emergent doctrine of "room for the river," a flood-control technique that operates by simply restoring the water's access to the territory. To help out the stranded landowners, The Nature Conservancy has partnered with the federal government to provide conservation payments for the land, which has become increasingly risky to farm since the 2019 breach.[49] What one can witness, year by year, is the growth of an old/new wetland, with a riotous influx of riverine species during the annual floods as well as a gradual reforestation of adjacent ground. Yet what's still missing on this stretch of the Mississippi is a biocultural transformation of human life: a new/old way of re-inhabiting the water and the land.

How fragile is the rebirth of an ecosystem? It's the question that people involved with restoration are beginning to dread. Like the 1990s, this is the decade of every danger, including a relaunch of the Hidrovía project in Latin America.[50] Yet at the same time, patches of biocultural desire keep re-emerging across the earth, even as the climate crisis deepens. As this article is being finalized, social movements in the La Plata basin are organizing a floating protest down the Paraguay-Paraná from Asunción to Rosario to celebrate the living memory of Cosita Romero and renew the demand for regional autonomy and sustainable development. Meanwhile, in the Mississippi basin, just think about the Anishinaabe on their rice lakes in the headwaters, the anti-pipeline activists attending trainings, the prairie restorationists scattered across the Midwest, those who still travel the great river in canoes, and everyone in Louisiana who struggles to save their land from simply collapsing into the sea under the onslaught of an obsolete petroleum economy that destroys inhabitable territory. As climate change doubles down, it's time to reach out with empathy and start talking to each other across species, languages, continents, and other great divides. We can do it just as rivers do: through an overflow of liquid expression and an undertow of geographical sensitivity.

Bioculture now!

A version of this article was originally published in the journal Open Rivers *(Winter/Spring 2025).*

ENDNOTES

1 The concept was developed in the transdisciplinary research project "Mississippi. An Anthropocene River," organized by the Haus der Kulturen der Welt and the Max Planck Institute for the History of Science in 2019. See https://www.anthropocene-curriculum.org/project/mississippi.

2 Luisa Maffi and Ellen Woodley, eds., *Biocultural Diversity Conservation: A Global Sourcebook* (Earthscan, 2010); Karl M. Wantzen, ed., *River Cultures: Life as a Dance to the Rhythm of the Waters* (UNESCO, 2023), https://unesdoc.unesco.org/ark:/48223/pf0000382775/PDF/382775eng.pdf.multi.

3 "Home," Wetlands without Borders, accessed October 17, 2025, https://humedalessinfronteras.org/en/.

4 Wolfgang J. Junk, Peter B. Bayley, and Richard E. Sparks, "The Flood Pulse Concept in River-Floodplain Systems," *Canadian Special Publication of Fisheries and Aquatic Sciences* 106, no. 1 (1989): 110–27; Cleber J. R. Alho and José Sabino, "Seasonal Pantanal Flood Pulse: Implications for Biodiversity Conservation—A Review," *Oecologia Australis* 16, no. 4 (2012): 958–78.

5 "Home," Territorios de Colaboración: Pedagogías de lo Anegado, accessed February 1, 2025, https://territorios.casariolab.art/home.

6 Charles A. Camillo and Matthew T. Pearcy, *Upon Their Shoulders: A History of the Mississippi River Commission from its Inception through the Advent of the Modern Mississippi River and Tributaries Project* (Mississippi River Commission, 2004), chap. 10–12.

7 John O. Anfinson, *The River We Have Wrought: A History of the Upper Mississippi* (University of Minnesota Press, 2003), chap. 10, 11 and Epilogue.

8 Nick Estes, *Our History Is the Future: Standing Rock Versus the Dakota Access Pipeline, and the Long Tradition of Indigenous Resistance* (Verso, 2019), chap. 4, "Flood."

9 Heather Dalton, *Merchants and Explorers: Roger Barlow, Sebastian Cabot, and Networks of Atlantic Exchange 1500–1560* (Oxford University Press, 2016), chap. 6.

10 Miguel Altieri and Walter Pengue, "GM soybean: Latin America's new colonizer," Seedling, January 2006, available at https://grain.org/en/article/588-gm-soybean-latin-america-s-new-colonizer; Xiao-Peng Song et al., "Massive Soybean Expansion in South America since 2000 and Implications for Conservation," *Nature Sustainability* 4 (June 2021): 784–792.

11 "Home," Secretaria Ejecutiva Del Comité Intergubernamental Hidrovía, accessed October 17, 2025, http://hidrovia.org/.

12 Griselda Capaldo, "South American Paraná-Paraguay Waterway (Hydrovia): An Environmental Diagnosis and Prognosis," *Yearbook of International Environmental Law* 14 (2003): 185–210.

13 Enrique H. Bucher and Paul C. Huszar, "Critical Environmental Costs of the Paraguay-Paraná Waterway Project in South America," *Ecological Economics* 15 (1995): 3–9. For an update, see Álvaro Álvarez, "Hidrovía Paraguay-Paraná: Entre el Río y la Autopista Fluvial" (published by the Humedales sin Fronteras member organizations CAUCE, FARN, and Taller Ecologista, 2022), https://tallerecologista.org.ar/wp-content/uploads/2022/11/hpp22web-oct.pdf.

14 Johan F. Gottgens et al., "The Paraguay–Paraná Hidrovía: Protecting the Pantanal with Lessons from the Past," *BioScience* 51, no. 4 (2001): 301–08.

15 Gisela Ariana Rausch, "Justicia Espacial, Políticas de lo Justo e Instauraciones Transversales. La Coalición Ríos Vivos y la Hidrovía Paraguay Paraná (Argentina, Década de 1990)," *A&P Continuidad* 7, no. 12 (2020): 52–61.

16 "Home," International Rivers | People, Water, Life, October 2, 2025, https://www.internationalrivers.org/

17 Colalición Ríos Vivos, *Sustentabilidad, Diversidad y Democracia* (ECOA, 2003), 28, https://ecoa.org.br/wp-content/uploads/2017/01/SUSTENTABILIDAD-DIVERSIDAD-Y-DEMOCRACIA-ilovepdf-compressed.pdf.

18 Gisela Ariana Rausch, "Proyectos Hidráulicos, Ambientalismos y Re-escalamiento Territorial: La Disputa en Torno a la Construcción del Proyecto Paraná Medio en el Proceso de Neoliberalización de Argentina, 1995–1997," *Revista de Geografía Norte Grande* 69 (2018): 169–90.

19 Marla J. Barnes, "The Story Behind the Sidney A. Murray Project," *Hydro Review* 10 (1990): 30–40.

20 Glen Switkes, "A River Runs Private: The Paraná Medio Project and the Coming Latin American Private Dam Craze," *The Multinational Monitor* 18, no. 10 (1997), https://www.multinationalmonitor.org/hyper/mm1097.06.html.

21 "Enamorados del río," interview with Raúl Rocco and Luis "Cosita" Romero, *Revista Barrilete,* August 4, 2016, http://revistabarriletesparana.blogspot.com/2016/08/enamorados-del-rio.html.

22 You can hear Cosita Romero in the series of four podcasts produced in 2020 by Humedales sin Fronteras member organization CAUCE: "Fluir Infinito: Viaje Sensible por el Paraná," https://cauceecologico.org/fluirinfinito.

23 Province of Entre Ríos, "Ley Anti Represas. Libertad de los Ríos Paraná y Uruguay, Ley 9022," Argentina Ambiental https://argentinambiental.com/legislacion/entre-rios/ley-9092-ley-anti-represas-libertad-los-rios-parana-uruguay. The law was integrated to Article 85 of the provincial constitution in 2008.

24 "Declaration of Curitiba," RiverNet by European Rivers Network, 1997, https://www.rivernet.org/general/movement/curitiba.htm.

25 Gottgens et al., "The Paraguay–Paraná Hidrovía."

26 On the North American bioregional movement, see Cheryll Glotfelty and Eve Quesnel, eds., *The Biosphere and the Bioregion: Essential Writings of Peter Berg* (Routledge, 2015), plus the cartographic and sociological work of David McClosky, available at https://cascadia-institute.org. For an example of bioregional thinking in the Southern Cone of Latin America, see Eduardo Gudynas, "El Concepto de Regionalismo Autónomo y el Desarrollo Sustentable en el Cono Sur," in Eduardo Gudynas, ed., *Sustentabilidad y Regionalismo en el Cono Sur* (Editorial Coscoroba, 200): 178–211.

27 "Bienvenidos a Alianza Sistema de Humedales," Alianza Sistema de Humedales Paraguay-Paraná, September 1, 2013, https://web.archive.org/web/20130901132403/http://www.alianzasistema.org/

28 Itaipú Binancional, *Acuerdo de Cooperación Técnica, Científica e Financiera (Itaipú Binacional, PNUMA/ORPALC, FPTI, CIC),* 2006.

29 See, for example, the panel on "Water—A Common Good" at the Third World Social Forum in 2003, moderated by Glenn Switkes and Elias Díaz Peña, in *Another World Is Possible: World Social Forum Proposals for an Alternative Globalization,* eds. William F. Fisher and Thomas Ponniah (Zed Books, 2015): 130–35.

30 J. Perea Borda, ed. *Los Ríos Nos Unen: Integración Fluvial Suramericana* (Corporación Andina de Fomento, 1998), https://scioteca.caf.com/handle/123456789/868.

31 J. Miguel Kanai, "The Pervasiveness of Neoliberal Territorial Design: Cross-Border Infrastructure Planning in South America Since the Introduction of IIRSA," *Geoforum* 69 (2016):

160–70; Daiana E. Melón, "The Integration of Regional Infrastructure in South America (IIRSA): Territorial Coloniality at the Service of Extractivism," *Alternautas* 9, no. 2 (2022): 209–21.

32 Walter A. Pengue, *Agricultura Industrial y Transnacionalización en América Latin: ¿La transgénesis de un continente?* (Grupo de Ecología del Paisaje y Medio Ambiente and Programa de las Naciones Unidas para el Medio Ambiente, 2005); Claiton Marcio da Silva and Claudio de Majo, eds., *The Age of the Soybean: An Environmental History of Soy During the Great Acceleration* (White Horse Press, 2022).

33 Rodolfo Chisleanschi, "The Lost Forests of the Argentine Gran Chaco," *Mongabay*, August 19, 2020, https://news.mongabay.com/2020/08/the-lost-forests-of-the-argentine-gran-chaco.

34 Germán Armengol, *El Conflicto del Campo de 2008: Consolidación del Modelo Sectorial de Agro-Negocios y Crisis de Hegemonía* (Bachelor's thesis, Universidad Nacional de La Plata, Facultad de Humanidades y Ciencias de la Educación, 2015), http://www.memoria.fahce.unlp.edu.ar/tesis/te.1183/te.1183.pdf.

35 John Bellamy Foster, *Marx's Ecology: Materialism and Nature* (Monthly Review Press, 2000); Brian M. Napoletano, Jaime Paneque-Gálvez and Antonio Vieyra, "Spatial Fix and Metabolic Rift as Conceptual Tools in Land-Change Science," *Capitalism Nature Socialism* 26, no. 4 (2015): 198–214.

36 Marcus Jorge Bottinno et. al., "Amazon Savannization and Climate Change Are Projected to Increase Dry Season Length and Temperature Extremes over Brazil," *Scientific Reports* 14, no. 5131 (2024), https://www.nature.com/articles/s41598-024-55176-5. The theoretical basis of this analysis was established by the coupled atmosphere-biosphere models of Carlos A. Nobre and his colleagues; cf. Nobre et al., "Amazonian Deforestation and Regional Climate Change," *Journal of Climate* 4 (1991): 957–88.

37 "Corredores Bioculturales (Marane'y Rape)," Casa Río Lab, accessed October 20, 2025, https://map.casariolab.art/#/valle/biocultural?center=-27.126,-60.130&zoom=3.830.

38 The groups Casa Río, CAUCE, FARN and Taller Ecologista define a biocultural corridor as "a clearly defined geographic space, located in urban, suburban or rural areas, that safeguards the natural and cultural heritage it hosts, whether material or immaterial, maintaining healthy interconnected ecosystems, favoring the connection of existing and future protected areas, fostering restoration processes, and promoting socially and ecologically responsible economic and residential uses of the territory." See "Corredores Bioculturales en la Estrategia Nacional de Biodiversidad," https://farn.org.ar/wp-content/uploads/2024/05/Corredores-Bioculturales-en-la-Estrategia-Nacional-de-Biodiversidad-HSF-Argentina.pdf.

39 "Corridors," Casa Río Lab, accessed February 1, 2025, https://map.casariolab.art.

40 Timothy M. Lenton, Sébastien Dutreuil, and Bruno Latour, "Life on Earth Is Hard to Spot," *Anthropocene Review* 7, no. 3 (2022): 248–72. For the original formulation, see James Lovelock and Lynn Margulis, "Atmospheric Homeostasis by and for the Biosphere: The Gaia Hypothesis," *Tellus* 26 (1974): 2–10.

41 Peter Veit, David Gibbs, and Katie Reytar, "Indigenous Forests Are Some of the Amazon's Last Carbon Sinks," World Resources Institute, "Insights" (2023): https://www.wri.org/insights/amazon-carbon-sink-indigenous-forests.

42 Bruce Clark, *Gaian Systems: Lynn Margulis, Neocybernetics and the End of the Anthropocene* (University of Minnesota Press, 2020).

43 "Sobrevivencia Amigos de La Tierra Paraguay," Sobrevivencia: Apoyo Integral a Comunidades Nativas y Ecosistemas, accessed October 21, 2025, https://www.sobrevivencia.org.py/.

44 "Instituto Gaia," Instituto de Pesquisa e Educação Ambiental - Gaia, accessed October 21, 2025, https://www.institutogaiapantanal.org/.

45 "Inicio," FARN | Fundación Ambiente y Recursos Naturales, September 3, 2024, https://farn.org.ar/.

46 "Home," CAUCE —Cultura Ambiental Causa Ecologista, accessed October 21, 2025, https://cauceecologico.org/.

47 "Inicio," Taller Ecologista, accessed October 21, 2025, https://tallerecologista.org.ar/.

48 For the most developed example of a biocultural corridor, see the map of the Greater La Plata Ring organized by Casa Río in collaboration with a large number of local inhabitants.

49 Shelly Morris, "Success Stories—Dogtooth Bend Restoration Project," uploaded by One Mississippi, July 27, 2020, YouTube, 53 min., 44 sec., https://www.youtube.com/watch?v=l6HjfHJyY2s.

50 Karl M. Wantzen et. al., "The End of an Entire Biome? World's Largest Wetland, the Pantanal, Is Menaced by the Hidrovía Project Which Is Uncertain to Sustainably Support Large-scale Navigation," *Science of The Total Environment* 908 (2024).

Planting a Seed Is a Revolutionary Act: A Blues Epistemology for the Anthropocene?

Jason Ludwig

Jason Ludwig celebrates the efforts of local activists in reconstructing the Black history of Natchez, Mississippi—long suppressed by the city—because its tourist economy is built atop its antebellum heritage. In doing so, an Anthropocene at the intersection of racial capitalism, enslavement, and environmental injustice can be revealed. Ludwig offers a "blues epistemology" (Clyde Woods) as a way to build a critical historical consciousness that is crucial for just futures.

A mural commissioned by Cooperation Jackson. Photograph by Jason Ludwig

I: THE VIEW FROM NATCHEZ

When I visit huge mansions
I run around to the back,
looking for the house
behind the house behind
the Big house where my origins
begin in this Republic.

—Sterling D Plumpp[1]

"Natchez was and is a segregated town," explained Jeremy Houston, a local tour guide and historian. This Mississippi city with a population of around 15,000 is also an unusual starting point for any effort to conceptualize the Anthropocene. Compared to the dramatic scenes of resource extraction usually associated with this term, Natchez is a slow and quiet place—seemingly far adrift from the global march of unmitigated extractivism that has harbored climactic and geological catastrophe on a planetary scale. Nevertheless, as Jeremy led our group of curious students, artists, and researchers through the town in October 2019, I found myself wondering: what exactly, then, can Natchez teach us about the Anthropocene?

Although once home to thriving paper mills and rubber plants, Natchez has since been left behind by an industrial economy that has sought cheaper labor abroad. Today the city depends for most of its money on a tourist industry that encourages visitors to spend days (and nights) on grounds once worked by enslaved people. The city's verdant meadows are dotted with grand manors sporting equally grand names like Longwood or Rosalie Mansion, former cotton plantations, and homes of cotton planters that have been converted into museums or bed and breakfast inns. These all aim to display to visitors to the city the wealth and opulence that once belonged to its antebellum, slave-owning elite. In Natchez today, tourists are invited to not only eat dinner on tables once owned by those who made their fortune in the trade of other human beings, but also—if one is so inclined—to take "haunted" Halloween tours through their plantation grounds, their bedrooms, and even the cellars of their mansions (although visitors are left to imagine for themselves the identities of the tattered and tortured ghosts who might be stalking the halls of the master's house).

If the concept of the Anthropocene points our attention to the future, Natchez on the other hand feels like a town designed to send visitors on a trip back through time. But as Jeremy was at pains to point out, the image of the past that the average tourist receives is an incomplete one. While Antebellum Natchez certainly was one of the country's wealthiest cities, its grandeur and wealth was produced by the labor of enslaved people—none of whom could enjoy the benefits of these riches. Theirs is the history you will not receive while staying at a bed and breakfast, Jeremy explained. And that is why he and other Black residents have taken it upon themselves to tell the other half of the city's history—the story of its Black past. They have invested many years of labor into doing so, erecting several placards and monuments throughout the city, marking sites of importance to the history of Black Natchez. These include slave markets, blues clubs, and the homes and business places of post-emancipation Black community leaders and civil rights activists. Jeremy himself has played a prominent role in recovering this long-ignored past, publishing a multi-volume history of Black Natchez, working as a docent at the city's African-American History Museum (opened in 1991), and founding his own historical tour company.[2]

The institutionalization of Black history in Natchez has only been possible thanks to long battles fought by local activists. The memorialization of the Forks of the Roads slave market is a case in point. The market, located at what was once a busy intersection along the city's eastern border, was founded in 1808 by the slave traders Isaac Franklin and John Armfield. Until 1845 it was a principal trading post in the global exchange of human bodies, with thousands of enslaved Africans and their descendants marched out on display under the brutal Mississippi sun, to be gazed upon by prospective buyers as well as a curious public. At its peak, around 500 enslaved persons were sold per day at Fork of the Roads, making it the largest Southern slave market outside of New Orleans. Such prodigious commercial activity was fueled by a developmentalist ideology that tied the economic growth of Natchez and the surrounding region to the expansion of the plantation economy as well as to the brutal bondage and exchange of enslaved bodies undergirding it. Its chief slogan—which made today's thriving plantation tourist economy possible—is captured in an old advertisement for the Forks of the Roads market (reproduced in facsimile on one of the placards that stands at the site today):"Buy More Negroes to Raise More Cotton to Buy More Negroes." And so on and so forth.

Despite this history, the grounds where the Forks of the Road market once stood remained empty of any historical markers until 1998 when local community members campaigned to memorialize the site. After a protracted battle with city leaders, who were worried that such actions might taint the city's reputation as the civilized and aristocratic "Jewel of the Mississippi" (which, they feared, would harm the tourist industry), the campaign succeeded, leading to the erection of placards that narrate the history of the Forks of the Road. Today, visitors to the site will find on display iron chains that once held enslaved people waiting to be sold into the brutal economy of Mississippi's cotton kingdom.

That this history remained silenced for so long is all the more egregious considering its relevance to present-day concerns. With his profits from slave-trading at the market, Isaac Franklin started his own cotton plantation in nearby Baton Rouge in the 1830s. With sardonic cruelty, he named it after the country from which he had imported most of his enslaved workforce: Angola. Nearly two hundred years later and in its current guise as the largest and most notorious maximum-security prison in the United States, the Louisiana State Penitentiary—the Angola Plantation—continues to operate as a site geared towards extracting maximum value from Black bodies in bondage.

That such connections to the past remained for so long hidden from public memory is no mere accident. Nor is it surprising. A plethora of

A historical placard at the Forks of the Road slave market memorialization. Photograph by Jason Ludwig

scholars have shown how, like murderers hiding the bodies of their victims, dominant institutions expunge the histories of violence that enabled their ascension in order to cover their hegemony under a veil of normalcy.[3] In Natchez, the image of the city presented by the tourist industry depends to a large extent upon such silencing of the past. As the work done by Jeremy and others who have sought to recover the history of Black Natchez shows, however, marginalized groups can and will contest the monopolization of historical narration.

The lessons this offers towards understanding the dynamics of the Anthropocene is that just like fossil fuels, just like cotton, just like tourism, history has a political economy too. And just as rethinking and reshaping our dependency on oil and coal is crucial for building a more livable future in the Anthropocene, it is also vital that we develop new forms of critical historical consciousness and institutions of public memory that place the injustices of the past on trial. Such work, which Jeremy and others in Natchez have long been engaged in, is an ineliminable step towards building a more just world. As the poet and native Mississippian Natasha Trethewey has written, confronting the challenges of the future means first "reckoning with our own blindness and erasures."[74] Put another way, reckoning with the Anthropocene requires not mistaking huge mansions to be our history, and searching instead for the stories hidden away in the house behind the house behind the Big House.

II: SINGING THE BLUES IN THE ANTHROPOCENE

One scholar whose life work equated to just such a colossal effort to uncover lost Black histories is Clyde Woods. In his writings on the history of the Mississippi Delta, Woods argued that the alluvial soils of the region gave birth not only to the logics of domination that justified the racial violence and ecological exploitation still prevalent in the United States today, but also to the most cogent forms of critique and resistance—what he named the "blues epistemology." Woods describes the blues epistemology as a Black intellectual tradition vested in collective deconstruction of the "plantation relations" that first destroyed Black identities and aspirations during enslavement, and which continue to do so over 150 years after emancipation. As a mode of knowing and expressing anguish at the Black past, indicting the injustices of the present, and imagining and building towards a more just future, the blues epistemology can be understood as oriented around social and personal investigation of two critical questions: "How did we get to where we are now?" and "How do we get to where we want to be?"

> DOMINANT INSTITUTIONS EXPUNGE THE HISTORIES OF VIOLENCE THAT ENABLED THEIR ASCENSION IN ORDER TO COVER THEIR HEGEMONY UNDER A VEIL OF NORMALCY.

And as those preserving the history of Black Natchez have shown, the blues epistemology and the forms of survival and resistance it has engendered have always been present in the city and the surrounding region. Its presence can be felt today in the Natchez Museum of African American History and Culture, where one can read the stories of the formerly enslaved who sought to build new lives for themselves while caught within a freedom that was not truly free; or about the musicians and writers, from Papa Lightfoot and Richard Wright to Anne Moody and the Ealey Brothers, who sought melodic and literary languages with which to express blues wisdoms; or even about Wharlest Jackson, whose life was stolen by a car bomb because he dared to speak up and fight for Black equality. Their stories all attest to the fact that as long as plantations have stood in Natchez, there have been voices courageous enough to indict the violence and exploitation that they stand for.

These voices must be amplified and their insights must inform every conversation concerning the Anthropocene. If the term "Anthropocene" conjures up apocalyptic images of ecological catastrophe, mass precarity, and the fragility of human life, who better to guide our thinking about these issues than those voices who have for generations engaged in critique and resistance against systems of violence and exploitation? Woods expresses this idea perfectly,[5] stating that future political and economic movements must take strides to

> celebrate and valorize the millions upon millions, living and dead who met the regimes of destruction with unshakeable dignity. In the same vein, the lands, rivers, streams, air, plants and animals of the region must be restored to their sacred status. Until then, 'every hill and molehill,' every blade of grass, every flutter of the flag, and every note that is played must be contested.

> THE PLANTATIONS STANDING ALONG THE MISSISSIPPI RIVER REPRESENT THE FOUNDATIONS OF THE MODERN HIERARCHICAL WORLD-SYSTEM, AND SIGNIFY THE VIOLENCES THAT ANNOUNCED ENTRY INTO THE ANTHROPOCENE.

From the viewpoint Woods offers us, the Mississippi Delta and its surrounding areas emerge as pre-eminent sites for understanding the historical forces that have shaped the Anthropocene. The blues epistemology offers the conceptual means for comprehending how this region never truly was the heart of an "empire of liberty," as Thomas Jefferson once dreamed of it, but was instead the epicenter of the nightmare that was American slaveocracy. Thinking the blues in the Anthropocene means attending to the history that tracks the expropriation of territories along the Mississippi, from Native populations and the radical reshaping of these lands into an ever-expanding regime aimed at extracting maximum value from land and from brutalized Black bodies. The tendrils of this regime stretched far beyond the banks of the river, its cotton and capital traveling across the Atlantic to fuel the industrial economies that European powers would later apply towards colonizing much of the globe.[6] Seen from the blues perspective, then, the plantations standing along the Mississippi River represent the foundations of the modern hierarchical world-system,

Richard Wright exhibit, The Natchez Museum of African American History and Culture. Photograph by Jason Ludwig

and signify the violences that announced entry into the Anthropocene. Only once the constitutive role that these historical violences against nature and people played in the development of the modern world is acknowledged can the important work of constructing more livable futures begin in earnest. This is the foundational truth to which the blues epistemology has always attested. The pantheon of blues thinkers enumerated by Woods—and indeed, Woods himself—demonstrate an express commitment to developing a new social order centered on the liberation of subjugated lands and people. No figure expresses this ideal better than Fannie Lou Hamer, who founded the Freedom Farm Cooperative in Sunflower County, Mississippi in 1969. Believing that true freedom would remain unattainable for the Delta's Black population so long as wealthy white planters monopolized land, Hamer started the farms in order to promote Black self-reliance in the region. For Hamer, the Freedom Farms expressed her philosophy that land should be communally-owned and that Black survival in Mississippi depended on seeking the necessary means for "channeling legitimate discontent into creative and progressive action for change," whether it be through practicing sustainable agricultural or organizing political movements.[7] To this end, the Freedom Farms produced food intended to feed Mississippi's impoverished and struggling Black families, while also offering affordable housing, educational opportunities, and various other services.

Although a lack of funding meant that the Freedom Farms were short-lived, such an experiment in envisioning and enacting a more socially and ecologically just world is instructive for our present moment, which is plagued as much by social injustice as by looming environmental catastrophe. Indeed, Hamer's work at the Freedom Farms has continued to serve as touchstone and guidance for those concerned with sustaining Black life amidst the future challenges presented by the Anthropocene.

III: BLACK AND BLUES FUTURES

Like Jeremy fighting to uncover the past of Black Natchez, others in Mississippi are reclaiming the legacy of Fannie Lou Hamer and the blues tradition in their efforts to develop a more liberatory Black future. The relevance of the blues epistemology to conceptualizations of the Anthropocene is most apparent in Mississippi's capital, Jackson. In the "City with Soul," Cooperation Jackson is organizing Black and Latino working-class communities towards building an environmentally sustainable, worker-owned cooperative. So far, this consists of the Freedom Farms (named after Hamer's cooperative), community maker-spaces, and a land trust upon which efforts are underway to develop worker-owned businesses and housing. Across these sites, the group seeks to develop the institutions and infrastructures necessary to sustain Black life in the face of the planetary devastation associated with the Anthropocene.

This work draws heavily on the inspiration of previous generations of Black radical thinkers and activists, ranging from Hamer to Kuwasi Balagoon, the radical Black poet and anarchist. The Cooperative's current work also builds upon the legacy of the Jackson-Kush Plan, a generations-old Black re-imagining of the city of Jackson and the Mississippi River Valley that envisions the region as a catalyst for a sweeping transformation of the living conditions of Black Americans. The plan envisions the creation of a Black-led New Afrikan Republic in Mississippi, Louisiana, Arkansas, and Tennessee that models itself after the Ancient Egyptian Kushite Civilization, with the Mississippi River serving as the fertile analog to the Nile.

Through their work, which blends Mississippi's long tradition of Black critical thought with expertise in twenty-first-century digital tools, Cooperation Jackson applies the blues epistemology towards developing what the historian Rayvon Fouché has described as a "black politics of

technology," a radical reshaping of technological processes in a manner responsive to Black needs. The result is in a broad vision of what radical Black future-making in the Anthropocene might look like.[8]
The cooperative's work is foremost concerned with addressing the resource deprivation that is a direct legacy of the ecological devastation and underdevelopment wrought by the plantation economy on Mississippi's landscape. Kali Akuno, one of Cooperation Jackson's founders, has written that the history of Mississippi's development "has fundamentally been contingent upon the extraction of natural resources such as timber...and cash crop agriculture, such as cotton, tobacco, sugarcane and rice, which were primarily sold as international commodities."[9] However, with the nineteenth-century transition from a global capitalist system structured around agricultural commodities to one structured around fossil fuels, formerly monocultural economies like Mississippi, lacking the capital and infrastructural networks of more economically-advanced regions in the United States, have since been locked into a state of resource scarcity and underdevelopment.

The burdens of this underdevelopment have largely fallen onto Mississippi's Black population. Despite the abundance of food across the United States and of agricultural land in Mississippi itself, working-class and impoverished Black populations in the state face a variety of food-access deprivations. This food scarcity, an ongoing legacy of the plantation economy, has left Black communities in Jackson and the surrounding region with little to no access to fresh and healthy foods. Addressing this racially-stratified scarcity motivates Cooperation Jackson's work, which applies new and sustainable technologies towards continuing Hamer's efforts to advance black food sovereignty in the region. Their plans to achieve this include the creation of an Eco-village in the heart of the Downtown Gateway section of West Jackson—a "comprehensive, interconnected and interdependent supply and value chains...our own network of cooperative farms, processing centers, food hubs, compost and soil generators, food processors, canneries, grocery stores, etc."[10]

The cooperative seeks to further develop Black resource sovereignty by building the material and infrastructure for the Eco-village with tools created in their Centers for Community Production—maker-spaces that use open source sharing and 3D printing in order to develop sustainable, worker-controlled manufacturing. Through work like this, Cooperation

Jackson contributes a Black radical vision of technoscientific practice in the Anthropocene that imagines possibilities extending far beyond the visions of global "sustainable development" discourse, showing how new tools can be used not just to improve profit margins while cutting carbon emissions, but in order to catalyze the democratization of the economy, the transition to a sustainable economy, and the empowerment of vulnerable Black communities.

Like Hamer's Freedom Farms, Cooperation Jackson's work is as much about feeding impoverished Black Mississippians as it is about seeking out and enacting a more just world. Such undertakings locate the Anthropocenic task of the reshaping of our relations with the natural world as inextricably intertwined with the need to address and undo the legacies of centuries of racist violence. As Sister Imani Bridgeet Olugbala of the cooperative has put it: "planting a seed can be a revolutionary act." Through following this insight and earnestly engaging with histories of violence, as well as those of Black resistance, perhaps we can plant the seeds necessary to sustain and cultivate more just and ethical forms of life in the Anthropocene.

A version of this article was originally published on the website Anthropocene Curriculum (Summer 2020).

ENDNOTES

1 Sterling D. Plumpp, "In a Natchez Cemetery I...," excerpted in Clyde Woods, *Development Arrested: The Blues and Plantation Power in the Mississippi Delta* (Verso, 2017).

2 Plumpp, "In a Natchez Cemetery I...."

3 Michel-Rolph Trouillot, *Silencing the Past: Power and the Production of History* (Beacon Press, 2015).

4 Natasha D. Trethewey, *Beyond Katrina: A Meditation on the Mississippi Gulf Coast* (University of Georgia Press, 2015).

5 Clyde Woods, *Development Arrested: The Blues and Plantation Power in the Mississippi Delta* (Verso, 2017), 290.

6 Sven Beckert, *Empire of Cotton: A Global History* (Vintage, 2015); Walter Johnson, *River of Dark Dreams: Slavery and Empire in the Cotton Kingdom* (Harvard University Press, 2017); Eric Williams, *Capitalism and Slavery* (University of North Carolina Press, 1994).

7 Fannie Lou Hamer, "If the Name of the Game Is Survive, Survive," speech delivered in Ruleville, Mississippi, September 27, 1971, cited in Clyde Woods, *Development Arrested.*

8 Rayvon Fouché, "The Wretched of the Gulf: Racism, Technological Dramas, and Black Politics of Technology," *The Black Scholar* 36, no. 4 (2006): 7–12.

9 Kali Akuno, "Build and Fight: The Program and Strategy of Cooperation Jackson," in *Jackson Rising: The Struggle for Economic Democracy and Black Self-Determination in Jackson, Mississippi*, ed. Kali Akuno and Ajamu Nangwaya (Daraja Press, 2017).

10 Akuno, "Build and Fight: The Program and Strategy of Cooperation Jackson."

Fluvial Networks of Creative Resistance by Joe Underhill, page 42.
Photograph by Emily Sekine

Farmers' Markets, Community Gardens – Fighting Deserts with Greens

A recipe from the River Semester by MORGAN PIPER CORDOVA

Written for the Mississippi River Open School, this recipe is an excerpt of Mississippi Mud Book of Recipes, a collection of stories, reflections and recipes that Morgan Piper Cordova assembled while an undergraduate student on the Fall 2023 River Semester. Cordova traces connections between food sovereignty, environmental justice, and resistance, offering both practical recipes and deeper meditations on how "everything you need to live is around you" along the Mississippi River.

The Landmark Farmers Market in the East Orange neighborhood in Memphis had rules; co-founder and head gardener Mike Minnis made sure we knew them. No cussing or running was allowed in the garden, neither was smoking or consuming alcohol. "But most of all," he says, shifting from sincere to cautionary, "Do not–and I mean not hand, arm, or leg–do not touch the plants." There's a moment of silence before he gathers us in his arms breadth with a small smile and says, "Come on, let me show you how it's done."

We follow him behind the white store with orange trim into a volcanic eruption of stark green life. He leads us through the garden, leaning his weight on a cane but strong as the rows of fruit trees that tower over the neighborhood. He explains how to cure depression and Alzheimer's with coriander and describes the benefits of an annual bodily detox (gives the organs a break in their constant exercise of moving processed foods through our body). He gestures to the loofah vines that canopy the garden as a community member shells black walnuts in pecan-colored water. He describes the three best fertilizers that he's tested and been able to produce from livestock in pools and earthen mounds on the property (red worm, fish, and chicken poops). He describes the year-long growing cycle in Memphis and the volcanic rock minerals that the river deposited on his land for the past millennia. "These rocks make these plants grow like crazy!" He explains how horses and gorillas are both vegans "and can carry their own weight at birth. Huge, strong creatures!" He takes us to the apiary. "I've been beekeeping for years, and I always get stung. I taught my daughter how to take care of the bees, and she never gets stung. You know why? We have different prerogatives. She wants to take care of the bees, I just want the honey." He shrugs and we move on. He mutters again, almost to himself, "Do it for the bees, not the honey."

The Landmark Farmers Market is the work of married couple Mike and Karen Minnis, and the whole garden is only situated on a half acre of land. Mike told us, "You only need a half acre to have a sustainable farmers' market." They make five tons of produce a season, and distribute it to East Orange, a Black neighborhood in southeast Memphis. The community helps them, and they give back through training in agriculture, fresh produce and herbal medicine.

Community gardens are described flippantly by the ignorant as "sustainable" forms of agriculture. But for most, especially those without access to fresh produce in their community, sustainability extends beyond just environmentalism buzzwords. As Mike Minnis made sure to remind us, "Another aspect of sustainability is self-sufficiency." I heard this mantra echoed in Black and Indigenous gardeners up and down the whole river valley. Self-sufficiency is the key to community survival. Another aspect of sustainability is finding a means for passing down narratives and knowledge about the land and the biodiversity that grows on it, and that's largely done through food for Black and Indigenous people. Kinship is no longer something that is merely a goal for marginalized communities, but necessary for survival.

Dail Chambers runs a few community gardens under the name North Saint Louis Nutritional Resilience. In some places, North St. Louis resembles a rural farmstead, large vacant lots are left where there once stood infrastructure for Black communities; torn down by the city to sell to developers in an act of "urban renewal." During COVID, Chambers began buying up land that the City planned to offer to developers for $28 an acre. She began to introduce an abundance into the neighborhood through these "Coahoma Orchards" and frequent neighborhood meals as she told us over the phone in one of her gardens in the Jeff VanderLou Neighborhood, "The garden is about taking care of each other."

Community gardens like Landmark and Coahoma Orchards exemplify kinship ideals present in Native cosmologies. The Lakota live by the principles of "being a good relative," kinship is recognizing that a sustainable system of living cannot be a result of domination. When Mike Minnis speaks of taking care of the bees rather than the honey, he speaks of a relationship that goes beyond commodity. Kinship requires a relationship that doesn't disconnect us from our sources of food and all of the factors that go into making that food accessible. That doesn't mean we need all of our food to grow in our backyard. Kinship today requires us to go beyond optics. Community groups, like A Red Circle in North St. Louis, find food shares through grocery stores and surplus from Black and Indigenous farmers outside of the city.

Kinship is predicated on social healing and the physical and mental health of the community. Respiratory illness is common in North St. Louis where chemical fires burn underground and particulate matter from industry turns the sky orange. Cardiovascular illness is also common in communities with high concentrations of commodity foods. Dale Chambers tells us about social pollination projects, where she interviews neighbors to ask what medicines they would like to see growing in the gardens. The goals of these orchards are to fight climate change and allow for shade in a hot, black concrete neighborhood. "The things that grow up around you are the medicine you need," Chambers says. Right now, Chambers has 40 perennial herbs and flowers growing in her gardens.

Along with fostering communities of care, these gardens work for the propagation of communal and cultural narratives. In North St. Louis alone, Chambers's social pollination projects give space for locals to request the native foods and medicines of their family and homeland. "Sioux Chef" Sean Sherman in Minneapolis has created the Indigenous Food Lab, effectively a test kitchen for pre-colonial ingredients and meals grown locally in Minnesota.

Not just in urban gardens, but in rural communities as well. Preserving narrative history also requires work and solidarity between farmers inside and outside the city. The urban gardens we encountered in Minneapolis, St. Louis, and Baton Rouge bridged the gap between rural and urban growers. There are many food hubs and cooperatives in North St. Louis, including organizations that teach people how to produce and process foods in their own communities, learning about history, culture and medicine. Basmin told us, "When we start eating native foods again–we will start to remember stories."

All of the Black and Indigenous gardeners and activists we encountered on this trip recognized the importance of food education as an exercise of sovereignty. St. Louis Indigenous artist and activist Saundi McClain-Kloeckener has a medicine program, reintroducing native foods and health products to communities. The Water Protector Welcome Center in Northern Minnesota is planning on hosting seasonal camps, run by the Wakemup family, for hunting, ricing, and sugar bushing. These Indigenous practices operate in a tense balance between US and Tribal Government licensing, family dynamics, and a lack of land and funds. But these practices are also necessary for life, as sustaining a lifeway is dependent on traditional practices. Land, food, and survival are intertwined and catastrophically threatened for Indigenous and Black populations in America. You control the food, you control the people. The first step to liberation is food sovereignty.

Monique Verdin, a Houma activist based in the Yakni Chito between the Atchafalaya and Mississippi Rivers, affirmed this sentiment. Between these two rivers live many different yet interrelated tribes, making the establishment of a single identity group potentially harmful to cultures and familial bonds. Because of this, Indigenous people in Southern Louisiana have struggled to receive recognition of their sovereignty. Verdin told us, "Many Indigenous people have realized they need to assert their sovereignty in this region... Sovereignty starts with food security." The largely Indigenous and Cajun residents of barrier island Isle de Jean Charles were, and are, subsistence farmers. In 2014, they were the first to receive a federal relocation grant in response to land displacement from sea-level rise and increased hurricane damage. They were moved 30 miles inland, into $200,000 houses that they were forced to pay taxes and insurance on. They are a people who built their communities and fed their families on fat fish and bottomless crawdad. Verdin says, "What are they gonna do now? Work at Walmart?"

Andeab + Mila Berhane's Hibiscus Tea

BATON ROUGE

Mila brought this out to us as we toured their garden, meandering around their own hibiscus and other plants native to Eritrea and East Africa.

HIBISCUS SABDARIFFA:

A Sorrel from Eritrea, steeped in hot water.

Add Cinnamon, sugar (or honey), + Ginger to taste, serve cold over ice cubes.

Mila says, "Better with rum!"

Andeab and Mila Berhane's Greenhand Nursery and Red Stick Farmers Market in Baton Rouge sits on a venerable international forest on the banks of a bayou in Northern Baton Rouge. As we move through the Mississippi River Valley south of St. Louis, year-long growing seasons give non-native plants from Africa and South America opportunities to thrive. Andeab is from Eritrea, and as he leads us through the garden, he shows us various plants from East Africa that he has grown from collected seeds. For every plant, he opens up a seed casing and offers us the seeded interior. Mila is from the Dominican Republic and teaches agriculture and decorative botany at Southern University A&M in Baton Rouge. It's clear during our tour of the greenhouse complex that her students and peers revere her. Many of the people there are alums who come to visit her and the space again. "This is my favorite place in the world," one says, "with my favorite people."

Their enormous, lush garden/forest sits on two acres. When I asked how many people work on it, Andeab pointed to the two of them, and then up towards the sky. In an equally important way, gardens are a journal, a record keeping of one's life and exploration of trauma. Michael W. Twitty writes that food for Black people is genetic, preparing and making southern "soul" food is a form of genealogy. The Berhanes' sons aren't interested in taking the garden from their parents when they die, but that doesn't seem to worry Mila and Andeab. For Andeab and Mila and Karen and Mike, their garden is their progeny, their love and their memory. The work of growing, sharing, and teaching about food is not a political action, but a practice necessary for being in community.

Speakeasy Farm's Peach Leaf Tea

NEW ORLEANS

Steep Peach Leaves in hot water overnight. The hot water releases the tannins in the Peach Leaves which will benefit our respiratory health.

It especially helps in moments of hot, angry grief, when a scream or cry feels necessary.

The Chemistry of Dirt: Reflecting on Three Years of the Mississippi River Open School

Jeremy Meckler

Reflecting on three years of involvement in the Mississippi River Open School's experimental and experiential pedagogy, Jeremy Meckler offers examples of efforts to "evert" the university, including riverboat storytelling, a pyramid of spectacular capitalism, and the confluence of people from the river's headwaters to the Gulf. What connects these activities is a radical openness to the critical exploration of the legacies of coloniality, environmental injustice, and creative resistance.

There is no such thing in nature as the chemistry of cobalt. There is dirt, but nobody wants to have anything to do with the chemistry of dirt because dirt is in fact genuinely complex. Photograph by Jeremy Meckler

I started working with the Mississippi River Open School for Kinship and Social Exchange around its inception. Having known and worked with many of the core organizers already, and bringing a background in the humanities academy, I like to think that I was a natural fit. But I didn't really know what I was getting into and, as it turns out, neither did anyone else.

I'm still not really sure how to describe this project or my role in it. The Open School is loosely conceived by design, inclusive rather than limited, and more than anything else I've ever been involved with in the academy, willing to work through and even embrace uncertainty. As we often reiterated in the first year of the Open School, our strategy was to build the boat while we paddle it. That approach has come with a variety of challenges. Half-built boats don't typically follow clear nautical trajectories, so getting off the shore can be challenging. But by building the boat together, by developing and engaging community inside and outside of traditional academic spaces, and by discovering together what the Open School can do and be, we ended up with a project that is radically open, useful and productive for those who are typically excluded from academic and creative spaces. The Open School is about connection, collaboration, and solidarity, in an increasingly alienated world. Sticking with the metaphor, a boat that is built while we paddle it might look different from a traditional vessel, but it also might be able to do things or take us places that we've never seen before. And importantly, it belongs to all of us who built it and continue to build it together. A wave might send our boat off course to wash up on a new shore that a more rigid course would have hidden from view entirely. Someone might help us as our prototype boat runs into an unexpected issue, as prototypes do, and then join us for the rest of the journey.

In other words, the Mississippi River Open School is, by design, experimental, an attempt to develop new community-engaged and community-designed pedagogies and epistemologies within the often calcified space of academic teaching/learning. (Disrupting conventional hierarchies between teacher and learner is a central part of this experimental design, which is why I am deliberately conflating teaching and learning throughout this essay.) This radical formulation is perhaps best articulated by one of our guiding "themes," which was so central that it was included in the title of the project: open school. According to its extended description, a lofty statement of principles, the Open School aims to "evert" the university, to turn the systems of the university inside out, reversing the extractive nature of academic incursions into the objects of its research by making the resources of the academy accessible beyond the confines of the ivory tower. How to enact this guiding principle is one of the things we've been trying to figure out.

The Mississippi River Open School is a descendant of a variety of other similarly constructed projects, most centrally several ongoing projects structured around the Anthropocene, a term that refers to the geologic epoch in which human activity has dramatically affected life on earth. The Anthropocene Commons, the Anthropocene Curriculum, and the several Anthropocene Campus* events that have happened around the world have all been organized by members or partners of the Open School. What I have come to realize over the course of several experimental, experiential teaching/learning expeditions with the Open School and other Anthropocene projects is that an important key to achieving these goals, a key to working toward everting the university and enacting a mode of embodied, experiential learning, is embracing the contingency that comes from direct engagement in the real world and from truly open collaboration in community. This means designing teaching/learning events that are deliberately collaborative and open-ended, allowing an unplanned creative process to unfold with and among the participants. Sometimes this radically open nature will reveal things and sometimes it will allow pedagogical models to adapt to the rapidly changing world. The world is a complicated place and, in the Anthropocene, the pace of change is accelerating. New climate records are set nearly every day and our predictive models are increasingly failing to predict events, be they climactic, political, or social.

We have yet to reach a consensus on a name for the kinds of pedagogy around which this project has been oriented. It certainly seeks to challenge the traditional hierarchies and elitisms of the academic mode, as articulated in the open school theme, but what is this mode of teaching/learning and how do we describe it? We've organized a series of events—some called field trips, others confluences or camps, one particularly ambitious project called a semester, and others campuses or reading groups or field schools—but all have similar goals and a similar method. The best term I've settled on to describe this method is "experiential learning." Experiential learning is descriptive in many ways, but also frustratingly vague, too easily confused with its use across a wide range of educational institutions to mean anything from vocational training to industrial networking to counter-hegemonic expansions from the classroom. (We hew closest to this last definition.) But despite its broadness, experiential learning's strength is that it emphasizes the centrality of experience, of being in a place, smelling it, feeling it, and having that haptic input inform the theoretical and historical ideas that often dominate academic thought. Material presence ends up making the whole thing less cerebral and more impactful, more directly felt. At the risk of being a corny academic, it's an attempt to realize—in a pedagogical context—the goals Karl Marx laid out in his early writings, a movement from the airy cerebral theories of German idealism to a materialist conception

* Anthropocene Campus is a series of public events and activities designed to explore the concept of the Anthropocene and its implications for knowledge, research, and education. It has brought together scholars, artists, activists, and others to examine the Anthropocene in order to develop new approaches to understanding and addressing the challenges of this geological epoch. The initial Anthropocene Campuses were initiated by Haus der Kulturen der Welt and the Max Planck Institute for the History of Science starting in 2014. They continue to be organized with the participation of the Anthropocene Commons and other partners.

of history. As he put it so incisively in his 1845 *Theses on Feuerbach*: "The philosophers have only interpreted the world in various ways; the point, however, is to change it." By engaging directly with the world being studied, by dropping the pretense of the academy as somehow separate from the world it studies, these experiential learning models aim to interact directly and materially with the many crises we are all living through. Our explicit goal of everting the university is deeply tied to this material teaching/learning model.

In science, there is often a distinction drawn between the classroom, where teaching is conducted, the lab, where research is conducted, and the field, where subjects of research are observed or collected; in our experiential model, these three spaces are inseparable, messy, chaotic, and impossible to control in the way things might be in a climate-controlled space, but more honest, interconnected, and true. It is by leaning into the contingency, by welcoming and embracing fluidity, and by designing pedagogical methods that are collaborative and community-centered that we can make this form of teaching/learning really work, and by doing so, stumble into experiences that are profound and interconnected, experiences that extend the classroom out into the world beyond. To borrow a metaphor from experimental filmmaker Hollis Frampton, this mode aims to engage with what he calls "the chemistry of dirt." As he put it, describing his own messy, complex, modernist film project *Magellan*:

> Inorganic chemistry purports to study such things as "cobalt." Well, in a certain sense, yes, there is such a thing as cobalt, but it is a product of the laboratory. It's a fiction. There is no such thing in nature as the chemistry of cobalt. There is dirt, but nobody wants to have anything to do with the chemistry of dirt because dirt is in fact genuinely complex.[1]

Following Frampton, the only way to achieve meaningful engagement with the real world, to tear down the imaginary boundaries between academy and research subject and grapple with the genuinely complex world around us, is to get our hands dirty.

Scenes from our symbolic and performative workshop with Dakota astronomy professor Jim Rock. Photograph by Jeremy Meckler

So in reflecting on one of the Mississippi River Open School's goals—everting the university through a new kind of pedagogy—and the early mantra of our project—building the boat while we paddle it—it seems appropriate to begin by thinking about specific, embodied experiences where a pedagogy that embraced contingency and radical openness led to revelation. The rest of this essay, accordingly, is organized around two personal stories, pulled from my involvement with this project. These were moments where we extended the space of learning beyond the classroom and saw connections more broadly and more clearly than we could have planned it.

THE ONLY WAY TO ACHIEVE MEANINGFUL ENGAGEMENT WITH THE REAL WORLD... IS TO GET OUR HANDS DIRTY.

SCENE I: THE RIVERBOAT

In May of 2023 we hosted the Open School's second "confluence" in the Twin Cities, a gathering of local partners and those affiliated with hubs up and down the Mississippi. As the first confluence in 2022 was virtual, this second confluence was the first time many of us were meeting in person, a joyful weekend of encounter and exploration. In addition to conventional meetings, the three-and-a-half-day event was deliberately organized around open-ended collaborative experiences that could blur lines between researcher and object of study, teacher and student, and the academy and the "real world." We taught/learned about history, community, and resistance

Lock and Dam No. 1, with its large cantilevered observation tower, is particularly carceral when viewed from the lower river level. Photo by Little Rock District Public Affairs

at the nascent Welcome Water Protector Center in Palisade, Minnesota, a site near the headwaters of the Mississippi where a major Stop Line 3 action camp had been based; we entered new worlds together at the Indigenous Futures Lab at the University of Minnesota where virtual reality visualizations approximate Indigenous ways of knowing; we joined with Community Members for Environmental Justice for an environmental justice tour of the redlined and historically disinvested Black neighborhoods on Minneapolis's northside that highlighted the group's recent legislative accomplishments; and we spent time at several Saint Paul sites important to the Dakota people and the history of Indigenous land theft in the region. In truth, we probably planned too many events, with not enough down time for participants to situate themselves or reflect on their experiences; the weekend was action-packed. But in our defense, we wanted to make the most of our teaching/learning time together and we had never done this as a group before.

Accordingly, by the end of our last full day people were pooped. Our early afternoon session, a fascinating, if at times overwhelming, symbolic and performative workshop with Dakota astronomy professor Jim Rock, had run over our allotted time (in direct sun, no less) and we had rushed our way through a tour of Waḳaŋ Ṭípi Awanyankapi, a native-led environmental stewardship organization working to preserve a neglected historical Dakota village in Saint Paul. Attendees had spent three days being shuttled around Minnesota, meeting with researchers, activists, organizers, and artists, and connecting with the disparate blend of people that the confluence brought together, all working on similar themes.

That final afternoon we had planned for a session with two traditional Indigenous storytellers at the Waḳaŋ Ṭípi Awanyankapi site before dinner on the *Magnolia Blossom*, a charming if kitschy riverboat that would take us out for a dinner on the water as a celebration of the confluence as a whole. Squeezed for time, generally wiped, and embracing the contingent flow of the event planning, we invited the storytellers onto our river cruise. The result was unexpectedly magical.

First, being on the river itself in the Twin Cities was something of a revelation. We had visited the riverbank up north in Palisade, where the river is only a few yards across and where we spent most of our time swatting at the mosquitos that swarmed us on the muddy shoreline. And it was hardly our first time thinking about the river. Many of us live close to the river and cross it regularly, and it was the Mississippi that brought us all together. (I live blocks from the river in

Minneapolis and walk my dog there most mornings before crossing a bridge to work in Saint Paul.) But even with this near-daily interaction, I seldom get down to water level to experience the cities from a river-eye-view. Riding the *Magnolia Blossom* through the Mississippi River gorge separating Saint Paul from Minneapolis was eye-opening. The urban architecture of the cities loomed overhead, in particular two major pieces of industrial infrastructure built to control the river: Fort Snelling, the U.S. Military fortress constructed in 1825 at a Dakota holy site, and Lock and Dam No. 1, the 1929 cement structure that controls river flow through the Twin Cities.

Fort Snelling has a well documented history as a site of colonial atrocities. It was the primary military base from which the U.S. Army waged the U.S.-Dakota War of 1862, it was the site of a horrifically inhumane post-war wintertime internment of over 1600 Dakota non-combatants (primarily women and children, at least 300 of whom died during their internment), and its construction overlooking Bdote, the site which Dakota people have venerated for over 10,000 years as the center of the earth, makes it stand out as a stark example of the forms of economic, military, and psychological persecution that were emblematic of the westward expansion of the United States. But given the broad pedagogical aims of our project and the intention of tying together the various historical strands that weave together to make our contemporary extractive systems, it also serves as a sterling example of the ways in which anti-black racism and coloniality were and are intertwined. Despite being located in a free state, the northernmost of northern states, Fort Snelling was a site at which slavery was actively practiced. In fact, Fort Snelling played a key role in the events precipitating the U.S. Civil War as one of the people enslaved there was Dred Scott, the plaintiff in the contentious 1857 U.S. Supreme Court decision, *Dred Scott v. Sanford,* which excluded Black people from American citizenship, dramatically escalating interstate tensions and more or less making inevitable the conflict that would break out in the Civil War four years later. The specific history of Fort Snelling as site was not an explicit focus of the confluence weekend, but broader histories of Black and Indigenous displacement up and down the Mississippi were strongly emphasized throughout, so the hulking specter of Fort Snelling looming over us felt both appropriate and valuable to our reflection on the weekend.

A couple of miles up the river from Fort Snelling sits Lock and Dam No. 1, the northernmost lock on the Mississippi that remains in operation today. Originally constructed in 1917 and rebuilt in 1929, Lock and Dam No. 1 controls the river level as far north as the Lower Saint Anthony Falls Lock and Dam in downtown Minneapolis, which was permanently closed to boat traffic in 2015 to stop the northward incursion of several invasive species of Asian carp up the Mississippi watershed. The two dams that bookend the river in the Twin Cities turn its surface into a pristine, navigable, lake-like waterway. The lock in Lock and Dam No. 1 seldom operates today, as most of the northernmost industrial traffic on the Mississippi ends a few miles downstream in Saint Paul's Lowertown. Lock and Dam No. 1 is colloquially known as the Ford Dam as it contains a hydroelectric power station which provided electricity to the adjacent Ford Motor Company's Twin Cities Assembly Plant in Saint Paul until its closure in 2011. The cement water control edifice, like all public infrastructure from nearly a century ago, requires regular maintenance which represents a significant expense, and given how little the lock is used anymore, the Army Corps of Engineers (which owns and manages the lock and dam) is currently engaged in a disposition study to try to decide what to do with this aging structure. It is possible that the Corps will recommend removal, a relatively drastic and expensive step, but one that would cut off the ongoing costs associated with maintaining a century-old piece of civil engineering. If removed, the thirty-six-foot height difference of the lock would be reincorporated into the flow of the river, "rewilding" the river and restoring the stretch between downtown Minneapolis and Saint Paul from an easily navigable flat industrial channel into its original form, a stretch of dynamic rapids. Such a drastic change comes with many potential side effects being explored by the disposition study. The existing lock and dam is an interesting physical reminder of the ways in

Despite a dubious conception and a tumultuous construction process involving a split between the two financiers, bankruptcy proceedings for the construction company, and reportedly, a cursed crystal skull welded to the tip of the pyramid, the Memphis Pyramid was completed in 1991. Photograph by Jeremy Thompson (CC BY 2.0)

which the American economy has changed in the last few decades—now more historical than industrial, this huge hunk of concrete is a monument to shipping, manufacturing, and car culture that has now become something of a white elephant to the Army Corps.

Seeing these structures from the river was instructive, the extreme low angle emphasizing the panoptic qualities both structures possess as prison-like observation sites overlooking the river valley. Fort Snelling's site on a bluff overlooking the river makes it look impregnable and the cement bulk of Lock and Dam No. 1, with its large cantilevered observation tower, is particularly carceral when viewed from the lower river level. Their authoritarian positioning, craning over the river to monitor and control the flow and use of the largest watershed in North America, serves as a strong visual metaphor for the settler colonial practices that undergird the expansion of European settlers into the Upper Midwest. But the other thing that was striking, and that doesn't present itself so readily from the city-level infrastructure surrounding the river, is just how little of the space of the river is effectively controlled by these measures. For all of their bulk, Fort Snelling and Lock and Dam No. 1 are dwarfed by thousands of acres of wooded hillsides, tiny tributaries, and other natural infrastructural elements that long pre-exist the incursion of European "development" into the area. For thousands of years, the river served as a major canoe thoroughfare, connecting the Dakota and Anishinaabe people to others across the sprawling Mississippi rivershed. While physical attempts to control the power of the Mississippi have undoubtedly affected it, they also seem so paltry in comparison to the river's own intentions. The first Lock and Dam No. 1 was completed in 1917 and after roughly one hundred years of operation, it could be removed in the next few decades. It will be a blip in the long history of the Mississippi's flow. The incursion of colonial and neocolonial practices on the river were felt directly as we floated along the river on a kitschy riverboat, but after a weekend engaging with new ways of thinking about the river, it was nearly impossible not to see the possibilities that alternative lifeways and knowledgeways present for living on the industrialized Mississippi.

> AFTER A WEEKEND ENGAGING WITH NEW WAYS OF THINKING ABOUT THE RIVER, IT WAS NEARLY IMPOSSIBLE NOT TO SEE THE POSSIBILITIES THAT ALTERNATIVE LIFEWAYS AND KNOWLEDGEWAYS PRESENT FOR LIVING ON THE INDUSTRIALIZED MISSISSIPPI.

And so, wiped out from a long three days of engagement, we all gathered on the top deck of the *Magnolia Blossom* and ate dinner, catered by a local Hmong restaurant, while we listened to stories from the Salish and Dakota people. The eastern cottonwood trees (*Populus deltoides*) that line the river were in bloom, releasing their seeds as snow-like fluffs that drifted around us on the early summer evening. And unlike our experience up north, mosquitos seemed to leave us alone, as far out as we were in the central river channel. The whole experience, although we didn't plan it this way, was a magical and comprehensive aggregation of our goals for the weekend: we engaged with the river itself, with the histories and existing systems of colonial extraction that plague it, and with the alternative knowledgeways that present potential solutions to the late capitalist death spiral we find ourselves in. And these revelations, magical as their concurrence felt at the end of a long weekend, were the result of the connections that we had built together over our time together; the sense of community that comes out of collaborative open-ended experiential processes, the sense of solidarity and collectivity, as if we are all part of a movement and in this together, is what made these collective revelations possible. In short, this moment was the Open School in its process of becoming. We had all built the boat while we paddled it, and we just happened to reap the rewards of that experience on a paddle boat on the Mississippi. What had originally been conceived of as a celebratory fête after a weekend of engagement ended up, for me at least, leaving the strongest teaching/learning impression of the whole weekend.

SCENE II: THE PYRAMID

In October 2024 the Open School hosted our third confluence, this time in Memphis, Tennessee. A variety of programming was planned around environmental justice, Indigenous sovereignty, and the history of institutional racial discrimination that is so visible in the city of Memphis. A few blocks from Beale Street, the historic downtown blues district, is I Am A Man plaza, a memorial to the pivotal 1968 sanitation workers strike and to Dr. Martin Luther King Jr., who was assassinated in Memphis after delivering his famous "I Have Seen the Mountaintop" speech in favor of the striking sanitation workers. A few blocks from there is the Lorraine Motel, the actual site where King was shot which is now a civil rights museum. Another few blocks from there is the Black church where a young Aretha Franklin sang in the choir; the Stax recording studio where Isaac Hayes and Otis Redding recorded soul records; and on and on. Histories of America crop up throughout downtown Memphis and all of it is within a stone's throw of the Mississippi river, the major transportation corridor that is the reason that Memphis was developed where it is. The third confluence, which took us to several of these sites, aimed to draw out these themes for attendees, to show how the American slave system, racial capitalism, Indigenous land theft, and environmental exploitation are all intertwined, symptoms of what K. Wayne Yang, writing under the avatar la paperson, would call the "set of technologies" that make up settler colonialism.[2] Put more colloquially: same shit, different century.

On this trip, I made the (perhaps controversial) decision to bring my family—my wife and our two-year-old son. As any parent knows, a two-year-old is too young to sit still for a long presentation, discussion, or bus tour, so our trip operated on toddler time. We dipped in and out of the official confluence itinerary, sometimes rushing back to the hotel for a nap to meet up with the group later on and sometimes taking a morning or afternoon off to explore the city and entertain our toddler on our own. My wife took on the lion's share of childcare responsibility and we happily welcomed other confluence attendees who wanted to

A two-year-old sits on a camo-printed ATV overlooking an indoor cypress swamp. Photograph by Jeremy Meckler

run around and play with a rambunctious two-year-old. It was a fun, sometimes frantic, weekend with a lot of moving pieces, but it was in one of these off-script moments that I experienced one of the purest revelations of the trip. This moment was the afternoon we spent in what is likely the most unique building in Memphis: the 321-foot-tall, mirrored Memphis Pyramid.

Conceived as a symbol of the city by Memphis-based artist Mark C. Hartz in the 1950s, the construction of the pyramid was actualized decades later with the financial backing of Sidney Shlenker, a businessman and professional sports team owner, and John Tigrett, the founder of the House of Blues and Hard Rock Cafe. The dream was ambitious. As Shlenker told *The New York Times* in 1989, "it's going to be a monument like the Statue of Liberty or the Eiffel Tower, a signature for the city. The difference is this will have something to do inside it."[3] The aim was to build a sports arena and concert venue that could pay tribute to the original Memphis, the ancient Egyptian capital. Memphis, Tennessee was named after the Egyptian Memphis in 1819, mere months after the signing of the Treaty of Tuscaloosa which ceded the Chickasaw Nation land on which it stands to the United States. Memphis's founders included future president Andrew Jackson, who oversaw the signing of the Treaty of Tuscaloosa and who, along with fellow land speculators, immediately bought up much of the acreage that would become the city of Memphis. Jackson thought the river in what would become Memphis resembled the Nile, never having been to Egypt himself, and thus he named his new land speculation settlement after the Egyptian capital. That same year, the first municipal charter was submitted for Cairo, Illinois, 150 miles upriver at the confluence of the Mississippi and Ohio rivers. That region, for a variety of reasons, earned the moniker "Little Egypt." These dubious Egyptian origins, an almost bald-faced attempt to associate the expansionist American colonial project with the grandeur of an ancient civilization by way of a loose river metaphor, are reflected, literally, in the design of this opulent glass pyramid on the Mississippi. Philip J. Deloria's landmark 1998 book *Playing Indian* chronicles the ways in which white Americans forged a national identity by impersonating Native Americans, from the Boston Tea Party to the Boy Scouts, but perhaps on this stretch of the Mississippi, American identity was forged (on coercively ceded Chickasaw land) by "playing Egyptian."[4] If so, we might see the 30-story glass pyramid as a 20th century continuation of this legacy of impersonation.

Despite a dubious conception and a tumultuous construction process involving a split between the two financiers, bankruptcy proceedings for the construction company, and reportedly, a cursed crystal skull welded to the tip of the pyramid, the Memphis Pyramid was completed in 1991. It was briefly the largest pyramid in North America until it was surpassed two years later by the Luxor Hotel in Las Vegas, another quintessentially American attempt at stolen cultural valor. The Memphis Pyramid, a bizarre architectural folly on the Mississippi, served as a basketball arena for a decade for the University of Memphis men's team, as the site for many concerts and events, including some of Mike Tyson's biggest boxing matches, and as an enticement for an NBA team, the Vancouver Grizzlies, to relocate to Memphis in 2001. Within three years, however, due to strict contract stipulations with the Grizzlies, Memphis had constructed a new stadium, the Fed Ex Forum, a few blocks away, and they were left with an empty 321-foot mirrored pyramid on the eastern shore of the Mississippi.

In 2008, the city found a new and profoundly strange tenant for the edifice—the hunting and fishing retailer Bass Pro Shops. The pyramid now operates as a Bass Pro Shops superstore, replete with a staggering number of amenities. The facility includes: an extensive indoor cypress swamp, a saltwater aquarium, live alligators and enormous fish, the tallest freestanding elevator in America which takes visitors up to the pyramid's observation deck, ATVs, boats, a gun museum, hundreds of taxidermied animals, a shooting range, archery range, laser arcade, and bowling alley, a hotel, and at the heart of it all, a Wahlburgers restaurant, the burger chain founded by Mark Wahlberg and his brothers that is also the subject of the A&E reality series *Wahlburgers* that ran for ten seasons from 2014–2019. In keeping with the experiential quality of the teaching/learning we've been building, it's difficult to truly experience the chaotic grandeur of what is colloquially referred to as the Bass Pro Shops Pyramid without actually being there.

For a two-year-old, relatively sleep deprived from nights in a hotel and shaken from a disruption to his regular routine, this place was a paradise, with animals to look at, fishing reels to spin, and dozens of ATVs and boats to climb in and out of. But beyond the opulent in-your-face Americanness of this space there were other clues to understand and experience late-stage capitalism within this highly concentrated American context. Throughout the cypress swamp were kiosks, where Bass Pro Shops employees pitched passersby on special deals—to join our members' club or to sign up for a discounted stay at the hotel. "Would you like to come back and stay here?" said one snake oil salesperson as we walked by. To be literally hailed into a self-evidently predatory scheme while we wandered through a pyramid seemed, if anything, a little on the nose. The slogans on apparel and the range of deadly equipment was mildly shocking for us urban northerners. (This is of course not to say that Minnesota, where we live, lacks its own hunting and fishing culture, just that we spend more time at REI than at Cabela's, the biggest regional Bass Pro Shops competitor in our neck of the woods.)

In general the vibe was disconcerting. The place was packed, and the parking lot was full of gleaming pickup trucks and suburban Americans deeply invested in cosplaying as rural. Midway through our sojourn around the cypress swamp, my wife turned to me, struck by a revelation, and said, "Trump is going to win, isn't he?" But as we chased our sprinting toddler from fishing rod display to boat to ATV, trying to guide him away from the all-too-alluring firearms section, it was the Wahlburgers at the heart of the pyramid that seemed particularly striking. Here is a restaurant chain, conceived, bankrolled and promoted by the movie star/pop hip hop frontman of Marky Mark and the Funky Bunch, raised in Boston and spending most of his adult life in Los Angeles, targeting an American burger chain at a self-consciously middle-America crowd. (There is also a prominent location in the Mall of America in Bloomington, Minnesota.) Jean Baudrillard couldn't have dreamed up a simulacrum this dizzying.

This prime example of the vacuous nucleus of late capitalist American identity presented itself in a moment when we strayed from the itinerary. This third confluence, organized around the importance of place and engaging with the Anthropocene crises facing the region, around how the logics of institutional racism and colonial expansion continue to dominate our public lives, and highlighting the many grassroots attempts to resist these persistent forces, found (for me) its most impactful and lasting example in this shining pseudo-Egyptian edifice overlooking the river. The fact that this excursion wasn't actually a planned part of the confluence events didn't limit it as a moment of revelation. In fact, the radical openness of the whole confluence experience, the deliberate blending and loosening of boundaries between teacher/student, observer/participant, and family/parent/child/community helped to extend the teaching/learning experience beyond the strict confines of officially planned events.

We'd spent the whole weekend thinking about the river, its history and possibilities, and the way its uses have conditioned the European development of the central strip of North America. We had spent time in contemplation and community at Chucalissa Mounds, a Chickasaw holy site that long predates the incursion of Western ideologies of development into the region; we experienced beautiful examples of Black and Indigenous creative resistance, from a screening of an experimental documentary made by a Black filmmaking collective in Cairo, Illinois about Black bodies and the confluence of the Mississippi and Ohio rivers to Art House Cafe, an arts-centered community and economic development organization that also makes phenomenal smoked turkey ribs; we explored College Park, Soulsville and other southside neighborhoods with the leader of the Memphis Interfaith Coalition for Action and Hope; we contemplated the river and our relationship to it from an enormous picture window at the Church of the River; and we played and explored Tom Lee Park along the river's east shore, a newly redeveloped public park with a playground where kids can climb on giant versions of animals that live in the river (otters, lizards, sturgeons) and where sports equipment can be checked out for free to use in shaded public basketball courts, pickleball courts, and more. We even walked down to the river to conduct a water blessing, led by an Indigenous leader from Saint Louis.

But through these experiences, the radical openness of the event design, and the spirit with which we were encouraged to enter collectively into these spaces and to think creatively and collaboratively about how we all fit into the flow of this massive waterway around which our project has been organized, allowed and actively encouraged my thinking to extend beyond the official boundaries of the itinerary. In fact, the ability to see an afternoon spent entertaining a toddler at a spectacle of a sporting goods store as inherently connected to the extractive colonial development of the lower Mississippi basin, highlighting the myriad problems that we are struggling with today, is a testament to how well the Open School is working. The gleaming modern pyramid, itself an iconographic element of a regressive nostalgia campaign that aims to associate American identity with ancient empire, is an attempt to disguise the histories of violence and dispossession that actually mark the site on the Mississippi's eastern shore. The fact that my little family saw that history buried in between all the fishing ponds and four-wheelers shows that our new experimental pedagogy is working and that our radically open pedagogical project is succeeding in tearing down boundaries between the academy and the "real world."[5]

THE GLEAMING MODERN PYRAMID IS AN ATTEMPT TO DISGUISE THE HISTORIES OF VIOLENCE AND DISPOSSESSION THAT ACTUALLY MARK THE SITE ON THE MISSISSIPPI'S EASTERN SHORE.

CONCLUSION

What I hope to have illustrated in these two examples is simple. It is the value of experience—in its most haptic and specific sense—the value of entering into the design of any teaching/learning process with an engaged sense of community, and with a willingness to embrace contingency and the complicated mess of the real world, which is not something to be studied but something to be a part of. In Minnesota and in Memphis, we found impactful and transformative moments and we found them by both engaging and by being open to broadly conceived possibilities of experience. If life in the Anthropocene tells us anything for certain, it's that we desperately need new ways to understand the world. We can't avoid it; we must adapt to the changing environment or be left behind. Our modes of teaching need to adapt too. By embracing contingency and by adopting an approach that is radically open and community-centered, we can develop a pedagogy that can help us to recognize, understand and survive the current and imminent crises and build sites of solidarity and resistance in the Anthropocene.

ENDNOTES

1 Hollis Frampton quoted in Scott MacDonald, *A Critical Cinema: Interviews with Independent Filmmakers* (University of California Press, 1988), 73. I adopt this rhetorical metaphor, proffered by a polymath experimental filmmaker and scholar in the humanities, with sincere apologies to any real chemists who might take issue with Frampton's mischaracterization of their field. Whether it is accurate or not to discussions of organic chemistry, it remains a useful framework for thinking about pedagogy.

2 la paperson, *A Third University Is Possible* (University of Minnesota Press, 2017).

3 Peter Applebome, "Era of the Great Pyramid Is Dawning in Memphis," *The New York Times*, July 23, 1989, https://www.nytimes.com/1989/07/23/us/era-of-the-great-pyramid-is-dawning-in-memphis.html.

4 Philip J. Deloria, *Playing Indian* (Yale University Press, 1998).

5 An extended version of this essay, incorporating a third scene in Brazil, is available at our website: www.mississippiriver.school.

Gulf South

The Gulf South includes the confluence of the Mississippi River with the Gulf of Mexico, the seventh-largest river delta on Earth. The Gulf South Open School is the southernmost river hub and comprised of artist organizers, activists, and educators. Together they explore how to learn and create collectively in the face of climate change, sea level rise, land loss, and environmental injustice.

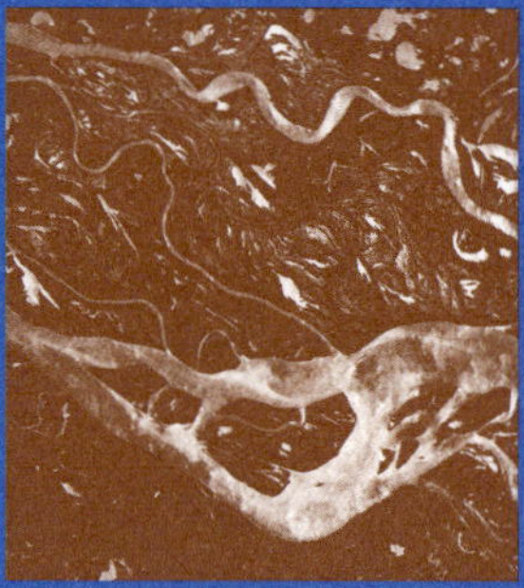

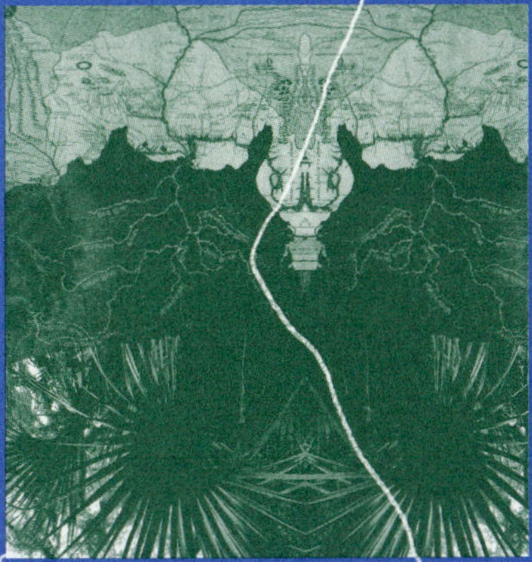

Geographies of Black Displacement: A Walking Discourse in Reading the Landscape Against Itself

Shana M. griffin

The Mississippi River is a colonial and carceral landscape. This is perhaps nowhere more apparent than New Orleans, which was strategically built along the river's banks. Shana M. griffin describes her development of walking as a critical spatial practice to reveal the city's hidden patterns of violence, geographies of displacement, and sites of resistance.

SITUATING THE PRACTICE

Walking is a method of knowing. A way of seeing what is often deliberately hidden or lingering in plain sight, yet waiting to be seen. As a critical practice, walking allows us to read the landscapes we traverse, recognize racial and gender constraints, interrogate spatial violence and inequality, and examine colonial assumptions embedded in the spaces we occupy. Walking restricts and facilitates new encounters and perspectives on what it means to "arrive," revealing who becomes visible and who is made to disappear.

Space, as critical geographer Camilla Hawthorne reminds us, "is not a blank slate on which human activity unfolds; instead, it is actively produced through power-laden processes. As such, space is always a site of struggle and contestation."[1] For black people, this struggle is embodied in everyday movements. Writer and landscape scholar Garnette Cadogan explains that walking makes him most alert to the world—to its "surrounding dangers and nearby delights"—as blackness necessitates a different reading of racialized urban spaces, one that is readily attuned to threats, adventures, surveillance, freedoms, and myths of safety. Walking, he writes, becomes "a complex and often oppressive negotiation," never neutral but always a spatial exercise in how race and gender structure access to public space.[2]

Walking draws attention to the racial and gendered experience of moving through space, transforming the mundane into a methodology for tracing how colonial violence becomes marked in the environment, how policy materializes in landscape, and how black communities create insurgent spatial knowledges. This includes what feminist historian Stephanie M. Camp refers to as "rival geographies"—movements by enslaved women against the plantation design's intended use, contesting "geographies of containment"[3] and displacement—alongside what black studies scholar and geographer Clyde Woods calls a "blues epistemology," vernacular ways of knowing place through lived experience and creative resistance.[4]

These frameworks, alongside the organizing efforts of black women public housing leaders, including my mother, Irene B. Griffin, shape my practice and inform the Geographies of Black Displacement walking discourse.

The author leading the Geographies of Black Displacement walk with members of the American Association of Geographers at their annual conference, 2018. Photographs by jazz franklin

WALKING AS DISCOURSE

Geographies of Black Displacement, a nearly three-hour walking discourse, traces the violence of displacement, containment, and disposability in land-use planning, housing policy, and urban development impacting black communities in New Orleans and the surrounding region.

Geographies of Black Displacement is not urban history packaged for tourist consumption, nor a walk for architectural appreciation of the colonial city, nor a narrative delivered to passive audiences. This discourse uses walking as a method to produce spatial knowledges, as an embodied investigation of how violence and inequality become spatialized, and as a pedagogy for reading the landscape critically across three neighborhoods: the historic French Quarter, the Bienville Basin neighborhood in Tremé, and the edge of Lower Mid-City.

Central to this practice is reading the urban landscape against itself. During the walk, we interrogate the built environment to reveal geographies of displacement, patterns of violence, and sites of resistance. Monuments, slave quarters, vacant lots, street names, and architectural mismatches bear traces of suppressed histories.

In 2018, I designed Geographies of Black Displacement as a walking field trip for the American Association of Geographers annual meeting, which that year focused on the theme "Black Geographies" and the work of Clyde Woods.[5] What began as an academic excursion evolved into an ongoing public practice engaging diverse audiences across multiple contexts.

This practice draws from and is situated within two interconnected projects that center black feminist spatial knowledges: DISPLACED, an interactive, multimedia, public history project documenting displacement in New Orleans and the surrounding region, and PUNCTUATE, an interdisciplinary project that combines research, art, and activism to challenge violent planning logics.

When the Gulf South Open School launched as a hub of the Mississippi River Open School for Kinship and Social Exchange, focusing on the river as a site of extraction and radical possibility, this framework deepened the walking discourse work by providing crucial context for understanding New Orleans' displacement geographies within watershed-scale systems.

The Mississippi River is not a backdrop but a watershed of infrastructure—an Indigenous trade route and site of sustenance, transformed by conquest into navigational technologies to build empire and support the slave trade. New Orleans exists where deltaic land, shaped by geological forces and seized through colonization, enabled plantation economies to extract wealth, labor, and resources. Walking the streets of New Orleans with attention to the river makes visible how decisions about water, land, and infrastructure have always determined who can live where and under what conditions, which communities thrive, and which are systematically dismantled.

This work analyzes how New Orleans was formed as a carceral landscape and colonial enterprise, fueled by the imperial logics of extraction, enslavement, and conquest. The discourse begins with the city's founding as a designed environment of control, of people, and of place. It moves through time examining the spatial logics of displacement that persist in the present, not as isolated tragedy but as ongoing violence: from architectural violence, residential confinement, and technologies of racial management and surveillance, to zoning restrictions, discriminatory housing patterns, and policies that make people disappear.

WALKING THE STREETS OF NEW ORLEANS WITH ATTENTION TO THE RIVER MAKES VISIBLE HOW DECISIONS ABOUT WATER, LAND, AND INFRASTRUCTURE HAVE ALWAYS DETERMINED WHO CAN LIVE WHERE AND UNDER WHAT CONDITIONS, WHICH COMMUNITIES THRIVE, AND WHICH ARE SYSTEMATICALLY DISMANTLED.

CRAFTING THE ROUTE AS ARGUMENT

The route of Geographies of Black Displacement is not arbitrary. Every site, every sequence, every transition between locations makes visible a continuum linking colonial land theft to enslavement to Jim and Jane Crow segregation to urban renewal to contemporary displacement. By moving through these sites in succession, participants see displacement as a repeating pattern across time.

Throughout the walk, with the support of print publications I have designed and distribute to each participant, we engage with the theoretical frameworks of scholars, poets, and activists alongside source materials: historical timelines and maps; restrictive antebellum ordinances; New Deal policy maps; planning documents; the Federal Housing Administration's underwriting manual; and contemporary legislative accounts.

BIENVILLE MONUMENT: COLONIAL VIOLENCE AND PLANTATION LOGICS

> "they ask me to remember / but they want me to remember / their memories / and I keep on remembering / mine."[6]
> —Lucille Clifton

The tour begins at Bienville Place, a triangular strip of land bordered by North Peters, Conti, and Decatur streets, where a monument of Jean-Baptiste Le Moyne, Sieur de Bienville, the founder of New Orleans, stands elevated above a priest, Father Athanase Douay (who accompanied Bienville on his expeditions), and a submissively seated Indigenous figure.

The casting and installation of sculptor Angela Gregory's three-figure composition in 1955 reveal how mid-twentieth-century New Orleans, with support from the French government, chose to celebrate its founding: by absenting enslaved Africans who built the city and disrespecting the Indigenous tribes of the region.

At this site, we acknowledge the past and ongoing presence of Bvlbancha, an Indigenous trading village that predates the violent formation of New Orleans, and

The Transatlantic Slave Trade to Louisiana plaque, New Orleans, LA. Photograph by Shana M. griffin

recognize the African burial grounds—of blood, bones, chains, separation, erasure, social death, and resistance—upon which the city stands.

We examine the monument and consider Lucille Clifton's poem, asking whose memories are inscribed here and what narratives of blackness it communicates through what it shows and what it erases. Looking at the figures depicted, their positionality, and implied meaning, I provocatively ask: Should we remove it? Or amend it? What would an amendment even look like here—an additional plaque? A counter-monument?

We discuss differences between a statue you can see, a street name we walk daily, and neighborhoods named after enslavers and colonizers. As we leave this monument, I encourage participants to consider what it would mean to read it against itself—to see what it's trying to hide and what fantasies it is trying to convey.

MISSISSIPPI RIVER: A MOVEMENT OF BODIES AND AN ABSENCE OF ACKNOWLEDGEMENT

At the Moonwalk, a riverfront promenade along the Mississippi River, the tour engages New Orleans' role in the slave trade—a trade of stolen lives on stolen land to build empire—facilitated by the river and the Middle Passage.

We stand at the 'Transatlantic Slave Trade to Louisiana' plaque, which the New Orleans Committee to Erect Historic Markers on the Slave Trade established in 2018. We discuss the movement of enslaved people under French, Spanish, and American rule; ways enslaved people resisted through escape, poisoning, marronage, work stoppage, and cultural preservation. We examine the centrality of the Mississippi River, slavery, land theft, commerce, and technological advances in cotton production, sugar granulation, and steamboat navigation in driving the city's growth. We reflect on the enormity of the city's involvement in the slave trade and the glaring absence of

memorials, markers, and museums that acknowledge how "the violence of slavery made actual bodies disappear."[7]

> "If you just step back for a second, the whole city is a memorial to slavery...The levee is a slave-built levee.
> The entire economic development of the city was premised upon slavery. All the buildings were built by enslaved people or free people of color. You could memorialize the city of New Orleans with a million markers of which enslaved people lived there, which enslaved people worked there, which enslaved people built this."[8]
> — Walter Johnson

The exhibition *Purchased Lives: New Orleans and the Domestic Slave Trade, 1808–1865* stated that approximately one million people were forcibly moved from the Upper South to the Lower South, with many traded and sold in New Orleans, the nation's largest antebellum slave market. Unlike other Southern cities, enslaved people were sold throughout the city—on sidewalks, in exchanges, at private homes, in open markets, at slave pens, on auction blocks, during estate sales, and as tourist spectacle.

The tour connects this commodification of violence and bondage to contemporary disaster tourism, and asks: How was control and disappearance designed into this landscape from the beginning—as architecture and policy, and then publicly erased?

Building with attached slave quarters at Conti and Dauphine Streets, New Orleans, LA. Photograps by Shana M. griffin

SLAVE QUARTERS: ARCHITECTURAL VIOLENCE AND RESIDENTIAL CONFINEMENT

In the French Quarter, slave quarters and sites of servitude are everywhere—and nowhere. Attached to the rear of elegant townhouses, hidden behind courtyards, and tucked above carriage houses, these structures housed the people who built and maintained the wealth displayed in the main residences. The quarters themselves are small, often consisting of two floors: a kitchen and workspace on the lower level and sleeping quarters on the upper level, where multiple people were forced to live with lower ceilings, minimal ventilation, and no running water. The spatial message to ensalved people forced to reside in them is clear: you are property, not a person.

Today, developers have converted many into boutique hotels, restaurants, short-term rentals, and artists' studios. Tourists drink cocktails in places where enslaved people once lived. While preservation and tourism have nearly aestheticized the violence encoded in these structures, the architecture remains.

At the intersection of Conti and Dauphine, where rows of slave quarters are visible, I reference an 1817 City ordinance regarding "slaves in the city and suburbs of New

Orleans" that forbade enslaved persons from residing in "any house, out-house, building or enclosure" not owned by their master without documented permission. Enslaved persons who did not comply faced imprisonment, twenty lashes, and a five-dollar fine.[9] This law, and others that followed, regulated and limited the geography and spatial interaction of enslaved persons to the physical structures owned by enslavers through residential confinement, architectural violence, and policing, while subjecting enslaved persons who 'violated' the law to beatings, incarceration, and fines. These policies reveal how slavery required constant spatial control and remains, materialized, in the landscape. The built environment of the slave quarters functioned as an apparatus of surveillance and containment. Though supposedly "domestic spaces," they operated as sites of carceral control, where enslavers could watch and listen for signs of resistance.[10]

At this site, I ask:

- How do these buildings communicate their purpose even now, 160 years after emancipation?
- How does architecture function as a technology of surveillance and control?
- What does it mean that these spaces of captivity are now marketed as "authentic New Orleans" experiences?
- What's the relationship between nineteenth-century ordinances regulating where enslaved people could sleep and contemporary laws criminalizing unhoused people or regulating the lives of public housing residents?

The conversation often turns to what's not here—the plaques that don't exist, the histories that aren't told, the names we don't know. A brass marker might identify the architect who designed the main house, yet nothing identifies the people who built it or those who were imprisoned within it. This erasure is also architectural. The decision to preserve buildings while erasing the histories they contain, to market "historic charm" while sanitizing violence, and to convert spaces of captivity into spaces of leisure is jarring.

Historic buildings with attached slave quarters at the intersection of Conti and Burgundy, New Orleans, LA. Photographs by Shana M. griffin

FUGITIVITY AS SPATIAL PRACTICE, RESISTANCE ACROSS TIME

> "Enslaved women and men created what I call rival geographies—alternative ways of knowing and using plantation and southern space that conflicted with planters' wishes and demands."[14]
> — Stephanie M. Camp

> "Enslaved Africans in America quickly recognized the connections between race and place...[they] constantly found themselves forced to negotiate spaces of containment and confinement in the land of their captivity...The strong desire to move freely across space formed an important part of the Black spatial imaginary."[11] — George Lipsitz

At the intersection of Conti and Burgundy streets, three French Quarter buildings stand within sight of each other, each with attached

Mariah, Negro/dark griffe woman, aged 28
Caroline, Mulatto woman, aged 20
Nannan, Black woman, aged 24
Mary Ann, Jet Black teen, aged 16
Eliza, Negro woman, aged 35
Jenny, Negro woman + two children, aged 34
Judy, Negro woman, aged 22
Nancy, Mulatto teen, aged 18
Caroline, Yellow woman, aged 27
Rose, Negress + infant, aged 25
Maria, Negro woman, aged 35
Elizabeth, Griffe woman, aged 30
Elisa, Mulatto teen, aged 16
Victoria, Negro woman, aged 50[13]

slave quarters visible from the street. The proximity is striking—you can stand at this corner and see all three simultaneously. This is the same architectural logic encountered at the previous site: slave quarters positioned for surveillance and control as mandated by city laws.

But architecture designed for control also created opportunities for resistance. These three buildings, with their quarters across from each other, enabled what was forbidden: communication between enslaved people housed in different structures, coordination across households, the exchange of information, and the potential for self-emancipation. The sight lines that allowed owners to monitor their property also allowed enslaved people to see each other, to signal, to plan. The proximity of concentrated surveillance also created confined networks of knowledge and sharing within communities.

Here, I reference Kimberly Juanita Brown's work in *The Repeating Body: Slavery's Visual Resonance in the Contemporary*, where she states, "the repeated bodies, narratives, and names make clear that it takes many generations to grasp the horrendous event of slavery. And in order to 'remember everything,' black women, alive, dead, and in-between, linger and loiter, waiting to have their stories told."[12]

Using Brown's words, I share names of women and girls who engaged in self-emancipation and fugitivity as recorded in runaway slave advertisements:

I encourage participants to imagine the relationships between enslaved people at these sites and what they needed to know to navigate freedom. They had to memorize routines: when owners slept and when streets were empty; read architecture: determine which walls were thick enough to muffle sound, which staircases creaked, which doors could be opened quietly; and map the city in their minds: identify routes to avoid patrols, locate safe houses, calculate distances between checkpoints, and move through space without detection in plain view of surveillance.

This spatial knowledge was insurgent and crucial for survival. They turned architectures of captivity into maps of possibilities. Women and girls' rebellious yearning for freedom revealed the places that sought to constrain them, as well as the unimaginable circumstances and spatial challenges they navigated to achieve liberation. This capacity to imagine movement beyond constraint, to envision freedom within captivity, persisted across centuries. The conditions of confinement they sought to escape are similar, if not the same, as those experienced by black women, centuries later, leading public housing advocacy efforts.

As we transition from the French Quarter to Bienville Basin in Tremé, I ask participants to consider what public housing resident leaders like Crystal Jones, Cynthia Wiggins, Sharon Jasper, Irene B. Griffin, Ursula Spencer, Barbara Jackson, Debra Davis, and others needed to know—how to read architecture: which courtyards were conducive for convenings and events,

Bienville Basin neighborhood, showing the original 1940s brick building, adjacent to newly constructed apartments built between 2014 and 2016, New Orleans, LA. Photographs by Shana M. griffin

which corners were heavily policed, and which routes were safe for children to walk to and from school; how to read policy: which loopholes could be exploited and which regulations could be challenged; and how to map power: which city council members might listen, which media outlets would cover their concerns, and which allies could be mobilized for support. They turned architectures of abandonment into platforms for resistance.

Both groups engage in practices that Stephanie M. Camp theorizes as rival geographies and that George Lipsitz frames as Black spatial imaginary—the desire and capacity to move freely, to imagine space differently, to create geographies beyond constraint.[14] The architecture didn't change its purpose—the women changed how they inhabited the architecture, enacting spatial possibilities the design was meant to foreclose.

TREMÉ/BIENVILLE BASIN: FROM BLACK PLACE-MAKING TO ORGANIZED ABANDONMENT

As we shift from the French Quarter to Bienville Basin in Tremé, the spatial strategies of resistance we've been tracing don't disappear—they evolve.

Tremé, built by black people, enslaved and free, is one of the oldest and largest free people of color neighborhoods in the United States and an exemplary site for examining how spatial containment evolved from slavery through Jim and Jane Crow policies to slum clearance and urban renewal. Claude Tremé was a white French hatmaker who married into one of the wealthiest planter families in the region. He became an enslaver and land developer, sectioning off and selling plots from the Morand Plantation (also referred to as the Morand-Moreau or Morand-Tremé Plantation) to create Faubourg Tremé, which became a racially

Fenced off development site since 2013, where homes once stood in the Basin courtyard on a former burial site, New Orleans, LA. Photograph by Shana M. griffin

mixed neighborhood with a significant population of free people of color and enslaved residents fifty years before the Civil War.[15] Ironically, one of the most important black neighborhoods in the United States bears the name of a man who profited from slavery.

The tour enters the section of Tremé that became Storyville, a city-sanctioned red-light district that regulated prostitution through spatial zoning from 1897 to 1917. The historic homes of Storyville were razed in the late 1930s as part of slum clearance policies to build public housing. By the time the United States entered World War II, the Housing Authority of New Orleans (HANO) built six segregated public housing developments, four for black families and two for white residents. The Iberville Public Housing Development included 75 buildings with one-, two-, and three-bedroom apartments with backyards, balconies, and communal courtyards. It was named after Pierre Le Moyne d'Iberville, a French-Canadian who, with his brother, Jean-Baptiste Le Moyne de Bienville (the colonial governor and enslaver we encountered at the start of the walk), led the seventeenth-century colonization of Louisiana.

In the aftermath of Hurricane Katrina, public housing was viewed with disdain, despite organizing efforts to stop demolition plans that solidified in the wake of disaster.

At this site, I often quote the words of activist and former St. Bernard Public Housing resident, Sharon Jasper, from a 2007 New Orleans City Council meeting, when the Council unanimously voted to demolish 5,000 public housing apartments. Jasper makes an explicit connection between slavery and policies that legitimized the mistreatment of low-income black women: "I'm tired of being disrespected. I am a Black woman. If I got to go to jail, if I got to die for what I believe in, I will not be treated like a slave! I'm a human being. A United States citizen."[16]

I ask participants: What is she naming? What continuities does she see that officials do not—or choose not to?

Between 2013 and 2014, HANO demolished 59 of the 75 buildings in the Iberville development, renovated the remaining 16 structures, and surrounded them with new apartment buildings in dull pastel colors and inferior materials. These designs were out of sync with the original development, not to mention the historic homes demolished in the 1930s.

In 2016, the city renamed the redevelopment "Bienville Basin." A neighborhood where black people built institutions, raised families, organized resistance, and created culture has been three times named after men who participated in the subjugation of black people.

As we move through the development, participants are asked: How do we take this down—not merely the physical monuments, but the names that saturate the landscape, the streets that honor enslavers and colonizers, and the invisible monuments embedded in the language itself? What is remembered when we name places after enslavers, and what is forgotten? Can removing names remove inequality and violence?

The sixteen renovated buildings stand today as structurally sound architectural guards within a "mixed-income" landscape driven by market forces and lacking its pre-Katrina vitality. Some apartments have been replaced with retail spaces; a yoga studio and a coffee shop reflect the shift from community to commodity.

While the former Iberville neighborhood housed over 800 families, Bienville Basin now houses fewer than 200 low-income families, many of whom are not original residents of the development. This illustrates what Ruth Wilson Gilmore calls "organized abandonment":[citation number 18] the systematic withdrawal of collective support, the transformation of a community into real estate, and the erasure of the people who made this neighborhood meaningful.

Here, as we finish the walk, I ask participants: What would it mean to rename this place for the people who built community here, who organized tenant councils, who fought displacement? To honor people like Irene B. Griffin or Beverly McGee instead of the men who benefited from slavery? What would it mean to build architecture that assumes community rather than designs it out?

The author leading a walk and conversing with students enrolled in "Displacement and Environmental Change," an anthropology course at Tulane University, taught by Nathan Jessee. Photograph by Nathan Jessee

WALKING AS GEOGRAPHY

Geography itself makes arguments. The distance between stops demonstrates scale. The route of the walk traces infrastructure: a monument of colonial erasure; the river that serves as an economic engine and a port of trade and control; sites of slavery marked in architectures of terror; neighborhoods once redlined; segregated public housing; and a highway that severed black communities. What's visible from each location matters. At one site, you see a historical marker acknowledging the violence of the transatlantic slave trade. At others, you notice a city designed to accommodate slavery, observing structures and homes with attached slave quarters. At the end, you walk through a redeveloped public housing neighborhood named after an enslaver. These spatial relationships produce knowledges that move beyond written form, as the walk allows us to stand in multiple geographies simultaneously.

Geographies of Black Displacement also traces the production of black spatial knowledge. The walks move through sites where violent policies were enacted and places where black people created geographic knowledge systems, organized spatial resistance, and built infrastructures of care. Displacement is not only about what was done and destroyed—but also about "rival geographies" created, kinship networks and mutual aid systems established, vernacular epistemologies enacted, and spatial arrangements that enabled black life to flourish despite violence.

DISPLACEMENT IS NOT ONLY ABOUT WHAT WAS DONE AND DESTROYED — BUT ALSO ABOUT "RIVAL GEOGRAPHIES" CREATED, KINSHIP NETWORKS AND MUTUAL AID SYSTEMS ESTABLISHED, VERNACULAR EPISTEMOLOGIES ENACTED, AND SPATIAL ARRANGEMENTS THAT ENABLED BLACK LIFE TO FLOURISH DESPITE VIOLENCE.

CONCLUSION: WALKING AS ONGOING PRACTICE

Geographies of Black Displacement invites participants to intervene. People learn to read landscapes as policy-made material, to see that every sidewalk, every vacancy, and every highway cut decides who can be where and under what conditions. This spatial engagement is transferable across place. Participants are encouraged to apply these analytical frameworks in their own neighborhoods and cities, in their professional work, and in organizing real-time fights against displacement. The practice doesn't just transmit information —it builds capacity for intervention.

This project has evolved significantly since 2018. Early versions focused more heavily on chronology—moving through time as well as space. Over numerous iterations, I've learned to include quotes, punctuate questions, and emphasize spatial patterns and relationships across sites. I select sites based on several factors: accessibility by foot and within the specified timeframe of the walk; representation of different historical periods, urban typologies, and policy mechanisms; documentary evidence, even if fragmented; and legibility, however subjective—some trace must be present that allows us to read the landscape, even if what's present is absence.

Absence becomes legible through walking, revealing the city as a graveyard with hundreds of unmarked graves: Indigenous routes of exchange rendered nearly invisible. The unacknowledged lives of enslaved people who built the city and its environs. Historical squares and buildings of terror and brutality coated in glory. Slave quarters turned coffee shops and hospitality centers with no reference to the lives imperiled by their violence. Parking lots where black institutions and homes once stood. Burial grounds unaccounted for. Neighborhoods built over and renamed. Silent corners where stores once anchored neighborhoods. The vacancy of these unmarked sites is evidence—not of natural decline but of deliberate policy.

I continue this work because walking makes displacement legible as a system while also honoring the specificity of place and the particularity of loss. Walking enables structural analysis and holds the human scale. And walking creates relationships—not just between the participants and me, but among the participants themselves, who continue conversations after the walk ends and connect around a shared commitment to spatial justice. Distance matters. Walking, sometimes for up to three hours, across three neighborhoods registers in tired legs, thirst (especially on hot days), and disorientation from moving between sites and from the accumulation of examples that become patterns reproducing violence.

Again, Geographies of Black Displacement is one methodology within a larger constellation of practices that includes DISPLACED and PUNCTUATE. Each approach centers black spatial knowledges and has particular affordances; and together they constitute an interdisciplinary feminist practice that intervenes in how displacement is understood, recorded, and challenged.

View of the Mississippi River at the site of the Transatlantic Slave Trade to Louisiana plaque, New Orleans, LA. Photograph by Shana M. griffin

Within the Mississippi River Open School's framework, the walking practice connects New Orleans' displacement geographies to a watershed-scale. The river is always present on these walks—sometimes visible, always implicated in how it carried enslaved people into the city and enabled the plantation economy that shaped regional land use. This is not the final work. The practice continues to adapt and to generate new questions. Each walk adds to an archive of encounters, demonstrating that another spatial politic is possible—one that centers black geographic knowledge, learns from Indigenous knowledges of refusal, embraces feminist urban designs, and imagines cities organized around kinship rather than extraction.

ENDNOTES

1 Camilla Hawthorne, "Mapping Black Geographies," *Transactions of the Institute of British Geographers* 50, no. 1 (2025): 1–6.

2 Garnette Cadogan, "Walking While Black," in *The Fire This Time: A New Generation Speaks About Race*, ed. Jesmyn Ward (New York: Scribner, 2016). Originally published as "Black and Blue" in *Freeman's: Arrival*, ed. John Freeman (New York: Grove Atlantic, 2015).

3 Stephanie M. Camp, *Closer to Freedom: Enslaved Women and Everyday Resistance in the Plantation South* (Chapel Hill: University of North Carolina Press, 2004).

4 Clyde Woods, *Development Arrested: The Blues and Plantation Power in the Mississippi Delta* (London: Verso, 1998).

5 Tia-Simone Gardner, John Kim, and Monica Moses Haller participated in a test run of the walk two days before the AAG conference.

Their observations and questions during this initial walk helped shape how I structured the tour as discourse.

6 Lucille Clifton, "why some people be mad at me sometimes," in *The Collected Poems of Lucille Clifton: 1965–2010*, ed. Kevin Young and Michael S. Glaser (Rochester, NY: BOA Editions, 2012), 427.

7 Melanie J. Newton, quoted in Marisa J. Fuentes, *Dispossessed Lives: Enslaved Women, Violence, and the Archive* (Philadelphia: University of Pennsylvania Press, 2016), 7.

8 Walter Johnson, quoted in "As New Orleans Turns 300, City to Mark Slave Trade Sites," *The Chronicle of Higher Education*, 2017.

9 Richard Campanella, "Two Centuries of Paradox: The Geography of New Orleans's African American Population" from Antebellum to Postdiluvian Times," in *Hurricane Katrina in Transatlantic Perspective*, ed. Romain Huret and R. J. Parks (Baton Rouge: Louisiana State University Press, 2014), 12.

10 Camp, *Closer to Freedom*; and Saidiya Hartman, *Scenes of Subjection: Terror, Slavery, and Self-Making in Nineteenth-Century America* (New York: Oxford University Press, 1997).

11 George Lipsitz, *How Racism Takes Place* (Philadelphia: Temple University Press, 2011), 53 and 66.

12 Kimberly Juanita Brown, *The Repeating Body: Slavery's Visual Resonance in the Contemporary* (Durham: Duke University Press, 2015). 6.

13 Pulled from an abbreviated list of 228 names of women and girls researched and compiled from the Freedom on the Move database (https://freedomonthemove.org), accessed July 2023, March 2024, and October 2025, as part of the author's multimedia project, *Fugitivity & Black Feminist Spatial Imaginaries*.

14 Camp, *Closer to Freedom*, 7 and Lipsitz, *How Racism Takes Place*, 53 and 66.

15 Brenda Marie Osbey, "FAUBOURG TREMÉ: Community in Transition," Brenda Marie Osbey (website), accessed November 29, 2024, https://www.osbeynola.com/treme-1.

16 Sharon Jasper, comments at New Orleans City Council meeting, December 20, 2007.

The Remote Sensation of Disintegration

Excerpts from the short film by IMANI JACQUELINE BROWN

The projects of colonialism, genocide, slavery, and fossil fuel production are phases of a single system of matter, wealth, culture, life, and soul dislocation known as Extractivism.

In January 2020, I flew in a three-passenger plane to survey oil and gas access canals in Plaquemines Parish, Louisiana. This was the first time that I witnessed the violence waged by the fossil fuel industry against my wider ecological body through a bird's eye view.

It was also the first time that I had been home in one year—the end of a self-imposed one-year moratorium on flying. I had spent the past year in London, in pursuit of an MA from the Centre for Research Architecture. Over the course of hundreds of hours, I had pored over satellite images of these same oil and gas canals and organized spreadsheets listing tens of thousands of permits for wells, canals, and pipelines, striving to comprehend—and identify accountability for—extractive violence.

For one week in September 2019, I travelled down the Mississippi River via a voyager canoe. It was the first time that I was offered the opportunity to meet the beginning of the River that gave birth to my land, my people, and my self. I realized that I could sense my home in the sediment and water that flow from the River's beginning in Lake Itasca to build land as she merges with the Gulf of Mexico. I realized that the very notion that Louisiana's land could be restored in isolation is an absurdity and an affront that maintains the segregation of our ecological communities.

How might we sense the
multiscalar,
multispecies,
multigenerational,
multidimensional
disintegration of our ecological body
by Extractivism?

By stepping beyond my grassroots perspective
and adopting the view-from-afar,
as well as the technological view-from-above,
I have not abandoned an ethical position of
local agency in favor of one that
"sees like a state"...

I have accepted my inheritance:
the ecological perspective of diaspora.
I am
seeing like a bird
seeing like a river
seeing like an ancestor.

And still, it was only from my newly remote
position, that I regained touch
with my body's sensors
and noticed that being-in-place is
fundamentally a condition of being-place.

The gaps between subjectivities are full...
of dark matter,

also known as kinship,
which holds existence together.

Once the Levees Break

Rebecca Snedeker

On the twentieth anniversary of Hurricane Katrina, New Orleanian Rebecca Snedeker recounts multigenerational stories of the precarity of living in close proximity to water. Coastal climate migration is a more fitting cultural marker, or golden spike, of our entry into the Anthropocene, because the history of increasing control over the river and human bodies–via levees and prisons–parallels the history of increasing control over time.

Quilt of Uncertainty, by Rebecca Snedeker, 2023. Digital photo collage. Tropical Storm Ida, August 27, 2021, 11:00 AM EDT, Advisory 5, archival image courtesy of the National Oceanic and Atmospheric Administration (NOAA) National Hurricane Center. All images courtesy of the artist

When I was five, my father explained to me that our city, New Orleans, could fill up with water like a fishbowl. Not long after receiving this surprising news, I heard the story of Noah's Ark at Sunday school and understood it to be the most useful tale of all. I was raised—home, school, and church—in the fancy Garden District, a village of sorts where everyone knew each other. My parents had just renovated a raised cottage, and we'd moved a few blocks from our modest shotgun home. It was the late 1970s, and their friends were Preservationists, white activists for New Orleans's architectural heritage.

The raised cottage style was designed to allow for a full story of floodwaters to rise and fall under the house. Many of these elegant homes were built in the early to mid-nineteenth century by free or enslaved craftsmen of African descent. A wide, central flight of stairs led up to a deep front porch and then the front door. Rain and river waters could pool under the house amid a grid of brick pilings, then eventually drain. By the time my family moved into our new home—after two hundred and sixty years of levee-building to contain the Mississippi River and seventy-five years of pumping stormwaters and sewage toward swamps in the back of town—domineering engineering had conquered the urban mindset, memories of routine floodings had subsided, and the open space under our house had been walled in with siding, beams, and sheetrock to create a low-ceilinged apartment for tenants: ripe for deluge.

On May 3, 1978, while I was at school, an epic rain arrived. The wetness was far more than the city's historic pumps could handle, and the streets began to flood. Carpool started early, and the kindergarten teachers formed a bucket brigade, passing each kid from one teacher to the next, like sandbags, to the cars. I was delivered with my carpool mates to our neighbor Lady Reiss's Cadillac. Lady drove slowly for a few blocks, like a captain trying to leave no wake, but the car stalled out by the Keenans' house, and we all took refuge inside. The afternoon stretched timelessly, accented by rounds of clapping thunder and

Colonial Time, 2023. Digital photo collage of found object assemblage and Plan of the City and Suburbs of New Orleans by I. Tanesse, William Rollinson, Charles Del Vecchio, and P. Maspero (1815). Archival image courtesy of the Library of Congress, Geography and Map Division, Louisiana: European Explorations and the Louisiana Purchase

board games in a sunroom surrounded by thrashing palmetto fronds. Then the rains stopped, and my dad glided up to the front steps in a canoe to paddle us home. Once there, I learned that our tenant's apartment had flooded.

In the wake of that storm, I asked for a Noah's Ark mural in my bedroom to help me sleep. My godmother, Mary Sue, obliged. There are no photos of the mural, only memories of falling asleep across from the floating zoo, the creatures braving extinction, with a rainbow and a dove with an olive branch above. My dad—a lifelong sailor who sold diesel marine engines—processed the flood pragmatically, digging in the backyard and building a bilge pump so he could drain the dank apartment swiftly if the waters were to rise again.

Two years later, we drove out to the 1980 grand opening of the Louisiana Science and Nature Center in New Orleans East. I stood mesmerized by a large model of a river delta. One slightly elevated end had a source of water, and the model sloped downward toward the lower end, where water pooled, drained, and circulated. The gushing water wove its way, cutting channels down the slope of silt. Toward the bottom, sediment would splay and then build up around a stream, forming a blotchy lobe. When the surface of the lobe grew high, the stream would slow and then, quick like a switch, change course to cut a shorter and more efficient path to the pool below. Over time, another lobe would form, and the pattern would repeat. This is my first memory of observing a physical model that represents a planetary pattern in smaller scale. The model illuminated how deltaic lobes build up over spans of time, and how hungry a river mouth is to reach the pool below.[1]

I was told this model related to the Mississippi River, yet there were no traces of humans in it. The model did not include earthen mounds built by the Indigenous nations that migrated to active floodplains here or the meeting grounds on the natural levee when the area was first called Bvlbancha. The model did not include levees and water-control structures, built under French, Spanish, and U.S. American rule—often by African-descended people who were enslaved and incarcerated—to straightjacket the existing channel. The model did not include miniature forced labor camps lining this channel, drawing its waters for irrigation

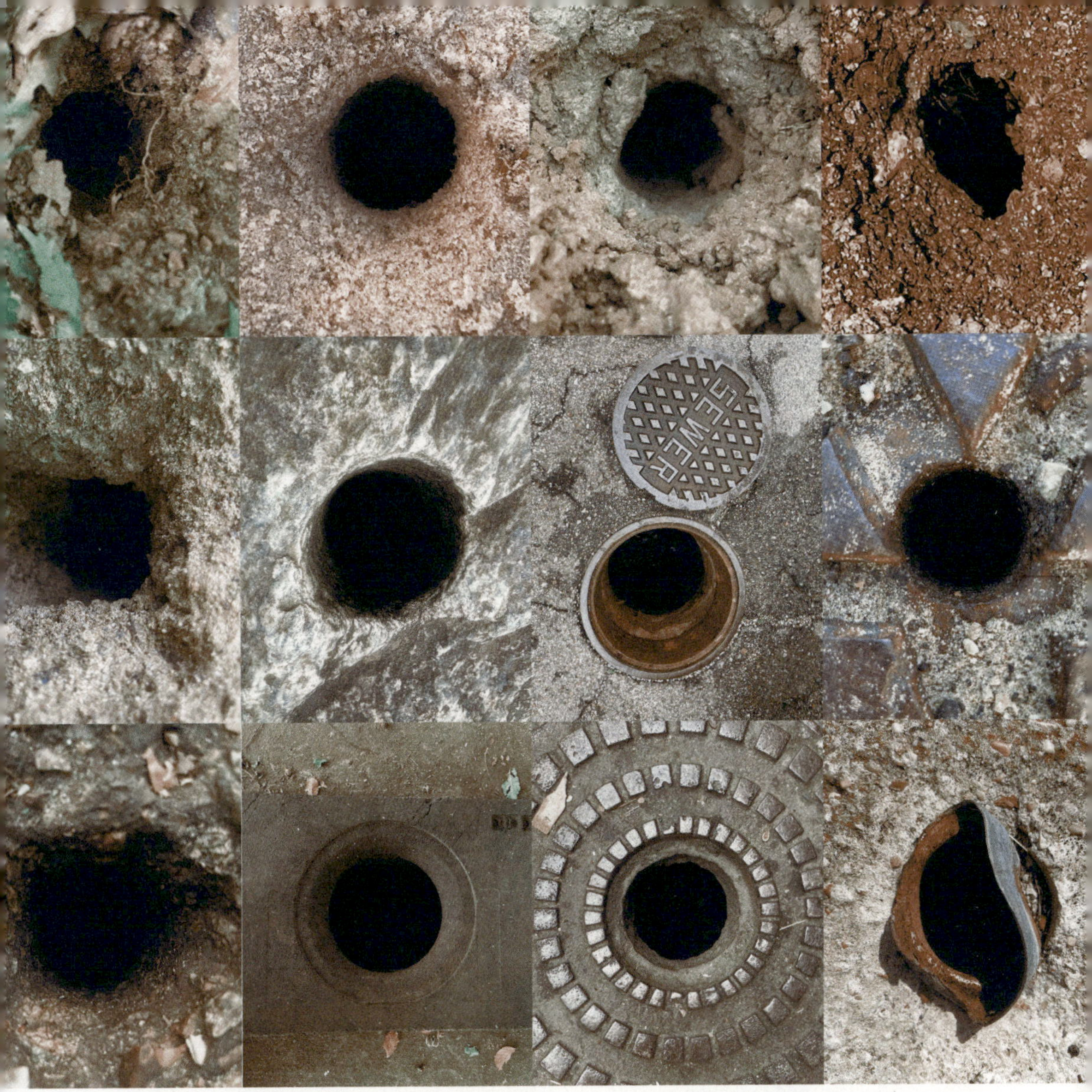

and commodity transportation, or polluting petrochemical refineries erected where those plantations once stood. The model did not contain the colonial settlement established around this corseted channel nor the nearby New Orleans East neighborhoods developed for first-time Black New Orleans homeowners from the 1950s to the 1970s, thousands of homes built on cement slabs on silt. The model did not reveal that, a quarter century later, those slabs would be broken, cracked from soil desiccation caused by pumping, and then saturated by floodwaters fifteen feet deep. The model did not include helicopters with ropes unfurled to rooftops or dead bodies in attics, when 80 percent of the city's previous land surface swiftly became water surface in a man-made disaster called Katrina. But certainly the model could have predicted such a collapse.[2]

That collapse occurred in 2005, when I was in my early thirties. I had returned home after college and forged a life as a documentary filmmaker when a ferocious Category 5 hurricane was approaching. On an eerie Saturday in late August, I evacuated to Dallas and landed with a distant relative. She had a

TV in her bedroom with the news running, but I didn't watch because her comments made my head explode. On Monday night, as I was on the cusp of sleep, she came to the guest room door with big news. The Mississippi River levees in New Orleans had failed. And then she left. I lay awake all night long, imagining the rush—six hundred thousand cubic feet per second—pouring into the city. The arrival of the overdue apocalypse. I wondered who had died, where the rest of us would go, who I would be. This remains the most mournful night of my life.

Come morning, I learned my relative had misunderstood the news. Stormwater drainage canals and a shipping canal's levee walls had been breached, but the river's waters were still locked in place. The city was not completely gone.

Throughout that week, we died and we were rescued. We supported each other and we shot each other. We shared whereabouts and grief by learning to text on cellphones, and we watched our entrenched poverty and racism exposed on televisions around the world. We grasped that our lives and our city would never be the same due to this singular event, and we referred to historic hurricanes and floods, aware this was an old story in new clothes. We lost so much that cannot be repaired or replaced, and we gained an understanding of how catastrophe can transform a place. We had the highest nativity rate in the country—the percentage of people living in a place who were also born there—and we were refugees.[3]

My home had flooded, and on Friday I relocated from Dallas to Austin to meet up with a close collaborator and his husband. My godmother Mary Sue, the Noah's Ark muralist, landed with her husband in arid Wyoming. My mom told me that Mary Sue saw a fossil of a palmetto frond at an exhibit on the geological history of the region. Apparently, Wyoming once had a tropical climate, too—with crocodiles! Sue was reminded that all places are changing all the time, that maybe it was OK that New Orleans flooded, if you took the long view. This was the first and only time I have thought her callous, even cruel.

In the aftermath, New Orleanians knew that we were the canary in the coal mine of coming failures of twentieth-century infrastructure and urban policies in the United States. After projecting a romanticized past, everything turned, and we were now futuristic. A childhood schoolmate of mine made wildly popular stickers that summed it up: "So far behind, we're ahead."

I joined a film project, *Land of Opportunity*, about this phenomenon: how, through Katrina, New Orleans had become emblematic of the future of U.S. cities. The director, Luisa Dantas, had grown up between Rio de Janeiro and New York City, with an international perspective on the American Dream, and she was curious about how people were seizing opportunities in the post-Katrina landscape and how these efforts would pan out over time. Her crew was documenting public housing residents fighting for their right to return to homes that had been fenced off and condemned despite suffering relatively little damage; Brazilian migrant workers laboring around the clock to rebuild the Superdome before the August 2006 NFL season; a Cuban urban planner leading charettes amid city-wide meetings where residents would circle around a model of their neighborhood and imagine how to "Build Back Better!"; a Creole urban gardener cooking with a cast-iron pan in a formaldehyde-laced FEMA trailer, while his family awaits permission to demolish their gutted home and rebuild; and a Black teenager who landed in Los Angeles for ninth grade—"Katrina, you did something!"—and then went on to UCLA with a Gates Scholarship.[4]

Despite the fact the film was more about opportunities and conflicts in urban America than an exceptional New Orleans event, most film funders and distributors cited "Katrina fatigue" from the flood of media already in the market, and we struggled to continue. Eventually, we compressed and interwove eight protagonists' lives over five years into a ninety-minute film, with the tagline: "Happening to a city near you." We understood that most people in other places, at that time, didn't know what was coming. This remains largely true today.[5]

River Mouth Kiss, 2023. Digital photo collage. "Mississippi River Basin–the World's Third Largest," courtesy of the United States Army Corps of Engineers and "La Riviere de Missisipi et ses Environs, dans l'Amerique Septentrionale," Nicolas de Fer, 1715

On August 29, 2010, the fifth anniversary of Katrina, the film aired in Europe. The anniversary was a major milestone at home, among others throughout an intense summer. Eight weeks earlier, I had given birth to my daughter, Lulu. Eighteen weeks earlier, the Deepwater Horizon rig had exploded, unleashing an estimated 134 million gallons of oil in the Gulf of Mexico, followed by 1.8 million gallons of carcinogenic Corexit "clean-up" sprays applied underwater and on water and land surfaces nearby. I heard that an old friend, an environmental investigative reporter, and his pregnant wife were moving away due to the impact of Corexit on mammalian health, particularly for newborns. The landscape was too toxic.[6]

°

Cut forward nine years to 2019, to the banks of the Industrial Canal, where I stepped into a long canoe, held the gunnels, found my seat, and was launched toward the mighty Mississippi River. I was joining the final leg of a program called River Semester, during which college students canoe down the Mississippi River, from its headwaters in Minnesota to the Gulf of Mexico. The plan was to do the last leg from New Orleans to Venice, Louisiana, a.k.a. "the end of the world," in four days and to charter a motorboat from the Venice marina to the

Gulf and back on the fifth day. There were two canoes, and each canoe fit eight to ten people. I'd said yes to this adventure, but almost every New Orleanian I had told thought I was crazy, since we are taught not to touch the waters. I'd asked if canoeing on the river was even legal. The director of the program got down on one knee to promise my daughter, who was then nine years old, that we would return.

I was participating in this journey in my role as director of the New Orleans Center for the Gulf South, a regional studies center at Tulane University. Our team had begun collaborating deeply with two German institutions that had posited the Mississippi as an "Anthropocene River" and funded a two-year study of the river as part of an ongoing investigation of the human impact on earth. The project was driven by the question of how to forge new forms of interdisciplinary knowledge production needed to address the complexities and impacts of human-induced climate change.

The Mississippi River study and pedagogical experiments were culminating in a season of programming that started at the headwaters in Lake Itaska and moved downriver to New Orleans, all timed to coincide with the River Semester canoeists' schedule. The day the paddlers arrived in New Orleans via the river and carried the canoes up the wide steps on the levee by Jackson Square—arguably the oldest and best way to enter this city, or the very worst, if you were enslaved—the events commenced in New Orleans.

That first weekend, two gatherings took place: a closed meeting of the Anthropocene Working Group, an international group of climate scientists seeking to formalize the Anthropocene as a new geological epoch, who were also funded by the Germans; and Slave Rebellion Reenactment, an historical reenactment of the 1811 Slave Revolt, the largest known slave revolt in North American history. I toggled between the climate scientists, with their hockey-stick graphs and chemical compound analyses—charts measuring carbon dioxide, methane, plutonium, and more, embedded in corings of lake bottoms, peat moss, coral, stalactite, and soil from several continents—and taking my daughter to see the "Army of the Enslaved," the all-Black group of reenactors who chanted "On to New Orleans! Freedom or Death!" as they marched from an upriver plantation, across a river spillway, through the French Quarter, and finally to Congo Square. Both the Anthropocene Working Group climate scientists and the Army of the Enslaved reenactors were tactical and revolutionary; riding frictions and time scales cultural, racial, geological, and cosmic; sounding battle cries for truth-telling.[7] That weekend was followed by a dense week of seminars, programming, and, as finale, a Saturday festival in an urban forest.[8]

I'D SAID YES TO THIS ADVENTURE, BUT ALMOST EVERY NEW ORLEANIAN I HAD TOLD THOUGHT I WAS CRAZY, SINCE WE ARE TAUGHT NOT TO TOUCH THE WATERS.

The second Sunday, I was finally seated in a River Semester canoe, heading from the Industrial Canal into the Mississippi. Those in the bow set the pace, arms churning rigorously like wheels ahead of and behind me. Exhausted from the previous months, I considered disembarking. Yet I was exhilarated by a sense of transgression as we crossed the border of the banks and entered the river, and I finally fell in sync with the other paddlers. I was enthralled by the view from the river's surface and the sheer volume of water flowing with and around us in the channel two hundred feet deep. I was carried by divine camaraderie, songs, laughter, and stories. We passed willow plants and petrochemical plants. We passed paddling ducks and swooping pelicans—descendants of dinosaurs. We passed tankers carrying fossil fuels, frozen poultry, and plastics around the planet, and we headed into daunting waves from their wakes.

Camping on the riverbanks at night, I felt like I had stepped into a nineteenth-century *Harper's Weekly* etching. Around a driftwood fire on spongy silt, we talked about time. I confessed to the students that, for most of my life, the timeline on which I had understood this place was just a quick blip: the three centuries since French colonists had named it New Orleans. When I was their age, I could describe British feudal systems from the

Tuned to Key of "River," 2022. Digital photo collage

Middle Ages and Italian art patronage during the Renaissance, yet I did not even have a name for those same time periods here. More recently, I had been studying geological and Indigenous histories of the region and was slowly gaining a sense of the longue durée, of a timeline that holds it all.

In my job, our team often organized immersive, site-based learning experiences open to scholars and the public. When we brought people together to learn from one another, often at sites related to cultural and environmental histories, I would hope we could imagine the future, but often what we were really doing was catching up to the present. So much of the built infrastructure our lifestyles depend on is hidden to the naked eye. Witnessing sites helps us understand our surroundings, across time. Visit a giant pile of refined sugar to consider slavery, diabetes, pleasure, and addiction; or a mound of radioactive phosphogypsum to contemplate that nitrogen-based ammonia fertilizer is produced—with radioactive byproducts—in Louisiana, shipped upriver and injected into agricultural fields, then drained back downriver and out to the Gulf, causing a "dead zone" there that is the size of New Jersey. This can help reality sink in and provide a refreshed foundation from which we can make decisions and act. I liked asking others, "In what timeline do you operate? In what timeframe is your imaginary?" I heard my friend Shana M. griffin ask: "When is your New Orleans?" And Monique Verdin: "What do the stars see when they look down at the Mississippi?" Under the stars with the River Semester students, we spoke of how extending the timelines of our imaginations, learning more and daydreaming and recreating how things worked before extraction reigned, may help us mitigate or even repair some of the damage that has been done.[9]

During the day, the paddlers sang together, in rounds. Somewhere along that chorus, it hit me how completely those of us who live by the river had given up on, or never even conceived of, personal access to its waters or hope for protecting them. I envisioned a blockade of boats spanning the river, Greenpeace-style, to block commerce and reclaim the waters from industry and capitalism. I finally understood that the Lower Mississippi isn't a "river" anymore. It was and is a shipping canal for multinational corporations. A pipeline. As I heard architect and planner Dilip da Cunha say just this last fall: "The river is a colonial construct."[10]

On our fifth and last day of the River Semester journey, we reached the Venice marina and hired two motorboat captains to bring us to the Gulf. From the dock, I climbed onto a fiberglass deck and sat next to a friend from New Orleans who had joined us for the day and would drive some of us back to New Orleans in her car that evening. The

Plasticene (-cene with pink chiffon, pinecones, Slinky, ceramic tile), 2023. Digital photo collage of found object assemblage. Louisiana Salt Dome Diorama Cross-Section, by Brian Lewis, courtesy of Louisiana State Exhibit Museum Shreveport

boat captain cranked a rock radio station, the first recorded music I had heard all week, and we took off. The bow leveled, and we zipped down a small distributary. After a week of manual motion, the speed was astonishing. Never have I felt the power of fossil fuels so clearly: They make everything go faster. It was intoxicating to feel this Great Acceleration, full throttle.

°

> blatt einer palme
> neben dem blatt ist ein kleines insekt auf
> der sedimentaplatte zu finden
> Wyoming/USA eozan
>
> leaf of a palm tree
> next to the leaf a small insect can be
> found on the sediment plate
> Wyoming/USA Eocene

Two years ago, I was invited to Vienna to contribute to a conference on music and race. One afternoon, I snuck away from the conference to visit Vienna's Natural History Museum, which I'd heard was a treasure chest of Habsburg Empire loot. Across a room of wooden showcases, skeletal tableaus, and clusters of ancient bivalves, a tall palmetto frond beckoned from between two high windows. My jaw dropped when I read the marker: "Wyoming/USA Eocene."[11]

I recalled Mary Sue's exodus to Wyoming and her fossil encounter seventeen years prior. This palmetto, alive at least forty million years ago, before tectonic clashes pushed the Rocky Mountains skyward, reminded me that Earth is ever-changing. Louisiana may one day be a jagged mountain range, or a glacier or magnetic pole. I released my judgment of Mary Sue. I released my anger that everything is changing.

Once home, I began making sketches and sculptures about local, planetary, and cosmic time, grounded in Gulf South materialities. My anxieties about running out of time in

Louisiana were salved by reading histories of human conceptions of time and gathering materials that make them tangible: circular hoops and spiral slinkies (seasons, recurrences), sailing lines and various strings (linear time, arrow of time), grains of sand and mesh fruit produce bags (quantum physics, space-time nets). I find the more I can touch time and make it tangible, the more I am able to stay light, creative, and agile. I see these artworks as tools for looking ahead and behind, for supporting playfulness, agility, imagination, to fight denial and stultification. We each build our survival kits and spells, and how we imagine and relate to time is fundamental.

I also started building synchronologies of river deltas around the world, frameworks that contain multiple chronologies in one chart, allowing a viewer to observe concurrent events and characteristics across continents. Upon seeing some of the sculptures and charts, a graduate student working in Pondicherry, India, near the Kaveri River delta, asked: "If you couch everything in this longue durée, does this mean it's not really worth taking any action?" I tried to explain: Seeing this big picture is the only thing that loosens me up from the paralyzing anxiety that being in constant climate precarity can cause, that helps me to live, that helps me to swim around and surface with any joy.

∘

One of my favorite places to surface is the Nanih Bvlbancha, an earthen mound on the greenway between Bayou St. John and the French Quarter. The Nanih was conceived of by a group of Indigenous friends who collaborated with an arts organization, a golf course construction crew, an urban youth farm, and many more groups and peoples. They welcomed everyone to help. Two of the golf course specialists were Mayan men who knew how to build the stairs to the top, which provides a view toward the river and distant skyscrapers. Many of us contributed soil from places that are significant to us. I visit the Nanih frequently on my bicycle route to the gym. Perched there, I imagine the past and a future time when the river will have its way, once the levees break.[12] As Dilip da Cunha observes, the water is not the problem; the idea of a flood is just a cultural condition because we think the river is a line that is supposed to stay in place, and we have designed infrastructure, real estate, and cities dependent on this human-imposed line that we read as reality. The flooding is a false construct, only possible if humans have come to believe the river is supposed to stay in one place and be a certain size. da Cunha reiterates: The very concept of a river is a design "imposed on" a place. A place imposed on a place.[13]

The last time the Mississippi almost had its way was a century ago, during the Great Flood of 1927, when the river nearly jumped westward to the Atchafalaya River, quick like a switch. This took place at a juncture two hundred miles upriver from New Orleans, right across from the Louisiana State Penitentiary—a.k.a. "Angola," a prison imposed on a plantation imposed on a floodplain. After the Great Flood, the Army Corps of Engineers built the Old River Control Structure complex, which continuously diverts one third of the Mississippi River to the Atchafalaya River Basin like an ongoing release valve, to fortify the status quo and prevent the Mississippi from changing course. It stands as a massive Brutalist-style monument to patterns of maintaining control and containment. I now see this monument as a time machine, too—locking the river in this lobe it wants to leave. Doing time.

The history of increasing control of the river and human bodies via levees and prisons parallels the history of increasing control of time. Today's obsession with time management, busyness, and the technologies we've developed to measure time in smaller and smaller increments, now to the atomic zeptosecond, are considered scientific, but of course they are also cultural.

Our language is doing time, too. New Orleans has been the name of the place for the past three hundred years, with the river locked in place by the French, Spanish, and U.S. Americans. When the river jumps course, the place will need to be renamed. New Bvlbancha? Does each placename specify only a phase of the life of that place, its matter for that time being?

°

In the Biblical story of Noah, in the scriptures of the Old Testament, in acrylic paint on my childhood wall, the ark is battling extinction.
In this cosmography, the entire planet is water, with only Noah and his ark carrying humans and terrestrial animals. A friend sends me an online lecture by a British archeologist who collaborated with Indian marine architects and shipbuilders to build the biblical specs of Noah's ark, as described on a clay tablet cuneiform dated 1750 BCE. It turns out the ark was a coracle, a circular ship form familiar to Babylonians, according to this tablet. Some say a circular boat leaves no wake; yet all movements move matter. I read the circularity as temporal, too. How facing extinction comes round and round. Will we decide to stop drilling for and burning oil?

Does a model of the earth have a wake? In Jena, Germany, and Tempe, Arizona, in a collaboration between the Max Planck Institute of Geoanthropology and Arizona State University, earth and social scientists have collaborated to build a Decision Theater where digital planetary models quantify, illustrate, and speculate change over time. This comprehensive, interactive modeling is based, in part, on artificial intelligence that draws from new and existing models and curated streams of research data.
In this cosmology, there are no simple answers. There are different interests and perspectives, and dozens of players can think through options together. "It looks like a war room, yet it is a peace conference," explains mathematical physicist and MPIGEA director Jürgen Renn, and "could help reveal what a stable consensus might be."[14]

Over the past twenty years in New Orleans, we have become experts in urban planning.

We have regional plans: the Coastal Restoration Authority Plan and Greater New Orleans Water Management Plan and the Changing the Course competition plans. We have personal plans: for hurricane evacuations, street water flooding, boil water advisories, power outages, and cancer tumors. But we can't plan our way out of the perils at hand. We can only mitigate, and we know each year may be the last. We have had twenty more years than I thought we would that night in Dallas, when I believed it was all over. Katrina wasn't the end, but I do see it now as the golden spike—the emblematic signal of the beginning of a time period—of U.S. coastal climate migration. The population of Greater New Orleans decreased by 20 percent between 2000 and 2015. And in the latest census estimates, New Orleans is the fastest-shrinking city in the United States.

When I fantasize about the river changing course, you may think me callous, even cruel. I am not going to dynamite the levees. But I have come to doubt that we can enter a new mentality, a less controlling and extractive

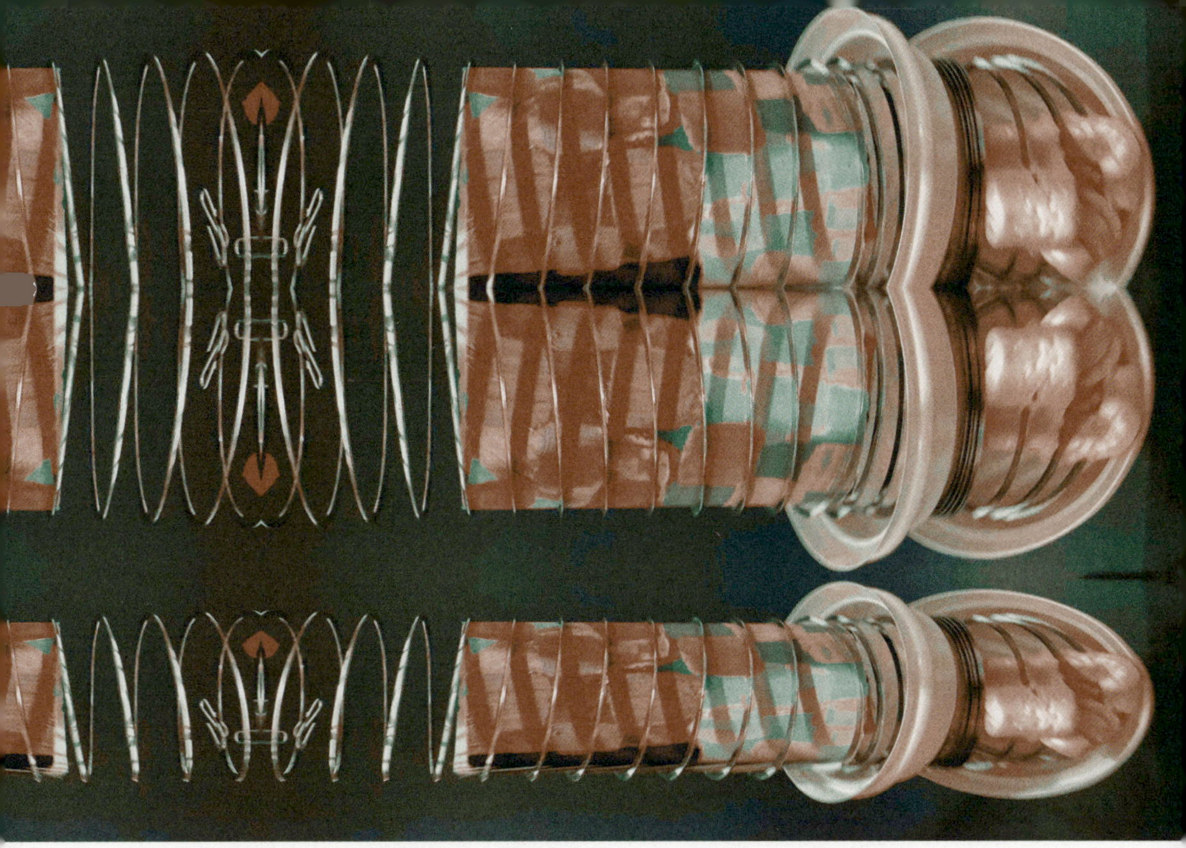

Carnival Zeptosecond, 2023. Digital photo collage of found object assemblage.

way of living, if the river remains locked in its existing channel. I don't know whether a change in human mentality will lead to releasing the river or the river changing course will quicken a societal shift, but I see the waters' freedom and health as inseparable from our own. And I'm no longer attached to this place in its current form.

Meanwhile, we connect the local to the bioregional, national, planetary, and cosmic. We collaborate with and learn from friends, old and new, in a growing, decentralized movement of mutual aid and vital relations. We are present and timeless, in a village of sorts where people know their neighbors.

I HAVE COME TO DOUBT THAT WE CAN ENTER A NEW MENTALITY, A LESS CONTROLLING AND EXTRACTIVE WAY OF LIVING, IF THE RIVER REMAINS LOCKED IN ITS EXISTING CHANNEL.

We resist Indigenous erasure, white supremacy, surveillance, censorship, voter suppression, deportation, and authoritarianism. And we cooperate and create open schools to learn survival skills. Because despite the precarity, this planet is our home.[15]

On the twentieth anniversary of Katrina, I imagine the levees breaking and the water pouring in. I imagine a dove above, with an olive branch. The olive branch is today. The gift is time, and the time is now.

For their support with this essay, I am grateful to Andy Horowitz (in the beginning), Kira Akerman (at submission, the point of no return), and Casey Ruble (during the end times), and to Doug Miller for his support with the illustrations.

A version of this article was originally published in the journal Southern Cultures *(Fall 2025).*

ENDNOTES

1 In the 1970s, concern about wetlands damage and coastal erosion caused by timber and petrochemical industry practices was rising. By 1980, the Louisiana Science and Nature Center, now known as the Audubon Louisiana Nature Center, was founded "to address an urgent community need for environmental education programming"; "Construction to begin at Audubon Louisiana Nature Center," FOX8Live.com, May 2, 2015, https://www.fox8live.com/story/28958503/construction-to-begin-at-audubon-louisiana-nature-center/.

2 As Jeffery Darensbourg notes, the placename Bulbancha/Bvlbancha is having a "resurgence," including its use in the names of several Indigenous collectives and media publications; "Bulbancha" 64 Parishes, May 1, 2024, https://64parishes.org/entry/bulbancha. The intersection of human racism and engineering in the Lower Mississippi River region and, specifically, the use of African-descended enslaved and incarcerated people in building river levees is addressed in many recent works, including Justin Hosbey's "Angola Prison's Black Ecologies," *Environment and Planning F* (2025), https://doi.org/10.1177/26349825241296077; Shana M. griffin's "DISPLACED New Orleans" project, accessed June 26, 2025, https://www.displacedneworleans.com; John Bardes's *The Carceral City: Slavery and the Making of Mass Incarceration in New Orleans, 1803–1930* (University of North Carolina Press, 2024); the Historic New Orleans Collection's *Captive State: Louisiana and the Making of Mass Incarceration* exhibition (July 19, 2024, to February 16, 2025), https://hnoc.org/exhibitions/captive-state; Kira Akerman's film *Hollow Tree* (2023), https://hollowtreefilm.com/about/; and Lydia Pelot-Hobbs's *Prison Capital: Mass Incarceration and Abolition Struggles for Abolition Democracy in America* (University of North Carolina Press, 2023) and "Lockdown Louisiana" in *Unfathomable City: A New Orleans Atlas*, ed. Rebecca Solnit and Rebecca Snedeker (University of California Press, 2013). The "plantation-to-pipeline" and "plantation to plant" landscape is described by many environmental justice–inspired organizations, activists, scholars, and artists from whom I've learned. Notable organizations include the Deep South Center for Environmental Justice, Human Rights Watch, Louisiana Bucket Brigade, Louisiana Environmental Action Network, Healthy Gulf, Rise St. James, Taproot Earth, and many more. See Richard Campanella, *Draining New Orleans: The 300-Year Quest to Dewater the Crescent City* (Louisiana State University Press, 2023), and Andy Horowitz, *Katrina: A History, 1915–2015* (Harvard University Press, 2022).

3 Media coverage of the federal levee failures, urban flooding, and rescues portrayed African-descended people living in systemic poverty and government neglect normalized in New Orleans, yet considered shocking to viewers in the United States and around the world. Further, ten years later, the Urban League announced that the income gap by race in New Orleans had grown by 37 percent since Katrina; "An Unequal Recovery in New Orleans: Racial Disparities Grow in City Ten Years After Katrina," *Democracy Now!*, August 28, 2015, https://www.democracynow.org/2015/8/28/an_unequal_recovery_in_new_orleans.

4 Luisa Dantas, *Land of Opportunity* (JoLu Productions, 2010). I believe the most important "Katrina film" that is not a documentary, but is as truthful as almost any, is Cauleen Smith's Afrofuturistic, Cli-Fi film, *The Fullness of Time*, a cauleen smith video, with Creative Time (2008).

5 The majority of our funding came from the Ford Foundation's former Metropolitan Opportunity program and through a broadcast deal with ARTE France. The film is now available through New Day Films and Kanopy.

6 "Estimating Chemical Dispersant Exposure for Deepwater Horizon Oil Spill Workers," University of Minnesota Twin Cities, June 8, 2022, https://twin-cities.umn.edu/news-events/estimating-chemical-dispersant-exposure-deepwater-horizon-oil-spill-workers.

7 *The Slave Rebellion Reenactment* project drew upon a lifetime of research by Leon A. Waters, director of the Louisiana Museum of African American History and Hidden History Tours and author of *On to New Orleans!: Louisiana's Heroic 1811 Slave Revolt* (Cypress Press, 1996); Dread Scott, Slave Rebellion Reenactment (Antenna, 2019): http://www.slave-revolt.com.

8 "Anthropocene River Campus: The Human Delta" was organized by the Haus de Kulturen der Welt, Max Planck

Institute for the History of Science, and the New Orleans Center for the Gulf South at Tulane University and included six two-day seminars: Claims/Property, Clashing Temporalities, Commodity Flows, Exhaustion and Imagination, Risk/Equity, and Un/bounded Engineering and Evolutionary Stability, each led by five to seven people who together brought local, regional, and international perspectives, as well as an evening public programming series that brought together local voices with participants based elsewhere. See "Anthropocene River Campus: The Human Delta," Anthropocene Curriculum, accessed December 15, 2024, https://www.anthropocene-curriculum.org/project/mississippi/anthropocene-river-campus-the-human-delta. FORESTival is an annual festival at A Studio in the Woods, a residency program and eight-acre hardwood forest on the West Bank of the river that exemplifies the ecological movement here in New Orleans. The site is a former sugar plantation where one can still visit irrigation ditches. That year, we set up an "Anthropocene Base Camp," with artifacts from the previous week and activities with Campus participants, such as tonal geologist Ryan C. Clarke, who took and discussed a muddy sediment coring with a small group of festivalgoers.

9 "A Walking Discourse on Black Geographies & Indigenous Futures with Shana M. griffin and Monique Verdin," presented by the Land Memory Bank & Seed Exchange and PUNCTUATE, with the Gulf South Open School, Mississippi River Open School, and the New Orleans Center for the Gulf South at Tulane University, April 16, 2024.

10 Joseph Underhill, "Navigating the Anthropocene River: A Traveler's Guide to the (Dis)comforts of Being at Home-in-the-World," Anthropocene Curriculum, July 27, 2020, https://www.anthropocene-curriculum.org/contribution/navigating-the-anthropocene-river; Dilip da Cunha, "Design Devices or Weapons of Colonizations," paper presented during "Rivers and Powers: A Conversation on the Imaginaries, Materiality, and Culture of Urban Waters," the keynote evening for the symposium "Geopoetics of Urban Rivers," Franke Institute for the Humanities, University of Chicago, October 17–18, 2024.

11 Rebecca Snedeker, "The L'Union Creole Spring Concert Series: Love and Life on the Cornerstore Dancefloor," paper presented at "Transculturality: Music and Racism," at the University of Music and Performing Arts, Vienna, Austria, May 6, 2023. The series was a collaboration between the Neighborhood Story Project, New Orleans Center for the Gulf South at Tulane University, New Orleans Jazz National Historic Park, and Preservation Hall Foundation.

12 The intertribal collective that instigated the creation of the Nanih Bvlbanha includes Dr. Tammy Greer, Ida Aronson, Jenna Mae, Ozone 504, and Monique Verdin; Nanih Bvlbancha website, accessed June 20, 2025, http://nanihbvlbancha.net.

13 Da Cunha, "Design Devices or Weapons of Colonizations"; Dilip da Cunha, *The Invention of Rivers: Alexander's Eye and Ganga's Descent* (University of Pennsylvania Press, 2019), xi.

14 "The Decision Theater, a Collaboration with Arizona State University," Max Planck Institute of Geoanthropology, accessed June 16, 2025, https://www.gea.mpg.de/77053/decision-theater; Jürgen Renn, "Geoanthropology – a Science for the Anthropocene," paper presented at "One Health and Geo-Anthropology in the Age of the Anthropocene," Interuniversity Center for the History of Science and Technology, University of Lisbon, and NOVA School of Science and Technology, University of Lisbon, Portugal, December 13, 2024.

15 Gulf South Open School, accessed June 20, 2025, https://www.gulfsouthopen.school/; Anthropocene Commons, accessed June 20, 2025, https://anthropocene-commons.org/; Monique Verdin, "Marooned Between Land and Water: Land Memory Bank & Seed Exchange," *Journal of Environmental Architecture* 79, no. 1 (Spring 2025).

Gulf South Open School

Part of the Mississippi River Open School network

Insurgent Ecologies exhibition at 3OneOne6 gallery

The Gulf South Open School is an exploration of how we, residents of the Gulf South, can come together to learn, explore, and create in the face of climate change, sea level rise, land loss, and environmental injustice.

The Gulf South we live in today is neither just nor sustainable. But there are people and organizations throughout the region who are showing us how to care for earth, water, ourselves, and other species; and who are showing us through writing, art, music, and direct action how we might work towards more just policies, systems, and environments.

Our goal is to help make sense of the myriad activities and possibilities that are available to us. We are seeking the common threads that connect us across different scales, geographies, communities, and issue areas. We are supporting each other in embracing complexity, tension, nuance, and change. We are building shared language, knowledge, and practices that can sustain us in the seasons ahead.

We organize outdoor activities, walking discourses, arts exhibitions, academic and public panels, monthly dinners, biweekly meetings, seasonal broadsheets, and time upriver with our Mississippi River Open School community.

Photographs by Christine "Cfreedom" Brown, Katie Fronek, and Shana M. griffin.

Summer Solstice herbal honey activity with Jenna Mae and Sprout Nola at the Nanih Bvlbancha

GSOS Community Table monthly dinner

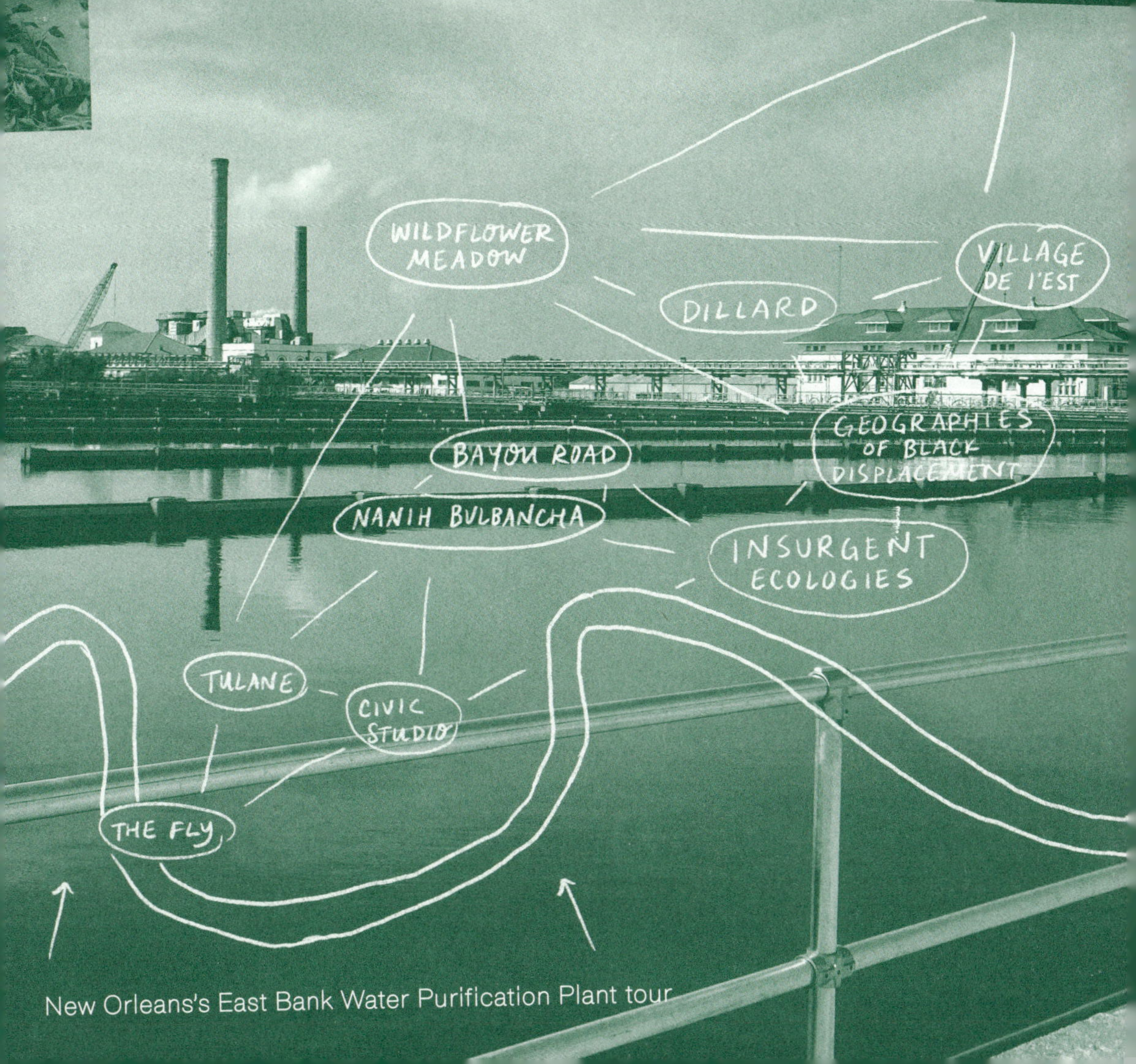

New Orleans's East Bank Water Purification Plant tour

The Four-Dimensional Mississippi

Catherine Russell, Colin Waters, Mark Williams, and Jan Zalasiewicz

Catherine is the founder and leader of the Anthropocene Sediment Network, which facilitates multidisciplinary research on Earth's surface materials and processes. Colin, Mark, and Jan have been members of the Anthropocene Working Group, a research team established in 2009 to provide scientific evidence for the formal recognition of the Anthropocene within the geological time scale. The authors ask: What does it mean to think of the Mississippi River as a geological artifact? Understanding the deep history of the river's topological formation, its shifting paths, changing sedimentation patterns, and formation of strata provides a baseline against which the human transformation of this Anthropocene River can be measured.

To think of the Mississippi River as geological, we must consider its past, present, and future. We must understand the deep history of the river's topological evolution, its shifting paths, changing sedimentation patterns, and deposition of strata, as this provides the baseline from which we assess present and future change. In the Anthropocene, the Mississippi River is an endlessly flowing superhighway of water, sediment, and pollutants that travel for some 3,700 kilometers from its source at Lake Itasca, a little south of the Canadian border, to its end in the Gulf of Mexico. The river is intensely altered and managed, contrasting with the ancient wild river that witnessed the human peopling of North America that started even before the beginning of the Holocene epoch, some 12,000 years ago. We know these histories from archaeological records, as well as from traces in the river's sedimentary deposits, so we can look at the river through a geological lens and consider how peculiar the present and future of this incredible river may be.

THE WIDER RIVER

The Mississippi River is the formal human-made interpretation of the entire river system, and its major channel was chosen and named from thousands of possible sources. The river is a dense network that branches out and drains from some 3 million square kilometers of land, which is about 45 percent of the area of the contiguous United States of America.[1] Almost any of these river tips that reach the outer edge of the drainage basin might have become the "main stem" of the river, rather than being artificially relegated as tributaries. Had the end of a Missouri River tributary been chosen as the main stem of the Mississippi River system, then the river would be about 6,000 kilometers long, such that it would have been the fourth longest in the world (after the Nile, Amazon, and Yangtze), rather than being about the seventeenth longest as the Mississippi is currently defined. The river discharges about one and a half cubic kilometers of water each average day (or 16,800 cubic meters a second).[2] In a nationwide drought this can slow to less than half a cubic kilometer, while in flood peaks it can exceed 5.6 cubic kilometers, as in the flood of May 2011.[3] Between 1940 and 2020 the average discharge has been increasing by about 4.5 percent per decade.[4]

The river is indeed ancient, first flowing south in the late Cretaceous, over 66 million years ago,[5] such that the initial river would have been paddled in by dinosaurs. The path taken by the river has shifted substantially over time, as it has become constrained, or connected to new basins, by mountain building or glacial activity. The Appalachian Mountains have always confined the Mississippi River from the east, as those mountains were built some 400 million years ago. The Rocky Mountains formed from about 80 million years ago to about 56 million years ago,[6] and it was their development that played a pivotal role in shaping the Mississippi River catchment today.

High up on the edges of the modern Mississippi River valley, there are discontinuous remnants of river strata that date back to the Pliocene Epoch, some 3 million years ago. In this time when the global temperatures were ~2–3°C warmer and sea-level up to 22 m higher than today,[7] the Mississippi developed into a very different kind of meandering river, but one that broadly followed the route of the modern river.[8] The sedimentary patterns are, however, far bigger with channels up to 5 km width and meanders of 9 km radius, compared with those of the modern Mississippi of 1 and 3 km respectively. This, and the typically coarser sediments, tells us that much more water flowed down the older river. Did the pre-ice age river have a greater extent, perhaps far into Canada? Or was there just more available water from more rainfall on the North American continent back then? It is a significant question because we already have a Pliocene level of carbon dioxide and Earth's heat balance is steadily changing towards equilibrium with this. As such, we are heading to a warmer and wetter climate, perhaps resembling a Pliocene kind of a climate. The Pliocene Mississippi deposits may hold clues to how the Mississippi will evolve as we move deeper into the Anthropocene.

The most recent major natural disruptions to the river were repeated glaciations that affected North America in response to about 50 cooler climatic intervals in the last 2.6 million years. In the most extensive of these, the Laurentide Ice Sheet periodically extended into the northern part of the Mississippi's course,[9] effectively bulldozing it out of the way, and leaving this part of the river to find a new course when the ice retreated. Each time the ice sheet melted on top or retreated, it formed

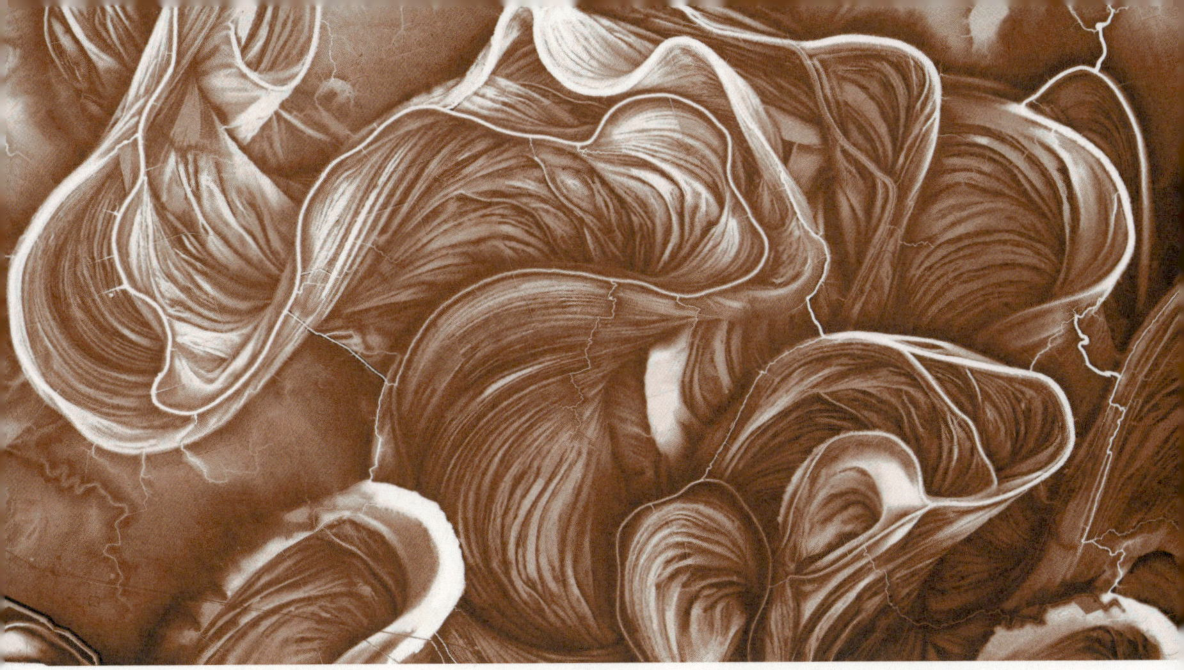

Lidar digital elevation model image of Mississippi River. Image by Daniel Coe

giant lakes that were held back by ice dams. When the ice dams broke, they caused huge volumes of fresh water to cascade along rivers towards the ocean.[10]

Along the Mississippi River, there were five major meltwater floods between 16,000 and 9,000 years ago, with one such superflood about 12,000 years ago estimated to have swelled the flow to 14 cubic kilometers a day, which could be sustained for decades or even centuries as these giant lakes drained.[11] Such flows, on a scale that is far above peak flood for the river today, caused disruptions to the major ocean-current systems and affected the global climate.[12] Throughout these fluctuations, the river itself has changed its pattern and course innumerable times, including many transitions from a multi-threaded "braided" channel, and a single-thread "meandering" channel. The sediment layers themselves show how in times of ice and permafrost, the swollen and sediment-choked river often split into the innumerable shallow and ever-changing channels of a multi-threaded braided river.[13] This kind of river is still common in the far north of the continent, where ice still lingers in the mountains and rivers pick their way across. Early gold prospectors cursed them as being "a foot deep and a mile wide." Fossilized relics of the more extensive Ice Age braidplains can be found as wide, low plateaus around the modern Mississippi. As the river then swept most of the mud it carried far downstream, the sands and gravels that remained are now avidly sought by humans for industries such as concrete manufacturing. Once the ice had gone, it left the Great Lakes, and a forever altered Mississippi River.

THE MODERN NATURAL MISSISSIPPI RIVER

Once the ice melted, the Mississippi River settled into the textbook meandering river pattern of the Holocene Epoch,[14] whose deposits overlie the sediment records of its extraordinary history. The river changed its character from many shallow channels into the single, sinuous, and deep channel of today's meandering river. A wild river of this kind forever meanders as it migrates across its wide floodplain through a constant process of erosion and deposition. As the current erodes sediment on the outer bank, sediment becomes deposited on the inner bank, such that each river bend shifts steadily over time. As the meanders shift and change over time, they can become highly curved and reconnect so that the river returns to a shorter path. These abandoned meander loops form crescent-shaped oxbow lakes, which become treasure troves of fossilized leaves and pollen, animal skeletons, and other remains that are buried within their soft, muddy sediments. During the larger floods, the channel can avulse, meaning that it abruptly switches its course to scour out and flow along an entirely different route within the floodplain. The sandy deposits left by the river are porous and permeable, and commonly contain oil and gas. It is a double-edged kind of treasure, as the exploitation of these hydrocarbon deposits in analogous places like Alberta helps power the changes that are now transforming the Mississippi of the Anthropocene.

By the mid-nineteenth century, the river had been modified by early civilizations so was already not wholly natural, though it flowed a good deal more freely than it does today. Since the start of the Holocene about 12,000 years ago, an average of 400 million tons of sand and (mostly) mud is estimated to have been carried annually in the Mississippi to the sea, building the Mississippi Delta year by year to a thickness of about 100 meters.[15] This figure is likely representative of the natural river in warm interglacial times, as the swollen river caused by glacial outbursts would have carried a far greater sediment load. Not all the sediment makes it to the sea, as much gets deposited along the way, in the beds and banks of river channels, or draped as swathes of mud and silt across the floodplain during floods. The floodplain in the Lower Mississippi River

Valley locally exceeds a hundred kilometers in width.[16] Such sediment redistributions have built wide landscapes and have concealed clues to the landscape's history and ecosystems, in the form of buried animal bones, plant debris, and relics of human culture, caught up in the sediment layers.

THE MISSISSIPPI MEETS THE SEA

The Mississippi River Delta extends over more than 30,000 square kilometers underwater, and a further 12,000 square kilometers is currently above sea level.[17] The delta wetlands include the city of New Orleans, which faces many challenges, substantially due to much of it being below sea level yet surrounded by water. The delta sediments and morphology represent another classic geological model that has been avidly studied, to help know where petroleum might be stored in ancient examples of these strata. In the deeper strata by the ocean's edge, there are highly productive oil and gas fields. The Mississippi Delta is a highly dynamic system with complex subterranean geometry. Gigantic fingers of sand mark where the channels flowed out to sea, with even larger ones below marking the shifting positions of "mouth bars" of sand just offshore, as they built out, like a slowly moving conveyor belt. These linear masses of sand are encased in muds so soft that the sheer weight of sediment can make masses of strata plastically deform and flow, even deep underground. However, sediments from the Holocene Epoch are just a veneer upon the surface of a mass of sedimentary strata. The weight of this enormous sediment mass has depressed the Earth's crust along the coast, causing it to flex and form mountains inland. The crustal depressions in effect create space for more sediment deposition, and as that has continued the surface of the delta throughout that time has stayed at or near sea level. When the sea level rises quickly, sediment deposition cannot keep up and much of its surface is drowned; when the sea level falls or remains steady, the delta wetlands build out seawards.

SEDIMENT REDISTRIBUTIONS HAVE BUILT WIDE LANDSCAPES AND HAVE CONCEALED CLUES TO THE LANDSCAPE'S HISTORY AND ECOSYSTEMS, IN THE FORM OF BURIED ANIMAL BONES, PLANT DEBRIS, AND RELICS OF HUMAN CULTURE, CAUGHT UP IN THE SEDIMENT LAYERS.

At the surface, the river has distributed sediment along some 300 kilometers of coastline, as it naturally switched (avulsed) to a different outlet every 1,000 to 1,500 years or so.[18] The currently active Balize Delta, upon which New Orleans is located, was initiated about a millennium ago and now covers an area of about 10,000 square kilometers.[19] Farther west, the Atchafalaya Delta has been developing for 1,500 years, and without the active involvement of the U.S. Army Corps of Engineers, it could become the new main route for the Mississippi River to the Gulf of Mexico.[20] The latest addition, the nearby Wax Lake Delta, is entirely human-generated, resulting from a new artificial channel cut in 1942 and since extended some eight kilometers out to sea.[21]

This Mississippi River and Delta system has been functioning and creating landscapes and strata since the Cretaceous Period, and rivers and deltas in general have been behaving along these general patterns for more than 420 million years, since the planetary revolution that took place when forests began to spread across the Earth's land surface.[22] Now, in the emerging Anthropocene, another revolution is transforming the form and function of river systems.

THE HUMAN-MODIFIED MISSISSIPPI RIVER

The human impact on river systems dates to before the Holocene when Indigenous North Americans fished and deforested areas for agriculture.[23] European settlers accelerated that change through further deforestation and agriculture, mining, and urbanization. In the last 100 or more years, the river has been engineered dramatically, such that its nature is now seemingly tamed, though the implications of this transformation are still being unraveled.[24]

More than 50,000 dams have been built across the USA, many of which are in the expansive Mississippi River catchment,[25] which store water for hydroelectric energy and irrigation, as well as building lakes for leisure. While these dams only briefly stop the inexorable flow of water, they trap as much as 20 million tons of sediment per year, which would otherwise build up the floodplains and delta downstream. Today's Mississippi Delta is sediment-starved, with estimates through 1987 to 2006 of only 145 million tons of sediment reaching the ocean per year, less than half the "natural" rates prior to 1900 of 400 million tons per year.[26] As a result, the delta is no longer growing normally so is yet more vulnerable to drowning through sea-level rise. Indeed, over the last century, a yearly average of about 50 square kilometers of land on the delta plain is lost through submergence, representing about 80 percent of coastal land loss in the U.S.[27] The delta surface is now on average about 0.6 meters lower in elevation than it was in the early 1950s due to average subsidence rates between 1965 and 1993 of 8–12 mm per year.[28]

The meanders of the Mississippi river have moved freely since the time of the dinosaurs, yet today are contained in sinuous concrete walls, notably thanks to the work of the U.S. Army Corps of Engineers from the 1920s onward. Whilst it is crucial to protect agricultural land and real estate, the Lower Mississippi River floodplain is now about 10 percent of its natural width,[29] which has consequences. Floodwaters are now prevented from taking their natural escape route onto extensive floodplains, so they attain higher flood heights and water-flow rates and make floods more hazardous when they do occur. Peak discharge past New Orleans is regulated at 3 cubic kilometers per day by flood diversion schemes.[30] Levee construction also prevents the river sediments from depositing onto river floodplains and delta tops, so they are not replenished and subside more rapidly, further increasing the risk of land drowning and reducing the natural fertility of the soils. Levees also cut off the supply of freshwater to the marshlands in the delta, which are increasingly threatened by intrusion of saltwater, with the potential to have a serious impact on this threatened ecosystem.[31]

THE MEANDERS OF THE MISSISSIPPI RIVER HAVE MOVED FREELY SINCE THE TIME OF THE DINOSAURS, YET TODAY ARE CONTAINED IN SINUOUS CONCRETE WALLS

The content of the Mississippi River today includes a range of new components, different from those of all preceding epochs. This begins with pollution caused by mining of the Mississippi Valley-type ore deposits, which are primarily lead-zinc ore. These were first recognized in southeastern Missouri, northeastern Iowa, southwestern Wisconsin, and northwestern Illinois, and mining of this kind first commenced in the mid-seventeenth century, becoming widespread in the mid-nineteenth century.[32] As lead extraction decreased after a peak of about 27,000 metric tons per year in the 1840s, zinc became the main metal mined from the region, with nearly 64,000 tons per year worked in the first decade of the twentieth century;[33] the last mine closed in 1979. The tailings from these mines have inevitably found their way into the rivers and accumulated in the sediment load transported by the river. More recently, a vast array of remarkably diverse human-generated materials has entered the river, including a range of plastic polymers, metals such as aluminum and titanium, concrete, and novel ceramics, with much of these fashioned into distinctive technofossils such as bottles and bricks. These objects, and fragments of them, are carried and deposited together with the river sediment. At the microscopic scale, there is now an influx of microplastics, fly ash particles, and glass microbeads. Novel chemicals such as persistent organic pollutants like pesticides and dioxins are not only dissolved in the water but also cling to sediment particles such as clays. The study of how these objects and compounds travel as part of the river system and become strata is in its infancy.

Since the middle of the 20th century, there has been a vast increase in nitrogen and phosphorus entering the river due to the runoff of fertilizers, livestock waste, and soil erosion from the major farming states of the Midwest, as well as human sewage from large urban population centers. Nitrogen and phosphorus are nutritious for algae, stimulating algal blooms that ultimately deplete the oxygen content of waters, especially those entering the Gulf of Mexico at the Mississippi Delta.[34] Such blooms create a "dead zone" that extends westwards from the delta with extent varying seasonally. Such dead zones started in the mid-1950s, accelerating in the 1970s and by the late 2010s were up to 23,000 square kilometers, extending as far west as Texas.[35] Additionally, there are many invasive species, including silver and bighead carp, which continue to have a substantial effect on biotic diversity in the river, which will in turn affect future paleontology.

THE FUTURE OF THE MISSISSIPPI IN THE ANTHROPOCENE

As the world warms and sea level rises from the buildup of greenhouse gases over the next century or two, much of the Mississippi Delta will likely disappear as it becomes inundated by the sea. A new delta will begin to form, perhaps somewhere near where Baton Rouge is currently located, which will itself step backwards upon the North American continent as sea levels continue to rise over centuries and millennia and Earth slowly adjusts to its new heat balance. The river, now shortened by losing its seaward portion, will likely adjust in other ways. How its corset of concrete, brick, and steel will develop depends on how the local population adapts to the trauma and disruption of losing the towns and cities of the delta. All other things being equal, the displaced people will have to move inland and rebuild, perhaps adding to the concrete, brick, and steel that holds the river tight. The drowned infrastructure of New Orleans and its neighborhoods, meanwhile, will become degraded and eroded at the sea surface, and buried materials may form future fossils. The upstream Mississippi will warm as the Earth enters its new, warmer climate state, leading to some physical and chemical effects, such as an increased rate of chemical weathering. The most obvious change will be the emergence of new communities of plants and animals that move in, which will be better adapted to the heat. Here, the array of invasive species may prove crucial, as among the thousands of invaders there will be some from hot climates elsewhere in the world, who will be better adapted to thrive in the new landscape. Under these adaptations and the flourishing of a new biota, the Mississippi River and delta will have transformed into a new river in a new Anthropocene world.

HOW ITS CORSET OF CONCRETE, BRICK, AND STEEL WILL DEVELOP DEPENDS ON HOW THE LOCAL POPULATION ADAPTS TO THE TRAUMA AND DISRUPTION OF LOSING THE TOWNS AND CITIES OF THE DELTA.

A version of this article was originally published on the website Anthropocene Curriculum (Fall 2019).

ENDNOTES

1 Jeffrey Nittrouer, Mead Allison, and Richard Campanella, "Bedform transport rates for the lowermost Mississippi River," *Journal of Geophysical Research* 113 (2008): 1–16.

2 National Parks Service (NPS), "Mississippi River Facts," February 15, 2025, https://www.nps.gov/miss/riverfacts.htm.

3 Franklin Heitmuller, Paul Hudson, Richard Kesel, "Overbank Sedimentation from the Historic AD 2011 Flood along the Lower Mississippi River, USA," *Geology* 45(2): 107-110.

4 Robert Turner, "Variability in the Discharge of the Mississippi River and Tributaries from 1817 to 2020," *PLoS ONE* 17 (2022): 1–18, https://doi.org/10.1371/journal.pone.0276513.

5 Sally Potter-McIntyre, Joshua Breeden, and David Malone, "A Maastrichtian Birth of the Ancestral Mississippi River System: Evidence from the U-Pb Detrital Zircon Geochronology of the McNairy Sandstone, Illinois, USA," *Cretaceous Research* 91 (2018): 71–79.

6 Joseph English and Stephen Johnston, "The Laramide Orogeny: What Were the Driving Forces?," *International Geology Review* 46 (2004): 833–38.

7 Kenneth Miller, James Wright, James Browning, Andrew Kulpecz, et al., "High Tide of the Warm Pliocene: Implications of Global Sea Level for Antarctic Deglaciation," *Geology* 40 (2012): 407–10.

8 William Cupples and Roy Van Arsdale, "The Preglacial 'Pliocene' Mississippi River," *The Journal of Geology* 122 (2014): 1–15.

9 Robert Fulton and Victor Prest, "Introduction: The Laurentide Ice Sheet and Its Significance," *Géographie physique et Quaternaire* 41 (1987): 181–86.

10 James Teller, David Leverington, and John Mann, "Freshwater Outbursts to the Oceans from Glacial Lake Agassiz and Their Role in Climate Change during the Last Deglaciation," *Quaternary Science Reviews* 21 (2002): 879–87.

11 Paul Aharon, "Meltwater Flooding Events in the Gulf of Mexico Revisited: Implications for Rapid Climate Changes During the Last Deglaciation," *Paleoceanography* 18 (2003): 1–14.

12 Teller, et al., "Freshwater Outbursts to the Oceans from Glacial Lake Agassiz and Their Role in Climate Change during the Last Deglaciation."

13 Tammy Rittenour, Michael Blum, and Robert Goble, "Fluvial Evolution of the Lower Mississippi River Valley During the Last 100 Ky Glacial Cycle; Response to Glaciation and Sea-Level Change," *Geological Society of America Bulletin* 119 (2007): 586–608.

14 Rittenour, et al., "Fluvial Evolution of the Lower Mississippi River Valley During the Last 100 Ky Glacial Cycle."

15 Harry Roberts, "Dynamic Changes of the Holocene Mississippi River Delta Plain: The Delta Cycle," *Journal of Coastal Research* 13 (1997): 605–27.

16 Gerry Galloway, *USA: Flood Management – Mississippi River* (WMO/GWP Associated Programme on Flood Management, 2004).

17 Roberts, "Dynamic Changes of the Holocene Mississippi River Delta Plain."

18 Roberts, "Dynamic Changes of the Holocene Mississippi River Delta Plain."

19 Roberts, "Dynamic Changes of the Holocene Mississippi River Delta Plain."

20 Harold Fisk, *Geologic Investigation of the Atchafalaya Basin and the Problem of Mississippi River Diversion* (U.S. Army Corps of Engineers, Mississippi River Commission, 1952).

21 Harry Roberts, "Delta Switching: Early Responses to the Atchafalaya River Diversion," *Journal of Coastal Research* 14 (1998): 882–99.

22 Neil Davies and Martin Gibling, "The Sedimentary Record of Carboniferous Rivers: Continuing Influence of Land Plant Evolution on Alluvial Processes and Palaeozoic Ecosystems," *Earth Science Reviews* 120 (2013): 40–79.

23 Bruce Smith, "Resource Resilience, Human Niche Construction, and the Long-Term Sustainability of Pre-Columbian Subsistence Economies in the Mississippi River Valley Corridor," *Journal of Ethnobiology* 29 (2009): 167–83.

24 Catherine Russell, Colin Waters, Mark Williams, Stephen Himson, Rachael Holmes, Annika Burns, and Jan Zalasiewicz, "Geological Evolution of the Mississippi River into the Anthropocene," *Anthropocene Review* 8 (2021): 115–40.

25 James Syvitski and John Milliman, "Geology, Geography, and Humans Battle for Dominance over the Delivery of Sediment to the Coastal Ocean," *Journal of Geology* 115 (2007): 1–19.

26 Robert Meade and John Moody, "Causes for the Decline of Suspended-Sediment Discharge in the Mississippi River System, 1940–2007," *Hydrological Processes* 24 (2009): 35–49, https://doi.org/10.1002/hyp.7477.

27 John Barras, Julie Bernier, and Robert Morton, *Land Area Change in Coastal Louisiana: A Multidecadal Perspective* (From 1956 to 2006). Pamphlet accompanying "U.S. Geological Survey Scientific Investigations Map 3019" (U.S. Geological Survey, 2008).

28 Robert Morton, Julie Bernier, John Barras, and Nicholas Ferina, "Rapid Subsidence and Historical Wetland Loss in the Mississippi Delta Plain: Likely Causes and Future Implications," *U.S. Geological Survey Open-File Report* (2005).

29 Paul Hartfield, "Engineered Wildness: The Lower Mississippi River, an Underappreciated National Treasure," *International Journal of Wilderness* 20 (2014): 8–13.

30 Nittrouer, et al., "Bedform transport rates for the lowermost Mississippi River," 1–16.

31 Jaap Nienhuis, Andrew Ashton, Douglas Edmonds, AJF Hoitink, Albert Kettner, Joel Rowland, and Torbjörn Törnqvist, "Global-Scale Human Impact on Delta Morphology Has Led to Net Land Area Gain," *Nature* 577 (2020): 514–18.

32 Allen Heyl Jr, Allen Agnew, Erwin Lyons, Charles Behre Jr, and Arthur Flint, "The Geology of the Upper Mississippi Valley Zinc-Lead District," *US Geological Survey Professional Paper* 309 (1959).

33 Heyl, et al., "The Geology of the Upper Mississippi Valley Zinc-Lead District."

34 Sergey Rabotyagov, Catherine Kling, Philip Gassman, et al., "The Economics of Dead Zones: Causes, Impacts, Policy Challenges, and a Statistical Model of the Gulf of Mexico Hypoxic Zone," *Review of Environmental Economics and Policy* 8 (2014): 58–79.

35 Nancy Rabalais and R. Eugene Turner, "Gulf of Mexico Hypoxia: Past, Present, and Future," *Limnology and Oceanography Bulletin* 28 (2019): 117–24, https://doi.org/10.1002/lob.10351.

Once the Levees Break by Rebecca Snedeker, page 256.
Photograph by Joachim Mueller Jung

Big River Drawings: In Support of Learning, Welcoming, and Community Engagement

An embodied spatial practice described here by ARON CHANG

A common directive in community engagement is to “meet people where they are.” One way to do that is to locate activities where the community already gathers. This might mean organizing a workshop inside a church or hosting a planning meeting in a school gym. Such spaces may be large, available, and conveniently located, but they may not be ideal environments for learning about the flow of the Mississippi River or imagining the future of drinking water systems. The challenge that arises, then, is: how might we create welcoming environments for diverse communities that support learning, dialogue, and creative activity? How might we change the scale and feel of a school gym?

Since early 2023, Civic Studio and the Water Leaders Institute have been creating large, temporary drawings of the Mississippi River in different public spaces using painter’s tape. A team of two or three people can create such a drawing in as little as two hours with materials costing less than $20. These drawings function in a few different ways.

Learning through drawing: The process of creating the river drawing is an opportunity to learn about and represent the flow of the Mississippi and to apply that knowledge to describe key features such as tributaries, distributaries, meanders, cutoffs, oxbows, and deltas.

A welcoming supergraphic: The river drawing becomes a supergraphic—sometimes hundreds of feet long—that transforms the space and invites people in. We use the river drawing to spark curiosity as participants follow the pathway of the river and try to make sense of what they are seeing. We use the scale of the drawing to ask participants to embrace the entirety of a space and to move and think expansively rather than asking people to engage at the scale of the eight-foot folding tables that we typically see at community events.

An armature for engagement: The river drawing also serves as an armature for community engagement by helping to organize the flow of people and activities in relation to the flow of water represented by the drawing. The drawing, like line markings on a sports field, suggests possibilities for direction and flow, and defines both a sequence of activities for participants to follow and the areas where participants will engage in those activities.

We will explain each of the above points in more detail, using images from events organized by Civic Studio and the Water Leaders Institute in 2023, to help illustrate techniques, impacts, and possible variations of big river drawings. We also hope to show how easily these drawings can be adapted to different spaces.

LEARNING THROUGH DRAWING

The first step for creating a big river drawing is determining the land across which the water will flow, as well as the aspects of the river that we hope to capture. We seek to incorporate visible topographical changes

All photographs courtesy of Aron Chang

in the landscape into the drawing. That is, we try to draw the flow of water in relation to the slope of the ground upon which the tape is affixed.

Whether inspired by USGS maps, Fisk maps, satellite imagery, lived experience, or other representations and ways of knowing the river, the task of drawing it requires identifying which aspects and qualities of the river to try to represent. What aspects of the channel and floodplain and major features like the Mississippi River delta might be shown? What proportions and spatial relationships are important to maintain, and where might distortions in scale and proportion be used to communicate something essential about the river? We are not simply attempting to represent the river as one might see it on a map—the relationship of the drawing to the space it exists in and the community it is engaging is more important. In this way, each river drawing is a completely different representation of the river, reflecting how the creators know the river and want to talk about it.

A WELCOMING SUPERGRAPHIC

One of our goals in creating a large drawing that spans a few hundred feet is to reshape the look and feel of the space we are gathering in. We want to momentarily shift attention from the gym-ness of the school gym in order to provide a more exciting context for the activities at hand.

We seek to create a lively composition. By rendering how tributaries come together, how a river meanders, or how a river spreads out to form a delta, we end up creating engaging forms and patterns.

The river drawing sprawls out and invites the viewer to follow along, eyes on the ground, to see where the tape leads. There are opportunities to take different paths, to jump across lines, and to move upstream or downstream. The river drawing enlivens the space and helps to span across different surfaces and scales. It holds participants' interest both as a large drawing and concept and in the specificity of how individual elements are rendered.

While the tape installations are meant to be temporary, returning the school gym to its everyday uses without leaving a trace, these big river drawings can also remain as evidence of the work and connections they inspire. At one of our events, the hosts were so pleased with the drawing that they asked us to leave the tape in place for people to continue viewing the drawing as a work of art.

AN ARMATURE FOR ENGAGEMENT

We use large river drawings to support different forms of learning, dialogue, and creative activities. By organizing individual stations along the river drawing, for example, we can encourage participants to follow a sequence as part of a larger narrative.

In one instance, we organized a series of Open Studios with the Water Collaborative and Total Community Action at three different locations (two gyms and a library).

The series focused on the topic of lead service lines in New Orleans's drinking water system. In this context, the river drawing represented the Mississippi River, which is the source of drinking water for the city. On the upstream end, a station invited participants to learn about the water cycle and the Mississippi. As participants moved downstream, they engaged with stations exploring drinking water infrastructure and what happens when human bodies ingest lead. The participants followed the journey of water from the river to the point of ingestion, engaging with a wide range of key interrelated concepts and terms along the way. Once the participant had made their way to the delta, they were invited to respond to a series of creative prompts.

In another Open Studio, we created a large river drawing across two stories at the Contemporary Arts Center in New Orleans. This event was part of the Water Map New Orleans / Water Map Bulbancha initiative, which seeks to build public knowledge of water and infrastructure and to support our delta city's residents in building a collective vision for what "living with water" will look like in the years ahead. Participants started at a station on the second-floor landing and followed the river around an oval ramp down to the first floor where the river spilled out into the lobby area as a widening delta. At the top, participants learned about how rivers change course. As participants made their way down the river, they were given painter's tape with which to apply what they had learned about meanders, erosion, oxbows, cutoffs, avulsions, and distributaries by making changes to the drawing and adding to the delta. In another event, focused on building understanding of the water cycle, we invited participants to use the movement of their bodies as they followed the path of water to understand and embody the water's flow in terms of energy, velocity, or sediment carried. Using painter's tape and a variety of graphic notations, we expanded upon the river drawing to represent the full water cycle, from precipitation to river flow to evapotranspiration. Along the path followed by participants, we brought additional senses into the experience by playing music created by Sly Watts to represent each part of the water cycle.

THOUGHTS ON ADAPTATIONS AND FURTHER EXPLORATION

We are using this approach to address other topics where describing flow is of pedagogical value. For instance, in another collaboration with Total Community Action, we are organizing Open Studios on the topic of incarceration, in which we ask participants to follow the path of someone moving through the criminal legal system (e.g., from apprehension to trial to prison to reentry) by following along a pathway rendered using painter's tape and stations arrayed along the drawing. We believe that by mapping out the system in physical space and having participants navigate one or more pathways through the criminal legal system, we can make it easier to comprehend the shape of the system and its impact on someone who is being incarcerated, and to make sense of terms and metaphors such as "pipeline," "double jeopardy," "reentry," and "recidivism." Furthermore, building broader understanding of the criminal legal system supports a holistic approach to reforming it, even as we seek to combat the most glaring injustices associated with specific parts of the system.

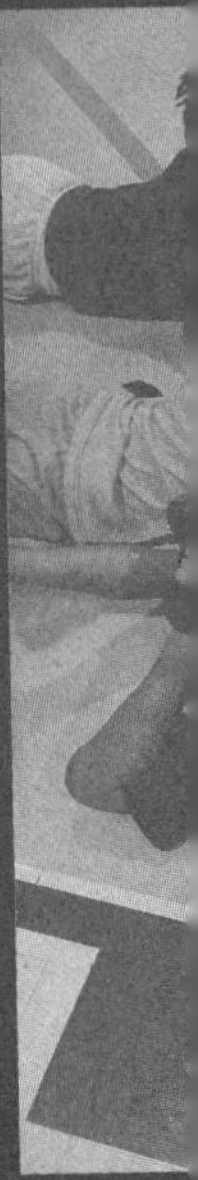

We will continue to explore the use of these large drawings as tools for learning and engagement. We are interested in testing different techniques and materials that are as easy to use as our current ones but result in no waste (the painter's tape becomes a bundle of trash at the end of each event, unfortunately). We have successfully used these techniques with youth, in family settings, and in other environments, and we believe that they can easily be adapted for use in classrooms, outdoor settings, and other places of learning and engagement.

Nanih Bvlbancha: Building New History in the Place of Many Tongues

Ida Aronson, Tammy Greer, Jenna Mae, Ozone 504, and Monique Verdin in conversation with Zane Piontek

Indigenous people have lived at the ends of the Mississippi River watershed as long as there has been land to live upon. Mississippian earthworks are found all along the watershed marking the stars, the seasons, trading grounds, settlements, ceremonial sites, birthplaces, and burial grounds.

Photograph by Hayden Legg

On April 6, 2024, Nanih Bvlbancha was unveiled at 1900 Lafitte Avenue. The earthen construct rises as a conspicuous podium among the grassy spread of the Lafitte Greenway. An installation of the triennial art exhibition *Prospect New Orleans*, Nanih Bvlbancha (called so after the original Chahta name for New Orleans, sometimes as "Bulbancha," or "place of many tongues"[1]) is rich in history and legacy: It is the latest to join the hundreds of similar mounds[2] constructed by Indigenous peoples that pepper the Southeast and that date back thousands of years to some of the earliest known man-made monuments on the American continent.

Nanih Bvlbancha is the product of a vast collective effort, generated and led by a team of Indigenous artists, academics, and community stewards who banded together as an intertribal collective to realize this shared dream. There's Jenna Mae, a poet, ethnographer, and herbalist of Cherokee, Eastern Siouan, and Mvskoke descent; Ida Aronson, a multimedia artist and member of the United Houma Nation who also works in Indigenous language restoration; Ozone 504, a social practice artist, radio engineer and DJ of Saponi, Monacan, and Lenni Lenape descent; Monique Verdin, a transdisciplinary artist, documentarian, and member of the United Houma Nation; and Dr. Tammy Greer, director of the Center for American Indian Research and Studies at the University of Southern Mississippi and a member of the United Houma Nation.

Photograph by Monique Verdin

I met with this collective to discuss the legacy of Indigenous earthenworks, the processes of constructing one in the past and present, and how Nanih Bvlbancha illuminates and uplifts contemporary Indigeneity.

What exactly is a Nanih?

Jenna Mae: Nanih comes from the Chahta (Choctaw) language, and it means hill or mountain. It's used in several different southeastern Indigenous languages. Our ancestors used it to describe our monumental earthwork culture as a hill or a mountain.

Ida Aronson: There were also different kinds of mounds. There were ceremonial mounds, there were burial mounds, there were mounds where important people would have lived in their houses. So we made this in the neutral ground as a monument both to our ancestors and our modern community, to say that we're still here, that we're still creating these things in a modern time, that we are not relegated to the past.

Ozone 504: There is beginning to be a movement among archaeologists to no longer use the term "mound" when describing these archaeological sites. You think of a mound just being kind of a pile of dirt, but these

are monumental architectural works. Some archaeologists are trying to revive the use of the word pyramid, so we were debating around that; but it turns out that the word pyramid was also a word the ancient Greeks used to kind of make fun of Egyptian monumental architecture works (It was a reference to a Greek pastry). So in the midst of this conversation, we were like: Why are we trying to use words from European languages at all? Why don't we use words from our own cultures? So that's when we decided to revive the use of Nanih as the name.

Tell me about the genesis of the idea for Nanih Bvlbancha.

Monique Verdin: In around 2013, Dr. Greer, myself, my grandmother, and another elder went down to Shrimpers Row in Dulac. There's a big old mound there. I want to say it's around 1,500 years old. And there was a tropical storm that was out in the Gulf, it was spitting rain on us, and we had decided we were going to go meet at the mound for whatever reason. We had this really sweet wander around it, seeing these old trees and all this life, and really thinking about how in this time when we're losing land at one of the most rapid rates on the planet, how these ancient mounds in the Delta that our ancestors built are still these high grounds where biodiversity is able to have a chance as everything around it is disappearing. For me, that mound visit, and just this curiosity for mounds, was where this project started.

I read that soil from all over the continent and across the world was used in constructing the Nanih. What's the significance of that international focus?

JM: We put a call out to ask people to send soil from their lands, or from a special sacred place to them. One of the reasons for that is to honor the Mississippi River and to recognize that the flow of the river carried soil here to form the land that we live on now. And also to acknowledge that we're losing land here in South Louisiana. We are the nation's wetlands, and we're losing land. We have a collective responsibility to do something about that, and so part of the call to send soil is an invitation to be a part of what's happening here, and be a part of the changes that are needed here to protect our coasts.

What is bagasse, and why did you choose to include that in the building materials?

O5O4: The bagasse was donated by the Alma Plantation in Pointe Coupee Parish. It's a byproduct of sugar production; it's what's left of the sugarcane after they've squeezed all the sugar water out of it. So we're tying that part of the history of Louisiana into the making of our earthwork.

MV: And Pointe Coupee Parish is the site of one of the earliest enslaved people uprisings dating back to the Poydras Plantation times. So I think about reimagining how these materials can be used as practices for liberation, as well as remembering how everything comes from somewhere.

Tell me about the design and architecture of the mound. How did that come together?

O5O4: We had to have permits from the city, so we had to have an actual architect sign off on the blueprint. One of their suggestions was that we put a drain down the middle, but the way we ended up doing it was based on the resources that we had. We built an oyster shell chimney all the way through the middle of it up to the top, and the water drains through the heart of the mound and is directed through French drains to drain off into the field around it.

IA: There's also a trench underneath the Nanih that is filled with more oyster shells, and that was covered with a layer of these woven palmetto mats that we made in community over the course of the January work days. So we had all these different community members creating pieces that we then put together in layers during the work days to create this unified drainage system.

How did the community work days go? What was the turnout like? What did it feel like for y'all to see people show up to contribute their time and energy to this project?

IA: We were putting out calls on social media and to our community through our own connections. They went great, we had different sections and areas that people could engage in. They could do some painting with

Dr. Tammy, they could do weaving of the palmetto mats, they could come shift dirt, do some education. The third work day in January was huge, we probably had about 80, 90 people. There was a lot of rain in January too, but people were still showing up.

MV: On our biggest day, which was that 80-to-90-people day in January, Grow Dat Youth Farm showed up with a truck bed full of soil that they gathered through their composting and soil practices out in City Park, so they brought some of the farm to the Nanih.

Did the community turnout exceed your expectations?

O504: Most definitely. It's been very inspiring. And part of the whole Prospect pad was, with all the removal of Confederate statues, particularly around New Orleans, this question of what is a public monument? What does it mean, and what communities aren't represented in the monuments around here at all? I think to have that many people turn up for our workdays—Quechua people, Mayan people, Navajo people, Choctaw people, Lenape people—it was truly, incredibly inspirational. That is what a public monument should do, it should really energize people and make them excited. I was definitely blown away by the amount of support that we have gotten and continue to get for this project.

JM: I have a child in the New Orleans charter school system, and the education around Indigenous people here in the state and in the region is almost nonexistent. So we're relegated to the past even in contemporary education. I know that my Indigenous child is not learning about his own culture in the school system, and other Indigenous children are not learning about themselves here. So to see a continued engagement at the mound, especially of the youth, is really heartwarming and hopeful and inspiring. I think people want to know more, but don't know where or how to engage or ask questions and find out more about contemporary Indigenous realities. I'm really grateful that the Nanih can be a site for that kind of engagement.

Ida, I know you're involved with the Houma Language Project. Tell me about that organization and its relation to Nanih Bvlbancha.

IA: The Houma language has been in slumber for probably over 100 years,

Photograph by Monique Verdin

and the Houma Language Project is working to revive it. It started in 2013, and in the past few years we've had a huge expansion of materials that are available for free online and learning modules that are all open for people to learn. The Houma Language Project has been super supportive of Nanih Bvlbancha. On one of the work days, myself and Jack Rittenberry [a linguist with the Houma Language Project] buried one of our original physical Houma Language dictionaries into the mound. This was an all-natural copy that Jack had made by hand, and we buried that into the mound for the posterity of both honoring our ancestors and honoring our modern reality.

Were any other items or artifacts embedded in the mound?

IA: One of our Atakapa-Ishak community members wrote a poem in his language, and that was placed in the mound, so there's multiple languages in the mound. There are woven palmetto mats and natural pigment art that were placed into the mound, so these feelings of welcoming and creation are imbued and embedded into the mound.

MV: In October of last year, Ida and I hosted a mini mound-making workshop at the Louisiana Children's Museum, and those items, those creations that the young people made were also part of that foundational layer of the Nanih.

It's interesting that Nanih Bvlbancha is at the same time a public artwork and a uniquely Indigenous cultural site. Who do you see it as being for, and what do you feel it means for different people?

IA: I think any time we can remind colonizers that we are still here and this is still our land is a worthy project. We get erased so often, not just from the state, but from this region and from this nation as a whole.

O504: While it is a project that's open to everyone, it's also very much an Indigenous-led project and very much for the upliftment of our people, but also the upliftment of everyone that lives in the Mississippi Delta. This is one of the cradles of civilization, and one of the reasons we're kind of considered a dystopian backwater these days is because of the greed and recklessness that's been imposed on top of this land.
We would like to hopefully someday lead a way out of this dystopia.

MV: It's not like we own this; it's more that we are stewards of this, and it's about remembering that and remembering that we need each other. Places of bio and cultural diversity are important, and Bvlbancha is that place. Indigenous people have never left. We are still here, and we have real solutions to offer in regards to how we can be more in balance with each other and the natural world around us.

So what does it mean to be building this mound today? How does Nanih Bvlbancha fit into the multi-millennia legacy that precedes it?

Dr. Tammy Greer: Part of the reason for building this mound was to elevate those other mounds, those ancient mounds that we have. And also, everyone comes from some Indigenous people somewhere. And what we're saying with this mound is that Indigenous people were not at all backwards or ignorant; they were architects. These things have lasted longer than many of our levees have lasted. They were architects and construction workers and physicians and astronomers, because some of these mounds align with the constellations, which takes a lot of planning and knowledge and understanding. And the complicated way that we were having to negotiate for the placing of this mound was the same as we would have done back in the day. So this is telling our youth, and really the youth of all people, that your people, where you came from, your Indigeneity, there were some brilliant people there. We want to get back to looking at our ancestors that way. They were brilliant, and in a lot of ways the way they were living was sustainable. That's where we need to go here. We need to get into that mindset again. We have put so much of ourselves into this mound, and now it's time to celebrate that, to move forward, and to learn the lessons from all we've gathered from building this mound.

A version of this interview was originally published in the magazine Antigravity *(July 2024).*

ENDNOTES

1 Jules Bentley, "Reviving Indigenous Histories with *Bulbancha is Still A Place*," *ANTIGRAVITY Magazine*, September 2018, https://antigravitymagazine.com/feature/reviving-indigenous-histories-with-bulbancha-is-still-a-place/.

2 Joe Saunders, "Native American Mounds," *64 Parishes*, n.d., accessed January 2, 2026, https://64parishes.org/entry/native-american-mounds.

Marooned Between Land and Water: Land Memory Bank & Seed Exchange

Monique Verdin

Monique Verdin's field notes reflect on interconnected sites in the Mississippi/Atchafalaya River Basin and speak to the power of interspecies collaboration and potentials for reciprocal relationships that sustain life for future generations. The text underscores the significance of nature's intelligence, lived experiences and ancestral knowledge, emphasizing the need for regenerative practices that honor the region's biological and cultural diversity. Collaborative efforts with the Okla Hina Ikhish Holo network of Indigenous Gardeners and the Land Memory Bank & Seed Exchange highlight initiatives aimed at preserving, propagating, and disseminating native plants, creating safe digital and physical spaces and developing strategies for adaptation.

I've been tending to the wild medicine that grows on my grandmother's land just south of the so-called city of New Orleans. This place I know as home borders a disconnected distributary of the Mississippi on a narrow tract of land that should be a coastal bottomland hardwood forest. It sits just inside a nineteen-foot-tall federal concrete levee wall, surrounded by open waters that have disappeared the trembling prairies, coastal wetlands and brackish estuaries. Our family land is near the historic colonial St. Bernard Catholic Cemetery, between the Kenilworth sugarcane plantation and Kinder Morgan's Southern Natural Toca Gas Plant, where pipelines connect us to the rest of the continental United States. Before the Toca site was a plant, it was a plantation; where enslaved people once labored in the cane fields, pipefitters now connect lines to a mega liquified natural gas terminal for global exports at the very end of the river.

WHEN THE LEVEES BROKE SO DID OUR FALSE SENSE OF SECURITY, LEAVING US TO WRESTLE WITH THE LEGACIES OF COLONIZATION AND REALITIES OF GLOBAL CORPORATE EXTRACTION.

"EVERY 100 MINUTES A FOOTBALL FIELD IS LOST FROM THE COAST OF SOUTH LOUISIANA"

This dire warning is perhaps an oversimplified calculation for visualization, but it is one we hear echoed again and again, and more importantly is something we are witnessing firsthand. To hear the facts, to see the figures, and to be haunted by the predictions regarding rising seas, sinking sediments and the rapid erosion of wetlands creates a kind of numbness. Bearing witness to the ocean reclaiming the Delta as its own makes some truths undeniable, though. Almost twenty years ago, Hurricane Katrina submerged our land with eleven feet of water when the Gulf of Mexico pushed in, forever changing our lives and ways of life in south Louisiana. When the Army Corps of Engineers levees broke, so did our false sense of security, leaving us to wrestle with the legacies of colonization and realities of global corporate extraction. The Corps now calls floodwalls "risk-reduction" levees as they cannot promise protection.

Twenty years ago, I thought the solution was for us all to pick up and move away from the ends of the bayous to higher grounds north of Interstate 10; the older I get, the more I realize there is nowhere that is

Terre Gaillarde. Shipping container studio, wild medicine garden, and water catchment found south of the banks of the old Bayou Terre Aux Boeufs, an ancient distributary of the Mississippi River. Digital collage created by Monique Verdin, USGS map from 1983 Black Bay, Louisiana

or will be safe from the unpredictable side effects and consequences of a rapidly changing climate. My Indigenous Houma ancestors dodged the "Trail of Tears" by retreating to those ends of the bayous, finding refuge on the oak ridges, and staying connected to networks through waterways and seasonal migrations. But my ancestors' refuge is disappearing at one of the fastest rates on the planet, forcing adaptations, new migrations and strategies for survival that have us resisting forced relocation, reconnecting circular trade networks and providing paths for us to retreat and return so we can remain and reclaim.

In collaboration with the Okla Hina Ikhish Holo network of Indigenous gardeners, the Women's Earth and Climate Action Network, Bvlbancha

Liberation Radio and the Land Memory Bank & Seed Exchange, I have been in community: planting seeds of possibility and growing gardens; activating civic spaces, physically and digitally; stewarding safe places to retreat to; and working to create neutral grounds that lean into learning from nature's intelligence and the multigenerational potential of visioning and building. All of this work is anchored and inspired by interconnected relationships, designed with regenerative reciprocity as a foundation.

In these times of uncertainty, I've been wondering how ecologies and technologies can support the most biological and cultural diversity for planetary well-being. In community we have been strategizing ways we can propagate good medicine and sustainable food systems for future generations—while questioning what it might look like to steward and preserve biodiversity in home territories found inside the "red zones" threatened with disappearance. We need solutions for survival that are possible/necessary for urban and rural adaptations, connections and collaborations, but too often there are too few models that feel practical and attainable.

Whenever a hurricane starts spinning in the Gulf of Mexico, I'm reminded of how fragile the conveniences of modern life are and begin worrying about my water source and usage, food security, communications, energy and community. Hurricanes always bring into focus what really matters. These field notes are reflections from interconnected sites in the Mississippi/Atchafalaya River Basin where adaptations and experimentations are in collaboration with nature and infrastructures in process, where regenerative coexistence and proof of concept strategies for survival are in practice.

TERRE GAILLARDE | LAND FULL OF LIFE

Terre Gaillarde (Land Full of Life) was the name of the fluid maroon community in St. Bernard Parish, led by the infamous leaders Juan San Maló and his wife Cecilia in the late 1700s. In remembrance of those who stewarded refuges of liberation, I have been calling the wild medicine gardens growing on my grandmother's land by the same name, as they grow in the same territory. Our family land is sinking, as south Louisiana's delta sediments subside, and sea levels rise. Annually, saltwater has been seeping farther up the Mississippi River threatening freshwater intakes. At the Terre Gaillarde site, I have been thinking through irrigation, drainage and mitigation strategies while investing in water banking cisterns and experimenting with plants and best practices for living through extreme drought and flooding scenarios. Additionally, Terre Gaillarde is stewarded as a living seed bank and experiential outdoor classroom, where food and wild medicine can be grown and shared to support folks in the city of New Orleans | Bvlbancha and beyond. The Land Memory Bank & Seed Exchange has been growing wild medicine and coastal prairie, and protecting bottomland forest, on this family land since 2015, sharing seeds and plants with community and supporting biodiversity specific to the subtropical delta riparian ecotone that is disappearing all around it. Knowing the need for wild spaces and the importance for seed stocks to adapt to be more salt tolerant and resilient to wind and flooding, I am working to heal this old sugarcane field and support its transition to being the land full of life that it is. Through work on this site, I am also propagating plants to be shared with other sites and community, knowing that this land may one day be taken back by the sea.

Nanih Bvlbancha. Portable network intranet system being tested at the Nanih Bvlbancha on the Lafitte Greenway in New Orleans. Digital collage created by Monique Verdin, United States Geological Survey map from 1983 Ponchatoula, Louisiana and 1983 New Orleans, Louisiana

NANIH BVLBANCHA | EARTHWORK IN THE PLACE OF MANY (BABBLING) LANGUAGES

Indigenous people have lived at the ends of the Mississippi River watershed as long as there has been land to live upon. Mississippian earthworks are found all along the watershed marking the stars, the seasons, trading grounds, settlements, ceremonial sites, birthplaces and burial grounds. *Nanih* means mound or hill in Chahta (Choctaw), *Bvlbancha* translates to place of babbling or many languages and was the name given to the territories of the lower coastal delta, as it was a site of trade long before the colonizers decided to rebrand as the global port city of Nouvelle Orleans. We are not sure when the last Nanih was built

Prairie des Femmes. Self portrait of Monique Verdin taken in 2021 shortly after purchasing Prairie des Femmes site as land was being cleared and reimagined from a fallow sweet potato field to Jardins Sauvages and place of refuge. Digital collage created by Monique Verdin, USGS map from 1984 Baton Rouge, Louisiana

Little-Big House. Little-Big House with solar generators and Swampnet portable network kit. Digital collage created by Monique Verdin, USGS map from 2024 Sunset, Louisiana and 2024 Arnaudville, Louisiana

in Bvlbancha, but when Prospect New Orleans offered an intertribal collective of artists, herbalists, educators, gardeners and researchers the opportunity to submit a proposal for a public monument as part of their Artists of Public Memory Initiative we committed to the work of birthing and building an earthwork. The Nanih Bvlbancha has been teaching us a lot about the need for neutral grounds and has acted as an antenna calling community to build, learn and grow together. The Nanih rests on the city greenway named after the pirate Lafitte, where enslaved and incarcerated men were once forced to dig Carondelet's colonial canal connecting the city to the bayou to the lake: filled long ago, reimagined as a twenty-first-century recreational park. Stewards of the Nanih are anchoring gatherings at the site every solstice and equinox and have witnessed it become a site of organized and organic community activations. Native medicine gardens are being seeded and the use of the site as a campus for the Gulf South Open School* is being developed. We are also experimenting with alternative communication systems using mesh network technologies and thinking through how the Nanih might be activated as a communication hub in times of emergency with the SwampNet project, in partnership with Community Tech NY. SwampNet is a collaborative project started in 2023 to bring alternative and autonomous communication systems to Bvlbancha | New Orleans and across the Gulf South. The Nanih Bvlbancha has given us the opportunity to lean into Indigenous futures, and the space to connect in contemporary times at a site that acknowledges Indigenous histories and traditional knowledge.

* Gulf South Open School is the name of a river hub that contributes to the Mississippi River Open School. The school explores how Gulf South residents can come together to learn, explore, and create in the face of climate change, sea level rise, land loss, and environmental injustice through hands-on activities, site visits, environmental stewardship, community dinners and conversations, and celebrations.

PRAIRIE DES FEMMES | WOMEN'S PRAIRIE

Three days after Hurricane Ida hit south Louisiana with 150 mph winds in 2021, I purchased twelve acres of land in southwest Louisiana, just north of Interstate 10, twenty-seven feet above sea level, in a place known as Prairie des Femmes (Women's Prairie). The land occupies the edge of an ancient Mississippi River distributary where the tall prairies once met the swamps of the Atchafalaya. As coastlands are disappearing to the south, this site is a place we can migrate to seasonally and in times of emergency; where we are relocating and propagating plants that are becoming hard to find and grow in our coastal territories due to saltwater intrusion, including maypop, yaupon, elderberry, wild

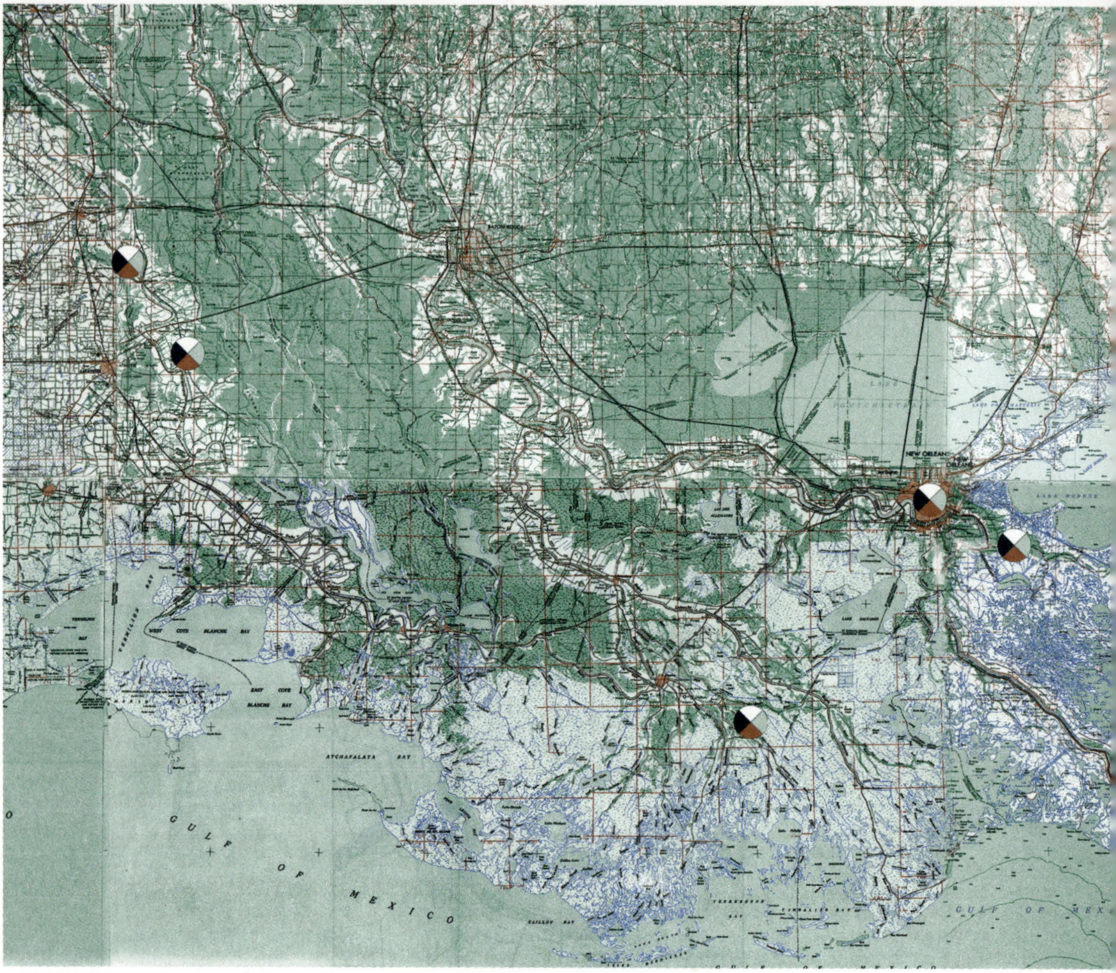

Okla Hina Ikhish Holo, garden sites of Okla Hina Ikhish Holo. Digital collage created by Monique Verdin, USGS maps 1954 Port Arthur, Texas; 1952 Lake Charles, Louisiana; 1953 Mobile, Alabama; 1957 Breton Sound, Louisiana; 1945 New Orleans, Louisiana; 1954 Baton Rouge, Louisiana

persimmon, life-everlasting and sassafras. The Prairie des Femmes property was an old sweet potato field for decades, left fallow for years allowing the wax myrtle and pine forest to flourish. This in-between swamp and prairie land provides opportunities to support symbiotic relationships that allow for the regrowth of prairie ecosystems for both carbon capture sequestration purposes and all the exponential beneficial reasons, including the coexistence of a fruit forest, a living seed bank and the preservation of biodiversity, for future generations. Seeds and plants from the Terre Gaillarde site in coastal St. Bernard Parish are currently being scattered and planted at the Prairie des Femmes site.

In the summer of 2022, we moved a little twelve-by-thirty-foot workers' cabin built out of hardwood, from the port of Krotz Springs, near the Atchafalaya River, out to Prairie des Femmes. Reborn as the Little-Big House, this infrastructure serves as a kind of welcome center/landing site/climate emergency hub/multipurpose space with an outdoor kitchen and bathroom addition. We have been incredibly fortunate to be in relationship with and learning from Footprint Project, a solar emergency organization that acts as energy first responders. At present, we have two solar generators being stored and used as primary power at the Little-Big House. The systems are on trailers and can be moved to other locations when needed, and we are currently researching microgrid possibilities with hybrid mobility. Ceramicist Mercedes Rodgers Thomin is in collaboration on site helping process wild clay, leading tile making and kiln building, and will be coleading future experimentation as we explore building with clay and bousillage (clay, moss, hair insulation) techniques. Additionally, the Land Memory Bank will be using sensors to monitor the land's nutrients and water consumption, as well as weather monitoring to build a land memory data bank. Digital memory materials, resources and a curated library will be uploaded onto a portable network kit. We are researching solar servers and hoping the Prairie des Femmes site might one day be a potential host for such technology. We envision the Little-Big House to be a site of learning and building together and look forward to cocreating experimental models for sustainable living.

OKLA HINA IKHISH HOLO | INDIGENOUS NETWORK OF GARDENERS

A network of Indigenous gardeners, rooted in the Atchafalaya-Mississippi River Basin and the Gulf South, has been in partnership with and supported by the Women's Earth and Climate Action Network since the summer of 2020. The Okla Hina Ikhish Holo—People of the Sacred Medicine Trail—mission is to reactivate ancient trade routes and to forge new paths that empower decentralized systems, nurture circular economies, foster local biodiversity, exercise food sovereignty, steward our traditional territories and build community around reciprocal relationships in the face of increasing climate impacts. We work collectively to serve the community at large through projects of mutual aid, public education, providing food and traditional plant medicine security, and collaborations with surrounding farms and coalitions to build networks of support. Prairie des Femmes and the Terre Gaillarde sites are connected to a network of Okla Hina Ikhish Holo gardens, including the Hummingbird Springs site in ancestral Mvskoke territory in southeastern Alabama, stewarded by Angela Comeaux; a medicine wheel garden at the University of Southern Mississippi in Hattiesburg and a home yaupon patch, tended by Dr. Tammy Greer; an urban Land Back garden in Bvlbancha, stewarded by Jenna Mae; Grand Bois Healing House and medicine gardens in Terrebonne Parish, Louisiana, being built out by Clarice Friloux; Raccoon Oak Farm in Breaux Bridge, Louisiana, cared for by Ida Aronson; Bochokwa Gardens in Lacombe, Louisiana, tended by Scierra LaGarde; and a number of other garden sites located in St. Landry and Orleans parishes. Each site of Okla Hina Ikhish Holo can be seen as part of a unified ecosystem of farmers in relationship and rematriating lands in the Gulf South region.

South Louisiana is on the map as a global port and tourist destination, known for jazz, carnival and crawfish, pirates, creoles and cajuns, and Cancer Alley. They say so-called Cancer Alley stretches from our Louisiana State Capital Baton Rouge | Iti Ouma | the Red Stick to New Orleans | Bvlbancha | Place of Many Languages, but I argue the alley extends south all the way to the oxygen-deprived "dead zone" in the Gulf. For many, this territory is a place that they call home. A place I call home. When you live in a place that is more water than land and inundated with industry and rising sea levels, it is concerning to have supreme court rulings that gut the Clean Water Act. Meanwhile, the Louisiana governor's office denies the existence of climate change, deregulating industry and handing out tax breaks to court carbon capture sequestration and liquified natural gas barons. We have been living on the frontlines as a kind of canary, sinking in the climate-challenged black-gold oil mines for a long time. We've witnessed extractive legacies play out and be perpetuated, always reckoning with what really matters.

WE ARE LEARNING FROM THE INTELLIGENCE OF NATURE HERE AT THE END OF THE MISSISSIPPI RIVER.

What really matters? Clean water, healthy soil, safe places to be, renewable and affordable energy, access to information and communication, and community. We are learning from the intelligence of nature here at the end of the Mississippi River. We are recognizing the power of interspecies collaborations and the infinite potential for real solutions built by the wisdom of lived experiences and ancestral knowledge that invests in regenerative relationships.

A version of this interview was originally published in the Journal of Architectural Education *(2025).*

Braid and Flow

A knowledge sharing practice by ARON CHANG, JELAGAT CHERUIYOT, DENISE FRAZIER, SHANA M. GRIFFIN, and REBECCA SNEDEKER

We each have relationships to the particular watersheds in which we live. How do we ground, learn, and share with people around the world who are dealing with comparable or different issues within their own watersheds? Braid and Flow is an online creative and knowledge sharing practice developed by the Gulf South Anthropocene Working Group (later renamed Gulf South Open School) members in Spring 2020, during the onset of the Covid-19 pandemic. In 2024, the planetary-wide Anthropocene Commons began to utilize this form for sharing across watersheds around the world.

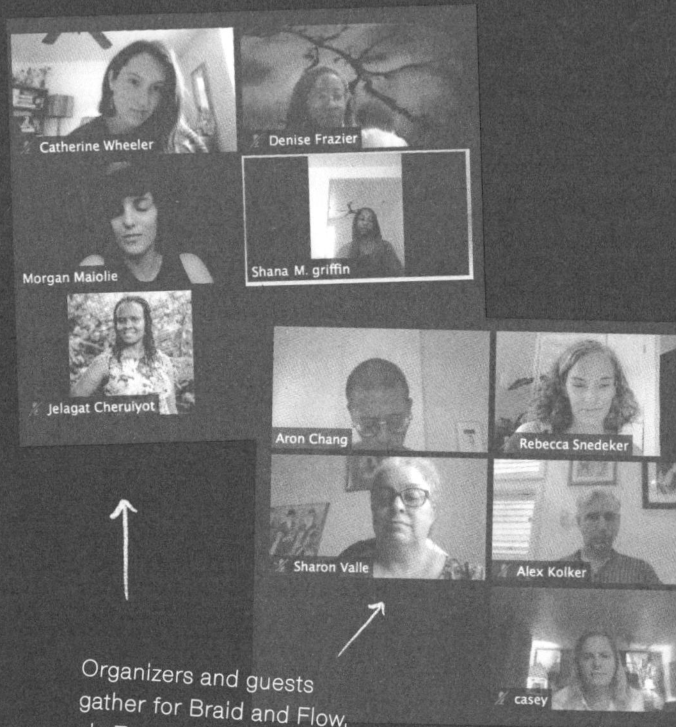

Organizers and guests gather for Braid and Flow, via Zoom, in June 2020.

EXCERPTS FROM PRESENTATION OF BRAID AND FLOW, REBECCA SNEDEKER AND DENISE FRAZIER, HKW THE SHAPE OF A PRACTICE, OCTOBER 2020

What do we create when we allow nature to inspire us; to shape our practice? Braid and Flow is a practice forged by members of the Gulf South Anthropocene Working Group in the wake of the Anthropocene River Campus.

Our practice is inspired by the structure of braided rivers and is named after their shapes. Some rivers meander, while others both split apart into myriad channels and weave back together across a broad floodplain. Similarly, we're creating a space for different disciplines and practices to come together around the biggest challenges we face as a society. Our conversations, like these braided rivers, flow from a source and then break away, but weave back together under the umbrella of a major topic.

Braid and Flow convenes twice each month to explore themes that stretch across scales and disciplines, such as food and food systems, racialized violence, climate, money, cultural institutions, technology and intimacy. Our goal is to strengthen the theories and the practices that guide our work as artists, activists, researchers, policy makers, writers, scientists, designers, teachers, students, and leaders, all working to navigate the Anthropocene and the challenges of climate change, white supremacy, and the global pandemic.

Each month, the first virtual event includes guided discussion of the theme with three breakout sessions led by experts. A second virtual event, three to four days later, includes a recap of the first event, a creative prompt, time to create and upload results to a shared folder, and then a round table of participants sharing their offerings. Each month's theme arises organically through conversation the preceding month. Meetings take place via the Zoom platform and all are welcome to join.

BRAID & FLOW

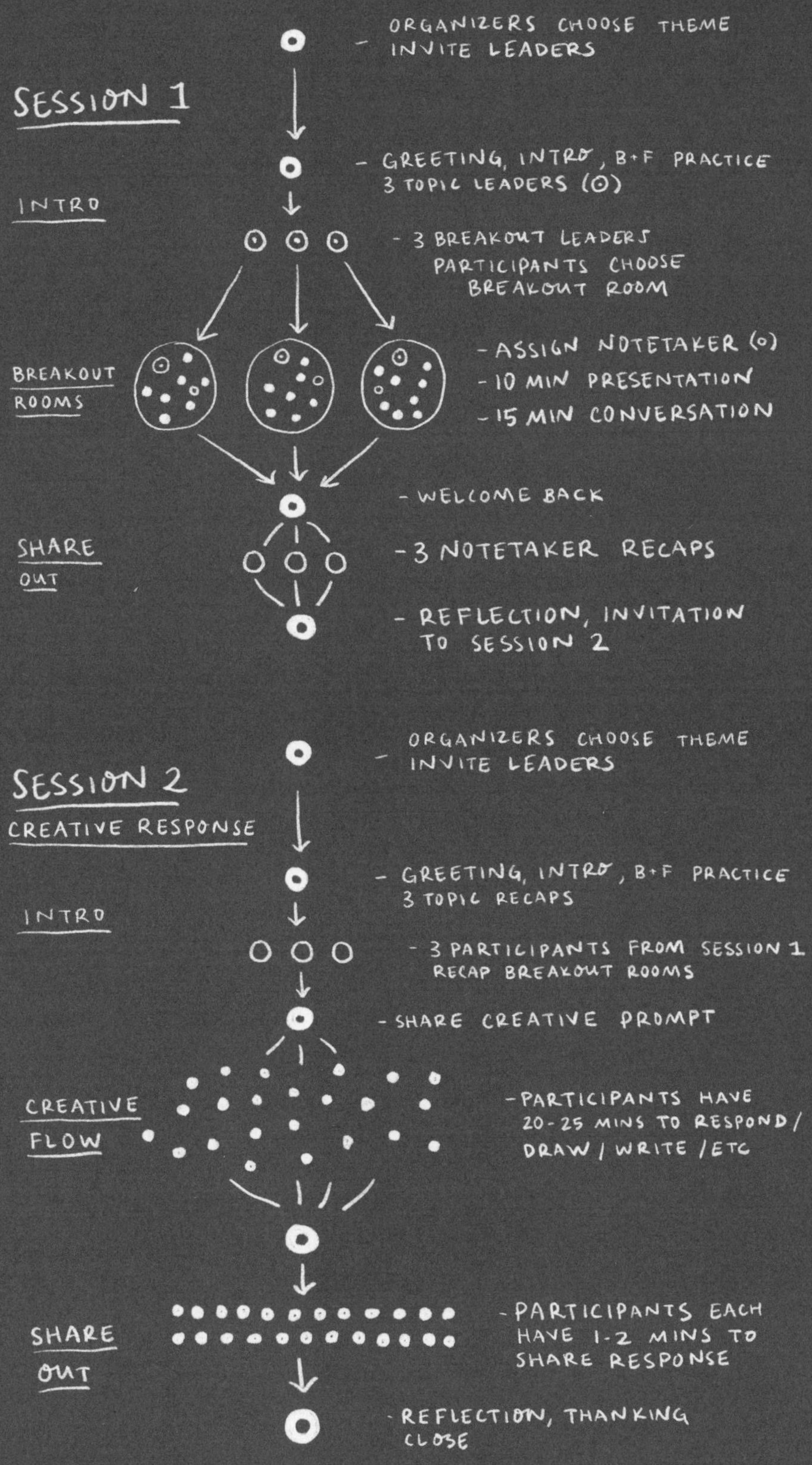
ORGANIZERS CHOOSE THEME
- INVITE LEADERS
SESSION 1
- GREETING, INTRO, B+F PRACTICE
3 TOPIC LEADERS (⊙)
INTRO
- 3 BREAKOUT LEADERS
PARTICIPANTS CHOOSE
BREAKOUT ROOM
BREAKOUT ROOMS
- ASSIGN NOTETAKER (◦)
- 10 MIN PRESENTATION
- 15 MIN CONVERSATION
- WELCOME BACK
SHARE OUT
- 3 NOTETAKER RECAPS
- REFLECTION, INVITATION TO SESSION 2
ORGANIZERS CHOOSE THEME
- INVITE LEADERS
SESSION 2
CREATIVE RESPONSE
- GREETING, INTRO, B+F PRACTICE
3 TOPIC RECAPS
INTRO
- 3 PARTICIPANTS FROM SESSION 1
RECAP BREAKOUT ROOMS
- SHARE CREATIVE PROMPT
CREATIVE FLOW
- PARTICIPANTS HAVE
20-25 MINS TO RESPOND/
DRAW / WRITE / ETC
SHARE OUT
- PARTICIPANTS EACH
HAVE 1-2 MINS TO
SHARE RESPONSE
- REFLECTION, THANKING
CLOSE

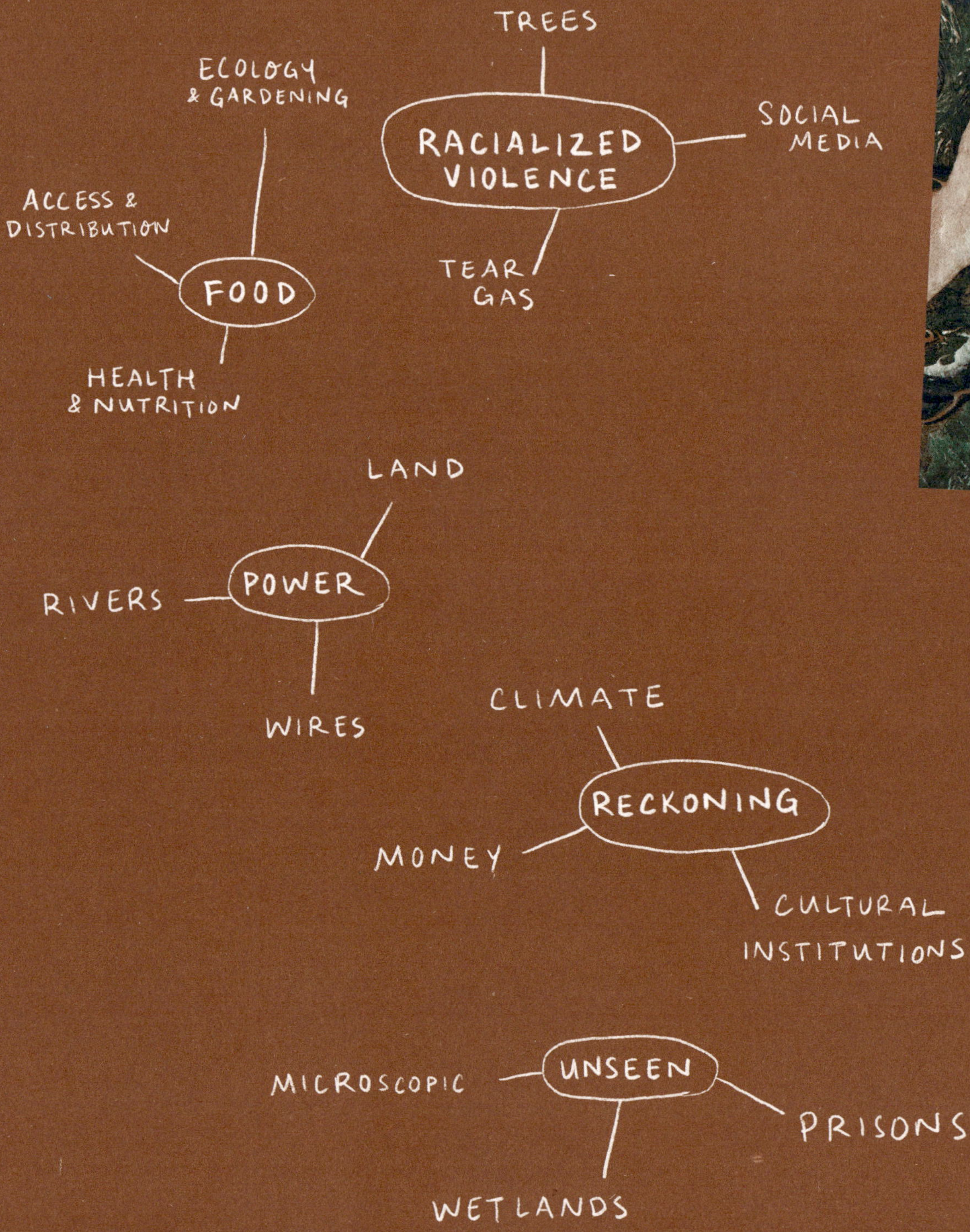
TREES
ECOLOGY & GARDENING
RACIALIZED VIOLENCE
SOCIAL MEDIA
ACCESS & DISTRIBUTION
FOOD
TEAR GAS
HEALTH & NUTRITION
LAND
RIVERS
POWER
WIRES
CLIMATE
RECKONING
MONEY
CULTURAL INSTITUTIONS
MICROSCOPIC
UNSEEN
PRISONS
WETLANDS

As we co-create this practice, we ask ourselves these questions.

How can we—
/ Gather together online to navigate the Anthropocene, resist white supremacy, and be transformed by pandemic,
/ Explore themes that stretch across scales and discipline,
/ Commit to sharing from our own work and life experience,
/ Shape a practice that de-centers intellectual hierarchies and white racialized spaces,
/ Create intimacy and resist digital isolation and fatigue through creative response,
/ Learn from one another, come to know one another, and emerge energized, knowing that each one of us have something meaningful and nourishing to give and receive?
/ Be like braided rivers?

AGS
241B

Glossary

Proposed as a new geological epoch to follow the Holocene, the Anthropocene refers to widescale earth systems changes caused by human activities, including climate change and mass species extinction. Within the span of a couple decades, the term has become pivotal in mobilizing new research and educational initiatives globally, public activism and engagement, art and documentaries, and more.

Anthropocene Campus is a series of public events and activities designed to explore the concept of the Anthropocene and its implications for knowledge, research, and education. It has brought together scholars, artists, activists, and others to examine the Anthropocene in order to develop new approaches to understanding and addressing the challenges of this geological epoch. The initial Anthropocene Campuses were initiated by Haus der Kulturen der Welt and the Max Planck Institute for the History of Science starting in 2014. They continue to be organized with the participation of the Anthropocene Commons and other partners.

Anthropocene Commons is a global, decentralized network of researchers, artists, educators, activists, and scientists who work collaboratively to foster a shared understanding of our planetary crises through transformative pedagogies, collective action, and the sharing of knowledge, skills, and resources.

Anthropocene Drift (or Over the Levee, Under the Plow) was a traveling five-day seminar in the context of Mississippi. An Anthropocene River on settler colonialism, industrial agriculture, Indigenous resurgence, and food sovereignty along the Mississippi River and its tributaries in the Upper Midwest.

Anthropocene River Journey was a collaboration in 2019 between Mississippi. An Anthropocene River and the River Semester to bring students, researchers, activists, artists, and others to journey by canoe from the headwaters of the Mississippi River to the Gulf of Mexico to research, document, and critically examine the Anthropocene as a site-specific concept on and along the river.

Field Stations were the name used to refer to the regional groups that convened as part of Mississippi. An Anthropocene River. The term "river hubs" came to replace it in the Mississippi River Open School.

Gulf South Open School is the name of a river hub that contributes to the Mississippi River Open School. The school explores how Gulf South residents can come together to learn, explore, and create in the face of climate change, sea level rise, land loss, and environmental injustice through hands-on activities, site visits, environmental stewardship, community dinners and conversations, and celebrations.

Mississippi. An Anthropocene River (2018–2019) explored the vast region encompassed by the world's fourth largest river. The project's aim was to make this landscape legible as a critical zone of habitation and long-term human-environment interaction. The project is manifest in a variety of field-research activities, public forums, workshops, and journeys on and along the Mississippi River.

Mississippi River Open School for Kinship and Social Exchange is an educational and research project spanning the Mississippi River from its headwaters to the Gulf for collaboratively imagining and practicing experimental modes of teaching and learning for the planetary emergency.

River Semester is a 100-day immersive undergraduate program run by Augsburg University, during which students travel from the headwaters of the Mississippi River to the Gulf of Mexico by canoe and sailboat. The curriculum focuses on environmental justice, social change, and interdisciplinary studies, incorporating experiential learning through field research, coursework, and interactions with local communities and experts along the river.

Stop Line 3 was a movement to halt the construction of the Enbridge Line 3 tar sands oil pipeline. Enbridge completed the construction of the pipeline in 2021.

Welcome Water Protector Center was an action camp and community hub in Anishinaabe territory (Palisade, Minnesota) that emerged during the Stop Line 3 movement to oppose the construction of the Enbridge Line 3 oil pipeline across the region. Related activities continue to be organized in a distributed way throughout the region.

Contributor Bios

AMBER GINSBURG

Amber Ginsburg creates site-generated projects and social sculpture that insert historical scenarios into present-day situations. Her background in craft orients her projects towards the continuities and ruptures in material, social, and utopic histories.

AMY LESEN

Based in New Orleans, Amy Lesen is Professor of Environmental Leadership and Participatory Change in the Antioch University PhD Program in Leadership and Change. Amy is a scholar-practitioner who does climate, environmental, disaster, and health justice work in collaboration with coastal communities across the Gulf Coast, elsewhere in the U.S. Southeast, in the Caribbean, and beyond.

ANDREA CARLSON

Andrea Carlson is an Ojibwe/Anishinaabe Indigenous futurist who challenges historical fictions through powerful mixed-media works that address authenticity, creativity, human universals, and the deep time of the natural world.

ARON CHANG

Aron Chang is an urban designer and educator who focuses on community-based planning and design practices. Aron is a member of the Civic Studio cooperative and co-leads the Water Leaders Institute as well as the Water Map New Orleans / Water Map Bulbancha initiative.

BRIAN HOLMES

Brian Holmes is an essayist, artist, and activist working on political ecology. Returning to the U.S. after twenty years in Europe, he helped form the group Deep Time Chicago, which uses earth system science to explore the markers of global ecological change in local institutions and daily life.

BRUCE BRAUN

Bruce Braun is Professor of Geography at the University of Minnesota. His research and teaching spans political ecology, settler colonialism and the environment, urban natures, and extractive infrastructures.

CATHERINE RUSSELL

Catherine Russell is a Visiting Fellow in Physical Geography at Loughborough University, whose expertise is in Anthropocene Sedimentology and river systems. She has been awarded a Fulbright-Lloyd's of London Visiting Scholarship and the Roland Goldring Award in 2023 for making a noteworthy contribution to sedimentology.

CLAIRE PENTECOST

Claire Pentecost is an artist and writer whose projects often address the contested line between the natural and the artificial, focusing for many years on food, agriculture, bio-engineering, and anthropogenic changes in the indivisible living entity that animates our planet.

COLIN WATERS

Colin Waters is an Honorary Professor at University of Leicester and a retired principal mapping geologist at the British Geological Survey, specializing in Carboniferous and Anthropocene stratigraphy and sedimentology. He was Secretary of the Anthropocene Working Group from 2011–2020 and its Chair from 2020–2024 and is current Yorkshire Geological Society President.

D. JELAGAT CHERUIYOT

D. Jelagat Cheruiyot is a Senior Professor of the Practice in Ecology and Evolutionary Biology at Tulane University. Born in Kenya, she studies elemental defense and heavy-metal transfer in ecosystems. Her work blends teaching, research, and community partnerships to advance urban gardening, environmental health, and sustainable neighborhood restoration through phytoremediation and ecological education.

DENISE FRAZIER

Denise Frazier is the Creative Director for the Jazz Generations Initiative-New Orleans, a multigenerational and interdisciplinary jazz studies and performance project based in New Orleans and New York. She received a PhD in Latin American Studies from Tulane University. Her research includes sound studies and the environments of the Gulf South and the Caribbean.

DIO CRAMER

Dio Cramer is an artist, geographer, and graphic designer living in the Mississippi River watershed, in Minneapolis, Minnesota. Their work is focused on placemaking, community building, and organizing through the arts, and facilitating collective and collaborative art-making in support of justice movements.

IDA ARONSON

Ida Aronson (they/them) is a multimedia artist, project manager, land worker, organizer, language worker, and citizen of the Houma Nation of Louisiana. They support many regional Indigenous projects, including Bvlbancha Public Access, Imagine Water Works, Nanih Bvlbancha, Okla Hina Ikhish Holo, Tasso Time, and more! Learn more: aronsoncv.carrd.co

IMANI JACQUELINE BROWN

Imani Jacqueline Brown is an artist, activist, and researcher from New Orleans, USA. Her work investigates the continuum of extractive environmental and economic systems, from settler-colonial genocide and slavery to contemporary gentrification, fossil fuel production, and police and corporate impunity.

JACOB LINDGREN

Jacob Lindgren is a graphic designer, web developer, and writer from Chicago.

JAMIE ALLEN

Jamie Allen is a cultural organiser and grounded researcher working across media, ecology, and infrastructure. His practice explores metabolic and infrastructural intimacies through technopoetics and experimental publishing. He develops collaborative tools and research platforms that examine how knowledge, energy, and technology shape collective life and planetary futures.

JAN ZALASIEWICZ

Jan Zalasiewicz is Emeritus Professor of Palaeobiology at the University of Leicester, previously of the British Geological Survey, and currently co-chairs the Anthropocene Working Group. His most recent book is *Discarded: How Technofossils Will Be Our Ultimate Legacy*.

JASON LUDWIG

Jason Ludwig is an assistant professor in the Department of Film and Media Studies at the University of California, Santa Barbara. His work examines histories of race, computing, and politics in the United States.

JENNA MAE

Jenna Mae is a poet, ethnographer, and herbalist of Cherokee, Eastern Siouan, and Mvskoke descent.

JENNIFER COLTEN

Jennifer Colten is a photographer whose work examines the representation of landscape, embedded cultural geographies, and environmental implications of land use. Addressing issues of cultural erasures and visibility is central to her practice.

JEREMY MECKLER

Jeremy Meckler is a scholar, educator, and parent working and living in Minneapolis. He is a PhD Candidate in Comparative Studies in Discourse and Society at the University of Minnesota and served as the Grant Coordinator and Editorial Manager for the Mississippi River Open School for Kinship and Social Exchange.

JESSE VOGLER

Jesse Vogler is an artist and architect whose work sits at the intersection of spatial practices, material culture, and political economy. He is the co-director of the Institute of Marking and Measuring and Professor of Architecture at the Free Univeristy of Tbilisi.

JOANNA FARLEY

Joanna Farley is an urban planner and resident of past/present/future New Orleans. She is currently doing a lot of learning from plants, making maps, and supporting youth to make radio.

JOE UNDERHILL

Joe Underhill's work focuses on experiential education to empower students in relation to the challenges of the Anthropocene. His research and writing examine the intersections of political culture and psychology, critical pedagogy, and environmental justice. He directs the River Semester program, the nation's only full semester program offered on the Mississippi River.

JOHN KIM

An educator, artist, and researcher, John Kim has written on topics including the environment, the Anthropocene, collective action, and critical media theory. He has also shown art, sculpture and video games in galleries and festivals around the world.

KATIE FRONEK

Katie Fronek is a resident of Bvlbancha / New Orleans and a member of the Civic Studio cooperative and Water Leaders Institute. She is a landscape designer with a practice focused on community based planning and environmental education.

KAYLA ANDERSON

Kayla Anderson participates in the art world as an interdisciplinary artist, a critical writer, a sometimes-curator, a precarious administrator, and an aspiring educator. Her work explores the ways that subjectivity shapes, and is shaped by, technology.

KIRISITINA SAILIATA

Kiri Sailiata is a professor of American Studies at Macalester College. Her teaching and research emphasizes Pacific history, environmental justice, visual culture, militarism, law, transnational feminisms and community based research.

LYNN PEEMOELLER

Lynn Peemoeller is a food systems planner. In her work, she utilizes fields of natural sciences, urban planning, policy, agriculture, food, culture, activism, and the arts in a social practice. She uses food primarily as an investigation into questions of identity, culture, and place.

MARK WILLIAMS

Mark Williams is Professor of Earth Sciences and Palaeobiology at the University of Leicester. He is the co-author of several books, including *The Cosmic Oasis* and *The Anthropocene: A Multidisciplinary Approach*. He is currently co-chair of the Anthropocene Working Group.

MEIRA SMIT

Meira Smit is an aspiring farmer, food sovereignty advocate, world traveler, textile artist, and storyteller from Eau Claire, Wisconsin. As a student on the 2023 River Semester, she discovered how her art practice could be a way to both digest and communicate human and nature collaborations and conflicts. She is currently traveling the world seeking to build solidarity networks with small farmers.

MONIQUE VERDIN

Monique Verdin is an art-maker, wild-gardener, storykeeper, citizen of the Houma Nation and steward of the Land Memory Bank. Monique co-stewards Bvlbancha Liberation Radio, an urban earthwork Nanih Bvlbancha, and is a SwampNet collaborator—experimenting with autonomous and alternative communications that operate as archives and channels for emergency community communications.

MORGAN ADAMSON

Morgan Adamson is Professor of Media and Cultural Studies at Macalester College, Saint Paul, Minnesota. She is a scholar-practitioner who works at the intersections of film and digital media, critical theory, and cultural studies.

MORGAN PIPER CORDOVA

Morgan Piper Cordova is a writer, musician, and amateur journalist from Petaluma, California. He was a student on the River Semester in 2023, where he undertook a project collecting stories about food, cuisine, and everything in between. Morgan is interested in researching the connection people have with their waterways. He works as a baker in San Francisco, California.

NELSON MONDALE

Nelson Mondale is a graphic and web designer living in Minneapolis, Minnesota. Nelson creates digital and printed tools to strengthen awareness around the Mississippi river, urban geography, and building community connections.

NICHOLAS BROWN

Nicholas A. Brown is a teacher, writer, and artist based in Boston, Massachusetts and La Farge, Wisconsin. His scholarly and creative work focuses on Indigenous and settler colonial landscapes. Brown is the co-author of *Re-Collecting Black Hawk: Landscape, Memory, and Power in the American Midwest* and is currently working on a book about the Pacific Crest Trail.

NICK HOLMES

Nick Holmes is a human rights activist, community engagement coordinator, historian, cultural preservationist, environmentalist, writer, and coop developer. His work focuses on overall sustainability for the Human Family.

OZONE 504

Ozone 504 is a social practice artist, radio engineer and DJ of Saponi, Monacan, and Lenni Lenape descent.

REBECCA SNEDEKER

Rebecca Snedeker is an artist and urbanist from Bvlbancha/New Orleans. She creates place-based, interdisciplinary, and immersive learning experiences that support humans in understanding and caring for one another and our surroundings. Snedeker is the co-author of *Unfathomable City: A New Orleans Atlas* and director of the documentary *By Invitation Only*.

ROOPALI PHADKE

Roopali Phadke is a professor of Environmental Studies at Macalester College in Saint Paul, Minnesota. Her teaching and research focus on water, energy and climate policy, citizen science, and community based research.

RYAN GRIFFIS

Ryan Griffis is an artist currently teaching in the School of Art + Design at the University of Illinois at Urbana-Champaign. He works collaboratively and across media to convey stories about the space-time of created, perceived, and contested landscapes.

SARA BLACK

Sara Black's work uses conscious processes of carpentry, woodworking, and craft as a time-based method; diseased or affected wood, inherited building materials, or other exhausted objects as material; and creates work that exposes the complex ways in which beings and things are suspended in worlds together, often generating forms that intend to push beyond human frames of reference.

SARA PAJUNEN

Sara Pajunen is a composer-improvisor and an audiovisual artist. Trained as a violinist and employing locally-responsive media ranging from field recordings to drone imagery, her work is motivated by interactions between her ancestral roots, American cultural histories, and connection to our environments through sound.

SARAH KANOUSE

Sarah Kanouse is an interdisciplinary artist and critical writer examining the political ecology of landscape and space. Migrating between video, photography, and performative forms, her research-based creative projects shift the visual dimension of the landscape to allow hidden stories of environmental and social transformation to emerge.

SARAH LEWISON

Sarah Lewison is an artist, and writer whose work invokes political-ecological relationships as rendered through law, history, and materiality, by using play, dialog, media, and public events. She is Professor Emeritus in the College of Arts and Media, Southern Illinois University, Carbondale.

SHANA M. GRIFFIN

Shana M. griffin is a feminist activist, geographer, and artist. Her work interrogates the built environment as technologies of control, and centers black women's spatial knowledges and the rival geographies communities forge against displacement and spatial erasure. She is the founder of PUNCTUATE, a feminist spatial initiative.

SHANAI MATTESON

Shanai Matteson is a public artist, writer, organizer, and community-based researcher. Since 2018 she has been working on a body of public art and advocacy work related to mining in her home region of northeastern Minnesota.

STEPHANIE LINDQUIST

Stephanie Lindquist is an artist and art educator. Through making, gardening, cooking, bathing, and medicine making Lindquist is learning about our diverse ancient roots and often overlooked knowledge systems that provide insight into our modern challenges around sustainability.

TAHANI NADIM

Tahani Nadim is a research professor at the College for Social Sciences & Humanities, Ruhr-University Bochum. Her research and teaching focus on collection histories, archival practices, digitization and transformative memory work.

TAMMY GREER

Tammy Greer is director of the Center for American Indian Research and Studies at the University of Southern Mississippi and a member of the United Houma Nation.

ZANE PIONTEK

Zane Piontek is a writer and musician from Baton Rouge, Louisiana. A graduate of Louisiana State University, he has written for such publications as *KLSU Radio* and *[225] Magazine* in Baton Rouge and *ANTIGRAVITY Magazine* in New Orleans. His work has explored the music and culture of Louisiana and the Southeast. He currently lives and works in New Orleans.

Collaborations

The work contained in this book has come to us from many lines and lineages of teaching. We've done our best to account for our partners and collaborators, but recognize that this list is incomplete:

3OneOne6 Gallery, A Studio in the Woods, Adam Bell, Adam Crosson, Albertine Kimble, Alex Kolker, Alyssa Fabia, Amalia Leguizamon, Amanda Lee Keikiahola Savage, Amelia Broussard, American Routes, Ana Hernandez, André Cailloux Center for Performing Arts and Cultural Justice, Andy Horowitz, Annie Humphrey, AnnieLaurie Erickson, Antenna, Anthropocene Commons, Anthropocene Curriculum, Anthropocene Working Group, Antioch University PhD Program in Leadership and Change, Aron Chang, Art of the Rural, ArtSpot Productions, Ashish Kumar, Autonomy is Not Freedom, Back to Indigenous Futures Lab (University of Minnesota), Bernd Scherer, Big Muddy Adventures, Bill Hart, Black Voters Matter, Brandon Ballengée, Brian Lozenski, Bruce "Sunpie" Barnes, Bruce Shoemaker, Bvlbancha Liberation Radio, ByWater Institute, Cait Bergeon, Cara Djonko-Moore, Carbondale Food Autonomy, Carlina Rossée, Center for American Indian Research and Studies at the University of Southern Mississippi, Center for Environmental Studies at Rice University, Chengwatana Farm, Christine "Cfreedom" Brown, Christine Taitano DeLisle, Christopher O'Loughlin, Christopher Oliver, Civic Studio, Community Engagement Center (Macalester College), Community Members for Environmental Justice, Community Tech New York, Contemporary Arts Center, Cory Diane, Crevasse 22, Cyndhia Ramatchandirane, Dancing Gnome Farm and Broken Paddle Guiding Co., Daniel Keefe, Deep Time Chicago, Dillard University Minority Health & Health Equity Research Center, Dismantle NOMA, DISPLACED Project, Dr. Alfred Frankowski, Dr. Anthony Fontenot, Dr. Austin Harrison, Dr. Ibrahima Seck of the Whitney Plantation, Dr. Jen Liu, Dr. Joseph Smith, Dread Scott, Duaba Unenra, EASEL Project, New Orleans, Ebony Aya, Ebru Bodur, Ella Robertson, Entergy, Fallon Samuels Aidoo, Farrah Freibert, Faye Dant of Jim's Journey: the Huck Finn Freedom Center, Fern Renville, Fernando Silva e Silva, Fire in the Village, FKA Welcome Water Protector Center, Fleury Clark Girimana, Geezis Humphrey, Geography of Robots, George Floyd Global Memorial, Giiwedin Indizhinikaaz, Grace Treffinger, Grand Marais at Frank Holten State Park, Greta Gladney, Guns Down Orange Mound, Hana Dinku, Hannah Chalew, Hasé Collective, Healthy Gulf, Heather Everhart, Historical Society of Brooklyn Illinois, Hollow Tree Documentary Film, Honor the Earth, House of World Cultures, Hyde Park Matters, Ibrahima Seck, Institutional Equity (Macalester College), jackie sumell, James Everest, James Rock, Jenna Grey Eagle, Jerri X, Jessi Parfait, Jihad Doucette, Joanna Farley, Joseph Mogul, Joshua Lewis, Juan Carlos Quintana, Juice Orange Mound, Jürgen Renn, Justice Jones, Justin Marcano,

Juxtaposition Arts, kai lumumba barrow, Karine Narahara, Katie Fronek, Katrin Klingan, Katrina Phillips, Keeli Siyaka, Kēhaulani Fagatele-Folau, Kira Akerman, Krista Langberg, Kristina Kay Robinson, Kwe Humphrey, Laia La Rue, Landmark Farmer's Market, Laura D. Kelley, Law Warschaw Gallery (Macalester College), Lealtad Suzuki Center for Social Justice (Macalester College), Leanna Goose, Leech Lake Reservation, LEEP, LLC, Les Cenelles, Lina Schwab, Lisa Anderson-Levy, Lisa E. Harris, Little Egypt Collective, Living Lands & Waters, Long Lake Conservation Center, Los Islenos Cultural Complex, Louisiana Environmental Action Network (LEAN), Louisiana Landmarks Society (LLS), LSU Center for River Studies, Luisa Dantas, Lynn Mizner, Macalester College, Macalester Native and Indigenous Initiative, Mads Clark, Marga Miller, Marianne Milligan, Matthew Rosenbeck, Max Planck Institute for the History of Science, Max Planck Institute of Geoanthropology, Melissa Ketter, Mellon Foundation, Men of Power, Meraux Foundation, Michael Ifeoma Esealuka, Michaela Harrison, Minerva Muñoz, Minnesota Marine Art Museum, Mondo Bizarro Productions, Nanih Bvlbancha, Native Canoe Program (University of Minnesota), Native Women's Care Circle, Neighborhood Story Project, Neli Wagner, New Orleans Center for the Gulf South at Tulane University, New Orleans for Lincoln Beach, New Orleans Mosquito, Rodent & Termite Control Board, Nic[o] Brierre Aziz, Nick Holmes, Okla Hina Ikhish Holo, Orange Mound Arts Council, Paper Machine, PATOIS, Pointe-Au-Chien Indian Tribe, Port of New Orleans, PUNCTUATE, Quanita Kendrick, Quapaw Canoe Company, Racial Justice Project Fund (Macalester College), Raymond "Moose" Jackson, Regina Cairns, Renee Royale, Rhodes College, Richie Blink of Delta Discovery, Riley Fletcher, Ripple Effect, Rise & Repair, Rise St. James, Roger Fernandes, Ron Bechet, Roxanne Gould, Roxxanne O'Brien, Ryan Clarke, Sam Wegner, Scott Eustis, Sedric McClure, SEEING BLACK, Sewerage & Water Board of New Orleans, Shruti Rao, Skyler Foy, Southern Illinois University Carbondale, Spill Paint Not Oil, Spillway, Stand for Children TN, Stephanie Lindquist, Swampnet, Teaching Social Action Institute, The Descendants Project, The Land Memory Bank & Seed Exchange, The Poche Family of Paulina, LA, The Tate, Etienne, and Provost (TEP) Center, The Water Collaborative, Thomas Halverson, Thompson's Event Center, Tia-Simone Gardner, Tom Turnbull, Tulane University's Newcomb Art Department, Vicente Diaz, Vivian Tran, Wakemup Productions, Washington University, Water Leaders Institute, Watershed Art and Ecology, Wendi Moore O'Neal, Western Illinois University's Kibbe Research Station, White Earth Tribal and Community College, Whole Child Strategies, Women for Change, Women of Strength, Women's Earth and Climate Action Network, Zaryn Prussia, Zoe Allen, and Zyanya Cruz.

Colophon

Editors: Dio Cramer, John Kim, Jeremy Meckler, Rebecca Snedeker

Book Designers: Dio Cramer, John Kim, Jacob Lindgren, Nelson Mondale

Illustrations: Dio Cramer, Nelson Mondale

Copyediting & Proofreading: Rebecca Snedeker, Griffy LaPlante

Printer: Graphius, Belgium

Published by Mississippi River Open School for Kinship and Social Exchange

Distributed by the
University of Minnesota Press
111 Third Avenue South, Suite 290
Minneapolis, MN 55401-2520
www.upress.umn.edu

This book is supported in part by the Mellon Foundation and the Max Planck Institute of Geoanthropology. The findings and conclusions contained within are those of the authors and do not necessarily reflect opinions or policies of either institution.

ISBN 978-1-5179-2192-7

A Cataloging-in-Publication record for this book is available from the Library of Congress

Photos on the cover (clockwise from top left): Sarah Lewison, 2022; Suzana Mallard, 2023; *The Herbarium Catalogue*, Royal Botanic Gardens, Kew, © The Board of Trustees of the RBG, Kew, 1976; Jennifer Colten and Jesse Vogler, *Mound [9182]*, 2018; Stephanie Lindquist, 2022; Louis Kaufman, 2023.

Inside front and back cover photographs by Louis Kaufman

Earlier versions of articles in this book were published in:

Anthropocene Curriculum (www.anthropocene-curriculum.org)
Antigravity (July 2024)
Imani (Spring 2024)
Journal of Architectural Education (2025)
Mississippi River Open School (www.mississippiriver.school)
Open Rivers (Winter/Spring 2025)
Southern Cultures (Fall 2025)